KENT

1800 - 1899

A Chronicle of the Nineteenth Century

In this book, Bob Ogley recounts great historical events as though they had just happened.
Here are the soldiers, the engineers, the explorers, the sportsmen and the artists, who contributed handsomely to an exciting but turbulent century of astonishing progress.
Famous names come alive: William Pitt, Horatio Nelson, Jane Austen, the Duke of Wellington, Charles Darwin, Charles Dickens, William Morris, Louis Napoleon and many others.
Interwoven with the tales of heroes and villains, triumphs and tragedies is the story of ordinary people and the changes in everyday life.
It is another vivid portrayal of life in Kent - and how Kentish influence came to dominate large areas of our Empire.

Froglets Publications

Awarded for excellence

Froglets Publications

Brasted Chart, Westerham,
Kent TN16 ILY

Tel: 01959 562972
Fax: 01959 565365

e:mail:
bobogley@frogletspublications.co.uk

website:
www.frogletspublications.co.uk

ISBN
Hardback 1 872337 51 1
Paperback 1 872337 56 2

Front cover: *The Old Bridge at Maidstone* by Albert Goodwin. Maidstone Museum. Back cover: *Train at Shakespeare Cliff* by George Childs. National Railway Museum York /HIP

Repro by One Thirteen, Whitstable. Printed and paperbound by Thanet Press, Margate. Hardbound by Biddles.

FOREWORD

THIS is a book about Kent of a kind never before attempted. With a feast of facts and illustrations it provides a panorama of the 19th century and, hopefully, an irresistible temptation to spend hours of browsing. It follows the success of the four-volume, lavishly-illustrated history of Kent in the 20th Century, which is still available in most bookshops and certainly from the publisher.

The story of the 19th century is no less dramatic because it opens with the threat of invasion from Napoleon, continues through the difficult years of riots and economic hardship, welcomes Queen Victoria with her strong Protestant faith and compassionate concern for the poor and shows how Kentish men played an important part in the development of steam-powered machinery, which transformed industrial productivity.

Many people in Kent lived in squalor, discomfort and danger. Men, women and children were employed for excessively long hours but they, too, played their part in the industrial revolution.

There was a massive shift in the balance of Kent's population. In 1801 people were spread evenly around the countyside; by 1891 more than two thirds had moved to the towns which, inspired by the coming of the railway, played host to a new urban culture.

This book tells the story of the changing face of the county, the understanding of childhood, the desire to seek recreation in the sea-bathing resorts and the appreciation of art and literature with Charles Dickens, William Morris, Alfred Lord Tennyson and J.M.W.Turner pre-eminent among the county's novelists, designers, poets and artists.

I have many people to thank, notably my wife Fern who has been involved in all stages, Mo Dyke and Avril Oswald, who read the proofs, corrected the text and made many useful suggestions, and Gillian John who organised the subscriptions.

I would especially like to thank the National Army Museum, Topham Picturepoint, Medway Archive and Heritage Centre and all the local history departments in the Kent libraries. The inclusion of more than 250 illustrations, many of them from library archives will, we hope, make this book more appealing. We are grateful to Kent Arts and Libraries for their efforts in preserving much of the heritage of Kent and this book has been published with their co-operation.

Bob Ogley

CONTENTS

ILLUSTRATIONS

By courtesy of the following:

The Director, the National Army Museum, London: pages 15, 26, 34, 35, 42, 43, 60, 126, 135, 136, 141, 143, 146, 151, 154, 197, 214.
Topham Picture Point: 12 (bottom), 14, 25, 28, 39, 78, 105, 106, 107, 113, 128, 131, 144, 161, 168, 184, 188, 199, 200, 220, 223, 226, 231. **NRM York /HIP:** 66, 111, 129. **Science Museum / HIP:** 80. **The British Library /HIP:** 12, 46, 208. **Corporation of London / HIP:** 49. **Public Record Office /HIP:** 140.**The British Museum /HIP:** 39
Rochester-upon-Medway Heritage Centre: 11, 65, 90, 92, 147, 149, 165, 236, 266. **Bromley Library:** 12, 24, 182, 186, 198, 216, 245. **Maidstone Museum:** 50/51, 95, 196. **Dover Museum:** 84, 173, 191, 206, 210. **Police Museum:** 105, 148, 187, 217 **English Heritage:** 132. **Museum of London:** 20/21. **Ashmoleum Museum:** 70. *Underriver SPGV:* 81.**Garden of England Cards:** 76
Kent Arts and Libraries: 7, 8/9, 97 (Canterbury). 23, 27, 29, 104, 123, 215, 219, 232, 240 (Folkestone). 30, 33, 73, 87, 213, 222 (Dartford). 32, 56, 115, 122, 227, 238 (Margate). 40, 194, 239, 241 (Ashford). 45, 54, 71, 79 (Centre for Kentish Studies). 47, 52, 63, 67, 169, 203 (Sevenoaks). 64, 88, 119, 185 (Gravesend). 74, 69, 110, 155, 175, 224, 229 (Tunbridge Wells). 137 (Whitstable). 83 (Sittingbourne). 83, 134 (Herne Bay). 160, 233, 242 (Dover). 100 (Tonbridge). 180 (Maidstone). 192, 205, (Ramsgate). **Faversham Society:** 85, 121, 172. **Author's collection:** 5, 19, 37, 38, 48, 53, 58, 59, 61, 68, 82, 86, 91, 93, 94, 103, 108, 109, 114, 116, 125, 150, 152, 153, 158, 162, 164, 167, 176, 178, 181, 190, 211, 212, 235, 248, 249. **Philip Lane:** 209 **Kent Fire Museum:** 189. **Shoreham Church:** 193. **Bexleyheath Library:** 234. **Frank Chapman:** 139, 237. **Ken Wilson:** 183. **Royal School for Military Engineering:** 36, 189, 228, 247 (bottom). **Private Collection:** 99. **National Maritime Museum:** 18. **The National Gallery:** 96. **Phyllida Warner Collection:** 98, 117, 230, 247. **Fern Warner:** 6, 124, 159, 163, 218. **The Pentland Group:** 133
In some cases we have been unable to trace the copyright holder despite every effort to do so.

BIBLIOGRAPHY

Kent Headlines by Alan Bignell, The History of Kent Cricket Club by Dudley Moore, Lady Sackville by Susan Alsop, Kent by John Vigar, Heroes and Villains by Adrian Gray, The Calender of Historic Weather Events, Bushell's chronology of Kent, The Kent Weather Book.

People and Places by Pat Davis, Teller of Tales by Pat Davis, Kent Murder Casebook by W.H. Johnson, Kent Police 1857-1957 by Kent Constabulary, Motor Bus Services of Kent by Eric Baldock, History of Combe Bank , Kent Women by Bowen Pearse, To Fire Committed by Harry Klopper, Kent (the King's England) by Arthur Mee.

The Chronicle of Britain, Kent by Pennethorne Hughes, Crime and Criminals of Victorian Kent by Adrian Gray, Smuggling in Kent and Sussex by Mary Wagh, Images of Ashford by Mike Bennett, Romney Marsh by Anne Roper, History of Gravesend by Robert Hiscock, Hopping Down in Kent by Alan Bignell, The History of Maidstone by Peter Clark and Lynn Murfin, History of Maidstone (1881) (reprinted John Hallewell Publications).

Canterbury by Marcus Crouch, Dover's Forgotten Fortress by Janice Welby, Kent: A Place in History by Alan Bignell, Wellington at Walmer by Gregory Hollyoake, Jane Austen in Kent by David Waldron Smithers, A History of Kent by Frank Jessop, Two Families at Fairlawne by Frank Chapman, Tales of Old Tonbridge by Frank Chapman, Tales of Old Tunbridge Wells by Frank Chapman.

Memories of Kent Cinemas by Martin Tapsell, Brains: Dartford Borough Council, History of J and E Hall, Nelson, His Private and Public Life by G.Lathom Browne, English Provincial Posts by Brian Austen, Chatham Past by Philip MacDougal, William Cobett's Rural Rides by William Cobbett, Rural Life in Victorian England by G.E.Mingay, In Quest of Hasted by John Boyle.

Religion and Society in Kent 1640-1914 (Yates, Hume and Hastings), The Victorian Archbishops of Canterbury by Dr Alan MG Stephenson, Napoleon III in England by Ivor Guest, History of the Weald of Kent, History of Greenwich by Beryl Platts, The Story of Greenwich by Clive Aslett, The English Prison Hulks by W.Branch Johnson, Pickwick Papers by Charles Dickens (and other Dickens novels), History of Kent Cricket Club by Lord Harris.

National Dictionary of Biography, History of the East Kent Volunteers, Royal Visitors to Tunbridge Wells by Don Foreman, The Crystal Palace by Patrick Beaver, Kent and the Napoleonic Wars by Peter Bloomfield, The Phoenix Suburb by Alan R.Warwick, Aspects of the Arsenal, ed by Beverley Burford and Julian Watson.

The Great Stink of London by Stephen Halliday, History of Sandwich, Policing Kent by Roy Ingleton, The Life and Works of Vincent van Gogh, by Janice Anderson, Charles Darwin, the Scholar Who Changed Human History published by Thames and Hudson

Preface

If only the French could play cricket

AS the nineteenth century dawns Kent is on a war footing yet again. Since 1793 when France declared war on Britain the county has braced itself for the possibility of an invasion and military camps are springing up throughout the county.

Some were set up during the American War of Independence including those at Coxheath, Chatham, Dover, Barham Downs and Shorne Cliffe. There are other camps at Mote Park where the Kent Volunteers are recruiting furiously and at Canterbury where one of the oldest English regiments, The Buffs is based.

So called because of the colour of the lining of their red jackets, breeches and waistcoats, the Buffs are now better known as the East Kent Regiment. When war was declared barracks were built outside the city along the road beyond Northgate transforming Canterbury into a garrison town.

John Frederick Sackville, Third Duke of Dorset, who died last year aged 54 was one of the best patrons of cricket ever known. The famous Vine ground at Sevenoaks belonged to him and he kept in his employ several famous cricketers including Bowra, Miller and Minshull. For many years until 1789 he was British Ambassador to France but, sadly, failed to teach the French the finer arts of the noble game.

The foremost military establishment in Kent and possibly in England is at Shorncliffe, Sandgate where the War Department has bought 230 acres. Here General Sir John Moore commands the Light Infantry Brigade and trains his men in tactics of mobility and speed.

Kent has many great houses whose titled owners are not only army officers and politicians but play a major role in the affairs of the empire. Typical of such aristocrats is Lord Cornwallis who was Governor General of India for seven years until 1793. He extended British control across most of the country and provided scope for Britain's industrial expansion despite the actions Tipu Sahib, the sultan of Mysore, who caused much of the trouble by supporting Napoleon Bonaparte. Thanks to the courage and skill of General Sir George Harris of Belmont near Throwley and his 73rd Grenadiers Tipu Sahib is now dead and an uneasy peace has returned to the sub continent.

William Pitt (the younger), born at Hayes Place in 1759, the eloquent, very able second son of Lord Chatham is Prime Minister. His family home is at Holwood Park, Keston but he has a country cottage at Westerham and stays frequently at Walmer Castle, traditionally the residence of the Lord Warden of the Cinque Ports. The war against revolutionary and Napoleonic France is occupying much of Pitt's time and energies. It is now 11 years since the first French refugee émigrés sailed into the Kent ports following the bloody Paris revolution and the storming of the Bastille prison which fell to an angry mob of peasants.

For some years Pitt has also been concerned with the health of George III, whose 'fever' involves delirious ramblings, sudden bursts of anger, sleeplessness, sweating and a fast pulse. But just as the Prime Minister urged the Prince of Wales to take over and set up the controversial Regency Bill, so the King's sanity has improved.

George III's court physician is Dr John Turton of Brasted Place — a great house near Sevenoaks built by Robert Adam. Turton has assisted with the King's recovery in which shock treatment was applied.

Neither the revolution in France, the possibility of invasion, nor the King's madness have failed to halt a pastime which is growing in popularity throughout Kent, cricket. It began as a village game some 200 years ago but today is played by the nobility and the gentry alongside their tenants. It provides an opportunity for gambling and many country gentlemen challenge each other and invite their more skilful gardeners and game-keepers to take part.

It has been suggested that if such a friendship link existed between the social classes in France, then the peasant revolution might not have taken place. But cricket is an English game and in the great country parks of Kent, where matches take place with stakes as high as 1,000 guineas, the servants share the interests of their betters.

Belmont with its beautiful park has been acquired by General George Harris in an auction.

Hero Harris returns home to Belmont

A KENT army officer, who was selected by Colonel Arthur Wellesley to lead the assault on the fortress city of Seringapatam, has returned to a new home at Throwley near Faversham with a stirring tale of the last days of Tipu Sahib, the corrupt ruler of Mysore, who was threatening to drive the British out of India.

Sahib had befriended the French, requested aid and promised Napoleon Bonaparte he would lead the campaign to end British rule on the sub continent.

Wellesley thought otherwise as did General Sir George Harris of the 73rd Grenadiers. In May last year he not only took Seringapatam but killed Tipu Sahib, annexed Mysore and has been showered with congratulations from the Government of India and from both houses of parliament in Britain for ridding India of such a dangerous ruler. In action with him was his 17-year-old son William.

General Harris received an eighth of the prize money from the capture of Seringapatam which amounted to £150,000. With this sum he has purchased Belmont, a neo-classical 18th century mansion and set himself up as a landed gentleman.

This is all a far cry from his early life as the son of a curate from the village of Brasted. Harris has enjoyed a distinguished military career which includes action at the Battle of Bunker Hill in the American War of Independence where he was wounded. Belmont was built by Samuel Wyatt in 1780 and was once owned by Edward Wilks, storekeeper of the Royal Powder Mills.

Many destitute as fire destroys 100 Chatham buildings

July 1: Three people have died and more than 100 buildings been destroyed in an inferno which raged through Chatham yesterday with amazing and irresistible fury. The famous Chatham House, Best's Brewery and 13 warehouses are damaged beyond repair. Scores of families are homeless and a greater part of them rendered destitute. It is believed the cost of the damage may exceed £30,000.

A committee of "gentlemen of the town" will be set up today to collect money for the relief of the sufferers. William Jefferys, the treasurer, has described the blaze in detail.

"It began in a building on the river bank in which was deposited a great deal of cordage and oakum. In a few minutes the shed, the adjoining forge and warehouses and a hoy, with her mast and sails which lay close to the side of the wharf, were one general blaze. The men employed on the wharf, endeavouring to extinguish the fire, exposed themselves to great danger and were scarcely able to effect their escape.

"The strength of the fire was so great that on the falling of the houses large flakes of fire were thrown up a prodigious height and carried to a considerable distance burning haystacks in fields to the south of the town.

"To describe this calamitous scene is impossible; parents searching after their children, whole families roofless and pennyless and such like spectacles were everywhere to be seen. But the most dreadful catastrophe was the fatal burning of William Bassett, a servant of Messrs Best, and the death of Mrs Dunk and her infant child who incautiously ventured too near a burning home and were struck by a falling chimney.

"To the divine interposition of Providence alone, can it be attributed, that no other lives were lost on this most melancholy occasion". *See page 13*

All roads lead to Canterbury where the ancient walls of Roman origin were rebuilt by the Normans and contained 21 watch towers and six gates. Too many for these worrying days. St George's Gate (above) is due to be demolished next year.

Major turnpike roads impassable in rain

THANKS to the "turnpike system" introduced by Parliament more than 100 years ago a network of roads takes traffic to almost every town and village in the county and a toll is charged for their use.

The first Turnpike Act was passed in 1709 for "repairing and amending the highway leading from Seven Oaks and Woods Gate (Pembury)". This, of course, is part of the main road from London to Rye which runs close to the fashionable resort of Tunbridge Wells so it is — and has always been — a principal highway.

Sadly, the section between Sevenoaks and Tonbridge where the road runs across the Wealden clay is in constant need of attention. Following the heavy rains earlier this year the road is now impassable.

However, most roads in the east of the county have been turnpiked. Those between Canterbury and Sandwich and on to Dover will be dealt with in a few years time.

In the majority of parishes public-spirited men, usually landowners, known as turnpike trustees, put up the money and then employ a body of labourers to undertake the maintenance of a length of road. and charge a toll. These are not always sufficient to cover the cost of turnpiking from end to end and the system is open to corruption.

The greatest concern is shown among those who live in the Weald where turnpike roads are virtually impassable for coaches and chaises in the winter and even the horse post has trouble getting through. There is a problem, apparently, in obtaining stone for road repairing from the clay vales of the Weald and often it has to be carried by hand for mile upon mile.

The Post Office hopes that fast mail coaches, such as those now operating on the London to Bath road, will soon be introduced to Kent. It really depends on Napoleon and his next move.

See page 103

Canterbury Cathedral, the cradle of English christianity whose Bishops are, historically, the Primates of All England. The cathedral stands on the site of the small church provided by Ethelbert for St Augustine and on the foundations of a Norman cathedral built in the decades after the Conquest.

The two west transepts are 15th century, as is the central Bell Harry Tower which dominates, not just the cathedral, but the city. Attached to the cathedral are the buildings of King's School which claims to be the oldest in the country.

5,721 guests at military party in Mote Park

THE Royal Review held in Mote Park, Maidstone two years ago, when King George III reviewed more than 5,000 members of the Kent Volunteer Force, will not be allowed to slip quietly into history. It was far too memorable an occasion for that.

So, this year, a commemorative pavilion has been opened in the park and East Street has been renamed King Street in honour of the visit of the royal party which included Queen Charlotte, the Princesses Sophia and Elizabeth and Prince William of Gloucester.

Although upwards of 19,000 Kentish men and Men of Kent have now responded to the call to arms, the strength of the volunteers at Mote Park amounted to 5,721 and they represented 42 towns and villages. Dressed in white vests, white trousers, red coatees and a sprig of oak leaves in their caps they marched past shops and houses festooned with garlands and flags.

The King inspected the volunteers, drawn up in double line from one end of the park to the other, and then saw them take part in a most realistic mock battle.The day ended with a feast prepared by Lord Romney of Mote House, Lord Lieutenant of Kent.

After the review the whole party sat down to dinner, the royal guests in an elegant marquee, the ministers of state in a second one and the volunteers in the open park. The tables were placed in two divisions, numbering 91 in all; the length of the tables was 13,353 yards and the principal dishes were:

Sixty lambs in quarters, making 240 dishes, 700 fowls, three in a dish, 300 hams, 300 tongues, 200 dishes of boiled beef, 220 dishes of roast beef, 220 joints of roast veal, 200 meat pies, 200 fruit pies, seven pipes of wine and 16 butts of beer.

Tom sailed round the world with Captain Cook

October 17: Lydd's heroic sailor Lieutenant Tom Edgar, who sailed round the world with Captain James Cook, died today aged 56. He will be buried in the village churchyard.

Edgar joined the Navy at 10 and two years later took part in the memorable engagement off the Brittany coast when Admiral Hawke destroyed the French fleet. Many years later in 1776 he joined Captain Cook on his last voyage in the exploration ship _Resolution._

Cook on an earlier epic journey had reached Tahiti and charted the coasts of New Zealand and eastern Australia. On this voyage he had circumnavigated Alaska as far as the Arctic ice pack and returned south to Hawaii.

Edgar and Cook were together in February 1778 when the legendary commander became involved, quite needlessly, in a skirmish with Hawaiian natives in Karakakoa Bay and was fatally wounded.

Tom Edgar and his crew came home and sailed into London with the body of Captain Cook in 1780.

Brasted physician will keep a wide eye on the King's madness

Dr John Turton of Brasted Place, near Westerham, has been appointed 'Physician in Ordinary' to King George III and will be responsible for keeping an eye on the dubious health of this most popular monarch.

Dr Turton, who enjoys the friendship of many of the leading figures in Georgian England, is deeply concerned about the recent so-called madness of the King and is anxious that his almost-miraculous recovery continues.

A few years ago the King's speech became hoarse, he sweated freely and behaved violently, terrifying the Queen.

One story alleged that he was seen talking to an oak tree in Windsor Great Park. Certainly he experienced hallucinations and was put under the medical care of Francis Willis who placed the King in a straightjacket, then gagged and beat him. Other doctors tried to blister his legs with mustard plasters.

Turton has impeccable references. In 1782 he successfully treated Horace Walpole for gout by prescribing a diet drink of dock roots. Other prestigious patients have included Oliver Goldsmith and David Garrick.

His house at Brasted — built from a design by Robert Adam in 1784 — should have included side wings. When George III proposed himself as a guest Dr Turton, dreading such an honour, hastily cancelled the order for the wings and informed His Majesty that his humble dwelling was quite inadequate to entertain royalty.

Turton still enjoys royal favour and has been presented with a striking clock from the turret of Horse Guards for his new estate.

Convicts make their home in Sydney

IT's a dubious honour for the Home Secretary, Viscount Sydney, but the new penal colony in a settlement in Australia — named after him — is now well established and home for hundreds of convicts.

Sydney lives at Penshurst — one of the noblest homes in England with a fine baronial hall that is sadly in need of sympathetic reconstruction.

It was in 1788 that Captain Arthur Phillip established a penal colony near Botany Bay which he described as "the finest harbour in the world". He called the colony Sydney and in that year commanded six transports carrying 736 convicts. Refusing to carry slaves, Phillip said Sydney was a fit place for these tough human beings to make a fresh start in life.

He returned home in 1791 and immediately gave Viscount Sydney a full account of his adventures in Australia. That included exploration of the interior and his discovery of the Hawkesbury River.

Several convicts left from Kent this year. They have been told that the Australia is an ideal place to start a new honest life but warned not to start any conflicts with the natives. The aborigines can be hostile. *See page 138*

Vice-Admiral Horatio Nelson who made a name for himself by smashing the French blockade at Copenhagen earlier this year has called upon William Pitt at Walmer Castle to discuss the turmoil in Europe.

Excise officers found 4000 yards of French lace and 246 pairs of gloves in a post chaise leaving Deal recently. In another incident a king's messenger was arrested for bringing in silk kerchiefs from a smuggler's lugger.

Wheat which was selling at 47 shillings a quarter 10 years ago is now 110 shillings, leaving many parishes stretched to provide adequate sustenance for widows, orphans and all those on Poor Relief.

Chatham is the largest town but the villages are growing

Home of the British fleet — The Royal Dockyard, Chatham founded by Queen Elizabeth.

FOR the first time in the history of Britain a census has been published in order to give an accurate figure for the population of each county. Census officials calculate there has been an increase of 77 per cent in the past 100 years. There are now just over nine million people living in England and Wales and, in each county, women are in the majority.

It will be of no surprise that Chatham, with its huge royal dockyard is Kent's largest town closely followed by the garrison towns of Canterbury, Rochester and Maidstone.

As the figures have been rounded off to the nearest hundred they are not completely accurate but there is little doubt that the population of Kent has increased rapidly due to the increased birth rate and falling death rate rather than any great influx of people from other areas of the country.

A few villages are also growing particularly those with a local industry, such as stone or chalk quarrying, but agriculture continues to be the main provider of work that sustains village life.

Some rural areas have a number of larger farms employing up to 12 people who "live-in" and have their meals cooked by the farmer's wife. This helps to swell the population of some Wealden villages such as Benenden (1,300 pop) and Biddenden (1,500) — both being much larger than the northern Kent villages of Beckenham, Erith and Sidcup. *See page 31*

Ashford	**2,600**	**Herne Bay**	**1,200**
Beckenham	**1,000**	**Hollingbourne**	**730**
Benenden	**1,300**	**Hythe**	**1,400**
Bexley	**1,400**	**Maidstone**	**8,000**
Biddenden	**1,500**	**Margate**	**4,800**
Broadstairs	**1,600**	**Mereworth**	**597**
Bromley	**2,700**	**Northfleet**	**1,900**
Canterbury	**9,500**	**Orpington**	**700**
Chatham	**10,500**	**Ramsgate**	**4,200**
Chislehurst	**1,200**	**Rochester**	**8,000**
Crayford	**1,200**	**Sevenoaks**	**2,600**
Dartford	**2,400**	**Sheerness**	**5,600**
Deal	**6,200**	**Sittingbourne**	**3,000**
Erith	**1,000**	**Sidcup**	**200**
Faversham	**3,500**	**Smarden**	**831**
Folkestone	**3,700**	**Tonbridge and**	
Gillingham	**4,100**	**Tunbridge Wells**	**4,400**
Gravesend	**4,500**	**Whitstable**	**1,600**

Holwood House, Keston. William Pitt diverted the course of the main road to London

Pitt forced to sell his home at Keston

March 14: William Pitt resigned today, after 18 continuous years as Prime Minister, following a head-on confrontation with the King over the issue of Catholic emancipation in Ireland, which Pitt supports. Henry Addington, Speaker of the House of Commons, has been invited to form a new government.

Relinquishing the premiership is a great blow but having to sell his beloved Holwood House at Keston is a bigger one for William Pitt, whose personal finances have never been in a healthy state. Twice in nine years he has been forced to take out a mortgage on the property; now it will be sold by auction.

Pitt is a Kentish man born and bred. He spent his childhood at Hayes Place where his father, the Earl of Chatham lived until his death in 1778. When Chatham suffered from his frequent attacks of gout, Cabinet meetings were held in his bedroom at Hayes and among visitors to the house was Benjamin Franklin, then agent of the

American Assembly.

William Pitt loved the house and that part of North Kent. He knew the surrounding countryside well and once recalled how he used to go bird-nesting in the woods of nearby Holwood — "a house I always wished to call my own".

The wish came true in 1785. Two years after becoming England's youngest-ever Prime Minister at 24, Pitt bought the Georgian-style Holwood House and the extensive grounds surrounding it.

Pitt increased the size of the estate by buying 30 acres of common land and paying £10 per year to the parish in exchange. He improved the property, added a large dining room with a bow window and diverted the course of the main road to London so it skirted the grounds. In a letter to his mother from Downing Street in 1780 he wrote: "Tomorrow I hope to go to Holwood where I am impatient to look at my works. I must carry there, however, only my passion for planting..."

That passion continued throughout Pitt's long service as Prime Minister. He spent many weekends at Holwood and particularly enjoyed planting by torchlight — an activity he inherited from his father.

See page 14

Anglo-French peace treaty signed by Lord Cornwallis

March 25: The constant threat of a French invasion somewhere along the Kent coast has been removed — for the time being. Today Lord Cornwallis signed the Treaty of Amiens ending the nine-year long war between England and France.

It is an uneasy peace and few people are made happy by Cornwallis' assurances. In fact many believe he has allowed Joseph Bonaparte, the brother of General Napoleon and France's first consul, to gain far more than Britain from the peace terms.

Most of the overseas possessions won by the British navy including Egypt and the Cape of Good Hope are to be handed back with the exception of Trinidad and Ceylon — and Naples which was gained from Nelson's Mediterranean victories.

Bonaparte has conceded nothing on trade; he controls the Low Countries and London merchants cannot hope for a revival of Euopean trade.

What's this? — A tunnel under the English Channel!

The Treaty of Amiens has prompted a brilliant French engineer to put forward an ambitious plan for linking France and England with a tunnel under the sea. Albert Mathieu-Favier says that passengers will travel in horse-drawn coaches and it will cost in the region of £1m to construct. In a special paper to the French Government Mathieu-Favier says the road will be lit by oil lamps, ventilation chimneys will rise above the sea surface and there will be a mid channel island where the horses could be rested in the fresh air. Although an uneasy peace now exists between France and England, war could flare up again at any time and the idea of French invaders marching through a tunnel into Kent is beginning to haunt politicians, military strategists and Kentish folk. Cartoon above shows how the mighty lion would flee from the beligerent French cock. *See page 206*

Volunteer fire brigade in Hythe

FIRE! The word strikes fear in every living person and little wonder, for Kent towns and villages have suffered conflagrations sometimes so severe that whole streets have been consumed — with lives lost, cattle burned to death, crops ruined and damage running into thousands of pounds.

A few years ago Gravesend was virtually razed to the ground in a blaze which destroyed 250 buildings and caused damage estimated at £250,000. The only engine in the town was unfit for service so the flames just spread and spread until a building was blown up to form a fire break.

In July 1762 Sittingbourne lost its beloved church in a disastrous fire. The residents petitioned the King and the Lord Chancellor to help them collect the sum of £2,250 necessary to rebuild the church.

In 1800 several lives were lost in the great Chatham inferno. There was no insurance and a great deal of money had to be collected for the "relief of the sufferers".

Such situations may soon be in the past. This year a Kent Fire Insurance company has been set up in Maidstone with the White Horse as the badge and a Volunteer Fire Brigade formed in Hythe where there is a much-improved wooden manual engine.

Protection is not yet completely adequate but every caring citizen knows what fire can do to life and property and there is no shortage of volunteers prepared to help. *See page 68*

Princess Caroline, who 'garters below the knee'

Boisterous princess of Montague House

PRINCESS Caroline, the estranged wife of the Prince of Wales, lives at Montague House, Blackheath which has been leased by her husband to provide a 'salubrious' upbringing for their daughter, Charlotte.

It is a modest house in comparison to the palaces occupied by Prince George but Caroline likes it and so does Charlotte who has recently completed her education at Shrewsbury House, Shooters Hill.

Here she received shock treatment to cure a speech defect and studied geography from a huge globe set into the floor of the house.

Princess Caroline amuses her friends by organising alfresco breakfasts and other more unusual entertainments which have delighted the gossiping society. On occasions she likes to single out a man to share her conversation and then retire from the party into a separate room. This action has invited much comment. According to Lady Hester Stanhope, her lady-in-waiting, one of the rooms contains a Chinese automaton which performs obscene movements. "How the sea captains colour up when the Princess dances about, exposing herself like an opera girl", she told a friend. "And then she garters below the knee - so low, so vulgar".

See page 53

Stronger defences as old enemies go to war again

May: With Napoleon's violation of all terms outlined in last year's peace treaty Britain has declared war once again on France and this time intends to place a war-weary nation in a much stronger position. One immediate action is to press ahead with more powerful fortifications at Dover where a French invasion force is likely to land.

More than 33 acres of land on the Western Heights have been purchased from Mr David Papillon for £6,000. They lie alongside the earthworks which were begun in the American War and then abandoned. It is a strategic point.

Responsibility for the fortifications rests with the Royal Engineers who propose to build a simple Redoubt with a ditch and semi-revetment together with a central tower like a Keep. General Twiss will supervise the programme.

Additional work includes closing the 'gorges of three salient works with lines reciprocally flanking each other'. From the left wing of the Citadel it is proposed to carry a 'line of parapet' down to the cliff's edge.

Hundreds of thousands of bricks have already been ordered and most of them come from Ipswich because local bricks cannot be produced in large enough quantities for this huge undertaking.

Feverish activity is also underway at Chatham where the fortifications built some years ago to defend the Thames, the Medway and, most important, Chatham Dockyard are being strengthened and the armament increased.

A vast sum of money is being spent on the Chatham Lines, as the fortifications are known. The work includes revetting all the ditches and ramparts in brick, constructing new magazine facilities and extending the Lines to include Rochester. The idea is to link up Fort Clarence, Fort Pitt and the unfinished Fort Amherst.

Barracks have also been constructed to house the infantry units and work is underway on barracks for the artillery at nearby Brompton.

See page 36

Pitt's Fencibles ready for action

ALTHOUGH he is no longer Prime Minister William Pitt is taking more than a keen interest in the recruitment of volunteers to the British Army. In his role as Lord Warden of the Cinque Ports — an office he has proudly held since 1792 — Pitt has created the Royal Cinque Ports Fencibles and promoted himself to Colonel.

This week his housekeeper Lady Hester Stanhope said: "Pitt absolutely goes through the fatigue of a drill sergeant...and I often attend him. The hard riding I do not mind but to remain still so many hours on horseback is an incomprehensible bore and

continued

Having crossed the Channel, Bonaparte and his men are intimidated by the sight of Colonel Pitt, of the Royal Cinque Port Fencibles, on the battlements of Walmer Castle.

Kent's message to the King: 'we'll never be conquered'

August 2: The war against revolutionary France is again dominating the lives of everyone who lives in Kent, rich or poor. This week a great county meeting, presided over by the Lord Lieutenant, was held in Maidstone to discuss the threatened invasion.

Satisfied with the fortifications and the determination of the militia and volunteers to put up a good fight a loyal address was sent to the King promising that *"in the event of an invasion the county would justify its traditional boast and prove that the men of Kent would never be conquered".*

There are military bases all over the county but the largest is at Coxheath which a few years ago was a vast, boundless tract of heathland where masked highwaymen often lurked and smugglers hid their ill-gotten treasures.

Since the war with America — and then France — the wilderness has become alive with thousands of red coated soldiers who quarrel frequently and arrange countless duels. A few years ago, when ten companies of infantry were billetted there, a Maidstone man set up a gambling table near the camp. He was caught and drummed through the lines to the tune of the *Rogue's March.*

Today a beacon fire stands at Coxheath. The beacon is composed of wood soaked in pitch and tar and a sergeant, corporal and four privates stand by in readiness to set it alight in the event of an invasion

There are other camps at Chatham, Dover, Barham Downs and Shornecliffe. The Kent Volunteers are still furiously recruiting at Mote Park, Maidstone and Canterbury is now the home to one of the oldest English regiments, The Buffs, whose association with Kent began in 1782 when they started recruiting here.

They are now known as the East Kent Regiment and massive barracks have been built outside the city along the road beyond Northgate transforming Canterbury into a garrison town.

continued from previous page

requires more patience than you can easily imagine..."

As Lord Warden, Pitt's official residence is at Walmer Castle. The honour was bestowed upon him by the King who thought the salary of £3,080 would help his favourite politician keep up appearances.

This week thousands more men volunteered to serve as soldiers following the introduction of the Army of Reserve Act. Dover has an additional 325 volunteers

See page 23

Engineer plans sea fortresses from Hythe to Rye

April: A military engineer, working on the great defences at Dover, Captain William Ford, has submitted a proposal for a chain of sea fortresses along the coasts of Kent and Sussex.

He believes the plan to evacuate people and livestock from Romney Marsh in order to deny Napoleon's troops food will not be sufficient to hamper their mobility and a more ambitious idea would be to build towers along the coast similar to the one on Mortella Point, Corsica which so hampered the British Army when it attempted to land on the island 20 years ago during the French Revolution.

Ford's plan is causing great excitement among military engineers who remember clearly how two heavily-armed British warships were successfully driven off at Corsica.

General William Twiss, commanding officer for the southern district is particularly enthusiastic. He believes "Martello" towers, as he calls them, will be mutally protective and offer a formidable defence against a French invasion force. He has invited a committee of the Royal Engineers to evaluate the possibilities and submit a report which he will put to a special conference at Rochester on October 21. William Pitt, Prime Minister, is also believed to support the scheme.

The meeting will also consider another revolutionary plan — the building of a defensive canal from Hythe to the River Rother to isolate Romney Marsh from the high ground to the rear. The mastermind behind this is another military engineer, Lt Col John Brown, who says that a construction team of several hundred men may be required but such a canal could be completed within two or three years.

There will be more recommendations for the committee to consider, including the modernisation of Henry VIII's castle at Sandgate.

See page 27

Kent doctors show faith in new smallpox vaccine

SOME of Kent's leading doctors and surgeons have managed to acquire the controversial new vaccine which can prevent the spread of smallpox — that most dreadful disease which has produced death and disfigurement in Kent's many epidemic years.

Four years ago a country doctor, Edward Jenner discovered that coxpox gave protection against smallpox. He took the alarming risk of inoculating an eight-year-old boy with the coxpox serum and then, a year later, with smallpox. The more serious disease failed to develop.

Jenner published his theory and was immediately criticised by doctors, attacked by the clergy and made fun of by the cartoonists who were opposed to the idea of humans being given an animal disease.

Within a year, however, 70 leading doctors came out in his favour including a few doctors from Kent who were suspicious at first but keen to see if the vaccine worked. It did.

It was in the second half of the 17th century that smallpox superseded the plague as the most feared disease. In 1729, more than 1,700 residents of Canterbury went down with the disease and 140 died. There have been massive outbreaks at Folkestone, Dover and Dartford. In the 30 years between 1736 and 1766 smallpox deprived Maidstone of almost 600 of its inhabitants.

Smallpox is particularly endemic in countryside areas among the poor. At Cowden, for example, there were recurring outbreaks on six occasions in 30 years. Of 192 who died in the village of Great Chart, "almost 100" resulted from smallpox.

Sadly, Jenner's cowpox serum will not eradicate smallpox in Kent until the vaccine is available to every child.

See page 67

Slave trade bill defeated

WILLIAM Wilberforce's bill to abolish the slave trade has been rejected by the House of Lords — but the great evangelist is confident he is close to success. He has now fought slavery for more than 20 years and argues the belief that all God's creatures must be free. Opponents to the lobby say slaves are better off than many free men and that other nations would take over British trade.

See page 24

May 10: William Pitt is Prime Minister again following the resignation of his one-time friend Henry Addington who took office three years ago. Pitt then had resigned in response to George III's refusal to accept Catholic emancipation.

A Society for Superseding Climbing Boys has been formed in order to register and licence apprentices and present parliament with a bill for reform.

In many parts of Kent children as young as six years old are being used as chimney sweeps and often work more than eight hours a day.

Should he land in Kent Napoleon will receive a warm welcome from John Bull and his friends as this cartoon shows. The pitchfork is not the only weapon. Bull's wife prefers the chamber pot!

Napoleon's army prepares to invade

May: The Treaty of Amiens, signed by Britain and France two years ago after nine years of war, lies shattered. Bonaparte has violated most of the peace terms, Britain has retaliated by declaring war and the people of Kent are bracing themselves for 'the invasion'.

Many of Napoleon's 100,000 carefully-trained troops can be seen from the white cliffs of Dover. On a fine day tents are clearly visible and hundreds of landing craft are ready for an assault on the Kentish coast.

There is frantic activity at Dover where a chain of semaphores has been set up on hilltops, capable of passing messages to London in just two minutes. Troops are also gathering in the county. More than 10,000 are stationed at Coxheath and Prince Frederick, the Duke of York, is preparing a review in August, when he will prepare them for the French invasion. The Duke has instilled a new spirit of professionalism into the army, introducing drill and exercise instead of flogging.

King George III, now recovered from his bouts of madness, says he will lead his defending army which, due to government economies, consists of 52,000 men. Following the introduction of the Army of Reserve Act, volunteers now total more than 30,000. They are untrained and badly armed but the men say they will be ready for combat when Napoleon's troops invade. Reports that the French are digging a tunnel under the sea are completely unfounded.

William Pitt, Prime Minister again, is determined to place a war-weary nation in a stronger position by building up stores and timber to remobilize the Royal Navy. He is delighted with the decision to build 73 "Martello" towers along the Kent and Sussex Coast and has authorised the building of the defensive canal. In fact he will superintend much of the work himself and plans to stay at Walmer Castle while the project is underway.

Reports from France indicate that Napoleon believes the invasion will be a success and has already had a medal struck *"Frappé à Londres"* for his brave officers. Earlier this month he wrote: "I want only for favourable wind to plant the Imperial Eagle on the Tower of London". First of all, his fleets must escape the blockade introduced by Addington.

Everything now depends on the Royal Navy.

Vice Admiral Horatio Lord Nelson lies dying on the busy deck of the Victory after being shot by a French sniper during the Battle of Trafalgar. "Don't throw me overboard", he said to Hardy. He died in the arms of the ship's purser, Walter Burke from Wouldham.

Victory at Trafalgar but Nelson dies

October 21: The great flagship *Victory*, built at Chatham Dockyard 46 years ago, played a crucial part in the crushing victory over the combined French and Spanish battle fleet off Cape Trafalgar today — but at a terrible price. Vice-Admiral Horatio Lord Nelson was mortally wounded and immediately the nation plunged into mourning.

This slight, battle-scarred son of a Norfolk vicar, who came to Kent as a teenager to join the Navy, was shot down by a sniper in the topmast of the French battleship *Redoubtable.* He fell on the quarterdeck and died in the arms of his purser Walter Burke.

Burke, well known in the village of Wouldham where he lives in a cottage near the church, said that he helped to carry the wounded admiral into the cockpit. "He asked to see Hardy so I ran onto the deck, found the captain and then returned to Nelson's side, telling him that the enemy was decisively beaten and I hoped he would live to bear the joyful tidings to his country."

"It is nonsense, Mr Burke, "to suppose that I can live", Nelson replied. "My sufferings are great but they will soon be over."

Despite the fact that a bullet was still lodged in his spine and the pain was immense, Vice-Admiral Nelson hung on to life through the last hour of the battle with Hardy at his side. "Don't throw me overboard", he said to Hardy "...take care of my dear Lady Hamilton... Kiss me Hardy". The captain kissed his cheek and Nelson said: "Thank God I have done my duty".

Victory was not the only ship of the British fleet to be built in Kent. Many of the stoutest warships were built in the great Kentish dockyards and their crews hailed from the county.

Several of the warships survived this great naval battle as complete wrecks. *Victory* lost several masts, her sails were shot to ribbons and the crew had to refit her rigging as bad weather threatened.

Nelson's flagship lost 57 killed and 103 wounded but by the end of November was able to sail from Gibraltar with Nelson's body in a rum cask.

Twenty six Kentish seamen were among the crew of the *Victory*. They included Jas Rawlinson, 14, a boy from Maidstone and Thomas Rawlinson (his father or uncle), 39, a private in the Royal Marines from Chatham.

Chatham remembers the launch of the Victory

October 24: Details are emerging of Britain's great victory at Trafalgar. Apparently the French fleet of 33 ships was attempting to sail from Cadiz into the Mediterranean to support Napoleon's planned invasion of Austria when they met Nelson's fleet of 23 ships and even saw his signal from the masthead — "England expects that every man will do his duty".

With the bands playing *Hearts of Oak* the British ships followed Nelson's revolutionary tactics of splitting into two squadrons and sailing through the French line. A great battle ensued, the French fell into confusion and the superior gunnery and seamanship of Nelson's fleet won the day destroying, at a stroke, Napoleon's sea power.

The whole nation is rejoicing at the news from Trafalgar but none more so than the people of Chatham who are recalling the glorious day of May 7, 1765 when the *Victory* was launched.

The dockworkers were given a day off and the whole town appeared like a fairground. William Pitt, the Elder, accompanied by his Cabinet ministers, coached to Chatham to witness the hustle and bustle which preceded the ceremony. He saw scores of men knock out the great wooden supports and then grease the shipway with huge slabs of Russian tallow and mutton fat.

Right along the dockyard, in the specially erected stands, were thousands of excited vistors. Mr Pitt and his ministers were in the grandstand and the military bands played *Rule Britannia* as the *Victory* slipped down the shipway into the water at Chatham. She had taken six years to build and cost £15,000.

The *Victory*, with 100 guns, had been part of a gigantic ship-building programme presented to the House of Commons by Mr Pitt in those worrying days before the threatened invasion. Immense quantities of timber were used in the construction, each timber being subjected to careful selection. Oak trees from various parts of the world were felled and shipped to Chatham. Most of her timbers came from the forests of Kent and Hampshire and many fine old seasoned oaks from Black Forest, Germany. Only trees 100 years old or more were used in her construction and her decks were made of the finest teak.

The *Victory* lay in her moorings for 13 years and eventually fought her first action at the *Battle of Ushant,* proving herself fast and quick to answer her helm and sail close to the wind. That was in 1778. She then returned to Chatham and, incredibly, became a prison hulk.

The young lady lighting the cannons was a serving sailor on the good ship,* Euryalus *and the only woman to fight at the battle of Trafalgar. Battle-scarred and triumphant she is now in great demand to tell her story to the customers of the New Inn, John Street, Chatham where her parents are the landlords.

Nelson, in one of his visits to the dockyard, found her and requested the Admiralty to recondition and recommission the noble vessel to serve as his flagship. She was refitted, given additional guns and was ready for action in the same month that Napoleon completed his preparations for the invasion of England.

The *Victory* sailed out of Chatham, down the Medway, made her way through the Downs, joined the English fleet at Spithead and found herself in the thick of the decisive battle of Trafalgar. Chatham is a very proud town.

January 18: John Moore, the Archbishop of Canterbury died today at Lambeth Palace. He will be succeeded by Charles Manners Sutton, the Dean of Windsor

December: The county of Kent did not breed Horatio Nelson but it certainly launched him.

It was in the early spring of 1771 that the sickly 12-year-old boy, determined to be a sailor, drove with his father from school in Norfolk to London. There he was put on a stage coach for Chatham and told to find his own way to the dockyard and the ship *Raisonnable,* whose captain was his uncle, Maurice Suckling.

Captain Suckling was not too certain about his young nephew enjoying a naval career. "What has poor Horace done", he wrote, "who is so weak, that he above all the rest should be sent to rough it out at sea?"

But Horace, as he was known at the time, was a determined lad. Alone in the strange Kent town he walked to the reach of the Medway where the *Raisonnable* was moored, passing, on the way, the old building slip where the *Victory* had been launched in 1765. His uncle was away at the time but junior officers were soon showing young Nelson the ropes.

For ten years this slightly-built boy, bristling with natural charm and an air of authority, sailed up and down between London and the North Foreland as a Thames pilot. By 1781 he had his own ship, the *Albermarle* and by the time the French Revolutionary Wars began in 1793 he was a senior naval officer.

Nelson lost the sight in his right eye in 1794 when attacking Calvi in Corsica and his right arm was shattered in an assault on Tenerife in 1797. By 1798 he was in command of a fleet in the Mediterranean and scored his great victory at the Nile.

In between his adventures and heroic deeds at sea he always returned to Kent. In 1801 the Admiralty appointed him "on a particular service" to watch the harbours of Boulogne and Calais where Bonaparte was preparing troops for the invasion. After a spell of desk work at Sheerness he travelled by post-chaise to Deal, stopping the traffic at Faversham as cheering crowds gathered around him.

A barge containing the body of Admiral Nelson leaves the Royal Hospital for
etched outline by Augustus Pugin, had

The weak boy sent to 'rough

On August 15 of that year he attacked shipping outside Boulogne but it was not successful. Two of his officers on the *Medusa* were seriously wounded so Nelson found a lodging house for them in Deal.

The great captain, now a viscount, did not take lodgings in Deal himself despite reports to the contrary. On land he preferred to stay at the Three Kings Hotel and it was there he was joined on occasions by Lady Emma Hamilton whom he had met in Naples.

He dined frequently in Deal with his new-found love and enjoyed excursions with her to Dover Castle and to Ramsgate where Lady Hamilton's friend, Lady Dunmore lived. He visited the beautiful Heronden House at Eastry, the home of the great naval family, the Harveys. And he dined with his friend Admiral Lutwidge who was living in Deal.

When Lady Hamilton left, Nelson stayed on his ship in the Downs. The weather was frequently poor and he wrote in his diary: "This is the coldest place in England, most assuredly".

Seamen at Greenwich on January 8, 1806. It is flying the Union Jack. Other barges, seen in this watercolour over an spent the morning manoeuvring for position.

it at sea' — welcome home, Lord Nelson

There were pleasant distractions. The Mayor of Sandwich came aboard to present him with the freedom of the town and on one occasion he went to Walmer Castle to dine with William Pitt, then Warden of the Cinque Ports, but found "Billy" asleep and left without seeing him.

During Nelson's final two years he saw little of Kent. Emma Hamilton certainly visited Ramsgate and Margate for the bathing while living at Merton in Surrey and she often visited Nelson's elder brother, the Rev William Nelson, who became a canon at Canterbury. She stayed with the family and sang in the Cathedral.

Today, Lord Nelson is on his way to Kent once more — this time in a coffin in the battered hulk of the ship he commanded so brilliantly. *The Victory* is making her way to the South Foreland where she will anchor before sailing for the Nore.

It was 34 years ago that the 12-year-old boy drove into Chatham, a town he came to know so well.

Welcome home, Lord Nelson.

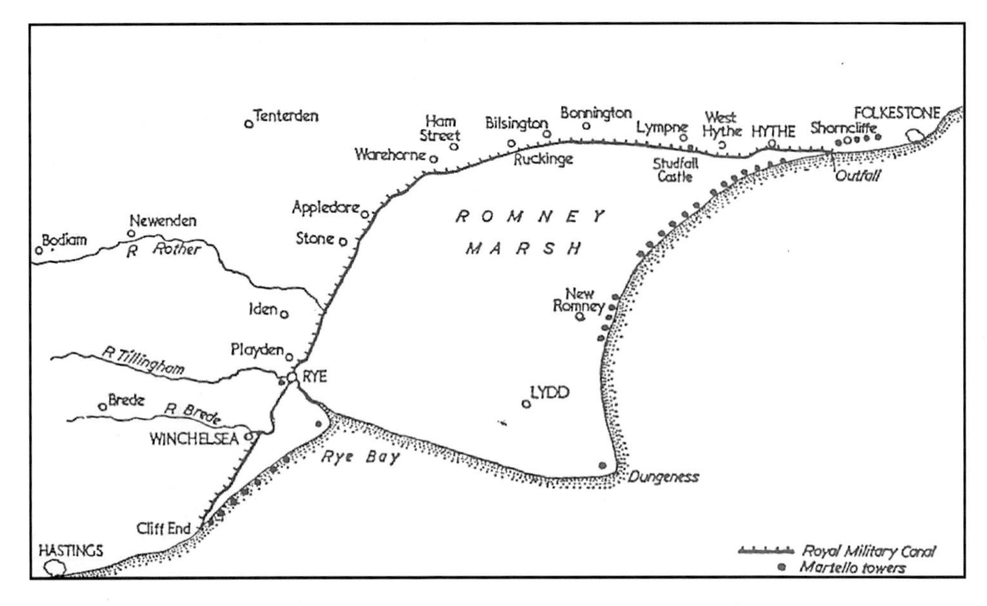

The line of the Military Canal from Shorncliffe via Hythe, Appledore and Rye to the sea at Cliff End, Pett, Sussex.

Nelson lies in state

January 9: **The funeral of Lord Nelson took place today in St Paul's Cathedral. Every member of the Royal family was present together with some of the oldest and ablest of Britain's admirals. Borne on the altar rails next to the coffin were the tattered flags of the *Victory.***

The ship arrived home from Cadiz on December 4 when she sailed from Spithead to the Nore. There, the corpse was transferred to the Admiralty yacht and conveyed to Greenwich. For four days the body of Nelson lay in state in the Painted Hall, Greenwich while crowds filed past from morning to evening.

Today crowds fill the streets of London. They are out in force in Chatham, too, and other Kent towns where people are in deep mourning. Great as the victory at Trafalgar was, it is almost forgotten in the grief for the loss of England's greatest hero.

October 8: **Meanwhile the war against France continues with Britain ruling the waves. Today the Royal Navy used rockets for the first time in the English Channel to bombard Boulogne. The French army, however, rules Europe following a series of victories on land.**

Military Canal open

April: The Military Canal which runs from Shorncliffe to Pett has been completed at last. It has cost £230,000, traverses 19 miles across Kent and part of Sussex and will serve as a defensive and navigable waterway.

Although the great civil engineer John Rennie gave valuable technical advice the project was supervised by Colonel John Brown, in command of the Royal Staff Corps, who employed up to 1,500 men and added many volunteers to speed up the operation in the final months.

There was really little need to hurry. Napoleon abandoned his plans to invade this part of England some months ago and ordered his troops — more than 100,000 of them — to strike camp and march to Austria.

However, the canal will still serve the purposes for which it was devised. Built in reaches, angled to one another it will enable enfilading cannon-fire to be brought to bear against assault troops attempting a crossing from the southern bank. More importantly it allows horse-drawn barges to carry troops, munitions and rations to any threatened point.

Colonel Brown is proud of his achievement. Last August he had the satisfaction of seeing the Commander-in-Chief inspect the canal from Hythe to Iden Lock where it joins the Rother. He travelled in a small boat drawn by horses which covered the distance at an average speed of seven miles an hour.

The canal itself is 60 feet wide. Excavated soil has been piled up on the landward side to form a parapet 35 feet wide that that will act as a protection for troops manning threatened areas and provide emplacements for cannons.

Beyond that parapet is the Royal Military Road made of shingle. On the seaward side is a narrower road which serves as a tow path for horses drawing barges up and down the canal.

The Military Canal at Hythe, 60 feet wide, a defensive and navigible waterway.

John Brown's navvies are rejoicing

The first sod was cut soon after William Pitt became Prime Minister again on October 30, 1804. Less than two years later the Rother was reached and then it was extended to Winchelsea. The final section, not connected with the main waterway, was completed this year. During that period bridges were built; following pressure by landowners and farmers, trees were also planted along the entire route.

The troops who dug the canal are known as navigators, or navvies. They were expected to excavate two cubic yards of soil daily which was removed by horse-drawn carts. The majority, spurred on by the attractive wages, rarely saw their wives and those that did found they did not have time to look after them.

According to a recent report in the Kentish Gazette, the county's oldest newspaper, one man decided that his young wife would be better off with a new partner so he took her to the market place at Hythe.

The report states: *"Last week the wife of one of the men employed in cutting the canal was conducted by her husband to the market place at Hythe with a halter round her neck and tied to a post; from whence she was purchased for 6d. She was a young woman, not more than 20 years of age, tall and of a likely form and figure. Her face, however exhibited evident marks of incompatibility of temper. Notwithstanding the new partner led her away with much apparent satisfaction."*

'How I leave my country' were Pitt's last words

January 23: **Prime Minister William Pitt who gave the orders to build the Military Canal and frequently superintended the work from his base at Walmer Castle has not survived to see the project completed. He died today aged 47 after a long illness.**

He was Prime Minister in 1784 aged 24 and immediately made a mark with forceful speeches. He urged Parliamentary reform and he restored the nation's finances after the War of American Independence. Pitt the Younger, as he was known, improved criminal administration, supported William Wilberforce's campaign against slavery and worked towards the Act of Union with Ireland.

He had strong connections with Kent. He was born at Hayes Place, kept a country home at Westerham, lived at Holwood House, Keston for several years and was Lord Warden.

His second period as Prime Minister began in 1804 as the French prepared to invade. That threat has faded but Napoleon is still growing in strength, especially after his victory at Austerlitz.

William Pitt's last words were: "Oh my country. How I leave my country!"

The Wilberforce Oak at Holwood Park, Keston — a memorial to the plans for the abolition of slavery

Kentish oak was privy to plans to abolish slavery

March 25: Some 13 years before the turn of the century William Wilberforce, social reformer and evangelical philanthropist, made a special journey to Holwood House, Keston to persuade Prime Minister William Pitt to support his Bill to abolish the slave trade. The two men walked the grounds and then sat under an oak tree while Wilberforce emphasised how Britain could lead the world in ending this lucrative trade.

It was such an historic meeting that Wilberforce made a note in his diary: *"I well remember after a conversation with Mr Pitt in the open air, at the foot of an old tree at Holwood, just above the steep descent into the vale of Keston, I resolved to give notice on a fit occasion in the House of Commons of my intention to bring forward the abolition of the slave trade".*

Convinced by the arguments put forward by this determined Tory and impressed by his long battle against slavery, Pitt agreed that "all God's creatures must be free". The Prime Minister and Wilberforce then worked out how they could overcome opponents in the powerful slave master's lobby, who contend that slaves are happy and better off than free men and that other nations would take over Britain's trade.

From that meeting at Holwood, when the great crusade was conceived, numerous attempts have been made to abolish the slave trade but they all failed — until yesterday. Despite opposition from West Indies merchants and George III, Parliament has, at last, passed the Abolition Bill.

Although Wilberforce has devoted his political life to the Abolitionist cause he was supported by a number of dedicated men including Pitt and Charles James Fox who both died before the Bill became law.

Holwood House — William Pitt's home for 15 years — was sold at auction in 1802 for £15,000 but the "Wilberforce Oak" still stands in the grounds. Sadly there is no memorial to the "Great Commoner" either in the estate or in Keston village which was Pitt's favourite retreat. Scores of statesmen from all over the world visited Holwood. William Wilberforce was the most distinguished. *See page 86*

William Wilberforce — he persuaded the prime minister to support his bill to abolish the slave trade.

The silk trade of Canterbury

MANY of the silk mills of Canterbury are being demolished following the death of James Callaway, who invested wisely and produced best-quality silk by traditional methods. He ran a successful business in the city for many years.

Some years before the turn of the century competition from the north of England was threatening his business so he experimented with new materials and invented Canterbury muslin.

It brought a new, but all too brief, prosperity to the craftsmen of the city. Callaway died last year and many of his workers — the labouring poor — have turned to making hop bags for a living.

See page 246

March 24: The Duke of Portland has been summoned by George III to form a new government following the collapse of Lord Grenville's coalition, which was formed to prosecute war against France following the death of Pitt. Grenville wanted to ease the restrictions placed on Roman Catholics in the army and navy.

Sir John Moore and 7,000 men of his Light Division which he raised and trained at Shorncliffe, have been ordered to Gibraltar to bolster the garrison there and constitute a mobile reserve.

This is only possible because of the increase in the size of the British army brought about by encouraging militiamen to join regiments of the line.

Lord Castlereagh, reappointed as secretary of war under the new Portland administration, has secured in parliament the Militia Transfer Bill, providing more than 30,000 extra men for the army.

See page 28

Attractive girl given credit for round-arm revolution

June: A new of style of bowling a cricket ball, in which the arm is straight and delivery made with a round-arm action, was introduced in an extraordinary match at Penenden Heath recently between 23 of Kent and 13 of England.

Although the match was won by Kent who triumphantly claimed the prize of 600 guineas, all talk is about the unconventional delivery which has shocked the cricket world and induced howls of protest from Lords.

The man responsible for introducing the new round-arm action is John Wiles Esq, a country gentleman and great all-round sportsman who lives at Totford, near Canterbury. But he gives all the credit to his sister!

During their regular practices together, usually in a large barn on his estate, Miss Wiles found it impossible to use a genuine underhand delivery because of the voluminous size of her skirt. So she delivered round-arm and found it very effective.

So did John Wiles. He practised the style himself with great success and persuaded Kent's leading professional bowler William Ashby to take up the idea. Soon it was being used by the entire Kent team and fully proved an obstacle in getting runs.

Will it stay? No official objection has yet come from Lords, but officials say a law is certain to be introduced to make it clear the ball must be delivered with the hand below the elbow.

A handsome range of substantial barracks have been built at Hythe to house the Royal Staff Corps. The barracks can accommodate 300 men and have officers' apartments and special rooms for married men. Facing the barracks across the Royal Military Canal are the new premises of the Royal Wagon Train. The three forts built in 1798 — Twiss, Sutherland and Moncrieff — reflect the need to defend this vulnerable stretch of coastline. In the hills above Hythe two 24-pound guns are manned by the Saltwood battery.

It's time to stop the poppet show'

January: With the exception of its twin towers, which still stand majestically on high, dry land, the ancient church of Reculver — a sacred shrine for more than 1,000 years — is to be demolished by order of the parishioners.

When Francis Drake sailed past in the Golden Hind the church stood almost half a mile away from the coast but the sea has claimed so much land that the precious monument will soon be totally engulfed.

One year before Trafalgar the chapel house slipped dramatically into the waves and people came from all over Kent to peer at the ruins and to surmise how long it would be before the church went the same way. The vicar's mother, considerably hurt by the constant presence of an excited mob, suggested that the few remaining villagers should demolish the church themselves. She said: "It must not be kept as a poppet show".

The parish clerk, Mr Brett made a note of the proceedings. *"The vicker took it into consideration and named it to the farmers in the parish about taking it down. Sum was for it and sum against. Then Mr Nailor wrote to the Bishop to know if he might have the church took down, and his answer was that it must be done by a majority of people in the parish. He got the majority of one, so down comes the church"* — signed (Mr Brett, clerk to the old church).

Some 1800 years ago Reculver was a sizeable Roman fort guarding the northern entrance to the Wantsum Channel. Known as Regulbium it remained the ecclesiastical centre for a vast area of Roman Kent.

Malevolent seas, kindled by unrelenting north-easterly gales have battered the north Kent coast for centuries and the headlands slipped into the sea taking with them the Roman buildings of Reculver.

Today the town has become total rack to the mercy of the waves as Mr Brett, the clerk, knows so well. He finishes his text with these words: *"And down came the church and what was His thoats about His flock that day no-one knows."*

Martello Towers in place as threat of war vanishes

ALTHOUGH the threat of a French invasion has all but vanished, seventy three Martello towers and two eleven-gun circular forts are in place along the Kent and Sussex coast.

Since work began in the spring of 1805 under the direction of the Board of Ordnance and the Royal Engineers several teams of local builders have been working almost non-stop. The towers are circular, bomb-proof, almost identical in design and present the most effective means of coastal protection.

The main contractor has been William Hobson who, to the delight of local builders along the coast, then sub-contracted.

The towers are some 33 feet tall and tapered, so that on the seaward side the walls vary in thickness from 13 feet at the base to six feet at parapet level. The bricks were shipped down the Thames and then bedded in a mixture of lime, ash and hot tallow so as to increase their ability to withstand bombardment.

Entrance to the towers is at first-floor level where there is a garrison for 24 men and one officer each equipped with muskets. The flat roof above forms a gun platform and is supported by a central column from the base of the tower. A 24-pound gun mounted on a carriage is capable of traversing 360 degrees.

The stock of ammunition is considerable — 100 rounds of solid shot, 20 grape-shot, 20 common shells, 20 8 lb powder cartridges, half a hundredweight of slow match and 40 junk wads.

If war with France does flare up again, extra men will be needed to man the guns. They will come from the fleet, infantry garrisons or county militia regiments.

Invasion seems unlikely. The towers, however, are impregnable with heavy siege guns. The 24 pounders will cause immense damage to lightly-built invasion craft as they near the shore.

Martello Towers as seen on the beach at Hythe.

Mutiny against Captain Bligh

CAPTAIN William Bligh who lives at the Manor House, Farningham when he is in England, knows all about mutinies. The former naval officer, chiefly remembered for his command of *H.M.S. Bounty* in 1789 and the mutiny on board led by acting lieutenant Fletcher Christian, has now incurred the wrath of British army officers in New South Wales where he has been the governor since 1805. Arrested by his deputy, William Bligh is on his way back to England to face the courts.

The trouble stems from his long fight against corruption in the army which made him extremely unpopular in the colony and led to a serious mutiny.

Bligh's friends in north-west Kent are still talking about the occasion when Christian Fletcher set him adrift in an open boat with 18 of his crew. After a journey of three months and some 3,500 miles he brought them to safety on Timor island.

There was another mutiny against Bligh in 1797 as part of the general unrest at the Nore. He made two more journeys to the South Pacific and saw service with Nelson before taking over as Governor in Australia.

The courts have twice vindicated Bligh and are likely to so so again. It is believed he will now retire and settle down in his peaceful Kentish village. *See page 49*

After a long retreat, Moore's ragged army turned to face the enemy at Corunna where a massive battle ensued.

General John Moore killed at Corunna

January 17: General Sir John Moore is dead. The charismatic Commanding Officer of the British Army in Spain — who, six years ago, commanded the Light Infantry Brigade at Shorncliffe — died from his wounds today after rallying his bedraggled troops to deliver the most stunning blow to his French pursuers.

With Lieutenant-General Sir Arthur Wellesley back in London, Moore had taken over and quickly proved to be one of the most remarkable men ever to lead in the field. The man who made his name in action in Corsica and Egypt and as a trainer of troops in Kent is said in just a few weeks "to have breathed the breath of a new life into the British army".

Moore came to Shorncliffe from Chatham in July 1803 and at the request of the Duke of York, formed a regiment for instruction in the new light infantry tactics. It was at Shorncliffe that these ideas were perfected. During this time he lived at Sir John Shaw's house in Sandgate.

His great campaign began last October when he drove north-east out of Portugal to help save Madrid and southern Spain from French occupation. Among his 30,000 troops was "upwards of a 1,000 men" of the West Kent Regiment (50th Foot). Sixty of them were accompanied by their wives, who had been chosen by ballot.

As the French armies collapsed in rapid succession Moore received intelligence that Napoleon had arrived and was advancing with a force of 250,000. It was no contest so Moore gave the order to "make a run for it".

For up to 17 hours a day, over the rocks and snows of Galicia, General Moore headed north-west towards Corunna followed by the superior French forces under Marshal Soult who dealt swiftlessly and ruthlessly with British stragglers. In fact 6,000 were killed.

The Kent men of the 50th Foot — now known as the "dirty half hundred," for their habit of wiping their faces with the black facings of their cuffs — crossed the Esla River near Valencia in full flood. With their arms and ammunition held high above their heads the men waded shoulder deep. The women and children suffered great hardship; one woman dropped dead in the road and a soldier carried her two-year-old child on his knapsack throughout the retreat.

Fighting various rearguard actions on the way the ragged army trudged on, many by now barefeet. After walking for 250 miles they reached Corunna where Moore discovered that most of the ships of the fleet, which were to evacuate his army, had not arrived. He turned to face the enemy.

A massive battle ensued with Moore riding up and down the front line rallying his troops. One officer of the 1st battalion of the 50th, today gave a dramatic picture of Moore's determination. "On one occasion he was talking to me when a shot tore off the leg of a man who screamed horribly and rolled around exciting agitation with others. The General said: 'This is nothing my lads. Keep your ranks. Take that man away. My good fellow, don't make such a noise; we must bear these things better".

Gradually the French were forced back with great loss and the 50th Regiment, led by Napier and Charles Stanhope of Chevening, were given the honour of entering Corunna. Behind them rode Moore shouting: "Well done, my majors!"

As the General urged them forward he received the terrible grapeshot wound which caused his death. He died this evening while 24,000 of his 30,000 troops were busily embarking for England. Stanhope was also killed and Napier taken prisoner.

Corunna, is a victory-in-defeat for the British who have completely thwarted Napoleon's plans. By invading Portugal, forcing the Spanish royal family to abdicate and placing on the throne his own brother Joseph Bonaparte, the French emperor was convinced he could conquer the whole Iberian peninsular and thus continue with his plans to deny Britain the use of every port in continental Europe.

Following the triumphs of Wellesley and then Moore it's all gone wrong for "Boney"who is on his way back home to Paris.

The war, however, continues.

See page 35

Thousands of soldiers who trained under General Sir John Moore (left) at Shorncliffe will remember how he made them run up the steep hill to the camp in an effort to train them in mobility and speed. This was to prove vital in Spain. The General rented Sir John Shaw's house while his mother and sister were in York Cottage, Castle Road. He died a hero's death in Corunna and there are plans now to place a memorial to him on the Esplanade at Sandgate.

September 26: The secretary for war, Lord Castlereagh, a contender for the premiership, has resigned from the government after fighting a duel with foreign secretary George Canning. They have been political rivals for many years. Canning was wounded in the thigh and Castlereagh had a button shot off his lapel.

See page 60

With the resignation of Castlereagh and Canning, the Duke of Portland's government has collapsed. Spencer Perceval is to be the new Prime Minister.

A Gull stream light has been placed on Goodwin Sands to protect shipping. Since the Middle Ages thousands of vessels have been lost. The Sands have the capacity to claim ships, break them up and swallow them without trace.

Frederick, the Duke of York and second son of George III, has resigned as commander-in-chief of the army following scandalous allegations concerning his mistress, Mrs Mary Anne Clarke.

Dartford as seen from East Hill. The proletarian rebel Wat Tyler, said to have been born in Dartford, started the insurrection against the poll tax here in 1381. It was to this town that John Hall came to seek his fortune.

Food preserved in cans — what a good idea!

SOME years before the turn of the century a 20-year-old millwright walked from Laverstoke in Hampshire to Dartford to seek work in the local mills. Today John Hall has his own engineering works, reputed to be among the finest in the country. He also owns a gun powder factory at Faversham, paper works at Horton Kirby, a flour mill at Chislehurst and a stall in Convent Garden.

This year, in association with his son-in-law Bryan Donkin, he has bought a French patent by a chemist called Appert for preserving meat and other food stuffs by canning. It cost him £1,000 but John Hall believes it could revolutionise the perishable food industry and aims to set up a canning factory at Bermondsey — the first in Britain.

John Hall still remembers those early days in Dartford. Accompanied by his father William on that long walk from Hampshire, he soon found work and his skill as a mechanic was quickly recognised by the mill owners, who persuaded him to start a small blacksmith's shop in Lowfield Street.

His business prospered and he acquired larger premises in Hythe Street. Next door lived a wealthy Flemish farmer who had four pretty daughters and John Hall admired each one but found it difficult to decide who should be his wife.

Paying a visit early one morning he found that three of the girls had not risen but Sarah was up, active and attentive so John said that she was the one for him. The couple were married in 1791. Today they have six sons and four daughters.

In 1801 John obtained permission to divert the stream in Waterside Street so that he could obtain power to drive his machinery. And from that moment his business went from strength to strength.

There are certain to be many improvements before the canning factory is running smoothly but John and Bryan Donkin are proud to be the pioneers on what promises to be a huge breakthrough in food preservation. *See page 33*

1810-1819

1810: Evangelical members of the Wesleyan Methodist movement split to form the Primitive Methodists.

1811: The Prince of Wales, the flambuoyant George, is appointed Prince Regent, due to the King's mental illness.

John Nash, an architect, designs a new road for London. It will be known as Regent Street.

The population of England, Scotland and Wales is 12,552,144, according to the second national census. Kent is growing rapidly especially at Chatham which continues to be the largest town.

1812: A company is formed which plans to install gas lights in Picadilly, Coventry Street and part of Prince's Street, London. *See page 40.*

The war has led to an exceptional rise in food prices— particularly bread and potatoes. There are riots all over the country.

An American pirate ship, *Argus*, is captured in the English Channel following a campaign of terror round the English coast.

1813: Various troops of yeomanry throughout Kent combine to form East Kent and West Kent Yeomanry cavalry.

April 13: The church of St Mary, Hillborough is consecrated, replacing the partially demolished church of Reculver

May 6: The spire of St Alphege, Greenwich is destroyed by lightning.

A steamboat service between London, Gravesend and Margate is inaugurated, using the newly completed stone pier at the latter port for landing passengers.

1814: Britain, Russia, Austria and Prussia sign the Treaty of Paris to bring "perpetual peace and friendship" between themselves and France.

The war between Great Britain and the United States which began in 1812, as a result of Britain's blockade of trade with Napoleon, ended today at Ghent with the signing of a treaty.

A Packet boat, *The British Queen* is lost on the Goodwin Sands with the loss of many lives.

1815: As the war with France ends and the peace treaty is signed work is completed on the fortifications on the Western Heights at Dover.

The passing of the Corn Law which prohibits foreign imports until the home price reaches £4 for 13 kg is greeted with riots in London. Farmers in Kent say imports are forcing down their corn prices.

Viscount Castlereagh, the foreign sectretary, proposes that a public monument should be erected to commemorate the Battle of Waterloo. Castlereagh lives at North Cray Cottage, Footscray, Kent. *See page 60*

General Sir George Harris of Belmont is raised to the peerage as Baron Harris of Seringapatam and Mysore and of Belmont, his family home. He is married to Anne Carteret Dixon of Bath and their eldest son, William George, 33, is the second baron. A soldier , like his father, William saw service in western Europe during the Napoleonic Wars and was shot in the shoulder at Waterloo.

1816: Richard Sheridan, the playwright who lives at Polesden Lacey, near Guildford, dies in poverty. Sheridan wrote *The Rivals* and *School for Scandal.*

Many small farmers in Kent, along with others throughout the country, have gone bankrupt and blame the new Corn Law. Agriculture, they say, is in a far worse position than it was before the war.

A protest meeting calling for radical land reform erupts into violence in Spa Fields, Islington as speaker after speaker voices his anger over high taxes, cuts in Poor Law payments and the Corn Law.

A twopenny edition of *The Political Register*, published by the radical William Cobbett, has already sold 60,000 copies. *See page 58*

Leigh Hunt is sentenced to two years' imprisonment for describing the Prince Regent as a "corpulent gentleman". The Prince's low level of morality has made him something of a laughing stock with middle-class British Society. *See page 49*

There is large scale emigration from Ireland in the wake of a potato famine that has killed thousands of people. A number are arriving into the hop gardens of Kent.

1818: 14,000 Londoners present a petition to the House of Commons complaining about the high price and poor quality of alcoholic drinks.

John Nash has completed Regent Street, a broad thoroughfare running from the Prince's residence, Carlton House, Pall Mall to Marylebone Park — now renamed Regent's Park.

1819: A peaceful mass meeting at Manchester turns into killing fields as a troop of Yeomanry charges into the crowd of 80,000 people, killing 11 and wounding 500. The incident is being referred to as the "Peterloo Massacre".

Rochester bridge is widened with a stronger central arch. *See page 147.*

Mill owners can no longer employ children under nine in textile factories and children under 16 can only work 12 hours a day.

A humorous look at sea bathing in Margate. This hand-coloured cartoon by Thomas Rowlandson is being sold to visitors to Margate for one shilling.

The 'genteel people who resort to Margate'

FOLLOWING the completion of a new stone pier and the introduction of a paddle steamboat service from London via Gravesend, thousands of visitors are pouring into Margate for a day, a weekend or, if they can afford it, perhaps a longer stay.

Visitors are conveyed from the hoys to the shore in small boats. One visitor, recalling the first steamboat arrival, wrote recently: "The inhabitants poured down in such numbers that they could be compared with nothing better than the savages on Cook's arrival at Otaheire. You could not have a parcel with a single night cap in it that was not immediately seized upon by some kind of ready hand, ready to convey it to your compartment or to their own. If Argos had a thousand eyes he had need of them all!".

Seabathing and the drinking of sea water, as an alternative to visiting Tunbridge Wells and other Spa towns, came into fashion more than 50 years ago but in that time Margate and Ramsgate have established themselves as Britain's premier seaside resorts. This is what the Kent historian Edward Hasted has to say about Margate, which he once described as "a poor fishing town".

"...When it came to be known that the shore here was so well adapted to bathing, being an entire level and covered with the finest sand, which extends for several miles on each side of the harbour, and the easy distance from the metropolis, with the convenience of so frequent a passage by water, it gave Margate a preference before all others, to which the beauty and healthiness of it and the adjoining country contributed still more..."

Hasted describes the excellence of sea bathing and the numbers of Genteel people who resort to Margate. "...Near the harbour there are several commodious bathing rooms, out of which the bathers are driven in the machines, any depth along the sands into the sea; at the back of the machine is a door, through which the bathers descend a few steps into the water, and an umbrella of canvas dropping over conceals them from the public view. Upwards of 40 of these machines are frequently employed..."

See page 45

Genius of the paper industry was an apprentice at Dartford

BRYAN Donkin, a skilled "mechanist" and a former apprentice to John Hall at Dartford, has revolutionised the world's paper industry by inventing a machine that produces continuous rolls of paper. Previously it was manufactured sheet by sheet — a slow and labour-intensive process.

Donkin left Dartford a few years ago and set up a factory at Fort Place, Bermondsey where he was financed by two brothers, Henry and Sealy Fourdrinier who managed London's leading firm of stationers.

They realised that such a machine had the potential to transform the paper-making industry and invited Donkin to work on the project. Within a few years he had perfected a continuous paper-making machine that was a technical and commercial success. The basic principle was the formation of paper on an endless belt of woven wire. This meant that separate moulds used in the hand-made process were no longer required.

The Fourdrinier brothers invested £60,000 but, sadly, have been declared bankrupt and a legal wrangle is taking place as to whom has ownership.

Genius: Bryan Donkin

Hester Stanhope leaves Kent for pilgrimage to Jerusalem

THE death of William Pitt at the age of 47 just four years ago was a sickening blow for the nation but chief among the mourners was the young lady who devoutly nursed him through his long illness — his lovely niece, Lady Hester Lucy Stanhope.

Seventeen years younger than Pitt and the daughter of Charles Stanhope of Chevening near Sevenoaks, Hester possessed such a cheerful and outgoing personality that she caught the shrewd eye of Uncle Billy.

He persuaded her to live with him at Walmer Castle "as", he later wrote, "an aristocratic ornament of drawing rooms and the confidante of statesmen".

Pitt admired her eccentricities such as blackening her face with cork. He also loved the way she tended the garden. "I let her do as she pleases", he once said, "for if she were resolved to cheat the Devil, she could do it!".

His death in 1806, quickly followed by that of her brother, Charles at Corunna, and General Sir John Moore, whom she greatly admired, was too much for Hester who left Kent and England earlier this year saying she will never return.

With a £1,200 pension from the King and accompanied by her faithful doctor companion, Miss Williams and an impressive entourage, Lady Stanhope is making a pilgrimage to Jerusalem. She yearns for adventure.

See page 99

October 18: Viscount Wellesley, now Lord Wellington, is back in Portugal and solidly entrenched at Torres Vedras with his army which now includes a battalion of The Buffs.

Numerically the French and British armies are well matched but Wellington has built stone walls across valleys and flooded the lines of approach. His position appears impregnable.

November 3: Following the death yesterday of his 27-year-old daughter Princess Amelia, George III's illness has taken a turn for the worse and physicians have forced him to wear a straightjacket. He is 72.

The King, who has just celebrated the golden jubilee of his reign, is so traumatised by Amelia's death that doctors hold out no hope for a complete recovery. It is now possible that the Prince of Wales will take over as Regent and there may even be a change of Government. *See page 56*

December 20: Prime Minister Spencer Perceval today introduced the Regency Bill. It is based on the original bill devised by William Pitt in 1788 when the King first became ill. Perceval took over as Prime Minister following the collapse of the Duke of Portland's government last year.

Churches in Kent set up schools for the poor

CHURCHES throughout Kent are making vigorous efforts to put education on their agenda by providing an educational system in place of the previous intermittent private efforts. The idea is to lift the clouds of ignorance from the minds of the poor.

Many children are now learning to read and write at Sunday School in the parish church or in classes arranged by the Baptist Church or Wesleyan Methodist classes.

Almost every child in the county now has the opportunity to attend school regularly and is expected to do so by the church and parish authorities. They are encouraged by the Church of England's new body, The National Society for the Education of the Poor.

Many village churches have monitoring methods by which half-trained children, under the controlling eye of a master, drill even younger children in the rudiments of the three Rs. This allows large numbers to be taught at one time at low cost.

Most village schools are financed by public subscription — 1d a week for reading and 2d for reading and writing. Additional income is coming from endowments and charity trusts.

In some parishes, teachers have been appointed and allocated money for books and testaments to teach children living in the workhouse.

Meanwhile children of the gentry continue to be schooled by governesses with a more formal education following on at small private schools. *See page 180*

Several serving soldiers with the Kent Regiments are allowed to take their wives with them to the war zone in Spain. Only six women per company are permitted and they are drawn by lots at the last possible moment, usually on the quay side at Gravesend or Chatham, to prevent desertion by men whose wives are left behind. The women are not paid but receive half rations in exchange for washing, cooking and mending. It is believed that 4,500 British wives are currently in Spain and, according to reports, have been a constant source of trouble — many drinking as heavily as the men. However, it has also been said that they show intense loyalty to the Regiment, officers and husbands. Those widowed have found new husbands.

Heroes all — Buffs' bloodbath at Albuhera

Saving the colour at the Battle of Albuhera. An oil on canvas painting by William Barns Wollen

May 16th: The Buffs have almost been wiped out. Yesterday, during fierce fighting on a ridge above the village of Albuhera in Spain, 643 men were massacred by French forces advancing under Marshal Soult. When dawn broke this morning it revealed the gruesome sight of the Kent men dead on the hillside. Most of them had been stripped naked by looters and scavengers. Rescuers picked up 12 officers and 229 men all badly wounded.

It was in September 1808 that the Buffs sailed for Portugal and immediately became heavily engaged in the Peninsular War — one company fighting with the rearguard during the retreat to Corunna. By February, 1809 under Sir Arthur Wellesley, who had returned to command the British Army, the Buffs were in the van of 20 Battalions hoping to drive the French out of Portugal.

Victory at Talavera was costly for the Kent boys who had 152 casualties and their commanding officer among the dead. So was the offensive at Doura — 50 casualties out of a British total of 121. This won a special commendation from Wellesley, now elevated to Viscount Wellington. Yet that was nothing compared to the tragedy at Albuhera where the Buffs led the 2nd Division in an attempt to block the French advance.

There were plenty of heroes. Ensign Thomas, a lad of 16, carried the Regimental colour and, at one time yelled: "Rally on me, men. I will be your pivot". He was killed by the French and the colour was captured.

Hours later the Brigade's Fusiliers made a magnificent attack from the right flank which sent the French cascading down the sodden hillside. In the process a sergeant regained the Buffs' Regimental colour. So grateful are the Buffs to the Royal Fusiliers that they are hoping to arrange honorary membership of each other's messes.

Another hero was a young lad, Lieutenant Latham, who managed to seize the King's colours from Ensign Walsh who lay dying. With hussars all around him Latham slashed out with a sword but a sabre blow split his face almost in two and another cut off his arm. As blows continued to reign upon him he sank to the ground and the hacking horsemen rode off.

Many hours later, as they picked up the wounded men, Buff officers found an unconscious and unrecognisable form. In his tunic, torn from its pike and heavy with blood, was the King's colours. One-armed and disfigured Lieutenant Latham had somehow survived.

Another hero of Albuhera is Viscount Beresford from Kilndown, near Goudhurst — one of Wellington's lieutenants who led the Portuguese into battle and helped to block Soult's advance while the Buffs scaled the ridge. *See page 38*

July 1: Latham has received surgical treatment at the personal expense of the Prince of Wales and despite his disabilities is making a fighting recovery.

He has also received a gold medal from his brother officers who are recommending "Albuhera Day" as the Buffs' regimental day.

A pontoon train troop proceeds under order to bridge a river. Real action for the Royal Sappers and Miners from the School of Military Engineering at Brompton Barracks, Chatham.

Engineers' school opens at Brompton

April: A School of Military Engineering has opened in the stylish new barracks at Brompton, Gillingham and a new corps — known as the Royal Sappers and Miners — has been established there.

The mastermind behind the scheme and first director of the school is Captain Charles Pasley, who fought with the late Sir John Moore at Corunna. He said this week that the lower ranks of the army are mostly drawn from the poorer classes and many are illiterate. They will be taught reading and writing while officers and other ranks will receive instructions in geometry and plan drawing.

Captain Charles Pasley

"NCOs and men", he said, "should be able to support their officers in the practical operation of siege warfare. They must have the ability to instruct the ordinary sapper".

Many local people are confused by the word 'sapping' but of all the military arts taught at the school it is one of the most important. It involves the cutting of zig-zag trenches or saps to provide a covered approach to the base of a fort and then mining beneath it to blow up the walls.

Army units have been stationed in Chatham and Gillingham since the dockyard was first established. In 1716 the Board of Ordnance, who supplied guns, rifles and ammunition, founded the Royal Regiment of Artillery and then the following year set up the Corps of Engineers consisting only of officers.

By 1787, the corps — then known as the Royal Engineers — provided officers for six companies of Royal Military Artificers based at Brompton.

The barracks were begun eight years ago, completed two years later in 1806 and for architectural elegance far surpassed other military establishments in England. Constructed on three sides of a quadrangle, they supplied accommodation for 1,200 men with apartments for officers. A handsome chapel and offices were built in the centre of the north side and stables established at the rear.

Two years ago Charles Pasley published a book on military policy which was critically acclaimed by such great writers as Coleridge, Wordsworth and Jane Austen. Thomas Telford also read it.

In it he stresses how his student engineers will conduct simulated warfare in the Medway and in the upper and lower Lines. They will learn elementary fortification. "In real seige conditions", he says, "they must be prepared to hazard life and limb in the performance of their duty".

Hasted spent seven years in a debtors' prison

Edward Hasted

EDWARD Hasted who has died penniless in a small charity hospital in Corsham, Wiltshire, will always be remembered for his monumental and brilliantly researched History of Kent. He was in his 80th year.

The last years of his life were troubled ones. After deserting his wife for another woman he fled to France and remained there until the war drove him back home and into a debtors' prison for almost seven years.

In his declining years, however, the earl of Radnor, a descendant of the Canterbury Huguenots, presented Hasted with the mastership of a small charity hospital endowed by Lady Hungerford at Corsham. He died in the lodge house.

Hasted was born in London, of Kentish stock, in December 1732. He trained at Lincoln's Inn, became a lawyer and moved to Sutton-at-Hone, near Dartford. By 1755 he was paying respects to the daughter of a neighbour, Anne Dorman. He married Anne, by special licence, in July of that year and the couple moved to Canterbury but quickly returned to Sutton-at-Hone where they acquired a large manor house, St John's — the home, in the days of King John, of the Knights Hospitallers.

At considerable cost Edward made great improvements to the house and then settled down to write a *History and Topographical Survey of the County of Kent.* It took him many years to research and write but was a great literary achievement and propelled him to the kind of popularity enjoyed by Chaucer and Lambarde in much earlier years.

These were happy years for Edward. Apart from his writing he took great interest in parish affairs, attended the village church regularly and sat on the West Kent quarter sessions' bench at Maidstone.

The couple who had five sons and two daughters moved back to Canterbury where Edward gave 19 years' service as a justice in east Kent.

However, by 1789 his finances were in total confusion and, despite selling his various estates, the historian found himself sinking deeper and deeper into debt. In 1790 he abandoned Anne and fled to France with another woman.

When the great historian returned — driven out by Napoleon — he was arrested immediately.

No longer the idle men of Cranbrook

AS the economic crisis, generated by the crippling Napoleonic War, continues to cause great misery here in Kent, one small town has come up with a novel idea to help the unemployment problem.

The overseers of Cranbrook have hired Friezley Farm and are setting the "idle men" to work on it. Farming can be a profitable business and the unemployed men are delighted. Cranbrook may well be pioneering a project that will spread rapidly across the county.

Following the opening of Margate Harbour two years ago which was designed by John Rennie, work is now underway on a new stone pier. It will be completed by next year.

March: *HMS Kent*, 74-gun third-rate cruiser of 1,964 tons, has been laid up at Devonport where she will serve as a training ship for the foreseeable future.

The fifth ship of this name, *HMS Kent* was commanded by Captain William Hope in 1798, the year of Nelson's great victory at the Nile. The following March she joined the fleet of the Admiral Lord Duncan and in 1799 deprived Napoleon of 25 good ships by forcing the Dutch fleet to surrender.

HMS Kent fought at Alexandria and Hope in 1801 and served under Nelson off Toulon in 1803.

May 11: Prime Minister Spencer Perceval was shot dead today in the lobby of the House of Commons. The assassin is believed to be John Bellingham who blames the British Government for his debts.

October: Arthur Wellesley, now the Duke of Wellington, looks certain to drive the French out of Spain after forcing them to fight for long periods of time.

October: Humphrey Davy, the chemist whose experimental methods led to the discovery of sodium and potassium, has been injured in a gunpowder accident at Tonbridge where he is in partnership with John Children of Ferox Hall and James Burton of Mabledon, Tonbridge.

The explosion could have blinded him but he is left with very sore eyes which scurrilous friends suggest may have been caused by his troublesome wife, Jane.

Napoleon retreats from Spain and faces defeat

December: The British Expeditionary Force in the Iberian Peninsula have finally routed the French army with stirring victories at Vittoria and Pamplona. With his hold on Germany also slipping, Napoleon is retreating towards the Rhine and there are reports that he is losing his troops' loyalty. After a brilliant military campaign Wellington is on the verge of a famous victory.

The 50th Foot of the West Kent Regiment were involved in the decisive battle at Vittoria at a cost of 27 dead and 76 wounded. No-one is saying whether the Kent boys were involved in the orgy of looting and pillaging which followed the victory but it is believed the temptation was irresistible. Apparently, Wellington's booty resembled that of Alexander the Great!

Earlier this year the 50th were detailed to guard Maya, one of two passes into the Pyrenees and found themselves facing 5,000 of the enemy. Undaunted by numbers they charged, crossing bayonets with the opposing column. Again and again they charged until the order was given to retire. There were many casualties.

The Buffs have also been in the thick of things. One of the first regiments to advance into France they lost 99 men and 12 officers during a valiant counter attack near the village of Vieux Mouguerre.

The breakthrough is close. Wellington has built up a position of enormous strength. *See page 41*

New canal will link Thames with the Channel

June: The nationwide network of canals, which is slowly linking industrial cities will soon provide the country with a complete waterborne transport system. Kent has not been left out.

This week the Kent and Sussex Junction Canal, linking Thames with the Channel via the already navigable Medway and Royal Military Canal, reached a stage nearer reality when Parliament approved the project.

The distance is about 28 miles and it is planned to start at the Medway end near East Peckham and rise to the Weald by means of nine locks. From Rams Hill, north of Horsmonden, the canal will remain on a 120- foot contour until it reaches Tenterden.

From there the canal will be taken down to Romney Marshes by 12 more locks as far as Reading Street and then on the level to the Royal Military Canal just south of Appledore.

For the engineers it will be a tremendous challenge for two feeder reservoirs are also planned in the grounds of Sissinghurst Castle at the half way mark. Parliament has given the promoters three years to raise the funds, believed to be in excess of £300,000.

When the canal opens 40-ton barges will carry chalk, lime and coal into the garden of England. Out will come timber, agricultural produce and, of course, hops. *See page 46*

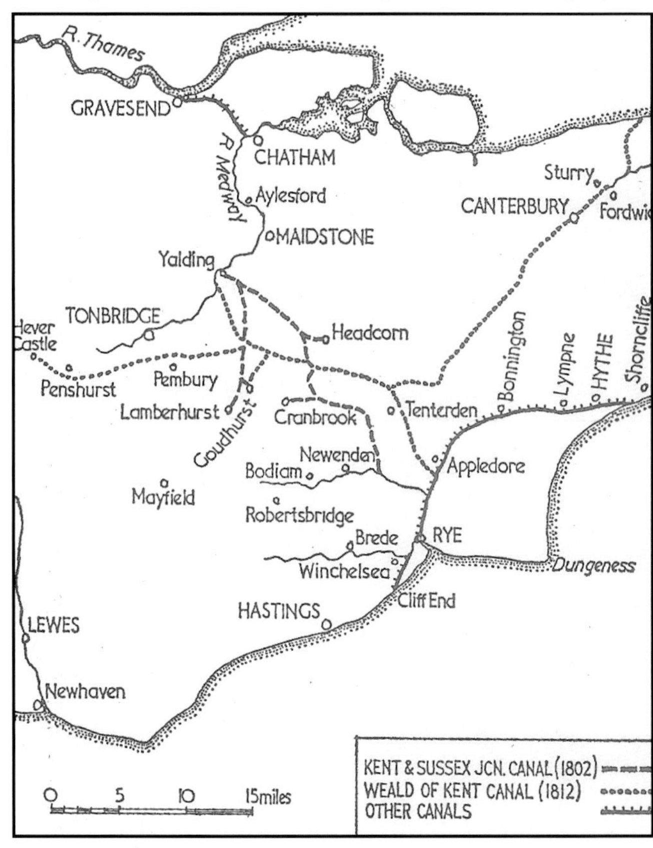

This diagram shows how the proposed Kent and Sussex Junction Canal will start at the River Thames, utilising the waterway that will soon link Gravesend with the River Medway. The Medway, navigible to East Peckham and Yalding, will then join the new canal which is planned to traverse the Weald until, south of Tenterden and close to Appledore, it will meet the Royal Military Canal and thence on to the sea.

An impromptu 'frost fair' is set up on the Thames with games for children and many colourful booths.

Frost fair is held on the Thames

January 31: The exceptionally harsh month, which has caused great hardship among the poorer classes, has enabled Londoners once again to stage an impromptu Frost Fair on the Thames.

As in previous years the arches of old London Bridge slowed down the ebb flow of the river which then froze solid. Having tested the thickness of the ice market men quickly built a "street" of colourful booths selling food and fancy wares. It is attracting a huge, enthusiastic crowd. Older people have been recalling earlier Frost Fairs but the greatest of them all is beyond living memory. In 1683 the river was frozen for a record ten weeks and an ambitious concern set up a printing press. Charles II and his party had their names printed while they enjoyed an ox roasted on the ice.

This year the temperatures have plummeted to 26F and the cold weather shows no sign of ending.

London streets are lit by gas

Londoners have never seen anything like it. Westminster Pier and a few streets around Piccadilly are illuminated at night by gas lamps. It was some years ago that pioneers managed to derive gas from coal but now a company has been established in London and Munroe and Co has erected gasworks at Bankside, Greenwich.

During the end of the last century there were several successful attempts to achieve lighting from gas. Employees of Boulton and Watt were the first to achieve a sustained practical application. William Murdoch lit his cottage by gas in 1792 and illuminated his factory in Birmingham to celebrate the Peace of Amiens in 1802.

July: The Yorkshire sportsman, Thomas Lord, has moved his Marylebone Cricket Club to a new ground just north of London in St John's Wood.

The MCC is now the principal authority of a game that is growing rapidly in the county of Kent.

County cricket is played at Canterbury, Rochester, Dartford Heath, Sevenoaks, Wrotham Naps, Hawkhurst, Coxheath, Penenden Heath and on the Common at Tunbridge Wells. *See page 61*

Henry Doubell has almost completed the building of his windmill which dominates the village of Cranbrook. It is one of the largest smock mills in England and the tallest in Kent.

Sir Henry Chudleigh Oxenden of Broome Park, Barham has formed a pack of foxhounds consisting of spayed bitches and organised a regular meet in East Kent. Hunting has been popular in West Kent for many years due to the enthusiasm of people like John Warde of Squerryes, Westerham and Squire Evelyn of St Clere, Kemsing who hunted fox and hare.

In 1793 Sir John Dyke of Lullingstone formed a pack which used to meet at Beckenham and Sydenham. That became known as the West Kent Hunt.

Godmersham, the lovely house near Ashford owned by Jane Austen's brother Edward Knight.

Exciting new novelist finds inspiration at Godmersham

January: The whole country has been trying to guess the identity of the author of a sensational new book published anonymously last year. Entitled *Pride and Prejudice* its opening sentence is: *"It is a truth universally acknowledged, that a single man in possession of a good fortune must be in want of a wife".*

Edward Knight of Godmersham certainly knows the name of the novelist who is causing such a stir. It is his 38-year-old sister, Jane Austen.

Pride and Prejudice was written about 16 years ago and then entitled *First Impressions*. It was not a success so Miss Austen, daughter of a Hampshire country parson, revised and republished it . Today she has admirers across the country, including the Prince Regent who wants to know her name so he can have his copy of the book dedicated.

Edward Knight — who changed his name from Austen — says Jane has written continuously from childhood using her relations as her enthusiastic readers. Two years ago she published, anonymously, *Sense and Sensibility* at her own financial risk. She is now working on a novel called *Mansfield Park* and there may be others.

Although Jane is based in Hampshire she visits Kent often. Her uncle lives at Sevenoaks, she has friends at Tonbridge and she has certainly visited Chevening; in fact many believe that the home of the Stanhope family was the model for the great house often visited by Elizabeth Bennet, the heroine of *Pride and Prejudice.*

Most of Jane's journeys into Kent, however, have been made to Godmersham to see her brother Edward. The house is rich in history and beauty and lies on the River Stour. Jane loves it.

She also shares her brother's love for driving around in fine carriages. She has dined at Goodnestone near Wingham, enjoyed a Ball at Chilham Castle and visited Ramsgate to see another brother, Francis who is a Captain in the Channel Fleet and engaged in fortifying the sea defences against Napoleon's expected invasion..

In her travels she has made numerous acquaintances. The majority see her as a witty, highly intelligent but frail little woman. Only a few are aware that she is England's exciting new novelist, quite brilliant in describing the everyday play of relationships within the leisured middle class. *See page 49*

Colonel gallops in with news of Napoleon's abdication

April 9: A young colonel who served with the 50th Foot in Gibraltar and Corsica is today the toast of Kent and England.

Attended only by a single Cossack, Hudson Lowe rode from deepest France into London to bring the news that Napoleon's rule over Europe has ended.

His dramatic ride across hostile territory was fraught with danger. He experienced many adventures, barely slept and managed to snatch only a morsel of food. Unscathed he sailed to Dover and, at full gallop, rode across Kent into London and almost demanded a meeting with the Prince Regent. Napoleon, he said, has abdicated.

Colonel Lowe's father had been regimental surgeon with the 50th for more than 30 years and Hudson was born into the regiment. A brilliant linguist and "political" soldier Lowe later served as the senior British liaison officer with the Prussian Marshal Blucher. He saw Bordeaux and Toulouse fall and the enemy scatter. For his bravery Lowe has already been offered a knighthood. *See page 42*

Kent rejoices as 'old Boney' sails into exile

April 20: The war is over, Napoleon has abdicated and is now on his way to Elba in the Mediterranean where he will live in exile over 86 square miles with just one battalion of the Imperial Guard. The end came on March 31 when the Allies — Britain, Austria, Russia and Prussia — stormed Montmartre and occupied Paris. France's military situation is now quite hopeless.

Today, as Napoleon Bonaparte, self styled master of Europe, said an emotional farewell to his guards at Fontainebleau Palace, there was rejoicing throughout England and particularly Kent.

For 22 weary years the county has faced the possibility of invasion and the tension at times has been almost too much to bear. The fortifications at Dover, the line of Martello towers stretching across the coast of southern Kent, the amazing military canal and the great build-up of volunteers is ample proof of the concern shown by the people of Kent towards an undisputed military genius.

Would they have been sufficient to stop this vastly superior army had it crossed the Channel? No-one knows but political commentators and cartoonists, who painted words and pictures of defiant cottagers armed with crude home made weapons, knew that Kent would fight to the end, even though many slept with their goods packed up on their wagons ready to flee. Even little boys who misbehaved and were told that "Boney will get you" grew up with a determination that this would never be the case.

Napoleon was obsessed by this defiance. He imposed his European-wide blockade on British trade and when Portugal refused to obey, France became embroiled in the Peninsula War. Russia also refused to co-operate and Austria began the War of the Fifth Coalition. The retreat from Russian encirclement at Moscow and the so-called Battle of the Nations at Leipzig signalled the turning of Napoleon's fortunes.

As Wellington's army and its ragged remnants of Buffs and the 50th Foot drag themselves home — the infantry by sea and the cavalry by easy stages overland — the Allied commanders are preparing to convene at Vienna to arrange a peace settlement. Flags fly in every Kent town and village. The county remains unconquered. *See page 44*

April 23: There were joyous scenes at Dover today as Louis XVIII arrived by stage coach from London accompanied by the Prince Regent and the Duke of Clarence. The King is on his way to France where the restoration of the Bourbon monarchy has been welcomed.

April 26: London celebrates peace at last with a party in St James' Park.

June 6: The Emperor Alexander of Russia, the King of Prussia and allied leaders landed at Dover following the festivities in France where they have been celebrating King Louis XVIII's return to the throne. With them was General Gebhard Leberecht von Blucher, the Prussian army commander who spearheaded the drive into Paris.

August: The Coxheath military camp, which once housed 15,000 soldiers, has been closed following an Act of Parliament. The clock house, used as officers' quarters remains, but the great heath has been enclosed.

October: Sheerness naval dockyard, first laid out by Samuel Pepys in 1665, has been totally and excellently rebuilt with warehouses, a garrison church, the Captain's House and various stores and workshops, all in pale brick with stone dressings.

Napoleon escapes from Elba — it's not over yet

May 31: **Napoleon's period of exile on Elba is already over. Aware of France's dissatisfaction with the restoration of the Bourbon dynasty the former emperor escaped from the island, sailed to Cannes, disembarked on March 1 and was greeted as the returning hero. Louis XVIII fled immediately.**

Napoleon occupied Paris and proclaimed peaceful intentions but the Allies (Britain, Austria, Prussia and Russia) were suspicious. After deliberating on the future shape of Europe they signed a quadruple alliance at Vienna and decided each to put 150,000 men into the field to suppress their old enemy.

Their fears are well founded. As the British and Prussians begin to mobilise their troops near Brussels it is reported that Napoleon with about 124,000 men — the majority veterans of many battles — is on his way north from Paris.

Wellington triumphs at Waterloo

June 24: In one of the bloodiest battles ever fought Napoleon's weary veterans have been humiliated. The former emperor rides for his life and the shattered remnants of his once-superior army are in full flight, pursued by Marshal Blucher and his Prussians.

It was on June 15 that a messenger interrupted a ball given by the Duchess of Richmond to tell Wellington and his officers that Napoleon had arrived in Brussels. The next day the French drove Blücher back at Ligny splitting the Allies. Marshal Ney attacked the British at Quatre Bras and Wellington withdrew to a ridge across the Brussels road near a village called Waterloo.

A few days after the Battle of Waterloo, Denis Dighton, military draughtsman to the Prince Regent, visited the Chateau of Hougoumont to make this study in watercolour of the battlefield.

By now the two Kent regiments were far removed from the action, the 50th Foot in Kent and the Buffs peacefully at camp in Montreal. But some Kent lads were in France and, among them, was a young colour sergeant with the Rifle Brigade accompanied by his wife and four year old daughter.

Yesterday the sergeant gave a vivid description of how the two great war leaders finally faced each other on the battlefield on June 18. He told how Napoleon attacked, attempting to drive Wellington's forces off the ridge. But the General, with 68,000 men and 156 guns, held his line. As successive waves of French infantry and cavalry continued to advance the carnage was appalling. One British regiment, the 27th Foot, was completely wiped out and victory for Napoleon seemed certain. But Wellington held on until eventually Marshal Blücher and his Prussians appeared from the north-east and the French scattered.

The fighting lasted all day with Wellington continuously rallying his troops. "Hard pounding, gentlemen", he said. "Let's see who will pound the longest". As the French disappeared Wellington said: "It was the nearest run thing you ever saw in your life".

It was indeed. The day's dead numbered 25,000 French, 7,000 Prussians and some 15,000 from the combined British forces.

See page 44

Wellington's skill as a military leader was confirmed during the Peninsular War and when he finally broke through the Pryrenees in 1813, his was the first hostile army on French soil since the rise of Napoleon. The painting above by Thomas Jones Barker shows him at Sorauren during the Battle of the Pyrenees. Today, after a long and exhausted campaign, he has achieved his greatest victory at Waterloo and the exiled emperor, as General Bonaparte, is sailing to live in exile on the remote island of St Helena in the south Atlantic with just four aides, 12 domestic staff and an Irish naval surgeon. As far as Wellington is concerned, the Napoleonic Wars have brought him great wealth. The financial reward from parliament alone amount to £700,000.

1815

Flags fly as the war with France finally ends

Vanguard of liberty! Ye Men of Kent,
Ye children of a soil that doth advance
Its haughty brow against the
coast of France,
now is the time to prove your worthiness

— WILLIAM WORDSWORTH

AS the foreign secretaries and diplomats of the great powers begin the task of redrawing the map of Europe, Kent is jubilant. Union flags are flying everywhere and in the great houses there have been endless balls and banquets. In the beer houses, soldiers and civilians alike are telling their personal stories of the war with France.

What would have happened if Napoleon's troops had sailed across the Channel and established a foothold in Kent? First they would have faced the regular army and, behind it, a miscellany of auxiliary forces, militia, volunteers and fencibles. Every man, woman and able boy in the county was organised to assist the military and carry out a variety of tasks.

Napoleon knew that the dockyard at Chatham was well protected and the coastal defences at Gravesend and New Tavern prevented a barrier against penetration further up the Thames. Had he landed near Romney Marsh he would have faced the heavily armed soldiers manning the sea fortresses, later known as Martello Towers, the newly-built but hardly impenetrable Military Canal, and further east, the intensive fortifications at Dover and those centred on the garrisons at Deal and Dover Castles — and Shorncliffe where General John Moore introduced his system of infantry training which was to prove so effective during the Peninsular War.

The first hint of the possibility of an invasion came in 1801 but the crisis passed and, with the Peace of Amiens in April 1802, all the corps were disembodied. A year later, however, the war resumed and this time more than 30,000 Volunteers enrolled. Pitt, as Lord Warden of the Cinque Ports, personally raised a regiment of three battalions. Again, the crisis passed.

The French emperor never entirely gave up the idea of an invasion of Britain although his thoughts kept turning elsewhere. In 1811, having rebuilt the French fleet, Napoleon said he had 80,000 men available for the assault. Then came his disastrous Moscow campaign, culminating in his retreat to France and abdication in 1814.

The role of the Royal Navy was crucial. They had to protect Britain and British shipping, including fishermen and then destroy the enemy's fleet. To achieve this the British had 92 ships of the line and 128 frigates, the majority operating from the county's four naval dockyards at Chatham, Woolwich, Deptford and Sheerness.

There was a near disaster when the navy mutinied at Spithead over poor food, low pay and refusal of shore leave. There was another mutiny at the Nore led by Richard Parker. When his support fell away the the ships returned to their allegiance, Parker was taken prisoner at Sheerness and with other leaders of the mutiny, hanged.

The lives of ordinary citizens were thrown into turmoil by the war and by the presence of so many troops in Kent. Not everybody approved of the restrictions placed upon them and there was rioting and violence in many towns. The greatest burdens involved the quartering of a vast number of soldiers and the constant requisition of waggons to transport military supplies.

One man who kept a diary of 'daily remarks and occurrences during the French Wars is Thomas Pattenden, a resident of Dover. Under the entry for August 4, 1801, for example, he wrote: "Very hot day. This morning at seven o'clock the ships and bombs under the command of Lord Nelson were seen from Dover Hill to have commenced a fire of shot and shells on the gun brigs and boats at Boulogne...The hills were full of spectators..."

For January 8, 1808 he said: "This morning three French prisoners got out through the wall of the town jail and took a small boat from the beach belonging to Mr Andrews who went in pursuit of them...they quietly submitted to be brought back".

Pattenden wrote about the frequent firing of heavy guns, the visit to Margate and Dover by the Duke of York, the information conveyed by Telegraph to the Admiral in the Downs, the sight of the French flotilla at Boulogne and how 60 ball cartridges were once delivered to each man should Napoleon launch a surprise attack by night.

Folkestone was not the only town to feel the presence of so many soldiers. There were barracks at Ashford, Hythe, Maidstone and Canterbury and many had to be quartered in nearby inns. One man, Edward Hopper of The Ship, Sandgate refused to take in soldiers and received a rebuke from Sir John Moore. His licence was withheld.

There is no doubt that the French War and the ever present threat of an invasion had a great impact upon the lives of Kentish folk but it is certain that, had Napoleon, landed on our shores, the people would have risen as one man.

One of the army officers who brought news of the victory at Waterloo back to Kent is Captain Percy who was due to land at Dover. Bad weather, however, forced him further north and his ship finally berthed at Broadstairs. A small crowd were there to greet him and take him to an inn at the top of Harbour Street where he was supplied with refreshment and a horse. Percy rode up Crow Hill, through St Peter's and on to London. All along the route he was greeted with great acclaim. This painting by R. Pollard shows the 'peace coach' crossing Rochester Bridge.

July 3, 1816: Dora Jordan, Britain's most celebrated actress-comedienne and for many years the devoted companion of the Duke of Clarence, died today almost penniless in obscure lodgings in Boulogne. She was 54.

Mrs Jordan, as she was always known, fulfilled many engagements in Kent and particularly at her favourite venue, The Theatre Royal in Margate. Here she played Peggy in David Garrick's *The Country Girl*, Lady Teazle in *School for Scandal* and was renowned for her spontaneous charm..

Town's farewell to a lonely woman

She lived happily with the Duke of Clarence for 20 years, bore his 10 children and, from her substantial earnings as an actress, paid his debts and helped to maintain his home.

Year after year she played at Margate staying at a local hotel and writing regularly to Clarence. On one occasion she told him: "I attend Methodist meetings whenever I can. My favourite preacher is a fisherman who is seeking souls all morning and sending them to the devil in the evening".

Last year the Duke of Clarence parted from his life-companion and Mrs Jordan, a sad and lonely woman, decided to retire from the stage. On July 29, 1815 she played Violante in *The Wonder* in her beloved Margate and the audience gave her a rousing farewell.

By now she was weary and overwhelmed by money problems. Fearing claims against her would lead to arrest she crossed to Boulogne under the name of Mrs James.

January 15: Emma, Lady Hamilton, the beautiful Ambassador's wife who captivated Lord Nelson and became mother of his daughter, died today in Calais almost penniless. Once known as a 'blowsy adventuress' who reputedly slept her way from obscurity to become wife of Sir William Hamilton and the mistress of Nelson, Emma constantly defied scandal. Her daughter, Horatia, now 14, has returned to England. Picture shows Lady Hamilton as Cerce by George Romney.

Red hills or white — where is the boundary of the Weald of Kent ?

July 29: All land within the Weald of Kent is, by immemorial custom, exempt from the payment of tithes. But where is the northern boundary of the Weald? It is a question which has been troubling Kent for years.

Land owners, including Lord Le Despencer, Lord Stanhope and John Warde say the boundary is just below the chalk hills of the North Downs. Clergymen and a few landed proprietors, who collect tithes and earn an income from the area, claim they are on the red hills of the Greensand Ridge.

This contentious issue which has dragged on for more than 10 years has, at last, been settled. Following a trial at Croydon before Lord Ellenborough and a special jury, which ended yesterday, it has been shown that, except in the case of Westerham, Sundridge, Brasted and Chevening, the boundaries of the Weald are on the red (ie sandstone) hills and not on the white (North Downs). Landowners can collect tithes from the area between.

Lord Le Despencer called 25 witnesses to support his case and one of them was Lord Stanhope who said: "If trees are blown down on the north of the Pilgrims' Road I can claim them as Lord of the Manor of Chevening but if they are on the south I should give them up to the landholders whose land stood nearest the trees in accordance with custom.

Serjeant Best, on behalf of the clergymen said that if Lord Le Despencer succeeded no less than 20 parishes within the limits of that district, where tithes of woodland had been immemorially paid, would be deprived of this right.

From the earliest period of Kent's history the northern boundary has never been clearly defined. They was no object in doing so in the early days when so much of the remainder of the Kingdom of Kent was either forest or woodland — and Weald meant Wild. Robert Furley recently summed it up: "So long as it was not cultivated the winds of heaven would continue to scatter the acorns and beech nuts, while the animals, insects and feathered tribes that inhabited it would extend rather than contract its natural boundary".

All that has changed. The real Weald of Kent lies below the red hills. And, in that vast area, no tithes can be enforced. The tradition continues.

Shortage of funds halts Weald canal

The ambitious plan to build a Weald of Kent Canal linking the Thames with the Channel has been abandoned after years of negotiation, controversy and considerable correspondence in the newspapers. Many believe its fruition was thwarted by the ending of the Napoleonic Wars and there is no doubt that was a major reason, but the plan was also beaten by lack of funds.

The Canal company was required by an Act of Parliament to raise £305,108 in three years — a sufficient sum to link the navigable Medway with the Royal Military Canal near Appledore.

In fact only £38,500 was ever subscribed and some of that by enthusiastic supporters of the Thames and Medway Canal which runs between Gravesend and Strood.

The majority of those against the scheme rightly see Kent as an agricultural county with little of the industry that is now so prominent in the Midlands and North of England. There, canal building continues in earnest. *See page 64*

Why Citizen Stanhope was 'the minority of one'

December 31: Some have called him the *Minority of One* and others *Citizen Stanhope* but with the death of Charles, the Third Earl Stanhope earlier this month, England has lost one of its most eccentric and charismatic characters.

An inventor, statesman and mathematician, Charles Stanhope lived at Chevening House near Sevenoaks and married the daughter of Lord Chatham, Lady Hester Pitt. They had three daughters, the eldest being the unconventional Hester, who acted as hostess to her uncle William.

Charles was widowed in 1780, married again and had four children including an heir, Philip. As a politician he introduced two bills in the House of Lords and in one he proposed to acknowledge the French Republic.

Chevening House — home of Charles, 3rd Earl Stanhope and Lady Hester Pitt.

Finding himself in a minority of one, Charles Stanhope protested against the defeat of his motion and withdrew from further attendance in Parliament wherepon a medal was struck with the motto *The Minority of One.*

In science he made a great reputation; he invented means for safe guarding buildings against fire, devised printing appliances which he presented to the public, perfected a process of stereotyping, had original ideas about electricity and shared lightning conductor experiments with his friend Ben Franklin. He also invented a microscopic lens which bears his name, devised a new way of making cement more durable and found a way of curing wounds in trees.

Charles Stanhope published notes on the tuning of musical instruments and on marine navigation, experimented with steam propulsion for warships, planned canals in Devon and advocated the development of railways. Other inventions included an iron printing press and a machine to do multiplication and division.

In the years before his death Charles would often be seen walking in the village of Chevening. He wore simple clothes and spoke at length to all he met. When he died, separated from his wife and at odds with his children, he was buried on Christmas Eve at St Botolph's Church.

The Waltz is 'obscene' but Prince Regent approves

A new dance, described by *The Times* as 'obscene' is becoming increasingly fashionable in the ballrooms of Kent's grand homes. Known as the waltz its most shocking innovation is the close hold in which each couple dance face to face with arms wrapped "immodestly" around one another.

The waltz requires little skill — six evenly accented steps with a full turn in two bars of music. It was danced earlier this year at Carlton House at the Prince Regent's request and is now set to dominate social dancing.

Princess Charlotte, heir to the throne, certainly approves of the waltz as does her husband Prince Leopold of Saxe-Coburg-Saalfeld. The couple were married earlier this year.

July 30: According to the *Kentish Herald* newspaper a dancer by the name of Miss Wagram shocked audiences at the Margate Theatre yesterday for "the indelicacy of her dancing". One step in particular brought howls of disapproval. She will not be invited to return.

1817

Kent fears revival of the smuggling trade

AS the army and navy begin to shed many of the fighting men they had recruited for the long Napoleonic wars and as the reunions, celebrations and jollifications begin to fade an economic hardship has hit the country and nowhere is worse than the county of Kent where unemployment is growing each month.

Many of those who have been unable to find work in the fields and harbours and docks have turned to the smuggling trade. An exciting and not unprofitable employment is that of evading the armed agents of the law and running a cargo of contraband ashore. No section of the Kent coast, it seems, is free from smuggling. The old business is back with a vengeance.

To deal with this a naval officer, Captain McCulloch, has been appointed to set up a blockade protecting the notorious coastline between Sheerness, Kent and Seaford in Sussex.

Parties of naval seamen will patrol offshore and man Watch Houses, sited at intervals of three or four miles. McCulloch will organise his team from his headquarters on a Man-of-War off Deal. He says he will not tolerate bribery of his men and he will "make the grass grow in the streets of Deal".

The heyday of the smuggling trade in Kent was in the early 17th century and it remained uncontrolled for years. Extraordinary high levels of tax imposed on imported goods and controls, designed to protect home industry, created the incentive to smuggle.

Restrictions on the export of wool had the greatest impact and the "owling trade" as it came to be known was a capital offence. In 1700 it was estimated that 150,000 packs of wool a year were being illegally shipped out from Kent within days of shearing.

The old business is back with a vengeance. Here are 'the owlers' at work

The first smuggling ring specialised in shipments of wool and even live sheep but within 20 years hundreds of new gangs were bringing in tea, spirits, tobacco and luxury items.

A labourer who earned no more than eight shillings for a week's work could expect 10 shillings for a successful night's effort carrying contraband. The sharp decline of the iron smelting and cloth-making industries in Kent meant that thousands lived in poverty. Smuggling, like poaching, was a form of social protest against their wretched existence.

The most notorious in Kent was the Hawkhurst Gang who created a network of "secret" routes through the countryside, synchronised the arrival of ships and landing parties, carried their contraband on horseback and sold their ill-gotten gains to the London market. They also took over other groups, forcing them at times to co-operate.

From its peak in 1780 smuggling decreased when William Pitt cut the duty on tea from 129% to 12 % and then increased window tax to make good the resulting deficit.

During the French Revolution, French aristocrats were smuggled to England as was the Duke of Orleans' valuable collection of pictures. The seamen of Folkestone and Deal specialised in running gold guineas to France where the economy had collapsed and money was needed to pay Napoleon's troops. A guinea in Paris could fetch 30 shillings.

The trade slumped during the war years but with the return, after Waterloo, of some 250,000 soldiers and seamen it is feared that smugglers will return to every accessible beach in Kent. The preventive service is designed to be tough but the custom houses know the smuggling trade will never be eliminated. *See page 58*

The Nelson, launched in great triumph at the Royal Dockyard, Woolwich on July 4, 1814, returned to dry dock this year for essential repairs.

Jane Austen, the 'anonymous' novelist is dead

July 18: The novelist Jane Austen, who spent much of her time at her brother's home in Godmersham and travelled widely in Kent, has died of Addison's disease at the age of 42.

Her work, which has been published anonymously to date beginning with *Sense and Sensibility* in 1812, now includes *Pride and Prejudice, Mansfield Park* and *Emma.* It is believed she has left two more novels completed.

Jane, whose admirers include the Prince Regent, made her first journey into Kent down the Rye Road to Sevenoaks aged 12. Most of her trips to the county since then were made along the Dover Road to East Kent.

The characters in her novels also enjoy a great deal of travelling and some of Kent's greatest mansions — Chevening, Broome Park, Evington Place, St Clere, Mersham-le-Hatch, Goodnestone, Nash Court, Chilham Castle and Eastwell Park have provided models for the homes that so delight her readers.

Starving rioters blame the Prince Regent

January: Rioting in Kent over the high price of bread — which has brought hundreds close to starvation — is now reflected in nationwide discontent.

More than 400,000 soldiers and sailors have been demobilized and most are now out of work. After a dramatic fall in testile exports the country is in recession.

This week a demonstrator threw a stone at the Prince Regent as he made his way to Parliament. The Prince's dissipated lifestyle, his secret marriage to Mrs Fitzherbert and his self indulgence has angered many radicals.

June 18: A new bridge is opened over the Thames on the second anniversary of Waterloo.

November 6: The Prince Regent's only daughter Charlotte died in childbirth today at the age of 21. Her boy was still born. Charlotte, second in line to the throne, lived at Shrewsbury House, Shooters Hill which has commanding views of the Thames and much of Kent.

December 7: Vice admiral William Bligh of Farningham House, who was the victim of various worrying mutinies, died today, aged 63.

1818

Northanger Abbey and Persuasion, written by the novelist Jane Austen have been published posthumously.

Elizabeth Fry, wife of a London merchant and well-known reformer has given evidence to Parliament that women in Newgate prison are cooped up in filthy rooms for crimes no more serious than petty theft. Some await the death sentence or deportation to Australia.

By an Act of Parliament more than £1m has been allocated to the building of more places of worship. Right across Kent new churches, chapels, temples and synagogues are being planned . Those falling into disrepair will be rebuilt or renovated.

Among the engineers making great improvements in the techniques of road building are Thomas Telford and John Macadam who has invented a road surface composed of a mixture of broken stones,sand and water

The county prisons at Maidstone have been completed at a cost of

£200,000. Prisoners will be transferred soon. See story page 52.

Hever Castle once the residence of the unfortunate Anne Boleyne (sic) during the halycon days of her courtship with Henry VIII, is notorious today as a hideaway for smugglers. This decaying property, seen here in better days, was built in the 13th century as a fortified farmhouse and later turned into a small Tudor manor house by the wealthy Boleynes and surrounded by a moat. After Anne's execution her old father was allowed to live on at Hever until his death when the property reverted to the crown. It has gone downhill ever since.

Treadmill installed in Maidstone's new gaol

PUBLIC EXECUTIONS TRANSFERRED FROM PENENDEN HEATH

January: After seven years of building work the county prisons at Maidstone have finally been completed for a cost of £200,000. Built of brick and Kentish rag, the boundary wall encloses 16 acres of land and contains both a gaol and house of correction. They are not excelled by any in the kingdom.

The first prisoners, removed from the old Bridewell in King Street, London, were installed last month. Those from the Old Gaol, Maidstone — overcrowded and frequently condemned by prison reformers — will follow within a few weeks.

The chaplain's house is within the boundary and corresponds in position and appearance with the porter's lodge. The chaplain, the Rev John Winter already attends the prisoners daily and, under his superintendence, schools have been formed for both adult and juvenile delinquents.

There is a treadmill house in the north-east part of the prison where inmates sentenced to hard labour work the wheels against retarding weights. On either side of the treadmill is a hospital and female prison, surrounded by its own perimeter wall.

The buildings have taken more than seven years to complete, much of the heavier work being carried out by French prisoners of war who carried the ragstone from quarries all over Kent.

It is hoped eventually to transfer executions from Penenden Heath to a site just outside the gaol for the benefit of the viewing public. Those who like to attend will be hoping to see the kind of executions for which Kent is famous.

In 1652 five women from Cranbrook and one from Lenham were hanged for witchcraft. In 1769 Susannah Lott was burnt to death on the Heath after being convicted of poisoning her husband amd during the latter part of the 18th century many smugglers were executed. *See page 53.*

Richard Barham — recovering at home.

Bedtime novel for recuperating rector

October: Richard Harris Barham, rector of Snargate and friend of all, including the "free traders" — those shadowy figures he often bumps into in the mists of Romney Marsh — is making good progress after his untimely accident last month.

The man of God was returning from a late night call when his gig overturned. He broke one leg, sprained an ankle on the other and was confined to bed. This gave Barham the time and impetus to put pen to paper and write a novel. Entitled *Baldwin,* it is due to be published early next year.

Richard Barham's life has been dogged by bad luck. At the age of 14 he was dragged along the road when the Dover Mail overturned and he nearly lost a hand. However, he went on to read law at Oxford and later swap silk for cloth. Ordained six years ago he endured (rather than enjoyed) a curacy at the "damp and dilapidated" parsonage at Westwell before promotion to the better living at Snargate.

In wishing him well with *Baldwin* his friends hope he finds a less painful opportunity for writing more novels. *See page 103*

Kents' new daughter, Victoria is fourth in line to the throne

May 24: A baby girl has been born to the Duke and Duchess of Kent who were married exactly a year ago. The child has been christened Alexandrina Victoria and will be fourth in line to the throne after the Prince Regent, her uncle William and her father.

Her parents, Prince Edward Augustus Duke of Kent and Strathern and Princess Victoria Louisa of Leningen, were married at Coburg on May 29, 1818 followed by a second ceremony at Kew in July.

Edward is the younger brother of the Prince Regent and the fourth son of George III who created a Royal Dukedom for Kent in 1799. It had been an Earldom since 1067 when William the Conqueror rewarded his redoubtable half brother Odo by making him Earl of Kent and Warden of Dover Castle.

The King is too ill to absorb the good news of his new grandaughter but the rest of the royal family are delighted by the arrival of Alexandrina Victoria.

November: Princess Caroline, the large, robust former wife of the Prince Regent is returning from Italy to "claim her rightful place as queen-elect of England".

The 81-year-old King George III is dying and, when the regent inherits, Caroline wants to be sure of becoming queen. She says she will renounce her title in return for a pay rise from £35,000 to £50,000.

Princess Caroline and Prince George were separated soon after their marriage in 1795. *See page 56*

Deal church has been enlarged and a windmill has been built at Willesborough, Ashford.

March: As 141 prisoners are transferred from the Old Gaol, Maidstone to the new prison at the end of Week Street comes the news that the crime rate in Kent is soaring. Many say this is due to the depression and unemployment as soldiers and sailors come home.

There is also a call to hang more criminals. In England only a third of those guilty of the 200 hanging offences are actually executed, a big drop from the previous year!

Maidstone prison officers say they can cope with more executions. *See page 82*

1819

Cranbrook - capital town that 'stands unrivalled'

THE parish farm at Sissinghurst Castle, which continues to provide work for the unemployed of Cranbrook, is helping this Wealden town achieve a standard that is the envy of neighbouring parishes.

The Saturday market enjoys considerable business in the sale of corn and hops and the town is well supplied with fish which comes from Hastings. There are also two fairs for hops, corn, cattle and pedlary.

Mr T.D.W. Dearn, in a brief account of the Weald capital, states: "For the salubrity of the air and the longevity of its inhabitants Cranbrook stands unrivalled. A stage coach from the George Inn, Cranbook to the George Inn, Borough (through Maidstone) is available every Sunday, Tuesday and Thursday morning at 10 o'clock. A stage wagon takes the same route every Monday.

"Farming is doing well, houses are being built and a new brewery has opened at Bakers Cross. Humphreys, the millwright has put up his new windmill, William Tooth is supplying the neighbourhood with his renowned beaver hats. The hop sacking, the Millhouse thread, tanners, braziers, printers, peruke makers and a bank are all witnesses to the prosperity of the town".

Leeds Castle, near Maidstone is currently undergoing a great extension — possibly the greatest since Henry VIII lavished money on its improvements many years ago. Leeds has been owned in turn by many famous Kentish families including the St Legers, the Culpeppers and the Fairfaxes, who have all played a part in settling the colonies of the New World. The sixth Lord Fairfax became a friend and confidante of George Washington and prospered so greatly in the colonies that he never returned.

No-one really knows how long the magnificent castle at Leeds has been standing in its large park on an island formed by the River Len, Perhaps 1200 years. Maybe longer?

The castle is believed to have been started by the Saxons, continued by the Normans, improved by the Plantagenets and then, of course, the Tudors. Today's extension will make it bigger and grander than ever.

1820 - 1829

1820: George IV is proclaimed King following the death of his father. Troops drawn up outside Carlton House cheer as George, 57, succeeds to the throne after nine years as Regent.

Forts Deke, Pitt and Clarence in the Chatham Line are completed.

The first steam packet between Dover and Calais is launched.

New church consecrated this year is St George's, Sevenoaks Weald.

May 1: Arthur Thistlewood and four other men who planned the murder of Cabinet ministers during a dinner in Grosvenor Square are beheaded for treason. The episode is known as the Cato Street conspiracy.

1821: A new building for the Bank of England in Threadneedle Street is completed by the architect Sir John Soane.

Michael Faraday, a scientist, develops an electric motor to show that electricity will produce a rotary motion.

1822: April 4: Four members of the North Kent gang of smugglers are executed following a battle with customs officers at Westgate.

A smugglers' tunnel is discovered at Margate.

July 22: The bodies of Percy Shelley, 30 and a friend are washed up on the shore near Lerici, Italy. They drowned when a storm upset their sailing boat.

September 9: George Canning is recalled to the cabinet as foreign secretary following the death of Lord Castlereagh.
See page 60

The West Kent Cricket Club moves to Chislehurst Common.

1823: October 30: Edmund Cartwright, 80, inventor of the power loom and the wool combing machine dies at Hastings.

Robert Peel, Home Secretary, introduces new prison reforms to end the death sentence on about 100 offences. It is no longer a hanging crime for stealing.

1824: March 4: The Royal Naval Lifeboat Institution is founded by Sir William Hilary.

June 16: A Society for the Prevention of Cruelty to Animals is formed after a meeting at the Old Slaughter House in St Martin's Lane, London.

October 21: Joseph Aspdin patents Portland Cement. This new product is impervious to water.

1825: A passenger steam railway opens for business between Stockton and Darlington. Locomotive Number One has been designed by George Stephenson.

The first section of a diary kept by Samuel Pepys, who was secretary to the Royal Navy under Charles II is published. It contains accounts of the Restoration, the plague and the great fire of London.

1826: A tunnel on the Manchester to Liverpool railway line is built.

An iron suspension bridge is built across the Menai Strait between Angelsey and North Wales. The engineer is Thomas Telford.

July 5: Sir Stamford Raffles, founder of the colony of Singapore dies aged 45. The island was uninhabited when Raffles extended the operation of the British East India Company there.

1827: February 17: Prime Minister, Lord Liverpool suffers a stroke at the age of 58. George Canning the Foreign Secretary is likely to be the new premier. Carlton House is coming down to be replaced by Carlton House Terrace. John Nash is the architect.

August 8: George Canning, Prime Minister for just four months dies from pneumonia. King George IV has chosen Lord Goderich to succeed him.

1828: January: The Duke of Wellington, hero of Waterloo and supporter of Catholic emancipation, has been invited by the King to form a new government. He follows Lord Liverpool (15 years as Prime Minister) and the brief interregnums of George Canning and Lord Goderich. Wellington has many personal reservations about his ability to take such high office but has reluctantly agreed. He will now have to guide Parliament through emancipation and electoral reform.

1829: January 28: William Burke, who sold the bodies of his murder victims to the doctors at Edinburgh, is hanged before a huge crowd. He was convicted on the evidence of his fellow criminals, William and Margaret Hare.

The painter John Constable is elected a member of the Royal Academy after 10 years as an associate member.

April 13: The Catholic Emancipation Act becomes law. Catholics may enter Parliament by taking an oath to say they accept the Protestant succession.

A horse omnibus is introduced on a route in London between Paddington and the Bank of England.

June 10: The two senior universities in Britain, Cambridge and Oxford today decided to test their superiority in the water. A hotly contested rowing race was won by Oxford. Cambridge plan to challenge that next year.

New churches consecrated this year are Holy Trinity, Tunbridge Wells and St Mary's, Riverhead.

Waiting for the miracle on The Lines at Gillingham

SOME time before the religious visionary, Joanna Southcott, died six years ago she predicted a date on which her loyal followers would be taken up bodily to heaven. That date was yesterday and hundreds gathered on The Lines, Gillingham waiting for the miracle. It never happened.

Uneducated and even illiterate Joanna Southcott spent her earlier years in domestic service but in 1792 she began to claim the gift of prophecy and her revelations attracted many followers.

She moved to Southwark after the publication of her first book *The Strange Effects of Faith* and opened a chapel where her predictions attracted many adherents. Later she announced that, as the woman in Revelation 12, she would be the mother of the coming Messiah.

Joanna took to her bed and six of the nine doctors who examined her said her symptoms would indicate pregnancy in a younger woman. This was news that thrilled her followers who began costly preparations for the birth of the spiritual man they called "the second Shiloh".

In November 1814 Joanna Southcott died of a brain disease, aged 64. Her followers continued to study the 65 tracts and books of her writings and the sect never completely died out. She left a locked box with instructions that it be opened only in the event of a national crisis.

George III finds peace at last

January 29: George III, Britain's king for a record 60 years, died today aged 82. Although his mental condition has rendered him incapable of ruling since 1811 he has, nonetheless, officiated over the most critical period in the country's history.

George died at Windsor Castle, deaf, blind and mad. He knew nothing of the death of his granddaughter, the marriage of his three sons or the passing of the queen. Neither did he know about the death of Edward, Duke of Kent in Sidmouth a week ago.

He will be succeeded by the Prince Regent, who is 57. Despite the present instability of the country and his own unpopularity, George IV's most urgent task is to start divorce proceedings against his estranged wife, Caroline who says she is returning to take up her duties as queen. *See page 57*

An attractive new pillared entrance has been added to the Margate seabathing infirmary which opened in 1796 and was financed by subscription. The infirmary is proving very successful and so is a dispensary for the poor opened this year at Ramsgate. Two more dispensaries are planned — at Tunbridge Wells and Maidstone.

June: A second great fire in Chatham has destroyed 73 dwellings and warehouses in the town centre and rendered hundreds of people homeless and destitute.

The elegant Chatham House has been destroyed and fire officers say "many other important buildings are a melancholy heap of ruins".

The fire was first spotted by the sentry at Chatham barrack gate and quickly attended by Sappers, Artillery, the Veteran Battalion, Royal Marines, the Navy and the East India Company.

Free traders snatched from gaol

A determined band of citizens from Dover marched to the town gaol in Biggin Street this week, climbed on the roof and began to demolish the building. The mayor and his entourage read the riot act and attempted to stop the men but were unsuccessful.

Within minutes they had rescued the imprisoned crew of a vessel who had earlier been found guilty of smuggling. The sailors were manacled but their rescuers paused briefly at the Red Cow, Dover where the irons were cut off.

The incident proved that the free traders can still count on popular support throughout Kent.

Grand Tourists love the Dover cutters

WITH the introduction this year of a regular steam packet crossing from Dover to Calais more and more of Britain's aristocracy are enjoying a "Grand Tour" of continental Europe and many are writing books about their travels and adventures.

The "Grand Tours" actually began some years ago when those fortunate enough to devote part of their time to leisure came to Dover in their post horse or chaise. The numbers increased in 1786 when the Royal Mail coach service to Dover was introduced. It took eight hours from London.

As shipowners improved their craft and the Dover cutters became known throughout Europe as the best of their kind, so the "Grand Tourists" greatly increased.

Bankers, merchants, politicians and lawyers travelled regularly to Europe and a vast volume of literature has piled up on such subjects as Renaissance art, the decline of Venice, adventures in the Alps and Gothic craftsmanship.

None has a better or sadder story to tell than the poet, Percy Shelley who, on July 28, 1814, eloped with 16-year-old Mary Godwin and crossed the Channel in the first boat he could engage.

The couple made their way to Paris and stayed in terrible inns before walking from Paris to Troyes and from there to Lucerne. Shelley wrote from Switzerland and invited his wife to join them but she declined and, in 1916, she committed suicide in the Serpentine. Shelley immediately married Mary Godwin.

Lord George Byron, the moody, bestselling poet and wildly unconventional and controversial peer also travelled from Dover to the continent four years ago — and has yet to return to England.

A caricaturist makes more fun of the plump and unloved royal couple.

Caroline — rightful Queen of England

There have been bonfires, bells and banquets in Maidstone and many other Kent towns following the news this week of Queen Caroline's victory over her husband George IV who has "scorned and publicly humiliated her for years".

Kent radicals have protested vigorously at the King's treatment of Caroline despite the fact that the Lords passed a bill to dissolve her marriage and deny her the title of queen. A group of women from the county were among those who petitioned parliament saying that George had vilified and persecuted his wife for years. Their protests have been successful. Given the small majority in the Lords (nine votes) and the fact that most of the public seem to be on the queen's side, government ministers have decided not to put the bill before the House of Commons. An 11-week inquiry into Caroline's alleged adulterous liaison with an Italian has not been proved. She is the rightful queen of England.

See page 59

July: A committee of 32 notables has been set up in Chatham to collect money for the relief of those who suffered in June's great conflagration. One of the committee members is John Dickens, a pay clerk in the dockyard who lives with his wife and eight children in a three-storey building in Ordnance Terrace.

A new turnpike road with toll gates at intervals is to be constructed between Gravesend and Borough Green, thus linking the Thames-side town with Tonbridge, via the small village of Ightham. This road will also link up with the Wrotham to Godstone turnpike, improving the east to west journey through the county.

Radical journalist begins his Rural Rides

October: William Cobbett, one of England's finest political journalists and self-proclaimed leader of the radical cause, has set out on horseback to "inspect the whole of England".

He plans to meet the people of Britain, expose corruption and see for himself how the crippling national debt caused by the Napoleonic Wars has forced landowners to become oppressors. He deplores the changes in the country way of life brought about by corrupt politicians and by the influence of London which he calls "the Great Wen".

Cobbett's findings will be published periodically in his own *Weekly Register* over the next few years and he hopes they will lead to reform.

Aged 59, Cobbett is over six feet tall and says he is the weight "of a four bushel sack of good wheat". He grew up in Farnham, Surrey and became the youngest sergeant major in the British Army where he attempted to expose corruption.

He travelled to Canada and the United States as a Tory pamphleteer and, back in England, established his *Weekly Register*. His dislike of the arrogance of Pitt led him towards Radicalism and he frequently wrote about the days when farmers and labourers drank beer and ate beef from the same table and there were no enclosures. His strong opinions were once interpreted as sedition and he spent two years in Newgate prison.

Cobbett is now known as "The People's Friend". Three years ago the Cabinet offered him £10,000 to retire from politics but he refused and briefly returned to the U.S.

Cobbett plans to observe the plight of the cottagers many of whom live in extreme poverty.

Back in England he became popular for his support of Queen Caroline against the "extravagant, overweight, self indulgent" King George IV.

Distrustful of the findings of the recent government commission on agriculture, Cobbett has decided to explore the countryside for himself. His first Rural Ride will take him to the heart of the West Country, then to Norfolk and Suffolk.

Next year he will journey into Kent and Sussex. *See page 60*

New leader for the Aldington Gang

February: Five men were killed and 25 seriously injured yesterday when a gang of smugglers from Aldington were involved in a running battle with preventive-men across Walland Marsh. Eye witnesses say it was the most savage encounter they had ever seen in the area.

Apparently some 250 men had gone to the coast east of Camber; a third of them were detailed to fight if necessary while the others carried cargo from the waiting boats.

They were spotted by Blockade-men and a party was sent from Camber Watch House to challenge them. In the battle which followed four smugglers and one preventive-man died. Those injured were treated by Dr Ralph Hougham of Pear Tree House, Brookland who was led blindfold to the scene. The leader of the Aldington Gang, Cephas Quested, was among those captured. He will be hanged.

This means the ruthless George Ransley will now be in charge. Ransley lives at The Bourne Tap, Brookland and frequently smuggles tubs of spirit from France. In fact he sells up to 100 tubs a week from his home and customers come from all over Kent.He also retains his own firm of solicitors and pays a surgeon to work exclusively for the gang.

The resurgence of smuggling has led to violent scenes in other coastal areas of Kent and fatalities are not unusual. North Kent gangs operate at Reculver and Seasalter and there are determined groups in Wingham and Canterbury. *See page 69*

April: **18 Kent men have been found guilty at the Old Bailey of attempting to smuggle goods into Herne Bay.**

The plan failed when a patrol surprised the men and in the battle which followed a midshipman was killed.

Three will be hanged and the rest transported. The dead man will be buried with full military honours.

Romantic poet found inspiration in Kent

February 23: With the death from consumption today of the poet John Keats, Kent has lost a great friend and England a genius.

It was just six years ago at the age of 20 that Keats left Regency London to find mental refreshment in the pretty resort of Margate.

Here, in a lodging house, he wrote three poems, a Sonnet and an Epistle to his brother George on the pleasures of poetry.

John Keats tells George how he thinks out his verse while... *"pillow'd on a bed of flowers That crowns a lofty cliff, which proudly towers above the ocean waves".*

He made more trips to Margate and then moved on to Canterbury where he hoped that the remembrance of Chaucer would set him "forward like a billiard ball".

At the time he was busy with his second book of *Endymion* and, although violently anti-clerical, found inspiration in the Cathedral city.

Endymion walks... *"oft turning his veil'd eye Down sidelong aisles, and into niches old".*

A year later Keats wrote the poem *Rossetti.* In a passage called *The Eve of St Mark* there is reference to old Minster Square where the fair maiden Bertha lived, her window looking out "far as the Bishop's garden wall" and within the sound of "the echoing Minster gate".

Keats' last visit to Kent was in September last year when he came ashore at Gravesend from the vessel *Maria Crowther* on his way to Italy in vain search for health.

John Keats — mental refreshment in Margate

Since 1818 when Keats fell in love with Fanny Brawne he has produced *Lamia, The Eve of St Agnes, Ode to a Nightingale, Ode on a Grecian Urn* and *La Belle Dame sans Merci.*

His output was small but of high quality. His creative genius has been cut short by his death at the age of 26.

September: Such an enthusiastic and spontaneously warm welcome was given to King George IV at Ramsgate today on his return from Hanover that His Majesty has decreed the harbour should be prefixed "Royal". To celebrate this honour the town will raise, by public subscription, enough money to erect a granite obelisk in Pier Yard. During his stay in the town the King was a guest of Sir W.M.Curtis of Cliff House.

Steaming down the Thames into Kent

Trips by steam-boat down the Thames are booming with twice as many passengers as eight years ago. Today The *London Engineer* arrived at Margate with a full complement. Return fares start at 5/-

May 5: Napoleon Bonaparte died today aged 52 at St Helena where he has been exiled for seven years. Among those who knew him well is the island's British chaplain, Richard Boys, who will shortly return to Kent to be vicar of Loose.

August 7: Queen Caroline died today at her house in Hammersmith to the west of London just two weeks after her husband's coronation. She was 53. For many years she ran an orphanage at Blackheath where, 15 years ago, allegations were made that she had an illegitimate child. She had been married to George since 1795 and, because of his distaste of her, won wide public sympathy.

A huge tower has been built at Victoria Parade, Deal as part of an anti-smuggling campaign to pass semaphore signals to Customs patrols.

October: A papermaking mill has been opened at Horton Kirby on the banks of the River Darent not far from the Shoreham Mill which is now well established. Some years ago the owner Thomas Willmott won a prize offered by the Society of Arts for producing paper from jute. Another main area for papermaking in Kent is along the Len and Loose valleys. Other mills exist at Little Chart, Borough Green, West Peckham, Penshurst, Hawkhurst, Chatham, Canterbury and Dover. Papermaking is a flourishing Kent industry.

December: The results of the national census this year show that more and more people in Kent are living, on average, beyond the age of 50 due mainly to the reduction in infant mortality and better clothing and food. Town populations in Kent are on the increase although most people still live in the country.

Loam on gravel, few trees and only 30 acres of Swedes

January 2: William Cobbett — the one-time soldier, prisoner, exile, journalist, farmer and politician — has reached the county of Kent on his country-wide horseback tour. His opinions, as recorded in his daily diary, may appear to be idiosyncratic and dismissive but he continues to show a clear compassion towards the sufferings of the rural poor.

"I came through Kent", he writes, "to get to Battle from the Great Wen (London). The first town is Bromley, the next Seven-Oaks, the next Tunbridge and between Tunbridge and this place you cross the boundaries of the two counties. From the Surrey Wen to Bromley the land is generally a deep loam on a gravel, and you see few trees except elm. The agricultural state of the country, or rather the quality of the land from Bromley, may be judged of, from the fact, that I did not see as I came along, more than thirty acres of Swedes during the fifty six miles. In Norfolk I should, in the same distance, have seen five hundred acres".

While riding through Bromley Cobbett wrote: Here there is a common, part of which has been enclosed...the women look rosy-cheeked. Seven-Oaks is a pretty little town with beautiful environs part of which consists of the Park of Knowle..It is a very fine place. Tunbridge is a small but very nice town and has some fine meadows and a navigable river.

Cobbett will spend the next few months in Sussex and hopes to return to Kent next summer when he will visit Tunbridge Wells and some of the Wealden towns.

See page 63

Lord Castlereagh kills himself with a knife

Lord Castlereagh, aged 53, is one of the few suicides buried in Westminster Abbey. His inquest was conducted in the drawing room beneath his bedroom by the West Kent coroner, who returned a verdict of unsound mind. Lord Byron has summed up the feelings of his enemies with his words:

*"So **He** has cut his throat at last! — He? Who? The man who cut his country's long ago."*

August 12: Robert Stewart, Viscount Castlereagh, the Foreign Secretary, died today by his own hand. He was found with his throat cut in the upstairs room of the small country house, North Cray Cottage, to which he and his wife loved to escape from the stress of politics.

Those close to Castlereagh cite overwork as the reason for his death. The Duke of Wellington, his comrade during the Peninsular War, told him only last week: "I am bound to warn you that you cannot be in your right mind". Friends have certainly been aware of a deteriorating condition with suggestions of homosexual conduct. He possessed a strange persecution mania.

Castlereagh was a popular foreign secretary who won international esteem when he led the coalition against Napoleon in 1813-14 but later his popularity waned. George Canning, his political rival, is tipped to succeed him.

The Castlereaghs married in 1794 and leased Woolletts Hall — later to become North Cray Cottage — in 1811. A childless couple, Amelia was content to look after her birds, beasts and rare plants while Robert enjoyed country pursuits and making a name for himself in politics.

The question that interests many people is why did this talented and industrious politician, who was also leader of the House of Commons, take his own life. Friends believe his mind became unhinged from the events of June and July this year when Castlereagh — or the Marquis of Londonderry as he was also known — received letters from conspirators who wanted to "impike his head". He showed them to the King and Wellington who both urged medical care.

Castlereagh has made many political enemies in the past few years. He did more than most to unite Britain and Ireland. He supported Catholic emancipation, applauded the efforts

continued in next column

Conspiracy took place in a house of ill-repute

to abolish slavery and opposed the persecution of Queen Caroline. He also instigated the repressive measures required to keep civil order so necessary in the hungry years following the Napoleonic wars.

Shelley, the poet, held him responsible for the so-called Peterloo Massacre three years ago and famously wrote: *"I met murder on the way, He had a mask like Castlereagh, Very smooth he looked yet grim, Seven Bloodhounds followed him".*

The other problem for Castlereagh concerned the gossip surrounding his private life and the accusation, a few months ago, of an homosexual act. In fact he was blackmailed.

On his regular stroll from the Foreign Office, Castlereagh often passed the haunts of several prostitutes and would, on occasions, enter a brothel. But on one such walk there was a conspiracy when he was accosted by a "young lady" who guided him into a place of ill repute. The prostitute took off her clothes and turned out to be a youth. Two men then appeared and told the noble Lord that if he did not give them money he would be exposed. Letters followed, threatening to expose his irregular conduct.

Castlereagh, trapped, went to see his good friend the Duke of Wellington who told him to return to Cray and see his doctor. He went home and slept with his wife who so feared for his life that she removed his razors and anything else with which he might injure himself. As the days went by his condition worsened.

Early this morning , his Lordship arose early and entered his dressing room. He then told his servant to fetch Dr Bankhead instantly. When the doctor arrived he caught Castlereagh as he fell having cut his carotid artery with a small curved knife.

Apparently death for him was preferable to his wife finding out about his sexual indiscretion. He will be buried in Westminster Abbey between Fox and Pitt.

A steam ship in Deptford

October: In years to come Deptford may rightly claim to be the cradle of steam navigation in England, thanks to Mr Thomas Brockelbank, of Westcombe Park who has built a small steam vessel on the former premises of the East India Company at Deptford Creek.

With financial help from a number of capitalists and gentlemen of influence the world's first steam navigation company has now been established and incorporated by an Act of Parliament .

The new Lords cricket ground — home of Marylebone Cricket Club.

Secretary of the MCC says: 'I'll trap them in the shrubbery at Lords'

March: Benjamin Aislabie, a wealthy wine merchant who lives at Lee Place has been appointed secretary of the Marylebone Cricket Club and promises to be most assiduous in collecting subscriptions from members. In fact this most clubbable man — mischievous in wine and song after dinner — promises that no-one will escape paying their dues and he will trap them "even in the shrubbery at Lords".

Aisalbie was educated at Sevenoaks School and is now such a jovial rotund character of 20 stone that he and his fine old house are known among friends as the "Elephant and Castle".

He has played cricket for years, although by his own admission he has never been very good. In 100 innings of "first class cricket" he boasts a highest score of 15 and averages 3.5. One tribute to this genial, corpulent cricket devotee is in verse: *"He still takes the bat and there's no better fun, to see him when batting attempting to run".*

"Old Ben", as he is known, advised Thomas Lord in the setting up of his second ground in 1808. This year he will work alongside the new owner, William Ward, a director of the Bank of England, who says the new ground will always be known as Lords. Ben Aisalbie and William Ward are genuine cricket lovers. After years of uncertainty Lords is safe from the property speculators.

Clarence recalls his naval days at Sheerness

September 6: Yesterday's visit to the new dockyard at Sheerness was a nostalgic and memorable one for the Duke of Clarence. As a midshipman —who joined the navy at the age of 13 and saw active service — the Duke was stationed at Sheerness and has fond memories of the dockyard which was laid out by Samuel Pepys more than 150 years ago.

The visit by this Prince of the Royal Blood to open the new dockyard was accompanied by fanfare and celebration. Having completed the formal honours Clarence paid tribute to John Rennie the great civil engineer who supervised the construction until he died in 1821. The work has been completed by John Rennie, the younger.

Sheerness has seen plenty of naval action as Clarence well knows. In 1797, before his time as a sailor, the naval forces rebelled against the barbarous conditions in which they served. The Nore mutiny was quelled in robust style but it drew the attention of the public to inhuman conditions and eventually led to some improvement.

The new work began in 1814 when the foundation stone of Admiralty House was laid.

January 17: Four smugglers were killed and six injured in a gun battle with preventive officers off the coast of Dungeness today. The smugglers — all Dutch — were carrying contraband worth £10,000 aboard a ship, *The Four Brothers* when they were intercepted by *The Badger*. The men will face a charge of firing at a King's ship.

Why Kent is now a county of paupers

The boom years which followed the end of the Napoleonic Wars now seem to be a lifetime away. A general depression has settled across the county and poverty is growing everywhere.

Nowhere is worse than the towns of Deal and Sandwich. The dispersal of the fleet in the Downs and the suppression of smuggling has brought a total suspension of trade. In Deal more than 500 pauper children are fed daily alongside the 450 inmates of its two poorhouses.

Sandwich, described by Daniel Defoe 100 years ago as "an old, decayed, poor, miserable little town" has hardly recovered. The shipyard is broken up, the malting business is crumbling and inhabitants long for a return of the days before the haven became silted up.

The manufacturing industry has virtually ceased. Wealden iron making collapsed long ago and so did the linen thread making of Maidstone, the cloth making of the Weald villages and the silk weaving of Canterbury. The coastal communities of Folkestone, Ramsgate, Whitstable and Faversham suffer from the seasonal maritime hazards caused by a succession of bitter winters. Unemployment is rife in Chatham while the towns of Gravesend and Milton are experiencing vast improvidence.

The Rev G.R.Gleig, vicar of Ash recently described the French wars as a "golden age" for East Kent. "During the good times of war", he wrote in his *Chronicles of Waltham*, "when the demand for labour was great, working men received half a crown a day, wheat sold for ninety or a hundred shillings a quarter, working people throve and were contented'

There was full employment during the wars. For Kent farmers every shilling expended brought back two shillings. That was followed by galloping inflation which had a devastating effect on real incomes. Kent today is a county of paupers. *See page 106*

Danish ship found in the River Rother

An ancient boat, excavated this year at Maytham in the channel of the River Rother, is believed to be one of the ships of the Danish invasion of AD 892/3 when a force of some 250 ships entered the mouth of the Rother which flowed out into the sea near Hythe. They cast anchor about four miles up river and built a fort at Appledore.

Antiquarians are delighted with the find. The boat is 63 ft 8ins long, 15 ft broad with a single mast and two cabins in the stern. Various domestic items have been found along with human bones.

October 30: Edmund Cartwright, the inventor of the power loom and the wool-combing machine has died at his home in Hastings, aged 80.

November: During a game of football this month, William Webb Ellis of Rugby School showed a fine disregard of the rules by picking up the ball and running with it. He was quickly pursued and the boys loved it so much they have adopted it as a new game. They are calling it Rugby Football!

George VI has given the British Museum his father's vast collection of 60,000 books.

William Cobbett rode through Sevenoaks and caught a glimpse of Knowle which he considered 'a very fine place'. The owner of this great house is Arabella, wife of the 3rd Duke of Dorset who died in 1899 leaving a great art collection. His son, the 4th Duke was killed in 1814 soon after his 21st birthday when his spine was crushed by a falling horse. Arabella's two daughters will inherit the estate.

Indignant radical rides through Kent

August 31: William Cobbett's horseback ride has finally taken him into the heart of Kent and through some of the most "delightful" countryside in rural England.

Entering the county from Sussex he had plenty to write in his diary about unusual rock formations and the large estates of Lord Abergavenny and the Marquis of Camden. "I soon got clear of Tunbridge Wells", he wrote, "and out of the contagion of its Wen-engendered inhabitants in time to meet the first rays of the sun on the hill up to Frant".

He then journeyed through Lamberhurst, Goudhurst, Milkhouse-Street, Benenden and Rolvenden into Tenterden.

In Benenden, Cobbett stopped to look at the stocks which were fitted with a bench "so that the patient while he is receiving the benefit of remedy is not exposed to the danger of catching cold by sitting!"

Cobbett commented that he had never seen a pair of feet peeping through stocks and was never likely to because this sort of mild, gentle good-humoured correction was not enough for our present rulers. "They want houses of correction, treadmills, hulks", he wrote, "gaols ten times as big as formerly..."

In Tenterden, Goudhurst, Appledore, Snargate and Brenzett Cobbett found something else to arouse his exasperation — the lack of people at service time in the parish church and evidence that the Church had little moral hold over the labouring classes.

"This Tenterden is a market town", he wrote, "and a singularly bright spot. As I entered the street, perhaps 200 feet wide, I saw the people coming out of church. It was a fine sight. Shabbily dressed people do not go to church. I saw, in short, drawn out before me, the dress and beauty of the town; and a great many very, very pretty girls I saw; and saw them too in their best attire."

As Cobbett rode on, his mind still full of appreciation for the Tenterden girls, he came to the coast and his first sight of the Martello Towers.

"Oh, Lord", he wrote, "to think I should be destined to behold these monuments of the wisdom of Pitt and Dundas and Perceval! Good G—. Here they are, piles of brick in a circular form about 300 feet circumference at the base...Cannons were to be fired from the top of these things in order to defend the country against the French Jacobins! "These ridiculous things cost five, perhaps ten thousand pounds each. One was, I am told sold the other day for two hundreds pounds.

"And that's not all. I crossed a canal at Appledore, made for the length of 30 miles, to keep out the French; for these armies which had crossed the Rhine and the Danube, were to be kept back by a canal, made by Pitt, 30 feet wide at the most!"

Cobbett's indignation was further aroused by more "expensive squanderings. Hills covered with barracks, walls of immense dimensions, incessant sinks of money— and much of it falling down.

"However, all is right", Cobbett wrote: "These things were made with the hearty goodwill of those who are now coming to ruin in consequence of the Debt, contracted for the purpose of making these things! The load will come, at last, upon the right shoulders." *See page 64*

Cobbett glad to leave behind the tarred and trousered

"THE wasteful policies" of Pitt and Dundas and the taxes which came from the Napoleonic Wars still rankle with William Cobbett.

He has ridden through Dover "which has less blackguard people than I ever observed in any sea port before". He has also seen the fortifications on the Western Heights.

"Here", he wrote, "is a hill....hallowed like a honey-comb. Here are line upon line, trench upon trench, cavern upon cavern, bomb-proof upon bomb-proof; in short the very sight of the thing convinces you that either madness the most humiliating, or profligacy the most scandalous must have been at work here for years.

"The question that every man of sense asks is: 'What reason had you to suppose the French would ever come to this hill to attack it, while the rest of the country was so much more easy to assail?

"However, let any man of good, plain understanding, go and look at the works that have here been performed, and that are now all tumbling into ruin. Let him ask what this cavern was for; what this ditch was for...and why all these holes and hiding places at an expense of millions upon millions?

"More brick and stone have been buried on this hill than would go to build a neat new cottage for every labouring man in the counties of Kent and Sussex".

Cobbett enjoyed the valley towards Folkestone but Deal he found a villainous place, full of filthy-looking people, great desolation of abomination, barracks tumbling down, partly occupied by soldiers. "Everything", he wrote, "seems upon the perish; I was glad to leave its inns to the tarred and trousered!" *See page 71*

Canterbury guards the head of Thomas More

THE lead box, containing the head of Sir Thomas More and kept in St Dunstan's Church, Canterbury, has been opened for the first time since his execution in 1535.

The head of this great statesman, author and one-time personal friend of Henry VIII is just a skeleton but those who had the privilege to see it are even more convinced that it is the noblest head that ever fell on Tower Hill. The story of how it came to be in Canterbury is an intriguing one.

In 1529 More succeeded Cardinal Wolsey as Lord Chancellor, the first in that office to be neither cleric nor nobleman. By that time he had been a member of the King's privy council, a Speaker of the House of Commons and had accompanied Henry VIII to the Field of the Cloth of Gold.

He helped the King to write his Latin attack on Luther and accepted his marriage to Anne Boleyn but was unable to deny the validity of the Pope and resigned as Chancellor in 1532.

As the distinction between the churches became urgent More refused to swear the oath following the Act of Supremacy in 1534 and was convicted for treason.

The trial was followed by execution and More's head was stuck on a pole at London Bridge. His daughter Margaret Roper, who lived in Canterbury, rescued the head and kept it by her in spices until her death. It was then placed in a lead box in nearby St Dunstan's where it remains to this day.

Thames to the Medway — the Gravesend to Higham canal.

Canal with a tunnel links Gravesend and Strood

April: The long-awaited canal between Gravesend and Strood, originally planned to provide a quick and safe means of carrying men and machines between the Thames and the Medway, has been opened at last.

Ralph Dodd, the mastermind behind the project, is naturally delighted. Various difficulties have blighted the scheme during construction but most of these have been overcome. New problems lie ahead but Dodd is confident that all will be well.

The work actually began 23 years ago when it was intended to bring the canal out to the Thames at Higham Bight but the great depth of the alluvial mud of the marshes meant that a new route had to be introduced.

continued on next page

The hulks on the River Medway at Chatham where "a generation of dead men arise from their tombs".

Hundreds buried alive in floating tombs

October: A revealing letter written by a French prisoner of war and smuggled from his prison hulk near Chatham is now in the hands of the French Government. It describes the harsh conditions suffered by those imprisoned on the hulks, moored stem to stern in disease-ridden marshland.

"The Medway", he wrote, "is covered with men of war, dismantled and lying in ordinary. Their fresh and brilliant painting contrasts with the hideous aspect of the old and smoky hulks. In these floating tombs prisoners of war are buried alive — Danes, Swedes, Frenchmen, Americans, no matter. They are lodged on the lower deck, on the upper deck and even on the orlop deck...400 malefactors are the maximum of a ship appropriated to convicts. From 800 to 1,200 is the ordinary numbers of prisoners of war heaped together in a prison ship of the same rate".

There is little doubt that conditions are bad and only the hope of revenge or the possibility of escape keep the men alive. A Chatham commissioner recently presented this report on the hulks: "What with the inadequate issue of clothes, prohibition of bathing, shortage of soap, skimped rations and overcrowding it is little wonder that the hulks are alive with vermin, that skin diseases and lung troubles are rampant, and that depression and debility cause the occupants to sink to the lowest level of manhood".

Other commissioners are just as scathing. One describes how gambling is permitted on the *Buckingham* and says: "A generation of dead men rise for a moment from their tombs. They are hollow-eyed, wan, earthy of complexion, bent-backed, shaggy bearded and of terrible emancipation".

An example of the overcrowding comes in this report on the *Brunswick* at Chatham: "The length of the orlop deck is 125 feet and the height 4ft 10 inches and in this space 460 prisoners are crowded at night. In the summer it is so unbearable that the inmates go naked to obtain relief".

Many French prisoners of war have attempted to escape only to be engulfed by the slime. Others have paid agents to procure them favourable positions in the lists of those to be exchanged with English prisoners of war. Those on board the *Bristol* and *Hero* have threatened mutiny.

Some prisoners have even bribed guards and bought the services of smugglers with the promise to take them back to France and then ended up with their throats slit. Only the clever and the lucky ones have escaped and they are rare." *See page 74*

continued from previous page

That was fine until constructors reached the hills of the Hundred of Hoo. Here they built a tunnel 2.5 miles long.

One difficulty still to be faced concerns the big difference in water levels between the canal and the river. Currently, barges have to wait in the Basin until tidal conditions are suitable for them. Many believe it is still cheaper to sail the long way round and risk falling foul of the privateers who are a constant source of danger for the supply ships moving between London and the Medway ports.

See page 120

Canterbury plans a railway and goes to Stephenson for advice

June: Canterbury's economic problems which have plagued the city since the collapse of its only manufacturing industry — the weaving of silk and cotton — could soon be solved.

This month the city fathers unveiled a revolutionary plan to build a railway line from Canterbury to the sea as an alternative to the expensive and dangerous Canterbury to Whitstable turnpike road.

This would mean that a steam- hauled locomotive could carry coal, other goods and even passengers on a short six-mile route to the sea.

Two years ago on the advice of William James, engineer, coalmaster and railway enthusiast, it was agreed to form a company, raise capital by means of 500 £50 shares and press ahead with the building of the railway. The only problem was how to traverse Tyler Hill — which presents a formidable barrier between the two towns.

An Act of Parliament for the line has now received Royal assent and the Canterbury to Whitstable Railway Company is officially incorporated. Sadly, James is no longer involved in the project. He was declared bankrupt a few months ago and now lingers in a debtors' prison.

The company now hopes to persuade George Stephenson to accept the position of engineer. He is already renowned for his locomotives and his famous *Rocket* has achieved the unbelievable speed of 30mph. Stephenson is the engineer and mastermind behind the world's first passenger steam railway which is due to open between Stockton and Darlington in September. *See page 78*

Robert Stephenson, who has assisted his father in providing the locomotives for the Stockton to Darlington railway which is due to open this year.

A diary kept by a man who achieved high office as secretary to the Royal Navy between 1669 and 1699 has been published to great acclaim. The diarist is Samuel Pepys who tells of such great events as the Restoration, the plague and the great fire of London.

Curse of the threshing machine

A FEW years ago Betteshanger farmer, John Boys invented a threshing machine. Driven by horses, rather than men, it enabled him to harvest and thresh his wheat in one day, grind it into flour overnight and make bread the following day.

The invention spread rapidly across rural Kent. Arriving during the period of economic depression, which followed the Napoleonic Wars, it was a blessing for farmers. But it has also led to large numbers of men being put on short hire and starvation wages. Many thousands more are now out of work and, in desperation, they have looked to the parish for relief. Some have been employed on the roads but, in the eastern part of the county, poverty is growing.

Cobbett has seen the poverty. In the account of his tour through the Isle of Thanet two years ago he mentioned how the labourers' houses looked beggarly in the extreme, ascribing the destitution to the fact that so much work on the farm was now undertaken by horses and by machines. He made no secret of his sympathy: "Never, let what will happen, will these people lie down and starve quietly".

There are more than 4,500 farms in the county — but with the price of food so high and wages (for those employed) so low, turmoil is growing.

See page 79

August 7: Great celebrations in Greenwich as the town and its neighbourhood is illuminated by gas lamps. The gasometer is in Bridge Street and the gas is supplied by the Phoenix Company of Bankside.

March: A Royal Naval Lifeboat Association has been founded by Sir William Hilary.

Speckled monster returns to claim more lives

November: A terrible sight faces those brave enough to walk the narrow, dirty streets of medieval Canterbury. Within the tightly packed houses — some, like those in Mercury Lane, almost devoid of daylight because of the overhanging buildings on either side — can be heard the terrible cries of dying children. Smallpox, that most dreadful disease, has returned to the city. This time the epidemic is so bad that many are comparing it to the bubonic plague which claimed so many Canterbury infants.

The sight of the dead and dying in the street is commonplace, despite the large-scale vaccination project carried out by the Kent and Canterbury Hospital only last year. No-one knows what the death toll will finally be; doctors say it will take months, maybe years to get the latest epidemic under control.

It was in the second half of the 17th century that smallpox superseded the plague as the most feared disease. Hundreds died in Kent until the introduction of inoculation in 1801 and even since then the "speckled monster" has continued to claim lives.

The people of Canterbury suffered badly during the national epidemic eight years ago. And they are suffering again.

Thomas R. Jolliffe has achieved what is believed to be one of the first balloon ascents in England. It took this year on a farm at Seal near Sevenoaks. The cubic capacity of the balloon was 14,000 feet and some 400 yards of best silk went into its making. The gas was manufactured on the spot. Although it was the wish of Mr Jolliffe to make his pioneering voyage in strict secrecy, a number of yokels formed a ring round the balloon, intent on causing mischief. They were thwarted by local farmers. **See page 171**

A wave of strikes is sweeping through the huge maritime-industrial conurbation of Dartford-Gravesend-Rochester-Strood and Gillingham as workers press for higher wages. Conservative politicians are blaming the unrest on the repeal of the Combination Acts which make possible, for the first time, the establishment of effective trade unions.

Scurrilous and almost obscene cartoons of the King and members of his Government has led to a revision of the Vagrancy Act which now has a clause prohibiting "every person wilfully exposing to view...any obscene print, picture or other indecent exhibition".

The new Act also consolidates the many laws for punishing "idle and disorderly persons and rogues and vagabonds". It has come about through the lobbying of William Wilberforce's Society for the Suppression of Vice.

It was the cartoons depicting the late Queen Caroline's complex domestic problems which really prompted the Government to revise the Act.

Kent's country banks are struggling for survival in the wake of a national credit crisis that is affecting financial houses in every major city.

October: The old porch together with the pulpit from Westminster Abbey, delicately carved with a canopy and supported on a graceful branching pillar, has been given to Trottiscliffe church.

Gas light comes to Dartford — via gun barrels

August: Dartford is about to become one of the first towns outside London to take advantage of the most modern innovation. Following a full survey of the town last year, and a successful appeal for subscriptions, a Dartford Gas Company has been established and no time will be wasted in bringing this most ambitious project to fruition.

It was just a few years ago that the town elders suggested that streets and buildings should be illuminated with gas. They appointed a Mr William Warcup to organise a survey and said the project should cost no more than £3,200.

Mr Warcup's specifications, now finalised, include the erection and installation of 52 public lamps and 120 private lamps. The gas pipes — made from gun barrels joined together — will be laid under the town's main thoroughfares. Work will begin next June and should be completed by October

The capital used to launch the company has been fixed at £4,000 divided into 200 shares of £20 each. This means that Dartford has found it possible to supply gas at a cost to the consumer considerably lower than that charged in central London. Shareholders can expect a good steady return.

It is now anticipated that other towns in Kent will follow Dartford's pioneering example.

No wages for the men of 'the best brigade in Kent'

January: A Fire Engine Association has been formed at Ashford and has great plans to become the finest in Kent with two engines and more than 40 members.

Unlike firemen in other brigades the volunteer members will not receive the smallest remuneration for their services. Inhabitants whose properties are on fire will be charged five guineas for the large and three guineas for the small engine. The rest of the funds will be obtained through private subscriptions and contributions from the offices of the Kent, Phoenix and Norwich Union insurance companies.

Fire fighting is a thirsty business and those members who retire to the Saracens Head and thereby fail to attend a fire will be heavily fined.

Why the Colgate family were advised to flee to America

July 6th: The people of Shoreham, Chevening and Bessels Green are mourning the death this week of Robert Colgate, a charismatic, outspoken Baptist who was forced to flee to America 29 years ago for showing sympathy with the American cause following the war of independence.

In Kent, Robert and his wife Sarah lived at Shoreham mill and farmed at nearby Filston . His involvement with politics was so stormy that Lord Stanhope advised him to leave before he was arrested. Colgate embarked on a sailing ship at Gravesend, reached America and settled down on a farm near Baltimore with his family.

Robert Colgate — from Shoreham to Baltimore.

After many years of hard work and aided by his sons, Bowles, John and George the farm yielded wheat, rye, flax, corn, potatoes, millet and oats. Robert also learned to make potash — a product in constant demand by his eldest son William who had started as an apprentice in a flourishing soap and candle-making business in New York and was now a senior partner.

Potash is an essential ingredient in making soap and Robert sent great quantities to William. He placed wood ash and tallow into large vats of water, then drew off and boiled them in a kettle. After being boiled for some time the soap was poured into moulds, cooled and packed into boxes.

In England Robert Colgate worshipped at Bessels Green Chapel. He called himself, at times, a Unitarian, worked hard for the Anabaptist Church and was known simply among his friends in America as Robert the Immigrant. The Colgate soap business now flourishes in the United States of America.

The steam packet* Rapid *leaves Gravesend for Margate

All over for leader of the Aldington Blues

December: George Ransley, the notorious sea smuggler and his motley band of fishermen, farm labourers and former soldiers, have been caught and sentenced to death at Maidstone Prison before a court agog with excitement.

Ransley, it was said, frequently crossed the Channel by the Dover Packet and purchased brandy, tobacco, tea and lace. His obedient team of ruffians would then load the valuable cargo into a boat with a false bottom while he returned to the Marsh in time to greet them on a deserted beach.

The leader of the Aldington Blues, as his land-smugglers were known, organised his men with near-military precision. Two thirds would carry the cargo from the boat after it had rowed in with muffled oars. A third, arranged on each flank and armed, would be protecting them. The cargo, in tubs, would be spirited away to secret hides (such as the Marsh churches) by hand and horse, pack mule or cart.

It was with his share of the profits that Ransley bought the Bourne Tap Inn. There, men and women would drink and dance — sometimes half naked — to celebrate success. Ransley, a tee-totaller took no part in such frivolities.

Between May and September this year seven successful runs took place. On the eighth the smugglers planned to land on Dover beach below the Castle casemates but this daring and ill-planned run went terribly wrong. Men of the Dover Blockade heard the boats and advanced towards the smugglers. In the ensuing fight two blockade officers were killed and Ransley and his men escaped.

Bent on revenge Lt Hellard of the Dover Blockade offered a reward of £500 for information leading to the arrest of Ransley. And he invited the Bow Street runners to question " suspicious strangers of the lower orders".

The bait was too tempting for the "lower orders" and details of Ransley's hideaway were soon known by a raiding party who took a circuitous route to Aldington, smashed through the door of his house, killed his dog and handcuffed him before he was able to scramble out of bed.

Seven other houses in the village received similar treatment and the prisoners were lodged aboard *The Ramillies* at Deal before transfer to Newgate prison, Bow Street and finally Maidstone.

So ends the successful career of the powerful leader of the Aldington Blues who controlled the smuggling trade from Deal to Camber. *See page 70*

Samuel Palmer — a self portrait

Blake meets Palmer in his green and pleasant land

WITH the death this year of William Blake, at the age of 70, England has lost its most individual poet and painter and one who, in recent years, had developed a close friendship with an eccentric group of young artists who call themselves the "Ancients".

Blake's passionate hatred of authority and the establishment is well known. So is his much-loved poem, *Jerusalem* which forms the preface to his book *Milton* (1804-8). Lesser known, however, were his frequent visits to the village of Shoreham to dine with a young artist called Samuel Palmer and his most creative friends.

They met for the first time four years ago when Palmer was 18 and a student at the Royal Academy School. For the younger man it was an awe-inspiring moment for Blake personified all that Palmer was looking for in art, literature and religion.

They became firm friends and when Palmer — with his cousin, Frederick Tatham, his father, brother William and his nurse, Mary Ward — moved to Shoreham for the fresh country air Blake decided to pay a visit.

He found the family at Ivy Cottage in Church Street and as there was no spare room Samuel had to sleep out at Mr Gregory, the baker's house.

Blake was soon to meet the "Ancients", so called because of the frequency with which they referred to ancient philosophers and artists. He found them swimming in the River Darent, revelling in youthful enthusiasm for new ideas and enjoying the fertile abundance of Shoreham's fields, woods, hills and valleys.

It may have inspired him to write the lines:

And by came an angel with a bright key, He opened the coffins and set them all free, And down the green plains leaping they run And washed in the river and shine in the sun.

Samuel Palmer has already had three paintings accepted for exhibition at the Royal Academy and two at the British Institution. At Shoreham the brilliance of colour and light which he sees in and around the village is firing his imagination. He calls it his Valley of Vision. More paintings, perhaps a masterpiece or two, is on the way. *See page 81*

New road in London will be Regent's Street

MANY hundreds of Kentish people have been travelling to London to see the new broad thoroughfare which runs from Carlton House in Pall Mall to Marylebone Park. Designed by John Nash, the Prince Regent's architect and surveyor-general, the road is called Regent's Street and the park will be renamed Regent's Park. Last year Nash redesigned Buckingham Palace

August: The Duke of Clarence has presented new colours to the West Kent Regiment at Portsmouth. The Regiment will now be known as the 50th Duke of Clarence's Regiment.

A new newspaper for London, *The Evening Standard,* published for the first time this year, will be available in many of Kent's northern parishes.

George Ransley, former leader of the Aldington Blues smuggling gang who was sentenced to death last year will instead be transported to Australia.

A view of the road between Maidstone and Mereworth — "the finest seven miles I have seen in England"

Gloom hangs over the ruined barracks

IN his strong radical, often dismissive and frequently arrogant style, William Cobbett has continued to paint a remarkable picture of rural life in Kent.

We left him three years ago in the "villainous" town of Deal. From there he took a "beautiful road to the rotten borough of Sandwich. It is", he described, "as villainous a hole as one would wish to see surrounded by some of the finest land in the world. Along one side is a marsh; along the other is land which they tell me bears seven quarters of wheat to an acre".

Cobbett rode to the Isle of Thanet — "a garden indeed, a county of corn but the labourers' houses all along, beggarly in the extreme. The people dirty, poor-looking, ragged but particularly dirty.

Travelling through Margate, Monckton, Sarr (sic) and Upstreet, Cobbett arrived in Canterbury and saw the remains of the Buffs Barracks at Northgate. They were falling down. The "horrible erections were crumbling; grass grew out of each crack, broken windows yawned everywhere and lamps were missing from all the lamp posts.

"Westminster Abbey is not the place for the monument of Pitt", he told his diary. "The statue of the great snorting bawler ought to be stuck up here". Canterbury is a city within its gates which stands upon less ground than those horrible erections, the barracks of Pitt, Dundas and Perceval. Here are horse-barracks, foot-barracks, artillery-barracks, engineering-barracks, a whole country of barracks but only, here and there, a soldier...It gave me great inexpressible pleasure to perceive the gloom that seemed to hang over these barracks which once swarmed with soldiers and their blythe companions, as a hive swarms with bees".

From Canterbury to Maidstone and then to Merryworth "and the finest seven miles I have ever seen in England or anywhere else. The Medway is to your left, with its meadows about a mile wide...There are hop gardens and orchards and plantations of ashes and chestnuts which adds greatly to the beauty.

And so onto Tonbridge " a common country town, though very clean and the people looking very well. The climate is warm here, for in entering the town I saw a large Althea Frutex in bloom, a thing rare enough any year and particularly a year like this".

Cobbett liked the villages which led to Westerham and especially the Weald "where I rode above a mile completely arched over by the boughs of the underwood growing in the banks of the lane. What an odd taste that man must have who prefers a turnpike-road to a lane like this?".

Archbishop deprives Canterbury of a party

July 28: The new Archbishop of Canterbury, William Howley has enraged many local residents by his refusal to be enthroned in the Cathedral last week. He claims he has no home in the city and little in common with the place apart from high ecclesiastical office. He will, he says, continue to live at Lambeth Palace and his country residence, Addington Park, near Croydon.

Archbishop Howley's decision to be enthroned by proxy has made him extremely unpopular. Very few Canterbury inhabitants are interested in the religious aspect of the ceremony but it always provides them with an excuse for merrymaking and Howley has deprived them.

There have been angry letters to the *Kentish Gazette* and the well-known wit, Sydney Smith writes "A proxy sent down in the Canterbury fly, to take the Creator to witness that the archbishop, detained in town by business or pleasure, will never violate that foundation of piety over which he presides — all this seems to me an act of the most extraordinary indolence ever recorded in history."

It transpires that Smith and Howley, who were boys together at Winchester, were playing chess one day when Howley was checkmated. In a fit of pique he hurled the chessboard at his colleague. Their friendship terminated that day!

Archbishop Howley — formerly Bishop of London — takes over the primacy from Charles Manners-Sutton who died a few weeks ago. Among his many ambitions is a plan to survey Lambeth Palace and carry out an extensive programme of reconstruction in the Gothic style.

He may, he says, even go to Canterbury one day. *See page 85*

Archbishop William Howley, 62 who was enthroned not in person but by proxy. A portrait by Sir Martin Archer Shee.

More Kentish families seek fortune in the New World

SINCE Britain made peace with the United States of America at the Paris Treaty in 1783 more and more families are following their forefathers by migrating to the former British colonies and swelling the ranks of English-speaking peoples in what has been described as "the land of opportunity".

Some years ago they were fleeing from Napoleon's expected invasion. Today, it is escape from rural turmoil and the decline in the importance of the land.

The parish of Biddenden has supported those who wish to spend the rest of their lives in the New World by collecting £53 to send six people to board a ship in Liverpool. The money will pay for their travel, buy provisions and there should be some left over for use on arrival.

Other Kentish families to leave are John Whitehead and his wife and John Hogbin, his wife and eight children, from the remote village Burmarsh. The two families have received grants from the parish.

In the New World they will join English labourers, carpenters, wheelwrights, millwrights, bricklayers and smiths.

John Marshall, a Dartford paper maker whose mill is sited on the banks of the River Darent just below Holy Trinity Church, has created a special device which can insert a water mark into a continuous roll of paper instead of sheet by sheet. His device is called a 'dandy roll' and has so impressed the Bank of England that they wish to appoint him to manufacture the moulds on which bank notes are made.

Protestant v Catholic on Penenden Heath

October 24: Kent has never seen anything like it. With the Catholic Emancipation Bill imminent, the High Sheriff of Kent, Sir Thomas Maryon Wilson, yesterday convened a county meeting on Penenden Heath in opposition to the "dastardly" measure. Between 40,000 and 50,000 Kentish Men turned up and petitioned Parliament that "the Protestant Constitution of the United Kingdom might be preserved entire and inviolate".

It was passed by a large majority but leading politicians say it is unlikely to carry much weight.

Roman Catholic Emancipation is almost certain to become law — so ending a controversy which has dominated British and Irish politics for more than 20 years. It led to the Gordon riots in 1780 and to the resignation of Pitt in 1801.

Those at Penenden Heath on behalf of the Emancipators included the Lord Lieutenant of Kent, the Marquis Camden and the Earls of Darnley, Cowper, Thanet, Radnor and Jersey; Viscount Torrington, Lord Say and Sele, Lord Clifton, the Right Hon J. Calcraft, Sir J.M. Tylden, Messrs Baring, Warre, Hodges, Brockman, Rider, Darell and Knight.

On the anti-Catholic side were the Earls of Winchilsea, Romney, Amherst, Abergavenny and Guildford, Viscount Sydney, Lords La Despencer, Teynham and Bexley, Sir Edward Dering and Sir John Bridges, the Hon J.W. Stratford, W. Deedes and W.O. Hammond.

Among those who spoke was Mr Shiel, a barrister and member of the Catholic Association who was made a freeholder of the county to enable him to address the meeting.

He spoke for half an hour and was met with incessant interruption. Eventually he was howled into silence. However, his speech appeared in full in two morning newspapers occuping four columns in space.

See page 75

A young journalist and would-be author, William Thackeray, has written the following *jeu d'esprit* about the demonstration on the heath.

Mister Sheil into Kent has gone,
On Penenden Heath you'll find him;
Nor think you that he came alone,
There's Doctor Doyle behind him.
"Men of Kent", said this little man,
"If you hate emancipation,
"You're a set of fools"; he then began,
A cut and dry oration.

He strove to speak, but the men of Kent
Began a grievious shouting,
When out of his waggon this little man went,
And put a stop to his spouting.
"What though these heretics heard me not",
Quoth he to his friend canonical:
My speech is safe in The Times *I wot,*
And eke in the Morning Chronicle*".*

530 prisoners saved after attempt to scuttle hulk

October 16: An attempt by prisoners of war to scuttle a hulk moored on the Medway has been thwarted by troops from the Chatham garrison.

According to *The Times* the lower deck of *The Dolphin* was covered by two feet of water before any alarm could be given and within minutes the ship was on her beam ends with 700 prisoners on board, many locked in and totally unconscious of their perilous situation.

The troops of the garrison were mustered and with the ship's crew engaged in strenuous efforts to save the lives of the convicts.

More than 150 were pulled through the portholes on the lower deck. They had kept their heads above water for nearly an hour. but some of them were almost dead. Another 380, wearing nothing more than a shirt, were taken from the vessel and marched along the beach by the military to the hospital ship *Canada.* Nobody knows who was responsible for the scuttling but there will be an inquiry.

September 26: The Home Secretary Sir Robert Peel has set up an organised police force. About 1,000 men, mostly ex-soldiers, paraded today in top hats and long blue coats to derisive cries from onlookers. Sir Robert said: "I want to teach that liberty does not consist of having your house robbed by organised gangs of thieves".

Five wonderful new churches are built in Kent

Taking advantage of generous parliamentary grants beautiful new churches have been built in five Kent towns during the past seven years. They are St John's, Chatham (completed in 1822), St George's, Ramsgate (1822), Holy Trinity, Maidstone (1828), Holy Trinity, Margate (1829), and Holy Trinity, Tunbridge Wells (1829).

It was in 1818 that two events took place which were to give a major impetus to new church building and the enlargement of existing buildings within the established Church of England.

They were the foundation of the incorporated Church Building Society and the passing of the Church Building Act for the erection of new churches in populous places.

Grants were then made available only on the strict understanding that at least half of the accommodation in the churches would be free. Before this date the bulk of sittings in town churches had to be paid for — some through annual pew rents and others through outright purchase of the sittings. That meant accommodation for the poor or for strangers was limited.

There is great excitement in Kent over the architectural quality of the new churches. Holy Trinity, Tunbridge Wells, for example was designed by Decimus Burton who submitted two brilliant plans for the arrangement of the interior.

More churches are currently under construction or enlargement in the county. They include Holy Trinity, Broadstairs, St Margaret's at Rochester and Sutton Valence.

The work of church building and restoration in Kent, a trickle before this year, is about to snowball. But a great emphasis will continue to be placed on the provision of free seating and liturgical innovation.

The new church at Pembury. ***See page 120.***

Wellington and Winchilsea meet in a duel of honour

March 21: To the astonishment of both the government and the opposition, the prime minister, Lord Wellington, today fought a duel of honour with his arch-Tory critic the Earl of Winchilsea.

The two men met at Battersea Fields, each armed with a pistol. The earl received the Duke's fire without returning it and then explained that he had not intended to impute personal dishonour to his opponent.

The dispute arose when the earl accused the Prime Minister of treachery and alliance with the antichrist over the question of Catholic emancipation. There was also a heated exchange between the two in connection with the recently-founded King's College.

With the duel over and no-one even close to being injured, honour was restored and the two men are friends again.

The north west view of Walmer Castle, the home of the Duke of Wellington.

Walmer Castle will be the Duke's home for life

April: One more honour has been bestowed on Britain's greatest living soldier and revered father figure to the nation. Alongside his duties as politician and Prime Minister the Duke of Wellington (the former Arthur Wellesley) is now Lord Warden of the Cinque Ports, Constable of Dover Castle and may enjoy Walmer Castle as a home for the rest of his life.

He took up office and residence in January this year and quickly described Walmer as "the most charming sea-residence I have ever seen".

With walls 13 feet thick, a deep moat and a squat concentric appearance Walmer was built in the reign of Henry VIII to give maximum fire-power and minimum target area for invaders. The gardens, laid out by Lady Hester Pitt, are magnificent and so are the great oak doors and drawing room where Pitt and Nelson met for the first time.

The Duke has already made changes and transferred to the castle some of his most treasured possessions. In his bedroom looking out to sea is his compact writing desk and the camp bed from Waterloo on which he always sleeps. The mattress is in its original silk cover and Blücher's velvet blanket adorns it.

The "Iron Duke" as he is known is too busy running the affairs of state and looking after his consituency of Rye to dwell on those brilliant campaigns in Spain and France which culminated in his brilliant victory at Waterloo.

He has other homes, of course, but Walmer, he says, is his favourite retreat and there he will enjoy the company of old friends and, perhaps, many new ones. *See page 106*

Drunk again at Marden — when we think of hops we automatically think of beer. Over indulgence or just a prank? Who knows?

Stocks: a very public form of chastisement

FOUR years ago Robert Peel, the home secretary, introduced new prison reforms in order to end the death sentence on more than 100 offences.

Prisons are now funded from the rates, administered by local magistrates and jailers will be paid salaries and will certainly not be allowed to take fees from prisoners which had previously been the case with some of the wealthy convicts.

Welfare reforms have also been introduced, including medical care, better diet, schooling, religious instruction and, in some, cases, even employment for prisoners.

The new reforms are welcomed by the prison managers at Maidstone and Chatham and certainly by the juries at the Kent Assizes who have often acquitted offenders rather than see them hanged. Until recently a man could be hanged for stealing a small amount of money, or for theft on a navigable river or even impersonating a Greenwich pensioner.

The pillory and stocks have not been abolished. But these instruments of punishment, in which offenders are exposed to public abuse and even missiles, are little used these days and only exist to remind would-be miscreants of the disgrace facing them for even a simple misdemeanour.

There is no longer a pillory in Maidstone. It once stood at the top of the High Street, near the Market Cross but in 1771 the corporation ordered it to be removed to a spot a few yards from the town hall. The last persons who are remembered to have stood in the pillory were two men who, in the first decade of this century, assisted French prisoners of war to escape while on parole.

The men were forced to undergo a very public form of chastisement. They were brought from the gaol at noon and stood in the pillory with head and hands held fast through holes in a cross bar. Their heads were shaved. The punishment lasted for an hour during which time the men were freely pelted with offal and rotten eggs.

The stocks are slightly less unpleasant in that the miscreant can sit out the sentence with only the ankles trapped. Stocks are still in place in many Kentish villages but, as Cobbett wrote four years ago, "they are never likely to be used because this mild, gentle, good humoured correction is not enough for our present rulers who want treadmills and hulks."

1830-1839

1830: William Cobbett publishes his *Rural Rides* in book form. It is the most fascinating report on the state of British life since Daniel Defoe.

September 15: The railway built to link Liverpool with Manchester opens but is marred by the death of William Huskisson, Liverpool MP. He is killed by the oncoming train as he crosses the track to greet the Duke of Wellington.

Agitation for electoral and parliamentary reform is growing in Kent as more and more radicals seek a greater say in the way money is spent. Prime Minister Wellington resigns saying "I shall always feel it my duty to resist such measures". Earl Grey is invited to form a new cabinet.

1831: September 8: Princess Victoria is absent from William IV's coronation because of a dispute between her mother, the Duchess of Kent and the King.

The first steam-powered omnibus goes into service between London city centre and Stratford.

A new London Bridge opens designed by Scottish engineer John Rennie. The stones from the old bridge will go towards building Ingress Abbey at Greenhithe.

April 22: Following the defeat of the Reform Bill, William IV dissolves parliament, backing the constitutional right of the Whig prime minister, Earl Grey to call an election.

1832: June: Cholera again strikes with frightening suddenness. It is estimated that more than 20,000 in Britain have already died this year. Doctors are divided over its cause.

June 7: Parliament finally passes the Reform Act by a majority of nine — 184 votes to 175.

An obelisk is erected at Telegraph Hill, Higham in memory of auctioneer Charles Larkin who gave much of his energy to secure the passing of the Reform Bill.

September 21: Sir Walter Scott, Scotland's premier poet and author dies at his estate, Abbotsford.

1833: The enabling act of parliament abolishing slavery is introduced by the colonial secretary, Lord Stanley.

The visionary artist, Samuel Palmer buys a house at Lisson Grove, London and falls in love with Hannah, daughter of the artist and "Shoreham Ancient" John Linnell.

1834: Six farm labourer from the Dorset village of Tolpuddle are sentenced to deportation to Australia for forming a Lodge of the Friendly Society of Agricultural Labourers. The sentence represents a fear among the gentry of the emerging power of trade unions.

July: William Lamb, 55, the Home Secretary and second Viscount Melbourne succeeds Earl Grey as prime minister. He leads a divided government.

October 16: The Palace of Westminster is gutted by fire. Both the houses, Commons and Lords are destroyed, including the chapel of St Stephen.

A new poor law is to be introduced to alleviate some of the problems faced by the poor — and the parishes which try to support them.

December: The Conservative, Sir Robert Peel is to be the fourth Prime Minister this year following the resignation of Viscount Melbourne.

1835: May 13: John Nash who died today leaves a fine legacy in Carlton House Terrace, Regent Street, Regent's Park, Marble Arch and the Royal Pavilion, Brighton.

Robert Peel resigns after trying for five months to govern without a majority. The Whig leader Lord Melbourne returns as Prime Minister.

William Cobbett, the author of Rural Rides and MP for Oldham dies.

A new Highways Act decides that all parish roads must be financed by the rates and trust roads by the tolls. Critics say there is still much confusion over what roads are trust and what are toll.

1836: The town hall at Gravesend is completed.

A Bath school teacher, Isaac Pitman invents a new form of writing which he hopes will make it possible for speech to be taken down at speed.

Charles Darwin, a 27-year-old naturalist returns from a trip around South America and the Pacific. It has taken five years and he says he has learned a great deal from detailed study of different animals, birds and plants.

1837: June 20: William IV dies at Windsor. His brother, the Duke of Cumberland, becomes King of Hanover and Princess Victoria, Queen of Great Britain and Ireland.

July 4: London's first main line railway terminus, Euston opens today with services to Birmingham and north-western England. Passengers flock to admire the sensational romanesque hall.

1838: April 14: Two British ships the *Great Britain* and the *Sirius* arrive in New York harbour. It heralds the beginning of a transatlantic passenger and freight service.

May 21: A People's Charter has been published demanding political reform and greater equality for the working classes.

1839: The Chartists present their petition with 1,280,000 signatures to parliament.

William Fox Talbot prints black and white photographs on paper.

Executioner says goodbye to Penenden Heath

December: Those malefactors who appear at Maidstone (Spring or Summer) Assizes rarely escape with a caution and small prison sentence. Here the criminal code is savage and ruthless in its operation. The presiding judge does not believe in allowing a felon to live so that he can continue to corrupt. "It is for your own sake as well as for society that you should be executed" is a typical comment.

That dictum was clearly demonstrated in the most ruthless way this month when three young men were hanged at Penenden Heath for setting fire to farm property. It will be the last execution on the Heath for new gallows are being erected in front of the county prison beside the porter's lodge.

The gallows at Penenden stand on the south side of the heath and hardly a year has passed without malefactors paying for their crimes with their lives.

At the Spring Assizes in 1786, 11 prisoners were hanged and in 1801 as many as 37 were condemned to death — two for murder, six for burglaries, 11 for highway robbery, six for felonies, eight for horse stealing, three for cow or sheep stealing and one for returning from transportation. Of the 37, 18 managed to win a reprieve and the remaining 19 were executed.

The notorious horse stealer, John Carpenter, alias _"Hellfire Jack"_, was executed in 1805, shortly after returning from transportation to Botany Bay, for the same offence. Jack confessed that he had stolen about 70 horses. ***See page 82***

William Hazlitt dies after 'happy life'

William Hazlitt, literary critic and essayist who was best known for _The Fight_, his famous account of a boxing match, _Table Talk_ (1821), The _The Spirit of the Age_ (1825) and _The Plain Speaker_ (1825).

WILLIAM Hazlitt, son of Maidstone, England's foremost critic has died at the age of 52. His last words were: "I've had a happy life".

Born in Earl Street, William was the youngest son of William Hazlitt, a minister of the Unitarian congregation. A few years ago he summed up his achievements as "having loitered my life away, reading books, looking at pictures, hearing, thinking, writing what pleased me best."

Hazlitt was the first regular drama critic of distinction and the subjects of his essays and lectures include the characters of Shakespeare's plays, the English poets and comic writers. He quarrelled with Wordsworth but was appreciated by Lamb and Keats who said: "If I am ever damned, I should like to be damned by him".

Maidstone will remember him as "morbidly self conscious, touchy and morose". None can deny he had taste, style and a withering irony.

'Here's a health to the brewer and God speed the plough'

December: A new law, introduced earlier this year, is changing the way in which the people of Kent enjoy their drink. Since the passing of the Beer Act — giving any householder the right to sell beer as long as he obtains the necessary licence — hundreds of beer houses have already opened in the county. The total of new licences in Britain in just six months is a staggering 24,000.

The Beer Act came in response to several decades of agitation for a change in the 200-year-old Licensing Acts. The licence costs two guineas, all duties on beer have been removed and opening hours have been set between 5am and 10 pm.

The high taxation on beer was first imposed to finance the Napoleonic Wars; in fact excise duties on beer and its ingredients, malt and hops,

continued on page 81

Captain Swing riots bring Kent close to rural collapse

The agricultural workers of Kent are hungry and their desire for a living wage has resulted in violent protests. Here, the landlord on horseback meets a desperate man, his dying wife and starving children. A hay rick burns in the background.

November: Kent is under siege. Every week for the past four or five months threshing machines belonging to wealthy farmers have been systematically destroyed by a mysterious, pseudonymous, vengeful character who calls himself "Captain Swing".

He doesn't exist. He is a name taken by the ill-fed, ill-clothed and quite desperate agricultural workers who, working together in gangs, have threatened to continue their trail of destruction and fear until they receive better wages and conditions.

The "Swing Riots ", as they are known, began in August when a threshing machine was destroyed at Lower Hardres, near Canterbury. Since then agricultural machinery in hundreds of farms has been battered into heaps of scrap metal or completely dismantled.

The uprising focuses on the poorest of labourers who have been receiving poor relief to supplement their wages. It is not enough, they say. Their homes have no heat, they are hungry and they are desperate.

The "Captain Swing" riot is not directed solely at the farmers. At each event of violence a letter is delivered urging farmers to do all in their power to force the government to reduce taxes and scrap the dreaded church tithes so they can afford to pay their workers more. The fictitious "Captain Swing" always signs the letters.

The riot at Lower Hardres was on August 28. The next day another threshing machine was destroyed at Newington and by the end of the third week more than 100 machines had been destroyed. A gang of men from Elham were charged and pleaded guilty. Edward Knatchbull, presiding at the East Kent sessions, gave them a three-day prison sentence and a caution.

The riots spread to the Isle of Thanet where 'General' Moore of Garlinge led men with blackened faces to destroy threshing machines at Monckton and St Nicholas. Six machines were smashed.

Since then more and more men have been brought to trial and magistrates who are landowners have found themselves under attack. Some blame the unrest on revolutionary Frenchmen who have crept into Kent to cause trouble where none had previously existed.

Agricultural machines are not the only target. Hay ricks and barns and a few houses have been burnt to the ground. The women joined in and one, Elizabeth Studham, set fire to the workhouse on the Isle of Thanet. It was completely destroyed. She has now been transported to Van Diemen's Land "for the rest of her life".

Methodist preachers say the burnings and attacks on particularly unsympathetic farmers are not part of any sinister plot. They are the spontaneous gestures of gangs of men whose families are deprived of the barest essentials of life.

"If Kent is close to a collapse of rural order", they say, "then the blame lies with the government and the exploitive landowners — not the workers." *See page 88*

Passenger railway line from Canterbury to Whitstable

Stephenson's steam locomotive, Invicta pushes the trucks with their VIP passengers the last two miles into Whitstable.

May 4: The Canterbury to Whitstable railway — the first locomotive passenger railway in the world — was opened yesterday amid the most lavish celebrations.

The opening ceremony took place at the Canterbury end of the line and huge crowds gathered in fields on both sides of the track to witness the excitement of passengers being hauled along by steam.

In the first carriage were the directors of the railway company. In the second were officials of Canterbury Corporation and in the third were their ladies. There was a band to provide music for the journey in the fourth truck and numbers five to ten were occupied by the proprietors of the Canterbury and Whitstable Railway Company which has suffered years of uncertainty about whether the line would ever be laid.

In all there were 20 carriages and 12 wagons carrying nearly 300 people. "It was", said the *Maidstone Journal*, "one of the most lively scenes we have witnessed for years".

As the train left Canterbury North Station, hauled by a rope and winding drum attached to a stationary engine at the top of Tyler Hill, a huge cheer reverberated around a city decked with flags. The bells of the Cathedral rang.

When the train reached Tyler Hill engine house the rope was unhooked and another rope was attached to haul the train to Clowes Wood where there was another stationary engine.

The line then went downhill and passenger carriages were detached from the wagons and allowed to freewheel. Behind ran the goods wagons with a roper attached to control their speed.

The 10hp locomotive *Invicta* — a replica of Stephenson's *Rocket* — was coupled to the train at Bogshole. It then pushed the carriages and wagons into Whitstable at a speed of 12 mph. The whole trip had taken just under 45 minutes.

Passengers who spoke about the historic journey said the most thrilling moment was travelling through the 828-yard long Tyler Hill tunnel in pitch darkness.

The day ended with a celebration dinner at the King's Head Hotel, Canterbury for 150 VIP guests. Among the speakers was Robert Stephenson, son of George, who actually supervised most of the work at Canterbury while the engine was being built by his father at Newcastle.

The Canterbury to Whitstable railway will open for official business today (May 4) with an hourly service of ten trains each way every day except Sunday. Adult passengers will pay 9d and children 6d. *See page 98*

Chiddingstone castle completed

April: Chiddingstone Castle has been completed, a pseudo-Gothic building faced in sandstone, towered and embattled, by the architect Henry Kendall. The village High Street has been diverted to make way for a lake of nearly three acres.

The sombre building is owned by Henry Streatfield, whose ancestors — Wealden ironmasters — have lived there since 1500. Beyond the Castle the Chiddingstone village centre is considered to be the prettiest in Kent.

'Everyone is drunk'

(continued from page 78)

made an enormous contribution to the British tax yield.

There was national concern about the prices. Along with bread, beer was the most important part of the daily diet. It was also seen as a patriotic drink and consumed by labourers, farmers and landowners alike. The most popular toast in rural Kent has always been: "Here's health to the brewer and God speed the plough".

Many well-established brewers with tied houses are enjoying this stiff competition. Among them are the two Faversham concerns of Henry Shepherd and Edward Rigden who say the new beerhouses have significantly increased the number of outlets for their products.

The last word comes from the Rev Sydney Smith: "Everyone is drunk", he writes. "Those who are not singing are sprawling. The sovereign people are in a beastly state". *See page 139*

On the accession of William IV as King of England, the name of the West Kent Regiment has been changed to the 50th Queen's Own in honour of Queen Adelaide.

Village is amused by the night-time antics of 'The Ancients'

THE inhabitants of Shoreham, the chalk village set in a river valley below the North Downs, must be quite amused by the antics of their most famous resident and his artistic friends. Samuel Palmer and The Ancients have been heard singing together in a deserted chalk pit as dusk falls. They have been seen and heard striding through the hills at night improvising a tragic drama and wandering off to the distant village of Underriver.

There is no doubt that the Shoreham countryside fires Palmer's dreamlike and almost hallucinatory imagination. It is richly depicted in his paintings of small rural scenes which show such an intensity of detail and a vibrant light.

However, there is a contrast to the peacefulness of Palmer's life and that is the agitation he feels over the outbreak of political fever caused by the destruction of barns and machinery by the eponymous Captain Swing. He is planning to write *An Address to the Electors of West Kent* in which he will put his arguments against reform.

His friends in Shoreham may be puzzled. He must have seen at first hand in the village and other places the misery of the agricultural classes and yet he is so strongly opposed to the proposed Reform Bill.

For almost 10 years now Palmer's pastoral idyll has been embodied in the countryside of Shoreham and district.

He is a visionary and a genius.

This painting by Palmer shows his Golden Valley — the village of Underriver — a good night-time stroll from his home in Shoreham.

1831

When the Evening Bell rang for a musical genius

THOMAS Attwood, a pupil of Mozart — but better known as the organist of St Paul's Cathedral — is rather excited by the talent of a young composer who has been lodging with him at Roselawn, Beulah Hill, Norwood. His young guest, just 21, is Felix Mendelssohn-Bartholdy and Attwood says he is a musical genius.

The story of how the young composer came to stay at Beulah Hill is fascinating. Soon after his tour of Scotland and Wales, Mendelssohn was thrown out of a cabriolet and severely wounded in the leg. He was taken to lodgings in London and a few days later receieved a generous hamper from Attwood containing flowers, a pheasant, a quantity of apples and pies and an invitation to be his guest at Roselawn when he was sufficiently recovered.

Mendelssohn stayed for a few nights and wrote in his diary: "This is Norwood, famous for its good air, for it lies on a hill as high as the cross of St Paul's...I have had a walk today of two miles and the air has really had a salutary effect on me...I can feel how much stronger and healthier I have become..."

During his stay a large party of his friends was invited to Roselawn and during the evening Mendelssohn played the piano accompanied on a harp by Attwood's daughter. While the music was in progress a ring was heard on the gate bell. It was the coachman announcing the arrival of his carriage which was to take him back to London. The summons was repeated again and again until at last he was able to drag himself away from his friends.

Back in his own lodgings that night Mendelssohn sat up all night composing a piece entitled *The Evening Bell,* the melody being frequently interrupted by a gate bell note. Later on he wrote another piece *E Minor Cappricio (op 16).*

Since November 1829 the young composer has enjoyed more musical evenings in Norwood.

Boy, 14 is hanged for murder

August: More than 4,000 people surrounded the gallows outside Maidstone gaol yesterday to witness the hanging of 14-year-old John Any Bird Bell for murder. It was the first public execution in front of the county prison and Bell was the youngest person ever to be sentenced to death. Encouraged by the enormous publicity this gruesome case had attracted the crowds stretched from the prison precincts all the way down to Week Street.

As the boy was led onto the wooden platform and asked if he had anything to say he was heard to mutter: "Pray for me. Pray for a poor boy". The trap door then opened and the spectators saw his neck break and the boy go into his death throes. In a moment or two it was all over.

John Bell and his younger brother James, 10, had earlier confessed to the murder of Richard Taylor at the top of Blue Bell Hill on March 4. Taylor was a young man who had left his Rochester home to walk to Aylesford to collect his incapacitated father's parish relief grant of nine shillings.

Some weeks later he was found dead in dense woods with his throat cut. The money — the sole income for his family — was gone.

The police interviewed hundreds of people about the crime and eventually narrowed the murder down to John and James Bell. They were committed for trial at Maidstone Assizes and found guilty. James was given a prison sentence and John sentenced to death by hanging. *See page 100*

The market town of Westerham, close to the Surrey border and the source of the River Darent. Standing back from the village green, behind the market house, is the church. Nearby is The Vicarage, the home of General James Wolfe, who died in the Battle for Quebec in 1859.

June 4: ***Thomas Telford, the Scottish engineer who has astonished the world with some of his aqueducts, bridges and canals can add another to his list of prodigious achievements — the pier at Herne Bay. The mile-long structure was formally opened today and to celebrate this great occasion the first steamboat*** **Venue** ***arrived to pick up VIP passengers. A harbour at Whitstable was also opened earlier this year.*** **See page 86**

Now cholera epidemic ravages Kent

September: Exhausted after their pre-occupation with parliamentary reform and the pacification of landowners after the "Swing" riots, many Kent boroughs are now fighting a new and even more deadly curse — cholera.

According to military medical officers it is "uncommonly rife" aboard the Medway warships, prison hulks and in soldiers' barracks. Scores of people are dying from a disease whose cause and cure are unknown and a strict quarantine has been imposed on all continental vessels in the Kent ports.

This week between 250-300 sail ships are under quarantine restrictions in the Medway station at Stangate Creek. Quarantine is also imposed at Dover, Faversham, Whitstable, Milton and Ramsgate.

With so many open sewers and filthy streets Chatham has one of the highest mortality rates in the country and it is here the disease was first reported in Kent. Cholera enters the body by way of the mouth and is contracted by consumption of food and water that has been contaminated by excreta of a cholera victim. It is also spread by flies that have fed on diseased excreta.

The first victims were those on the prison ship *Cumberland*. Within a few days cholera had claimed more than 80 convicts including the surgeon who was treating them. It then spread into the town killing an officer of the Royal Marines and sweeping through Rhode Street, The Brook, Full-A-Love Alley and Slickett's Hill. A senior naval medical officer this week said: "The continuing rampant fever is of a most malignant nature and scarcely second to the plague itself".

The deaths increased with the arrival of the warmer weather. The mayor of Queenborough was a victim. Two young children from Milton died along with the woman who had been employed to clean the filthy hovel where they lived. At Mile Town, Sheerness, 12 died within a few days — all persons of low circumstances. Minster has fared even worse with 47 deaths from 107 cases.

Last week the *Maidstone Journal* reported: "We are happy to learn that this frightful disease has somewhat abated in the last two days".

That is not the case in London where the disease has spread. It is believed that more than 5,000 have died and cholera is now spreading through the country at an alarming rate. *See page 124*

Following a chequered past, the 13th century building, Maison Dieu, Dover has become the home of the Commander of the Royal Engineers. Founded by Hubert de Burgh, Constable of Dover Castle, in 1203 it was originally the hospital of St Mary Domus Dieu and later provided accommodation for pilgrims visiting the shrine of Thomas à Becket in Canterbury. In 1534, an oath was signed accepting the supremacy of Henry VIII as head of the Church of England formally ending all religious connection with Maison Dieu. The building was later surrendered to the Crown and until this year used as a supplies base for the army and navy.

Famous Greenwich whaler has a 'piece of Antarctica'

FOR many years Samuel Enderby of Crooms Hill House, Greenwich has been known for his profitable whaling business in the icy waters south of Cape Horn. From this year, however, he will now have another place in history — for a black, mountainous region rising out of the ice caps of Antarctica has been officially named *Enderby Land.*

It was last year that one of his ships under the command of John Biscoe, sailing farther south than any Enderby ship before him, came across part of the enormous ice sheet of this vast continent. He immediately named it after his employer.

The Enderby story is a fascinating one. For years the family has been trading in whale oil and, on one famous occasion, a vessel voyaged to America to deliver oil gleaned by the whalers of Nantucket and returned with a cargo of East India Company tea. It was ceremoniously thrown overboard into Boston Harbour by local patriots — forerunner to the American War of Independence in 1773.

By the end of the 18th century Samuel and his brother Charles were deeply involved in the whaling industry. Their famous whalers would often take an outward cargo of convicts and return with sperm oil. It gave the family, not only an important stake in the development of Australia and New Zealand, but a chance to explore the Antarctic.

Samuel lives at Crooms Hill House and Charles in a lonely house besides the two landing stages at Greenwich. Nearby there are three cottages and a public house called the *Pilot*. The rest of the area is marshland.

18 MPs for Kent as Reform Bill is finally passed

June 8: Amid great rejoicing in Kent the Reform Bill has been finally passed. It will transform the shape of British politics bringing sweeping changes to a system that has roots in the Middle Ages. On average one in five adult males in the county will have the vote.

The number of parliamentary seats in Kent will remain unaltered at 18 but Queenborough (131 voters) and New Romney (eight voters) will each lose their MP while Hythe (126 voters) will be reduced from two to one.

Of these three vacant seats two have been given to Greenwich and one to Chatham which means parliamentary representation in Kent will be: Canterbury (2), Chatham (1), Dover (2), Greenwich (2), Hythe (1), Maidstone (2), Rochester (2), Sandwich (2), East Kent (2) and West Kent (2)).

The people of Chatham are delighted that they can now elect their own member of parliament and the contest will take place in December between T.E.Perry (Tory) and William Maberley (Whig). It appears the majority of people in the borough support the Whig coalition led by the Prime Minster Earl Grey.

There are many reformers in the county whose hard work and stirring speeches have had a marked influence on the passing of the Act. Among them is Charles Larkin of Higham who campaigned vigorously for the southern agricultural counties to have one third of England and Wales' 658 MPs.

The Guildhall, Faversham at the Market Place end of Court Street was built in 1574 but the top hamper of cream and brown was added about 18 years ago. Inside is a heavy Flemish overmantel from a merchant adventurer who died in 1533.

August 21: The tomb in Canterbury Cathedral of Henry IV, who was King of England between 1366 and 1413, was opened today and the remains of his face and red beard momentarily seen. There had been a growing belief for some time in the Yorkist story of the XVth century that the body of the king was thrown overboard on the sea journey from London to Faversham. This has finally been disproved.

October: To the delight of all sailors Trinity House has at last placed a lightship on the notoriously menacing Goodwin Sands, four miles off the coast of Deal. Since the middle ages the sands have had the capacity to claim ships, break them up and swallow them without trace. Estimates of ships lost in stormy weather vary between 1,400 and 5,000

December: Sir Walter Scott, Scotland's premier poet and novelist who died in September, has many admirers. Among them is the vicar of Horsmonden who has erected an extraordinary tower, 491 feet above the sea, in fields close to Gibbett Lane, Horsmonden. No road leads to the site. It is a lonely tribute to the poet. .

ARCHBISHOP IS STONED

IT will take a long time for the Archbishop of Canterbury, William Howley to forget his first visit to the city this year. Invited to dine with members of the corporation His Holiness found that a large, angry mob were gathered outside the Guildhall.

With abusive words and a hail of stones and mud coming from all directions the carriage stopped and Archbishop Howley hurried quickly into the building to meet his guests.

The reasons for Canterbury's displeasure are twofold. Many people are still furious that Howley deprived them of a party when he refused to be enthroned at Canterbury a few years ago. Secondly there is considerable agitation about the reform of parliament and the archbishop has made no secret of his feelings.

For him the reformers have been digging away at the foundations which hold up the established order of society.

Slavery abolished: Wilberforce and Hannah More die — contented with their life's work

WILLIAM Wilberforce, philanthropist, reformer and orator has died a happy man. Since his famous meeting with Prime Minister William Pitt in the grounds of Holwood House, Keston, Wilberforce has led the fight in Britain for the abolition of the slave trade. This year his dream came true.

It was on July 29 that Lord Stanley, the colonial secretary, introduced the enabling Act of Parliament abolishing slavery. Although it was outlawed in 1807, it continued in a clandestine way in order to meet British planters' needs in the West Indies and the former American colonies. Africans were shipped across the Atlantic in appalling conditions.

Soon after abolition became law Wilberforce died and no-one has mourned him more than the inhabitants of East Farleigh and Teston, near Maidstone where he has been a frequent visitor for so many years.

The Rev James Ramsay died in December 1787 aged 36

It was James Ramsay, vicar of Teston from 1781, who inspired Wilberforce to take up the abolitionist cause. Wilberforce became an Evangelical Christian and was tempted to take holy orders but was persuaded to remain in Parliament.

Not so his two sons. They have both enjoyed terms as vicars of East Farleigh and Wilberforce senior has made many visits to their charming 17th century vicarage.

Another Evangelical Christian and abolitionist who has died this year is Hannah More. As a feminist writer she pushed for reforms and wrote several bestsellers upholding the traditional virtues for women which she saw as being devout, modest, chaste and subservient.

She is known in Kent for starting, at Teston near Maidstone, one of the first Sunday Schools in the country. That was in 1789 and came about through her great friendship also with the inspirational James Ramsay.

Ramsay had been rector of two parishes on the Caribbean island of St Kitts and had seen, at first hand, the suffering of the Negro slaves brought over from Africa and the conditions under which they had to work on the sugar plantations. He decided to attempt to convert them to Christianity but this brought him into direct conflict with the majority of his parishioners who were the planters.

Feelings ran so high that Ramsay left the island. He came to Teston where he was reunited with an old friend, Admiral Middleton of Barham Court, Teston, MP for Rochester and later First Lord of the Admiralty. Still appalled by the conditions under which the negro slaves worked Ramsay wrote an essay entitled *The Treatment and Conversion of African Slaves in the British Sugar Colonies.* This was seen by Wilberforce and then Hannah Moore, who met at Teston vicarage and decided to devote their lives to the abolitionist movement. Barham Court was always available for meetings.

Hannah, known as "the bishop in petticoats" listened to the vicar's stories and wrote one of the first poems of the abolition crusade about a young slave who preferred to die rather than allow his skin to bear the marks of the whip.

William and Hannah are dead but the slaves are free.

Kent welcomes a new friendly seaside town — Herne Bay

KENT has a new seaside town — Herne Bay. It has now been officially detached by Act of Parliament from the ancient parish of Herne to the delight of inhabitants who have campaigned long and hard for this recognition. The new town is symmetrically laid out with broad promenades, bandstand, pavilion and kiosks to accompany the new mile-long pier — already the pride of Herne Bay. There is much to be done. Aware of the holiday potential, town planners want to make it a solid, friendly watering place with plenty of atmosphere and no Regency crescents.

Engineering genius dies in poverty at Bull Hotel

April 23: Few people know that Richard Trevithick, who died yesterday in poverty and was carried to his grave by employees of John Hall of Dartford, was one of Britain's greatest mechanical engineers.

In 1801, as engineer to the main Cornish tin mines, he built and successfully road-tested Britain's first full-size locomotive. A few years later he constructed at his own cost a circular railway track on a parcel of land at Euston in London. The engine, which he calls: 'Catch Me If You Can?' weighed 10 tons and attained speeds of 12 mph.

Known as "the Cornish giant" because of his superhuman strength, Trevithick spent his childhood absorbing all that he could about machinery and, as a young adult, very soon invented new types of pumping engines for the mines.

He was a pioneer of high pressure steam. His contemporary, the engineer James Watt, said at the time that Trevithick ought to have been hanged for his dangerous invention.

Trevithick came to work for J and E Hall at Dartford some years ago in order to experiment with steam turbines. His Dartford colleagues saw him as a genius — the greatest mechanical engineer of his time. In his workshop at Dartford he adapted steam power to ships, both by paddle and screw and to agricultural machinery.

He died yesterday (April 22) at the age of 62 at the Bull Inn where he was lodging and was buried by his fellow workmen in the churchyard of St Edmund, King and Martyr.

In order to thwart the body snatchers, who are currently active in north Kent long pieces of timber were placed at right angles to the coffin above and two pieces below. The coffin was then bolted and clamped between them. Any body snatcher wishing to remove the coffin containing the most prolific brain in England will have to excavate a huge hole.

No stone marks Richard Trevithick's grave.

West Kent Hospital opens in Maidstone

April: The dispensary which was established at Maidstone three years ago is now a hospital — thanks to overwhelming public support.

It was only last year that the funds were found to erect a new building at the east end of Marsham Street consisting of a physician's room, a surgeon's room, a dispensary, an operating room and four wards for the accommodation of 24 in-patients.

The West Kent General Hospital has only been possible because public support has been so liberally bestowed. Collections have been made in all churches and chapels in the town, subscribers have been most generous and legacies are promised. Already a large number of poor people are applying for medical aid.

There was no general hospital for Kent's poor until the opening of the Kent and Canterbury in 1793 which served the needs of both in and out patients. Financed initially by a legacy it has remained dependent on donations, legacies and annual subscriptions.

The patients at Canterbury are drawn from agricultural labourers and domestic servants and several parishes are prepared to subscribe for its use.

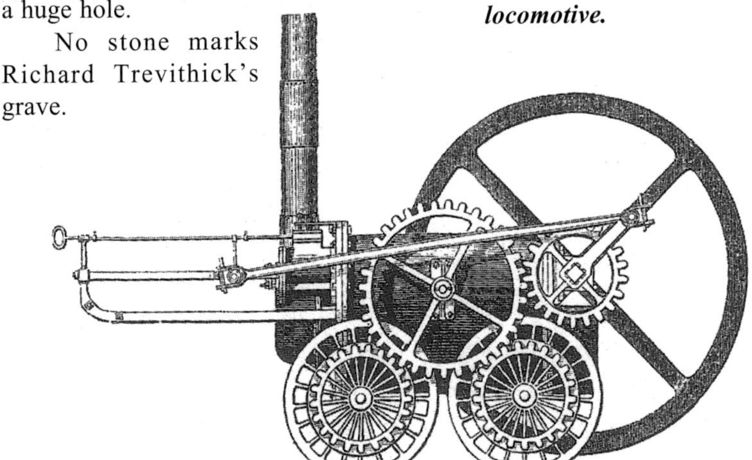

Trevithick's design for a steam locomotive.

The new town pier at Gravesend. Watermen have hampered construction throughout

Gravesend pier opens but the watermen are unhappy

ALTHOUGH the majority of inhabitants, including Lord Darnley of Cobham and all the civic dignitaries, welcome the opening of the new town pier at Gravesend, watermen are not at all pleased. Much of their living depends upon landing passengers from the steam vessels now plying the Thames between Gravesend and London. This will cease and they are very angry.

The watermen have hampered construction throughout. Damage was caused to the early work undertaken to prepare for the building and last year the West Kent Yeomanry were called to quell a riot. The watermen's arguments run parallel with those of Captain Swing. "Progress", they say, "is ruining our livelihood".

Although Gravesend's riverside traffic declined slightly when the London docks were opened a few years ago, trade is picking up again.. Approximately 290,000 passengers are carried annually by steam boats leaving Gravesend and are increasing. Borough officials believe they could soon hit the million mark. A pier, they say, is essential.

The Three Daws public house which stands next to the pier is one of the oldest inns in the town and believed to be a meeting place for smugglers and sailors wishing to escape the press gangs. Such customers have been notably quiet during the construction of the pier. *See page 113*

Riots over: convicts may soon be freed

THE violent reign of Captain Swing is over at last. With the Reform Bill in place and the introduction of the threshing machine abandoned, there should be better days (and wages) ahead for the unskilled labourer. For more than two years the threshing machine has become the unmistakeable symbol of this modern world and represents loss of work. Hundreds have been destroyed by rioters; fires have blazed away in farmyards and meadows in every corner of the county.

It is now estimated that 102 prisoners were tried by 12 different courts throughout Kent. Twenty five were acquitted, four executed for arson, 48 sentenced for varying terms of imprisonment and 52 transported.

Victims of the uprising — landowners and the administrators of poor law and tithes — do not agree with the moves for a general amnesty. But it is possible that Captain Swing convicts may soon be pardoned and released.

Those on their way to Botany Bay will be free to return home when they can find a ship. For arsonists who appeared before Maidstone Assizes it's too late.

Upper class are 'afraid of the peasants'

SIR Francis Bond Head, the man charged with the responsibility of implementing the new Poor Law in Kent, has begun his great task in the east of the county where the Swing riots began four years ago. But it isn't easy.

He said this week: "The peasants have succeeded in intimidating the upper classes and the balance of social life with their demands. The authority of the upper classes is sinking...most respectable people acknowledge they are afraid of the peasants".

The Poor Law was introduced earlier this year to alleviate some of the problems and distress faced by both the poor and the parishes who support them. In future outdoor relief will be restricted to the aged and the sick. Able bodied who seek poor relief must enter a workhouse, whose conditions will be spartan to discourage applicants. Families will be divided by age and gender. There will be little food.

Sir Francis, a former army major, is preparing his ground with military precision by inspecting all existing poorhouses and organising meetings with local magistrates. Opposition to the laws, however, is growing.

Great Chart refuses to join the proposed West Ashford Union. Smarden wish to remain independent. Bethersden refuse to elect a guardian. Bridge has voted to petition parliament. Dover, Margate and Ramsgate seek a degree of independence.

It is the same story in West Kent. Maidstone opposes the proposed amalgamation with Coxheath. Tonbridge prefers to form a union "of itself" and North Aylesford officers have been openly hostile.

This opposition is not confined to the proposed unions. The Radical and Liberal Whigs oppose it and the Kent Liberal MPs have fought it in Parliament. Even a Tory peer, the controversial Earl of Stanhope, is against the Laws. In a recent speech he said: "I dislike the grievous cruelties, the flagrant injustice and the intolerable oppression of the amended system".

Sir Francis Head aims to create 27 Kent unions run by newly-elected boards of guardians. He believes wholeheartedly in the new system and has told all the officers that "our wretched system of late Poor Laws has deprived the labourer and almost ruined the farmer".

He hopes to complete his task in about a year. During that time all Unions must agree maximum scales for outdoor relief and a uniform diet for the new workhouses. Iron bedsteads will be provided and aged paupers concentrated in one building per union. *See page 90*

Ramsgate mourns death of Coleridge

HIS many friends in Ramsgate are mourning the death of Samuel Taylor Coleridge, one of the leading poets of the Romantic movement, who has been taking his annual sea-bathing holiday in the Thanet resort for 14 years.

Coleridge, best known for *The Ancient Mariner* and *Kubla Khan,* took his first holiday in Ramsgate in 1819 at the height of the town's popularity. On that occasion he took a sea bath at Dumpton Gap and walked along the cliffs. Later he wrote a poem about the area called *Delinquent Traveller.*

A close friend of William Wordsworth, Coleridge travelled on the resort on the steam packets, usually *The Eagle* or the *Royal Sovereign.*

He stayed at Wellington Crescent or The Plains of Waterloo and wrote extensively on Ramsgate as a fashionable Georgian resort.

Lionel Lukin of Hythe — first man to built a lifeboat

February 16: The epitaph on the tombstone of Lionel Lukin, who died earlier this month aged 92, clearly shows his great contribution to the history of seafaring. It simply reads: "The first man to build a lifeboat".

Lukin died at his home in Hythe and is buried in St Leonard's churchyard. The epitaph is clear, simple and accurate but gives little impression of his great struggle for public recognition which began 46 years ago.

Lukin, a coachmaker and inventor, was distressed by the number of casualties at sea and intrigued by the concept of an unsinkable boat.

He experimented with several designs and eventually converted a Norwegian yawl with watertight containers at bow and stern and cork belt to increase buoyancy. He called the boat *Experiment*, loaned it to a Ramsgate pilot and later learned it had crossed the Channel several times before being seized in a foreign port.

Lukin constructed new crafts, arranged successful trials off the Kent coast and made several adjustments. In 1807 a 40ft boat, the *Frances Ann*, was built in Lowestoft under Lukin's supervision for the Suffolk Humane Society. With three masts, lug sails plus 12 short oars it performed perfectly in the most appalling conditions.

The *Frances Ann* was the first sailing lifeboat to be built and went on to save hundreds of lives during her service.

Other boatbuilders designing life preserving craft received grants and prizes for their efforts but nothing came Lukin's way — not even official recognition. It was, perhaps, because of this that he played little further part in lifeboat development.

Poor-law rioting erupts in the villages

July: As predicted by many Kent newspapers the introduction of the first county unions and the granting of relief have been accompanied by serious anti-Poor Law rioting.

The Faversham and Milton unions, created in March, were not only the first to be established in England — they were also the first to experience mob violence. When bread tickets were issued to the poor of Murston, Tong, Bapchild and Rodmersham on April 30 the relieving officer was mobbed and his books and papers destroyed.

The Bapchild uprising was organised by Sittingbourne traders who felt their livelihood threatened by union bread contracts. Ringleaders were immediately arrested.

The rioting has continued. There was a large demonstration at Doddington Poorhouse on May 4 in which a mob armed with bludgeons forced paupers to return their bread tickets. Similar disturbances have taken place at Upchurch, Hernehill, Lynsted and Teynham. At Rodmersham on May 7 a crowd of 150 took relief tickets from paupers and ordered them back to demand cash. The scene turned ugly but order was restored on the arrival of the 50th Foot from Chatham accompanied by the Yeoman Cavalry.

Many rioters have blackened their faces and appeared in parishes to which they do not belong.

Even before the violence erupted Kent newspapers roundly condemned the 1834 Act. The *Kent Herald* described it as "an attempt to drive the poor from misery to starvation". The *Kentish Gazette* predicted within 12 months "a scene bordering upon revolution of the most sanguinary description". The *Maidstone Journal* said the "fearful effects...will create a moral pestilence in our peasantry".

See page 106

Hop picking is the dominant industry in rural Kent and here on Millens Norton farm at Sittingbourne are the binmen whose job is akin to a sacred cult.

Wife swapping common in the hoppers' huts

September: Beer shops are booming in Kent, the consumption of ale is ever increasing and the demand for Kentish hops is now at an all-time high. Farmers, once struggling to make an adequate living, have converted to hop growing. Business is good.

It is estimated there are 40,000 acres of hops in the county this year and every acre requires up to 200 pickers. For this season's picking thousands of Londoners have flocked out of the city and into the Kentish countryside in search of work. It is a first come, first served business and hundreds have been unlucky.

The hoppers arrived, as usual, in waves divided by class — gipsies in their caravans, travellers who own house carts, 'foreigners' from London and home dwellers who work with hops all the year round.

The largest hop grower in Kent this year is Mr Ellis of Barming who has 500 acres and employs between three and four thousand hoppers. He gives them beer rather than water to drink beacuse of the risk of cholera. They live in hoppers' huts and survive mainly on potatoes.

Morality in the camps is low. Wife swapping is commonplace and many women have to lock themselves in at night to escape the attention of men. This year there have been several impromptu hopper weddings, supervised by the binmen who have allowed some men to take more than one wife.

See page 124

A lunatic asylum has opened at Barming not far from the new West Kent General Hospital, which opened two years ago at Maidstone.

Augustus Pugin

Ramsgate church architect will redesign House of Commons

AUGUSTUS Pugin, son of a French refugee but better known as the High Priest of Gothic Revival architecture, has been commissioned to design the interior of the Palace of Westminster following its disastrous fire last year.

Pugin lives at The Grange, Ramsgate and has designed many churches including the nearby St Augustine's church in sculpted stone.

The fire at Westminster in October last year was caused by workmen burning long disused wooden tallies.

The fire raced through the old building destroying much of the Commons and Lords and the chapel of St Stephen. Westminster Hall was saved by firemen.

Pugin will be responsible for designing the interior of the Palace — paintings, mosaics and stained glass as well as fittings and furniture. Charles Barry will design the exterior. *See page 133*

Fountain Hotel, Canterbury, oldest in England and the best in Europe

August 10: The Royal Fountain Hotel, St Margaret's Street, Canterbury, believed to be the oldest inn in Kent and possibly in England, today welcomed Princess Victoria as a guest.

The *Gazette* newspaper wrote: "Several elegant ladies congregated in front of the hotel and, on her appearance at the window, they loudly huzzaed her and waved their handkerchiefs in token of the pleasure they felt in beholding their future sovereign".

The Fountain Hotel dates back to 1029. In that year it is said that the wife of Harold Godwin was a guest while she waited for her husband to return from Denmark. Legend says that the four knights who murdered Thomas à Beckett met at the hotel. Hugh de Morville, William de Tracy, Reginald FitzUrse and Richard the Breton arrived in Canterbury on the fifth day of Christmas of 1170 and gathered at the Fountain before moving on to the Cathedral.

When Edward 1 married Queen Margaret of France on September 10, 1299 several European guests stayed at the Fountain Hotel and among them was the Ambassador to the Holy Roman Emperor who wrote to his master: "The inns of England are the best in Europe, those in Canterbury are the best in England and the Fountain, where I am lodged as handsomely as if I was in the King's Palace, is the best in Canterbury."

Criminals rampant: 'we have no civil force to put them down'

CRIME in many Kent towns, especially Maidstone and Chatham, has reached an unprecedented level. Small armies of pickpockets, burglars and prostitutes are living wholly or partly by crime. The vicar of Staplehurst said recently that "predatory bands...are causing manifest danger to life and property...We have no civil force (in Kent) to put them down.."

A monument has been erected at Bilsington to Sir William Richard Cosway, a key figure in promoting the Reform Bill of 1832. Sir William was killed in a fall from his coach during the election last year.

An obelisk has been erected at Telegraph Hill, Higham in memory of auctioneer Charles Larkin who gave much of his energy to secure the passing of the Reform Bill.

A Woolwich Steam Packet Company, established last year, is now providing a service three times a day between Woolwich and Hungerford Market by the steamers *Fairy Sylph* and *Naiad.*

The old Norman north west tower of Canterbury Cathedral, has been replaced with an replica of the XVth century south west tower.

John Reade has invented a kiln for the drying of hops which is an essential ingredient in the flavour of beer. He calls it a conical oast — a brick building, either round or square, with a tapering roof leading up to an inclined wooden cowl. This can be swivelled to improve the flow of air.

Kent Cricket Club secures a new home at Malling

August: The earliest recorded cricket match to be played in Kent took place on August 7, 1705 at Malling when 11 gentlemen of Kent played against as many of Chatham for 11 guineas a man.

How appropriate that, after 131 years and many hundreds of games, all played under the patronage of influential county personalities, an attempt should be made to form an official Kent County Cricket Club — and that the headquarters should be at Town Malling.

The key figures are Thomas Selby and Silas Norton who realise the days of the great patrons, such as Lord John Sackville, Sir Horace Mann, Lord Sondes and the Earl of Thanet, are passing.

They want Kent to play all its first class home matches against other counties at Malling and have secured the services of Fuller Pilch, undoubtably the greatest batsman in England today.

Pilch, aged 32, was born in Norfolk and has played at Lords for both the Players and England. In a match against Sussex in 1827 he was one of the first players to test the effect of round-arm bowling,

Another Kent player of great promise is a giant of a lad called Alfred Mynn. Born at Goudhurst in 1807 of a family of yeoman farmers he played early matches for Leeds village and made his debut for the Gentlemen against the Players in 1832. His first game for Kent was last season.

Mynn is a dangerous attacking batsman and also bowls with great pace and accuracy. In a match for Kent against Benenden earlier this year he took six wickets for one run. His victims included Fuller Pilch playing as a given man and three other county players.

The future of Kent County Cricket Club on their new ground at Malling looks well assured. *See page107*

Charles Dickens, aged 24. His Posthumous Papers of the Pickwick Club have been published in 20 parts.

Catherine Hogarth and Charles Dickens were married on the eve of the publication of the first issue of Pickwick Papers. They are living at Chalk.

Fame, tragedy and a wife: what a year for Dickens

September: Charles Dickens, the 24-year-old son of an improvident government clerk, has leapt to fame this year with the publication, in monthly numbers, of *The Posthumous Papers of the Pickwick Club.* Starting in April, the work has been published in 20 parts and is a fictional account of the comic adventures of a club founded by Samuel Pickwick whose fellow members include Tracy Tupman, Augustus Snodgrass and Nathaniel Winkle.

Dickens has many friends in the Medway Towns. As a young boy he lived with his parents in Chatham and Rochester and, at the age of 12, was boarded out while his father served a prison sentence for debt. For a while young Dickens was put to work labelling bottles in a London shoe-blacking factory but at 16 he learned shorthand and spent four years reporting law cases and debates in parliament.

continued on next page

Charles Dickens

continued from previous page

His first literary efforts came earlier this year in the form of a number of comic sketches, mainly about London life, which he contributed to newspapers under the pseudonym 'Boz'. They were successful but not so popular as his *Pickwick Papers*.

Dickens said this week that he is is indebted to Robert Seymour, a publisher who specialised in Cockney sporting plates. "The idea propounded to me", he said, "was that of a Nimrod Club, the members of which were to go out shooting, fishing and so forth and getting themselves into difficulties through their want of dexterity. Not being a great sportsman I said it would be infinitely better if I took my own way with a freer range of English scenes".

And so Pickwick was born with 'Boz', the nickname of his younger brother, appended to each edition of the magazine.

1836 has certainly been a memorable year for the young author. On the eve of the first issue of the Pickwick Papers he married Catherine Hogarth and spent his honeymoon at Craddock's Cottage, Chalk. After publication of issue No 11 his publisher, Mr Seymour, committed suicide out of, it has been said, pique because not he, but Dickens, became the dominant figure in his publishing enterprise.

See page 118

A Locomotive Act, which limits the speed of all trains to five miles an hour, is passed by Parliament.All steam engines must be preceded by a man carrying a red flag.

The portly, bespectacled Samuel Pickwick a moment before he falls through the ice. This etching by Phiz appeared in one of the early Pickwick issues by Charles Dickens.

Whitstable divers find the wreck of the Mary Rose

March 15: There was great excitement in Whitstable this week when it became known that the town's popular and enterprising deep sea divers, John and Charles Deane have found the wreck of Henry VIII's great flagship which sank less than two miles off Portsmouth harbour when sailing to engage the French fleet.

It was exactly 300 years ago, in 1536, that *The Mary Rose* was swamped. She was a bit too deep for salvage work but the Deane brothers have marked the spot on the map for future divers.

John said this week that he believes many of the ship's contents have survived, especially long bows and cannon and several musical instruments.

December 14: The first section of the Greenwich railway has been completed. It was opened today amid the firing of guns and the ringing of bells. A band, dressed as Beefeaters, travelled on the roof of the directors' carriage as the first train took its inaugural journey from London Bridge to Deptford. Meanwhile a South Eastern Railway Company has been formed to extend the new railway network across Kent. *See page 98*

December 27: A Christmas Day blizzard of great ferocity has claimed many lives in England including 20-year-old Sarah Port from Herne Bay who wandered off the track as she was returning home from Broomfield with her brother. She perished through cold and fatigue.

The new town hall at Gravesend has been completed.

The South Eastern Railway Company is formed.

A new church, Holy Trinity, Sheerness is consecrated.

1837

'Wake up Victoria — you are Queen of England'

June 20: Victoria, the daughter of the Duchess of Kent, was wakened at five o'clock this morning to be told by Dr William Howley, Archbishop of Canterbury, that she was queen of Great Britain and Ireland.

Dr Howley explained to the 18-year-old Princess that her uncle, William IV, the "sailor king" had died at Windsor. Seriously ill with asthma, which developed when his much-loved daughter Sophie died in May, his health has been in decline ever since.

The Princess, still in her dressing gown, heard how Howley and the Lord Chamberlain drove poste haste to Kensington Palace with the news. At first the staff had refused to let them in but were eventually persuaded to wake William's niece.

Victoria Alexandrina is under five feet in height and at 18 becomes the youngest monarch since Edward VI came to the throne in 1547. She will not require a regent; her uncle William had been a little distrustful of her mother and her confidante, Sir John Conroy. Her father, the Duke of Kent died some years ago.

Victoria is well known in parts of Kent. She and her mother have visited Ramsgate often. She has also been to Broadstairs (1829) and has fond memories of Tunbridge Wells, Greenwich and Blackheath.

Her many friends in Kent know her as a determined young lady who is clearly aware of her duty to the country. She is a good horsewoman and a fine dancer.

As Kent mourns the death of the King they will remember his 20-year liaison with Dorothea Jordan, the celebrated actress who so often stayed at Margate and appeared there at the Theatre Royal.

She bore King William's 10 illegitimate children and was heartbroken when he left her. William's wife Queen Adelaide gave birth to four children but all died in infancy. *See page 102*

Although William Aspdin claims he has been making Portland cement since 1811 he has only taken out a patent this year. His factory is at Northfleet.

October: Edward Hussey, a draughtsman and surveyor, has built a grand new house above the valley at Lamberhurst where the famous 14th century Scotney Castle stands.The new home, in Tudor style, has been designed by Anthony Salvin whose builders quarried all the stone from the nearby hills of the Lower Tunbridge Wells strata.

An Act of Parliament has been passed in order to make a new road from Pratts Bottom, near Bromley to Dunton Green, near Sevenoaks. The road will follow the steep gradient on the escarpment of Sepham Hill and will require considerable engineering skills.

When the Princess met the famous smuggler

THE accession of Queen Victoria to the throne of England has been celebrated throughout Kent and particularly in Ramsgate and Broadstairs where she is known as a girl who is fond of outdoor games and fresh air.

In 1823 Victoria and her mother stayed at Albion House and Townley House, Ramsgate. Four years later, in October 1927, they were invited to see Dr Manners Sutton, Archbishop of Canterbury, lay a foundation stone on St George's Church. The Princess, then eight, spent many happy hours on Ramsgate sands.

In 1829, aged 10, she stayed with her mother at Pierremont Hall, Broadstairs and was introduced to the famous Broadstairs smuggler, Joss Snelling. Victoria, anxious to know more about this infamous man, was told about his smuggling exploits and how he had once been arrested for landing 61 tubs of foreign spirits. At his trial more than 700 people turned up to see him

Victoria and her mother made more trips to Ramsgate, staying at West Cliff House owned by Thomas Warre and later *Bellevue Tavern* where the landlord was the kindly John Cramp.

Her uncle, William IV also visited Ramsgate on several occasions and it is said that he proposed four times to a Miss Long, who always refused him.

October: Joss Snelling, the 'famous smuggler', who met Princess Victoria, has died in Broadstairs aged 96. He was one of the oldest inhabitants of Kent.

'Dizzy' d'Israeli elected MP for Maidstone

October: A young man of great political ambition, who is also described as as an "eccentric and audacious adventurer" has been elected as one of the two MPs for Maidstone. He will represent the Conservative Party.

Benjamin Disraeli, aged 33 and the son of a middle class Jewish author, came to the town under considerable financial duress. He had lost money speculating on the Stock Exchange and run up considerable debts. However, it is believed that the sitting candidate, Mr Wyndham Lewis has loaned him the necessary £2,000.

It was Mr Lewis's wife, Mary Anne who persuaded 'Dizzy d'Israeli' as she knew him, to run as the second candidate. His first duty was to dictate his election address to the editor of the *Maidstone and Kentish Journal*, Mr E.P. Hall. As the editor was about to write down his name he said: "Leave out the apostrophe; it looks so foreign. Write it in one word - Disraeli."

Mary Anne, delighted by her friend's success at the polls, also had a message for the *Maidstone Journal*. "In a few years time", she said, "Benjamin Disraeli will be one of the greatest men of his day".

Mr Disraeli will not have an easy ride. Bribery and intimidation are an intrinsic part of the post-1832 Reform Act politics. *See page 100*

Benjamin Disraeli — MP for Maidstone.

Blackheath tragedy for 'parachute' pioneer

July 25: An extraordinary and most daring attempt to jump from a balloon above the fields of Blackheath ended in tragedy yesterday. Robert Cocking, wearing a folding, umbrella-shaped device made of fabric leapt out of the Great Nassau balloon, owned by Mr Charles Green hoping that wind resistance would slow him down sufficiently for a fairly comfortable landing.

The device was stored in compact folded form and had already been used on previous occasions. Cocking believed that the parachute — as everyone is calling it — would act as a kind of aerodynamic brake but, sadly, it collapsed in mid air and he plunged to his death.Cocking came down in Broom Field, Burnt Ash Road and will be buried at St Margaret's Church, Lee.

May: It has been a terrible spring — so late that troopers of the East and West Kent Yeomanry couldn't find any oak leaves to wear in their caps for the review at Mote Park.

Come to America is the oft-heard cry: 'Yes', says Fanny

FANNY Elizabeth Fitzwilliam, described by a recent critic as "the liveliest actress who ever trod the boards" is off soon to find her fortune in America. Her strenuous tour will include theatres in New York, Boston and New Orleans.

Fanny was born in Dover next door to the Theatre Royal where her father Robert was manager. She made her debut at three, sang professionally at 10 and at 12 became an accomplished pianist.

London eventually beckoned and she opened at the Haymarket in 1817 in the *Review* following by a string of starring roles. By 1832 — then manager of Sadler's Wells — she was Britain's best paid actress.

Come to America was the oft heard cry. Well, she's on her way!

DEFYING THE RULES

IN these tragic days of rampant sickness few ordinary people live beyond the age of 50 or 60 but defying the rules of life expectancy are Mr and Mrs Cross of Whitfield near Dover aged 79 and 80 respectively and still going strong. Not so their 12 children. Ten lived for less than 15 days and one for 15 months. A daughter lives on.

Turner inspired by the fate of the Temeraire

BRITAIN'S greatest landscape artist Joseph (J.M.W.) Turner has completed the painting which he affectionately refers to as "my darling". It is called *The Fighting Temeraire* and it shows the great gilded man-of-war being towed to her last berth, belching black smoke against the background of a brilliant sun.

The picture was inspired by the fate of the warship which was launched at Chatham in 1798 as a substantial 98-gun fighting ship built of 5,000 Kentish oaks and manned by more than 700 men. She fought alongside Nelson's flagship *The Victory* at the Battle of Trafalgar and distinguished herself.

Yet less than 40 years after that decisive victory she was no longer wanted. Sold to a London ship-breaker last year this "heart of oak" was towed to Rotherhithe.

J.M.H. Turner is 66 and is refusing all offers to buy the painting. Many critics say that Turner's later works are incomprehensible but here, out of a four foot canvas, he has created a "thing of beauty". Thackeray has likened it to "a magnificent national ode, or piece of music".

The Fighting Temeraire ***by Joseph William Mallord Turner. Picture courtesy of The National Gallery***

Darwin almost missed his voyage on the Beagle

CHARLES Darwin, secretary of the Geographical Society, is writing an account of the wildlife he encountered during his five-year voyage to the southern hemisphere on a naval brig, HMS *Beagle*. His book, *The Zoolology of the Journey of the Beagle*, will be published next year.

The naturalist has told friends at the Geographical Society that he had refused the first offer from Captain Fitzroy to travel on the *Beagle* because of the objections from his father who said: "If you can find any man of common sense who advises you to go I will give my consent".

Charles wrote his letter of refusal and the next day met his Uncle Jos, a man of good judgement, who was prepared to plead his cause. Robert Darwin then gave his consent and Charles set off as an unpaid volunteer on a voyage to circumnavigate the southern hemisphere. *See page 105*

'Messiah' and eight 'disciples' die: policeman and soldier also killed

The bloody battle of Bossenden Wood

June 1: Sir William Courtenay, the 'mad Messiah' and eight of his 'disciples' were killed yesterday in a furious battle with more than 100 soldiers at Bossenden Wood, near Dunkirk. A soldier and a policeman also died.

Courtenay, for some months, had been claiming divine status and prophesying that those responsible for the new workhouses would be destroyed by fire from heaven. He told his followers, mostly those in desperate plight and facing incarceration in the dreaded workhouse, that he was the returned Christ.

Yesterday morning he led his army of "disciples" on an aimless trek through the woods and then back to his headquarters at Bossenden Farm where he threatened revolt and civil disorder. Two policemen tried to arrest him but Courtenay shot one dead and then shouted to his followers: "I am the saviour of the world. You are my true lambs".

More than 100 soldiers from the Canterbury Garrison led by Lieutenant H.B. Bennett were sent to "talk" to the deluded madman but Courtenay shot Bennett dead and urged his men to fight. Armed with rough farm implements and oak cudgels they advanced on the soldiers who fired. Soon, the field behind Bossenden Farm was littered with the dead and dying. Courtenay was killed with a bullet through the lungs.

The truth behind this tragic character is now emerging. Courtenay's real name was John Tom, a solicitor's clerk, son of a pub landlord and, at one time, good at cricket and wrestling. In 1832 Tom left his home in Cornwall telling his wife he was going on a business trip. He then vanished.

Some months later with a new name and new personality he turned up at Herne Bay. His mother had died of insanity and now he was suffering. Madness had taken over.

At first he called himself Count Moses Rostopchein Rothschild but soon changed his name to Sir William Percy Honeywood Courtenay, Knight of Malta, Rightful Heir to the Earldom of Devon, King of the Gypsies, King of Jerusalem.

Courtenay got involved in politics and unsuccessfully fought two elections for the Tories. He was gracious and skilful at sloganeering. He supported the lower classes and he even produced a weekly paper called the *British Lion*.

In 1833 he took part in a trial of smugglers attempting to act as counsel for the defence. He was arrested for perjury — an act that precipitated near riotous scenes. He was released but transferred to the County Asylum at Barming. Released once more he began to make his prophesies, quoting at length from the *Book of Revelations*. His followers believed that no bullet could harm them.

Sir William Courtenay, the alias of John Tom.

The 45th Militia with musket shot and bayonet proved them wrong at the Bossenden battlefield. When it was all over hundreds flocked to the Red Lion at Hernhill to see the shattered body of their one-time hero. His shirt was ripped to pieces by "disciples" who wanted to remember their martyr. He was buried secretly in an unmarked grave.

A pier has been constructed at Deal.

New churches consecrated this year are Holy Trinity, Sissinghurst and Holy Trinity, Blackheath.

The lowest temperature of the 19th century — 14F — has been recorded at Beckenham.

The Palace of Otford, covered in ivy and little more than a ruin, was for many centuries one of the favourite manors of the Archbishops of Canterbury. Thomas à Becket lived here and Archbishop Winchelsea died here in 1313. The building began to deteriorate soon after Henry VIII's death and was stripped of its lead roofing. The ruined tower is all that remains.

Coronation feast

Carriages, equestrians and pedestrians poured in from every direction to the Barrack Field, Woolwich for a military feast in honour of the Queen's Coronation. Among the 100,000 persons present were Prince George, the Prince of Saxe-Coburg, the Duke de Nemours, Marshal Soult and the Prince de Ligne. Five lines of carriages were drawn up outside the line and 800 sat down for breakfast in the mess room. The toast to the Queen was announced to the multitude by a salute of cannon fired by officers, the men being engaged with their families at dinner on the barrack field.

London to Greenwich over 60 million Kentish bricks

THE first railway line linking London and Kent has been completed. It runs from London Bridge to Greenwich over a spectacular viaduct above the meadows of Bermondsey. It is being described as the toll gate to Europe.

The Lord Mayor of London, the Rt Hon Sir Thomas Kelly said: "The great object of the new railway is that of economising time; the great characteristic of modern commercial life is the value set upon time... time constitutes wealth..."

Kent has played a massive part in the construction. More than 60 million bricks were used in the construction of the viaduct and it provided work for hundreds of poor people in the Kentish brickfields.

There are 878 arches of 18-foot spans. Each arch is 28-foot wide and 22 foot high. The parapet walls are 23 inches thick.

The completed length was opened with little fuss for the main excitement took place last year when the first section to Deptford opened. On this occasion five trains took 1,500 passengers on the three mile journey with the Lord Mayor's train being drawn by the locomotive *Royal William*. On their return to London 400 guests were entertained to dinner at the Bridge House Tavern, Southwark where a spirit of optimism prevailed.

First steamships cross the Atlantic

April: Two British paddle ships, the *Great Western* and the *Sirius* have arrived in New York harbour in what is hoped to be the beginning of a transatlantic passenger service. Hundreds of American people were there to greet the ships. The *Great Western*, built in Bristol, is the brainchild of engineer Isambard Kingdom Brunel who is currently building the Great Western Railway. More wooden steam ships are under construction at Northfleet in the yard of William Pitcher. *See page 99*

Lady Stanhope, Queen of the Desert, dies alone and penniless

June: Lady Hester Stanhope died this month in a dilapidated house in a land many miles away from her spiritual home in Chevening. Eccentric to the last, disillusioned with the British government who had stopped her pension, she died alone in a former monastery, depressed and penniless.

It was a sad and tragic end for the bright lady who had been crowned Queen of the Desert, the first European woman to set foot in the mysterious city of Palmyra, linked with King Solomon. She was a legend long before she died.

Hester left Kent 29 years ago at the age of 34 with her entourage which included her lover Michael Bruce. The party travelled from Gibraltar to Constantinople and on to Egypt. They survived a shipwreck off the coast of Rhodes and lost all their possessions. Hester replenished her wardrobe and dressed as a Turkish man in breeches, boots and shirts. She never again wore western dress.

The party travelled to Damascus where Lady Hester ignored all the Muslim rules. She rode a horse into the city, unveiled and sensationally dressed but was allowed to pass unharmed. Here, at Djoun, high on the slopes of Mount Levant, she turned a decaying castle into a refuge for the sick and homeless. As time went on she became self-styled Queen of Arabia and ruled the nearby Druse villagers with a generosity that was to bankrupt her.

Hester enjoyed the attention of 30 Syrian attendants and continued a luxurious lifestyle, entertaining frequently and travelling often. Her biographer wrote: "Lady Hester's nose was a nose of wild ambition, of pride grown fantastical; a nose that scorned the Earth, it was a nose altogether in the air".

By now Michael Bruce had long since left. Her financial state deteriorated and last year the British government decided to stop her pension until one of her outstanding debts had been paid.

Hester saw this as an injustice. She invited friends in England to publicise her plight and even wrote to Queen Victoria. To no avail. In fury she renounced her British citizenship and threatened to shoot any English consul who approached her.

She died alone. She will be buried according to the rites of the Church of England.

Lady Hester Stanhope, the companion of William Pitt, who set off with an impressive entourage and a £1,200 pension from the King for a stately pilgrimage.

Brunel full of praise for screw propeller

THE outstanding entrepreneurial engineer, Isambard Kingdom Brunel, who is renowned throughout the land as a 'wizard' with ships and bridges, entered Ramsgate harbour this year in the experimental ship *Archimedes* which is driven, not by paddle, but screw propeller.

This revolutionery invention follows many years of hard work by 31-year-old Francis Pettit-Smith of Hythe. As a small boy Pettit-Smith sailed his toy ships in the Military Canal but he grew up to be a farmer and used to experiment for hours while watching his sheep on Romney Marsh. He believed that there must be a more efficient way of marine propulsion than the old paddle wheels.

Eventually he devised the screw propeller and earlier this year it was fitted to *SS Archimedes*. Brunel is delighted with Pettit-Smith's invention and wants it to drive his new ship, *Great Britain* now being built in Bristol. Brunel says it will not only be the first ocean-going ship constructed entirely of iron but the first to dispense with paddles.

Brunel, 33, is best known as chief engineer to the Great Western Railway between Paddington and Bristol. His design for the new Clifton suspension bridge was accepted in 1831 He says the screw propeller will revolutionise shipping.

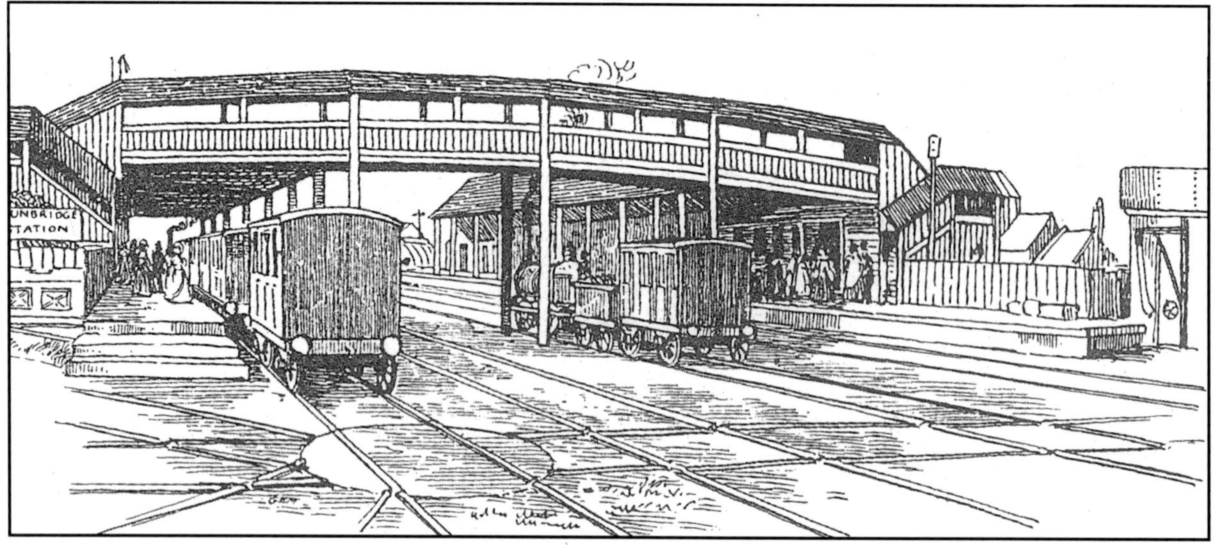

The Iron Horse will soon be coming to Tonbridge. A bill has been santioned by Parliament and a dead straight line is currently being constructed from Reigate Junction via Edenbridge. This line drawing, issued by South-Eastern Railway, shows how Tonbridge Station will look. *See page 108*

Jollity follows sound of the death throes

THE *Maidstone Journal* has made it clear how much they and sensitive townsfolk deplore public executions outside Maidstone Gaol. In July last year the usual crowd of ghouls gathered around the scaffold to see the hanging of George Willis, a soldier who had snapped under pressure and shot dead his sergeant major. The newspaper wrote:

"The melancholy scene appeared to have made very little impression upon the crowd, for, immediately after the execution, the public houses were crammed with inmates, and drinking and jollity appeared to be the only things thought of."

A few months ago Samuel Seager, a 30-year-old bachelor, was hanged for the murder of Hannah Giles. They both lived at Otterden, an isolated and enclosed hamlet a few miles from Charing. Otterden was typical of an unhappy rural community where passions and feelings ran high, morals were loose and violence commonplace.

Seager was full of repentance for his violent act and spent many hours praying in his cell. That did not appease the heartless mob of Maidstone and district who like to watch the death throes of the unfortunate. The execution was witnessed by thousands of people.

Seager's appearance was greeted with vicious comments, much laughter and later drinking and brawling. There were many men present but the majority were women and children

"What sort of mother", asked the *Maidstone Journal*, "would bring her family to such occasions?" *See page 174*

Disraeli marries for 'my money and love'

January: Benjamin Disraeli, the eloquent Member of Parliament for Maidstone, has married Mary Anne Lewis, the widow of his former colleague, who did more than most to persuade him to enter politics.

Mrs Lewis, 12 years older than Benjamin, was left a fortune by her late husband, Wyndham, which has enabled the newly-married couple to purchase the estate of Hughenden from the executors of the Young family and for Disraeli to assume the style and passions of an English country gentleman. Friends say it has been a calculated match but his wife recently said: "Dizzy married me for my money but if he had the chance again he would marry me for love".

His maiden speech in the House of Commons was not so successful. Soon after his return as member for Maidstone he rose from below the gangway — a dark complexioned young man with long black ringlets and dandified costume — and delivered an ambitious and eccentric speech. As he was howled down with shouts of derision, Disraeli called back: "I will sit down now but the time will come when you will hear me".

1840-1849

1840: Queen Victoria marries her cousin, Prince Albert of Saxe-Coburg-Gotha, at St James's Palace.

Elizabeth Fry, aged 60, sets up a nurses' training home in London.

May 6: A Penny Post is introduced. The idea comes from Rowland Hill of the Post Office who suggests that letters should be pre-paid with adhesive stamps affixed.

1841: June 30: Isambard Kingdom Brunel's 118-mile Great Western railway opens, just six years after plans were first discussed. It starts at Paddington, a new station in London.

September 21: The London to Brighton railway line opens.

Punch, a new satirical weekly magazine is launched in London.

1842: May 14: The first issue of *London Illustrated News* appears in the shops. The publisher is Mr Herbert Ingram.

A chartist petition, signed by more than three million people and six miles long, is dismissed by parliament by 287 votes to 49.

July 3: A would-be assassin is arrested after a failed attempt in Hyde Park to murder the queen.

1843: The huge monument to Lord Nelson is raised in Trafalgar Square. It is designed by Samuel Peto.

William Wordsworth, 73, succeeds Robert Southey as poet laureate.

HMS Worcester is built and launched at Deptford.

Charles Dickens publishes a book that is complete rather than in monthly parts. *A Christmas Carol* is a Christmas bestseller.

1844: Parliament sets up select committee to regularise new railways and approve the routes. The move comes in the wake of what is known as "railway mania".

The Government prohibits the use of female labour underground in a Mines Act, introduced by Lord Shaftesbury. There is to be no more exploitation of child labour.

In order to rescue young men from the evils of music halls and other vices, a Young Men's Christian Aid (YMCA) is founded.

1845: Hungerford Suspension Bridge over the Thames, designed by Isambard Kingdom Brunel, is opened.

An act of the enclosure of common land is approved by parliament to encourage large scale and more productive farming.

Eliza Acton, a middle-aged spinster from Tonbridge publishes *Modern Cookery*, which contains receipes for the standard fare. It is already a bestseller.

1846: Sir Robert Peel is recalled as Prime Minister by Queen Victoria, 15 days after resigning. He is poised to bring in a Bill to abolish the corn laws.

The Daily News is founded. The editor is Charles Dickens.

A new planet, Neptune, is sighted in the solar system.

1846: Sir Robert Peel, Prime Minister for five years, resigns following the repeal of the corn laws. John Russell, leader of the Whigs, is his successor.

September 12: Elizabeth Barrett, the poetess, elopes with Robert Browning in defiance of her father's ban on marriage.

1847: A Communist League is founded by Karl Marx, Friedrich Engels and Stefan Born.

Thousands of starving Irish people stream into towns in search of food following a terrible winter. More than 6, 000 sail to England.

Vanity Fair, by William Makepeace Thackeray, is proving more popular than Charles Dickens recent book, *Martin Chuzzlewit*. Another sensational novel called *Jane Eyre*, is launched. Its author is a 'mysterious' Currer Bell.

1848: April 3: Work on the Admiralty Pier begins at Dover.

March: A violent revolution is sweeping across the continent. It began without any warning when the French king, Louis Phillipe, was driven from his throne by a popular Paris uprising. France is a republic once more.

April 10: As events across the Channel inspire the Chartists to relaunch their campaign for political reform, a giant petition, said to contain 5,706,000 signatures, is delivered to the House of Commons. Queen Victoria, on the advice of her ministers leaves London.

July 7: The author of the best-selling novel, *Jane Eyre*, visits her publisher George Smith in London. Currer Bell, it turns out, is a 32-year old Yorkshire woman called Charlotte Bronte.

August 7: George Stephenson, father of the railway, dies at his home near Chesterfield. His greatest steam locomotive was *Rocket* which reached speeds of 30 mph in 1829.

December 28: Queen Victoria invites professional actors to join in the Christmas festivities at Windsor Castle, giving the much-abused theatrical profession a great boost.

1849: March: The Punjab and the Sikh nation falls to the British after a fiercely fought battle near Amritsar.

The cholera epidemic reaches a terrible peak, taking as many as 2,000 lives a week.

Welcome at Dover for Victoria's German prince

February 8: The inhabitants of Dover today became the first people in England to welcome to these shores the German prince who is to marry Queen Victoria.

After a stormy crossing of the Channel 21-year-old Prince Albert of Saxe-Coburg-Gotha, landed at the quayside and was driven to London via Canterbury in good time for the royal wedding at St James' Palace in two days' time.

Rumours about the Queen's love for her cousin, the handsome son of Ernest I, Duke of Saxe-Coburg-Gotha, have been circulating for some time and many of Kent's leading citizens do not approve of the liaison. Some recall the unpopularity of the five German Hanoverian kings — a dynasty which ended when Victoria succeeded her uncle William IV.

Now they wonder what influence the alien German prince will have on the royal household and the affairs of state.

It appears that parliament feels the same. They have refused to vote Albert more than £30,000 a year which the Queen feels is insufficient for his needs.

See page 161

February 10th: Queen Victoria and her new husband, Albert have arrived in Windsor for a short stay after their wedding at St James Palace. The service went well and it was followed by a magnificent wedding breakfast at Buckingham Palace.

Celebrations are currently taking place across Kent. At Woolwich the Commodore's residence at the dockyard has been illuminated by coloured lamps and a splendid display of fireworks is planned for this evening on the Barrack Field. Prince Albert has been invited to review the troops there in the spring.

Louis Napoleon's invasion force gathers at Brasted Place

April: For several months now Prince Louis Napoleon, nephew of the great Emperor, has been collecting together a small army which he intends should accompany him in his bid to overthrow the French government and restore the Napoleon dynasty to the throne of France.

One of the meeting places, where this great coup is being planned is Brasted Place, near Westerham, a fine 18th century house once owned by John Turton, George III's physician, and now let to Prince Louis.

There, under the care of a lady known as the Comptesse d'Espel — believed to be Louis's mistress — an extraordinary band of French and Polish refugees are gathering. Many of them have been engaged as servants in the great house.

Prince Louis, prince of the Imperial house of Bonaparte and son of a former King of Holland, arrived in England nine years ago in 1831 when he and his mother (Bonaparte's sister) disembarked at Dover from the steamship *Royal George* and rented a small furnished house in Hanover Square, London. They were political refugees and appreciated the tolerance shown towards them.

The prince stayed only for a year or so before leaving. He returned again to England two years ago and took a lease at Carlton House Terrace where his drawing room became a Napoleonic Museum. There were portraits of Empress Josephine and Queen Hortense and many personal souvenirs of his uncle all displayed in a glass topped cabinet. He became friendly with Mr Disraeli, the MP for Maidstone and devoted much of his time to political aspirations for he had always cherished hopes of returning to his native land.

With the march of events in recent weeks, Louis has been carefully applying the final touches to his preparations, confident of success. Brasted Place has provided cover for many of his trusted adherents. It is away from the glare of London publicity and the vigilance of French Embassy detectives. The south lawns are concealed by trees and well adapted for the secret training of recruits in preparation for commando operations.

Only the Prince knows the date of the planned invasion but he is concentrating his energy towards perfecting arrangements. Rifles have been purchased, uniforms acquired. A small hand press has been delivered to Brasted and there, proclamations, written by Louis have declared the Orleans dynasty overthrown. Insiders believe he will leave for France in the summer.

See page 112

Since the passing of the Municipal Corporations Act five years ago, town police forces have been formed in Canterbury, Deal, Dover, Gravesend, Maidstone and Ramsgate. Other towns will soon follow suit. Last year saw the introduction of the Rural Constabulary Act which has not been adopted in Kent. *See page 105.*

Mail robbers are warned: beware of the blunderbuss

MANY more post routes are now in operation and Kent is well served by mail coaches which were introduced some 50 years ago. There are daily departures on all major routes while others are served by the foot post. In addition letters are delivered to any house en route of the penny post which connect villages to the nearest post town.

A great advantage of mail coaches and one of the reasons for their introduction is the greater security they provide. The guard, usually a post office employee, is provided with a cutlass, a brace of pistols and a blunderbuss which are inspected by the Post Office armourer before each journey. Mail cart and foot post messengers are also armed — measures which have effectively foiled the highway robber who caused so much misery in the last century, particularly in the lonely marshes of southern Kent.

Highway robbery like this is not so common in Kent since post office and other employees have been armed.

Thieves are still attracted to the mail because of the number of letters containing coins or notes. The letter carrier employed between Southborough and Tonbridge was arrested in 1838 for embezzling a letter containing a guinea. In March 1839 a penny post messenger from Ashford to Brabourne Lees absconded with a letter containing five sovereigns.

Frequent delays to the post are caused by bad roads and by severe weather. Coaches on the Dover Road were suspended for several days in 1836 because of snow.

Two years ago the Hastings mail coach was overturned in Tonbridge High Street after striking a heap of manure which had been left on the roadway.

Foot posts still exist in many areas of the county but in some cases the lengths have been reduced. The messenger who served Sevenoaks, Kemsing and Wrotham for example travelled 26 miles a day until a shorter route was found.

One important route served by a foot post is from Sittingbourne to Sheerness. The messenger takes a path through the marshes close to the estuary which is a more direct route than is possible by horse. His average speed has been measured at 2° miles an hour.

The Ingoldsby Legends

A NEW book from the pen of the Rev Richard Barham is causing a stir in the literary circles of Kent.

Entitled the *Ingoldsby Legends* it brilliantly embellishes stories of the villages, churches and characters in Barham's own marsh-ridden corner of Kent.

One story is called *The Smuggler's Leap* and Barham writes of exciseman Gill "on his high-stepping mare and rascally Smuggler Bill" who both died when sea mist suddenly swirled about the Acol chalk pit. "Makes one's flesh creep where it yawns full 60 feet deep".

Barham was Rector of Snargate until a few years ago when he hurried to London to consult a specialist about his seriously-ill daughter. In the Strand he bumped into an old friend who urged him to apply for the vacant post of Minor Canon at St Paul's Cathedral. He did apply, in verse, and got the job.

Since then his life has been full of incident and tragedy; he has been chaplain of the Vintner's Company, founder member of the Garrick Club, contributor to *Blackwood's* magazine and has suffered the death of two children.

See page 115

A new town hall has opened in the thriving resort of Folkestone. Many more buildings are going up in time, it is hoped, for the arrival of the railway.

See page 108

Sandgate, the small resort next to Hythe, where villagers lived in fear of invasion and are still in danger from the encroaching tides. The castle, a bastion of Henry VIII's defence scheme, was adapted at the beginning of this century to meet the Napoleonic menace.

Trafalgar launched with Nelson's wine

May 20: Crowds flocked to Northfleet today to see the launch of the Royal Mail Packet Company's wooden steamer *Thames* from the shipyard of William Pitcher. Later this year she will become the first transatlantic liner to sail from the River Thames when she leaves Gravesend for Falmouth and the British West Indies.

It was only three years ago that the age of the engine-powered vessel began when the two British ships *Great Western* and *Sirius* sailed to the American harbour of New York. Today it is full steam ahead as more and more ocean-going liners sail off on maiden voyages to far away places.

Pitcher's yard has never been so busy. Three more launches will take place this year for the Royal Mail fleet. They are the *Medway* in July, *Trent* in October and *Isis* in November — all wooden steamers.

The dockyard was opened in 1788 by Thomas Pitcher on ground levelled as the result of chalk workings. The first launch was *The Royal Charlotte* (123 tons). In 1813 the Russian fleet was refitted and then, a few years later, the yard mysteriously closed.

It was reopened two years ago by William and Henry Pitcher and is set to become the largest shipyard on the River Thames.

June 21: In the presence of Queen Victoria and Prince Albert, *HMS Trafalgar* was launched today from Woolwich by the late Admiral Horatio Nelson's niece, Lady Bridport.

Using a bottle of wine which Nelson had on board *HMS Victory* at Trafalgar and accompanied by his sister, Mrs Matcham, and survivors of the memorable battle, Lady Bridport christened the 120-gun ship and watched the great leviathan glide slowly and majestically off the stocks.

One eye-witness to the ceremony described it as a perfect day. "The roads from London swarmed with carriages and pedestrians — coaches and four by dozens, coaches and pair by hundreds; barouches, gigs, phaetons innumerable; cornets and mitres, rich hammercloths emblazoned in silver, the more humble carriages and the patent cab passed before the eye in incessant line.

"Almost every shop in Woolwich was closed. From fifty to a hundred steamers and yachts carried joyous freights of people on the river and if ever there was a life upon waters it was on that day."

The naturalist Charles Darwin and his wife Emma are interested in buying Down House, Downe set in 18 acres of land, not far from Bromley. Darwin visited Downe (the 'e' has just been added) this week to look round the village and to meet the customers of the George and Dragon Inn. He writes: "The little pot house where we slept overnight while viewing the house is a grocers shop and the landlord is the carpenter— so you may guess the style of village. A carrier goes weekly to London..." *See page 107.*

Tower that telescoped for ever upwards

A TOWER, built in the Gothic style, which rises some 170 feet above the village of Hadlow is causing bewilderment and no little amusement among those who live in the Weald of Kent and have watched this spectacular folly climbing ever upwards.

The owner of the Hadlow Castle tower, Walter May, says he will go no higher. He was hoping for views of the sea from the top but apparently the South Downs are in the way. It is a spectacular ornament, although totally out of keeping with the surrounding countryside.

The castle, or castellated mansion, was built a few years ago by May. Rumour says that when his wife left him he wanted an ever-present reminder of what she had left behind so set to work on the tower with the help of George Ledwell-Taylor, a distinguished naval architect.

Henry Tufton, Earl of Thanet, is the new Lord Lieutenant of Kent.

New churches opened this year are Holy Trinity, Crockham Hill, Christchurch, Bexleyheath, St Margaret's, Lee, St Stephen's, Tovil and St Stephen's at Kilndown.

The Canterbury and Whitstable Railway Company has run into financial difficulties and is advertising both the railway and harbour to let at an annual rent of no less than £3,500 a year.

The population of England and Wales is now just under 16 million According to this year's national census the towns are growing rapidly and the number of agricultural workers are on the decrease. Chatham is still the largest town in Kent.

Queen Victoria has given birth to a son and heir, Prince Albert Edward, a brother to Princess Victoria.

With the formation of small borough police forces throughout the county, the old system of watchmen is no longer required. Here is one of the last, Charlie Roose whose job was the examine and secure property, raise the alarm of fire and apprehend all miscreants. **See page 148**

Holiday for the Queen in Walmer Castle

November 10: Her Majesty The Queen and His Royal Highness Prince Albert drove through Deal today on their way to Walmer Castle for their long awaited holiday. Every inhabitant in the small seaside town was given the day off work or school and thousands lined the route to give the royal party a joyous welcome.

The Queen arrived at Walmer Castle in excellent health and spirits where she was welcomed by the Duke of Wellington. Immediately the royal salute was fired by the guard of honour and the troops and this was repeated by eight guns on the upper, and six on the lower, rampart. The journey of 103 miles from Windsor had been achieved in nine hours with only two stops to change horses.

Walmer Church will welcome Queen Victoria and her entourage on Sunday.

It was in the autumn that the Queen first expressed her desire to "borrow" Walmer castle for a seaside holiday, as the outbreak of scarlet fever had rendered Brighton Pavilion inadvisable. "In any case", she told the Prime Minister, "I despise this garish Regency building and I regard the people of Brighton as indiscreet and troublesome".

She asked the Prime Minister, Mr Robert Peel, to contact Lord Wellington who replied by saying: "Walmer Castle is the most delightful seaside residence to be found anywhere, particularly for children. They can be out all day on the ramparts and the beautiful woods and gardens are enclosed and sheltered from severe gales".

The royal family left Windsor early this morning and travelled to Paddington by steam train. They journeyed through Kent in a procession, escorted by their children, Prince Albert Edward (the Prince of Wales) and Princess Victoria (the Princess Royal).

Also accompanying them were the Dowager Lady Lyttleton (Royal Governess), Lady Portman (Lady in Waiting), Viscount Sydney of Penshurst (Lord in Waiting), Lord Charles Wellesley (Equerry in Waiting on Prince Albert) and the Hon C.A.Murray (Master of the Household).

The royal party changed horses and escorts at The Green Man Hotel, Blackheath and The Fountain Inn, Canterbury. They travelled along the Dover Road via Shooter's Hill, Dartford, Rochester, Chatham, Sittingbourne and Canterbury and all along the route were greeted by loyal citizens anxious to express their devotion. Her Majesty had directed the royal nurses to sit on opposite sides of the carriage so that people lining the route should be able to see the royal infants, Vicky and Bertie.

At Sholden the party, preceded by a troop of the 7th Hussars and a guard of honour provided by the 51st Infantry, passed under a triumphal arch. *See page 135*

Cruelty in the workhouse: Kent's paupers are fighting back

December: Misbehaviour, drunken and disorderly conduct, wilful damage and refusal to work. These are some of the offences which make Kent's workhouses the most unruly in the country.

Inmates are supposed to work 10 hours a day if fit — and many do — but the rebellious few direct their anger and frustration at the workhouse officers. At Tonbridge a few years ago 80 out of 240 paupers ran away so the guardians raised the walls to prevent escape.

The paupers complain that their work is hard and monotonous and the masters are cruel. The only employment for the men of Medway workhouse is the picking of 8lbs of oakum a day for Chatham Dockyard. In Cranbrook the inmates break stones and at Sevenoaks the men operate a hand corn mill.

A few months ago 30 men were involved in a disturbance at Thanet. The master was attacked and a constable called. He, too, was assaulted. *See page 116*

Charles Darwin who revels in the isolation of Down House but does not want to turn into a Kentish hog!

Kent accused of 'selling' gala match at Canterbury

August 4: Without any known justification the cricket-mad supporters of Kent CC are accusing their players of "selling" the match against England which ended yesterday. It has impaired, but not ruined, what is hoped to be the first of many cricket festivals on the lovely Beverley ground at Canterbury

The facts tell the story. Kent, having gained a first innings lead of 22, completely changed the order of going in for the second knock. They were bundled out for 44 with four giants of the game, Mynn, Felix, Pilch and Wenman all failing to score. England went on to win by nine wickets.

With so much money at stake corruption on a grand scale is suspected. Betting and gaming among gentry and populace alike has reached alarming proportions since the days of Regency England when it was introduced. Today, cricket matches are often played for purses of 100 or 200 guineas. In addition spectators (and players) often have side bets on the number of runs scored or wickets taken.

However, tributes must be paid to England for their fine win. In Kent's first innings Fuller Pilch and Nicholas Felix added 154 runs for the fourth wicket. They were all out for 278 and England replied with 266.

The Beverley Club's new ground is just beyond the Cavalry Barracks on the Thanet Road. Marquees and tents were in a semi-circle on each side of the field and many ladies in beautiful coloured dresses were in attendance.

Today the Gentlemen of Kent will play the Gentlemen of England. *See page 120*

Charles Darwin buys Down in Downe for £2,200

September 14: Charles and Emma Darwin today completed their long-awaited move to Down House, a squarish Georgian building in the village of Downe, for the favourable purchase price of £2,200. They intend to alter the house and grounds to suit their needs and bring up their family there — the couple have two children and Emma is expecting a third.

The couple have lived in London since 1839 and, for most of that time, Darwin has been immersed in his scientific work, which assumed national importance when he returned from his five-year voyage to the southern hemisphere.

Three years ago he published an account of the wildlife he encountered on the journey, *The Zoology of the Voyage of the Beagle*. He described many of the living creatures he saw and the fossils and animals on deserted islands such as the Galapagos, off the coast of Ecuador. He believes his observations may have new implications for the way people think about links between the species.

Darwin wants to revel in the relative isolation of Down House although he intends "to spend a night or two in London occasionally "to keep up communications with scientific men and not turn into a complete Kentish hog".

This week he said: "The charm of the place to me is that almost every field is intersected by one or more footpaths — I never saw so many walks in any other country. It is extraordinarily rural and quiet with narrow lanes and high hedges and hardly any ruts. It is surprising to think that London is only 16 miles off".

See page 153

October 8: Mary Darwin, who was born just a few days after the move to Down House, has died. This week the couple heard that Emma's father, Josiah Wedgwood, is also very ill.

Sir William Cubitt — a man of dynamite

January 27: ***Sir William Cubitt, chief engineer of South Eastern Railway, solved the problem of the Round Down at Folkestone — which at 375 feet was even higher than the Shakespeare Cliff — by removing the entire mass with dynamite. At 9 am yesterday Cubbitt arrived with other engineers for an inspection of Shakespeare and Abbottscliffe tunnels before studying, for the very last time, the Round Down, rising defiantly in between.***

As William Cubitt took an early lunch he watched the crowds arrive while, out to sea, two steamships crowded with spectators dropped anchor. At 2.26 pm the detonation was made. The **Kent Herald** ***described what happened next:***

"A low faint, indistinct and indescribable moaning was heard, and immediately afterwards the bottom of the cliff began to belly out, and then almost simultaneously about 500 feet in breadth of the summit began gradually, but rapidly to sink, the earth on which a marquee was placed trembling sensibly under the shock. There was roaring explosion, no bursting out of fire, no violent crashing and splintering of rocks and, comparatively speaking, very little smoke..."

Trains through the heart of Kent as the age of the railway gathers steam

June: Passengers are now able to travel by train from London to the Kent coast. This month, amid great rejoicing, the South Eastern Railway Company's final section between Ashford and Folkestone was completed. It is an historic event for the county of Kent; the railway is certain to change the way we live.

There is still work to be done. The giant viaduct at Foord is not yet finished so trains will terminate at a temporary station. Meanwhile work continues on the line to Dover where three long tunnels are being bored.

To build a railway line from London to the Kent coast is a sensational achievement. Sanctioned by Parliament in 1837, following the abortion of many other highly imaginative schemes, the SER was obliged to share the first part of the route with the London and Brighton Railway Company. That line was opened on September 21.

The SER route begins at Reigate Junction and strikes eastward via Edenbridge and Tonbridge and through the rolling countryside of the Weald towards Ashford, which was opened late last year. For 45 miles the line runs straight and level and deviates only in its last stretch towards Hythe and Folkestone.

The stretch to Dover is unbelieveably difficult. Thousands of men are employed on the digging of the Martello Tunnel (532 yards), Abbotscliffe Tunnel (one mile 182 yards) and Shakespeare Tunnel (1387 yards) along a coastal route.

Between Abbotscliffe and Shakespeare tunnels Round Down cliff towers 400 feet and that has proved the greatest obstacle of all. William Cubitt, the contractor, wanted to remove a 70ft width of chalk over a 300 ft length so he sank three shafts and, off each, created a gallery 300 ft long. At the foot of each shaft he made a chamber and in them placed thousands of pounds of gunpowder. A thousand feet of wire connected each charge to a battery.

Cubitt needed approval from the Board of Trade who insisted that the Royal Engineers should supervise the firing. On January 26 this year the railway navvies stood clear as the charges were detonated. They heard a low faint rumbling and then saw the bottom of the cliff begin to belly out. Almost simultaneously a 500ft breadth of the summit began to sink.

When the dust had finally settled and chalk cleared the foundations for a track were made secure and the railway sections built along the beach. One is protected by a timber viaduct and the other by a concrete sea wall. Work continues on this section; it is hoped to open the complete line to Dover by the end of January next year.

With railway lines now being constructed all over the country Parliament is working hard to push each Bill through the Commons. In the last three or four years some 60 railway companies have promoted Bills that will create

The great Foord viaduct at Folkestone which was opened on November 14 this year

Spider's web from London

continued from page 108

thousands of miles of railway line. One anomaly is Parliament's desire to have just one terminal into London from the south. London Bridge is the only gateway to the Kent and Sussex coasts.

In a few weeks time permission is certain to be given for a single track branch line to serve Maidstone. A spokesman for South Eastern Railway said this week that capital is currently available at low rates of interest, investors believe their dividends will increase rapidly, there is political calm and the essential raw materials of copper and iron are falling in price.

Within a few years a spider's web of lines will stretch out from London.

See page 113

Peto prefers 'the railway jobs'

November 14: Samuel Morton Peto, who has achieved world-wide fame as the man who designed and supervised the building of Nelson's Column, completed last week, has added two more triumphs to his growing reputation.

Today, his great viaduct at Folkestone was officially opened and, as the navvies celebrated, the first train steamed slowly over the bridge of 19 arches.

A few weeks ago Peto and his cousin, Thomas Grissell, completed the final extension of Woolwich Dockyard which has taken labourers more than two years to build. As well as the immense graving dock, the great basins and the new slips, the dockyard embraces a steam-engine factory and a mast house. About 25 cottages have been pulled down to make way for a new road.

Peto, born in Woking, learned the building trade from his uncle to whom he was apprenticed. He and Thomas Grissell inherited the business and, showing a talent for draughtsmanship, began to win major contracts.

Between 1832 and the current day Peto has built Hungerford Market, the Reform and the Conservative Clubs, Nelson's Column, the Lyceum and St James' Theatres and a section of the Great Western Railway.

It is the latest work which pleases Peto the most. On the Folkestone contract he worked with Edward Ladds Betts and the two men have decided to form a new partnership, leaving Grissell to concentrate on buildings.

See page 223

Kent soldiers caught in Afghan bloodbath

December 30: As the county celebrates its great contribution to the 'railway age' it is easy to understand why many Kentish hearts and minds are far removed from steam trains, railway lines, screw propellers and other appendages of the industrial revolution.

They are more likely to be following the gruesome events in faraway Afghanistan where soldiers of the Buffs and the 50th Foot are embroiled in one of the deadliest conflicts since Waterloo. But news comes through agonisingly slowly.

Britain has been attempting to gain control of this vast, mountainous, inhospitable, landlocked, Islamic country before the Russians. But the British colonial authorities have found themselves drawn into a complex web of Sikh and Afghan rivalries.

In August 1839 the British Army captured Kabul. Two years later 15,000 British soldiers, under the command of Lord Auckland, were massacred as they began their retreat from the city.

This week the Buffs and the 50th Foot have been fighting side by side at Punniar under General Gough and General Grey respectively. The fighting reached its climax yesterday (December 29) when the Buffs were in action in the early afternoon. They were brought forward and from 5pm and for about three miles the 50th marched over the ground where the Buffs had been engaged, passing their dead and wounded.

Victory was gained but the enemy gunners fought with superb gallantry, firing their guns until the 50th were a mere ten yards away. Then, until the severity of their wounds actually prevented movement, they cut away with sabres and many of the 50th were severely wounded.

The war goes on. Britain is determined to keep Russia out of Afghanistan.

Penshurst Place, built in 1340 and little more than a romantic ruin by the end of the last century, is undergoing sympathetic reconstruction. The present owner, Lord de Lisle and Dudley, who was created a baron seven years ago, is restoring the Long Gallery, the Garden Tower and the Great Hall which is considered to be the best example of 14th century architecture in the country.

This wonderful house was the home of Sir Philip Sydney, the poet and soldier, who was born at Penshurst in 1559 and wrote about it in* Arcadia. *His tomb is in Westminster Abbey.

A view of the proposed station at Maidstone on the South Eastern (Mid Kent) railway. In this painting by George Hawkins, coaches are shown bringing passengers to the station. Work on the line from the Maidstone Road station has started but the voice of local controversy has not yet been stilled. **See page 113.**

Police believe artist killed his own father

August 29: The talented but tormented Kent artist, Richard Dadd, is being hunted by police following the discovery of the body of his father in Cobham Park. Robert Dadd had been stabbed to death.

It is known that father and son booked rooms in the Leather Bottle Inn at Cobham and had then gone for a stroll in the park where Richard Dadd enjoyed painting. It is also known that he booked in at the Crown Inn, Rochester on the night of the murder and then disappeared.

Richard Dadd is a brilliant artist. At the Royal Academy he was a student friend of Frith and three years ago became leader of a talented group called The Clique who all exhibited their work regularly.

Dadd, though, has been a tortured soul. Born in 1817 in Chatham, the son of an apothecary, he was one of seven children, of whom four have died insane.

Friends, however, believe that his recent exposure to the Egyptian sun, rather than genetic inheritance, was responsible for his recent gloomy, unpredictable and violent moods. They have told the police that, from June this year, Dadd has lived entirely on beer and eggs. He has drawn pictures of people with their throats cut. He is haunted by evil spirits, particularly the Egyptian god, Osiris.

The police are confident of capturing Dadd soon. They believe he may have taken a boat from Dover and may be linked to an attack on a coach passenger near Fontainebleau.

New Poet Laureate

THE people of Sevenoaks and Sundridge are delighted to learn that William Wordsworth has been appointed Poet Laureate in succession to Robert Southey. William, 73, is the brother of Christopher Wordsworth, a former Sevenoaks School boy, who was appointed rector of Sundridge in 1815 and went on to become Bishop of Lincoln.

Louis Napoleon's home is a fortress in The Somme

January: Prince Louis Napoleon, who embarked on his foolish and impractical 'invasion' of France in August 1840, is now languishing in an unhealthy swamp-bound fortress on the marshes of the Somme. With two years of his six-year prison sentence to serve he is busying himself with literary and scientific studies and has contributed several brilliant articles to newspapers.

He has also had time to re-live his extraordinary bid to overthrow the French Government and reclaim the throne.

It was on July 6, 1840 that Prince Louis chartered the steamer, *Edinburgh Castle* for a month for 'the purpose of a pleasure cruise'. At Deptford it was loaded with two carriages, nine horses, two trunks of uniform, many chests of rifles and pistols, hampers of food and wine and bundles of proclamations.

Louis himself boarded at Gravesend on the evening of August 4. There were more then 50 men on the boat but only a handful knew the reason for the expedition and they had difficulty in restraining the spirits of those who were gaily hailing every vessel that passed and gaining attention from the Clifton Hotel, where people could be seen staring out of field glasses.

The *Edinburgh Castle* reached Ramsgate in the early morning of August 5 where the remainder of the invading party joined and Prince Louis was able to reveal the purpose of the expedition. By then he also had an additional passenger in the form of a golden eagle which had been acquired from a ragamuffin of a boy at Gravesend.

Two days later Prince Louis and his followers were incarcerated in a Boulogne jail and Disraeli was writing in his diary: "Never was anything so rash and crude to all appearances as this 'invasion' by Louis Napoleon for he was joined by no-one. A fine house in Carlton Gardens, an Arabian horse and excellent cook was hardly worse than his present position".

Prince Louis had been arrested the moment he disembarked at Boulogne without a shot being fired. The British were suspected of collusion but Palmerston called on the French ambassador to assure him the 'invasion' had been neither encouraged nor connived at by any member of his government.

The Prince was tried in Paris and sentenced to perpetual imprisonment in France in September. It was on the very day of the trial, some 5,000 miles away, that one of the sons of Louis Philippe was casting anchor off St Helena in order to bring home to France the body of Napoleon I.

Prince Louis is now 36 and suffering from rheumatism which is hardly surprising in his present environment. His friends say he is thinner and his manner is "quite different from the gay, martial air he wore in London".

He has spoken frequently of making an attempt to escape.

See page 114

Constable killed in pub brawl with prize-fighters

September 8: Those who enforce the law in the town of Dover are searching for the cold-blooded villain who killed a constable during a brawl in a public house yesterday.

The incident followed an open-air prize fight which had to be cancelled because of heavy rain. Supporters and contestants alike retreated to the pub, consumed a great deal of alcohol and began to squabble violently. Two constables from Dover arrived on the scene, found themselves hopelessly outnumbered and sent for reinforcements.

Among the pub customers was Canterbury chimney sweep James Clark and his five sons who were all prizefighters. The belligerent sons, spoiling for a real contest, turned on the constables. One of them, Thomas Clark, grabbed a broomhandle and struck one of the constables so violently that he staggered across the pub floor, collapsed and died within seconds.

The furious struggle continued but eventually James Clark and four of his sons were arrested. Thomas, the man who struck the fatal blow escaped. It is hoped that he will be found in time to appear at the Maidstone Assizes in November.

St Augustine's Abbey buildings at Canterbury have been partially restored as an Anglican college for missionaries.

All Saints Church, Maidstone has been restored. Improvements include the removal of the galleries and the acquisition of new pews.

A wonderfully ornate pinnacled gate tower at Eastwell Park has been opened.

Sir Marc Brunel (pictured here in 1802), once a Normandy farmer, has run into a great controversy over the opening of the Rotherhithe Tunnel under the River Thames which he designed with his son Isambard. The Thames watermen, not at all impressed with this great engineering project, fear it will rob them of a living and hung out black flags as hundreds celebrated. It is the first tunnel under a navigable river and runs as little as six feet below the river bed. The tunnel was intended for road traffic but the Brunels have run out of money so it will be for foot passengers only.

Shrimp teas in a trippers' paradise

September: Gravesend today is a trippers' paradise — one of the most popular resorts in the country — where people come to sample shrimp teas, fresh air and enjoy a salubrious neighbourhood.

It was announced this week that the boats plying between Gravesend and London have carried two million passsengers in just a year.

It is not only the river which is an attraction. Most visitors to Gravesend take in the famous Rosherville Gardens and Windmill Hill.

At the summit a windmill provides the "best view in Kent" and houses a camera obscura. The nearby Belle Vue Tavern has a dancing platform and bowling alley

Others like to wander along Teapot Row built into the face of the short promenade adjacent to Rosherville Pier where almost every establishment offers shrimp teas.

There is another delicacy in the town, now famous throughout the country — Gravesend Grass. It is more correctly asparagus and reputedly the best in England.

Mayor warns: rail link will ruin Maidstone

February 7: There was great rejoicing in Dover today as the complete railway line linking the Channel port with London was officially opened. The South Eastern Railway Company proudly boasts they have opened the gateway to Europe.

Meanwhile a branch line from the Maidstone Road station, about half way between Tonbridge and Marden, is striking north through the orchards and hop growing districts of the Medway valley towards the county town.

For years now many people in Maidstone have been bitterly opposed to the railway coming anywhere near their town. When the Tonbridge to Ashford route was first proposed some eight years ago the mayor told a public meeting: "If a railway line is laid to the south then Maidstone will be ruined as a commercial town".

He was referring to the effect on Maidstone's wholesale trade fearing a decline in the number of wharfingers or corn and coal merchants because of the competition with London suppliers on price. In the end, of course, the South Eastern track was built through the Weald, passing some miles south of Maidstone

Opponents to the railway continued to be vociferous as the "spider's web" grew with Lord Marsham and the majority of the town council persisting with their view that trade would suffer.

However, as pressure grew for a line to Maidstone, some members of the corporation admitted they were wrong and supported the building of a single track from the Maidstone Road station giving the county town a slow indirect rail link with London and Ashford

In an effort to advertise the comfort and efficiency of this new line the SER have promised free rides to the inhabitants of Maidstone on September 24 — the day before the line opens. It will also be the first to be equipped with the electric telegraph system to give safer working. *See page 120*

New churches completed this year are St John the Evangelist, Chislehurst (now called Sidcup), St John the Baptist, Hildenborough and St Mary's, Platt.

From Greenhithe to the Northwest Passage?

May 18: Great was the excitement in Greenhithe today as the well-known Arctic explorer, Sir John Franklin said goodbye to his family on the quayside and sailed off on the long journey westward in a bid to find the Northwest Passage.

The British Rear Admiral, aged 59, has no doubts about its existence but is unsure whether it is available for navigation. He intends to find out and sails with the good wishes of the Admiralty who appointed him leader of this momentous naval expedition.

The search for the Northwest Passage has been a long and, so far, fruitless one. As early as 1534 Jacques Cartier, the French navigator, explored the St Lawrence River looking for a passage to China. In 1576 Sir Martin Frobisher discovered a body of water (Frobisher Bay) on what is now called Baffin Island and thought it was the passage. In the late 16th century John Davis made three voyages, exploring the western shores of Greenland, Davis Strait and Cumberland Sound. Henry Hudson reached Hudson Bay in 1610 and was abandoned there by his mutinous crew.

Iron resolution: Sir John Franklin

More expeditions were mounted in the 17th and 18th centuries and more territories and islands discovered. Sir John Franklin explored the Canadian Arctic coast between 1819 and 1821 and found the Barren Sounds. The story of the sufferings of his crew during this voyage is one of the most terrible on human record. Cold, hunger and fatigue broke down even the strongest in the party and many died. The survivors returned to New York having journeyed by water and land, 5,550 miles.

Little wonder there were so many people at Greenhithe for Arctic expeditions always excite special interest. Two ships, the *Erebus* and *Terror* have been fitted, for the first time in the annals of Arctic exploration, with auxiliary screws and provisioned for three years.

Franklin, a man of iron resolution and indomitable courage, instructed his captains to make their way to about 74 deg N, 98deg W. "We will sail in the vicinity of Cape Walker and thence to the southward and westward in a course as direct to the Bering Straits as ice and land might permit. If I find the Northwest Passage my work is complete". *See page 158*

Prince Louis escapes from his fortress in the Somme

May 26: Prince Louis Napoleon yesterday escaped from Ham Prison, the swamp-bound fortress on the marshes of the Somme where he had been gaoled for six years in 1840 following his abortive attempt to seize the throne of France.

The escape was almost as audacious as his 'invasion' plans but far more successful. When workmen arrived at Ham to carry out repairs to this dilapidated prison, Louis shaved off his moustache and beard, covered his head with a black wig, put on a builder's blouse and trousers and stepped into the courtyard with a plank on his shoulders. He then walked boldly past the sentries on duty into the countryside and on to the St Quentin Road where a carriage was waiting. He drove to Valenciennes, boarded a train for Brussels and from there made his way to London.

By the evening he was having dinner with Lord Malmesbury and friends and regaling them with the story of his great escape. The French Government is furious. *See page 122*

Anger as west Kent goes east

***October*: Despite vehement opposition from the clergy and in the face of considerable local hostility, the majority of parishes in the diocese of Rochester have been transferred to that of Canterbury.**

This follows an Act of Parliament amalgamating smaller sees. It means that Rochester will now embrace the counties of Essex and Hertfordshire, formerly in London.

Most people in Kent see this as an unsatisfactory arrangement. The bulk of the diocese and the residence of its bishop is separated from the Cathedral. ***See page 195***

The Foy Boat Inn was believed to be owned by Mrs Sophia Booth and is where Joseph Turner stayed during his visits to Margate. It stood at Coldharbour until 1835. Buildings to the left are Customs House and Harbour House.

Turner believes steam has potential for beauty

October: The landscape painter, Joseph Mallord William Turner, who is arousing prodigious passion among leading expressionists for his originality, has found great inspiration on the rugged clifftops of East Kent where he particularly likes to paint the shimmering effects of sunlight on water. His admirers are excited by his free use of colour.

Seascape Folkestone was completed this year. It is another in his series of seaside paintings . Turner has also painted in Margate, Deal and Dover, along the banks of the Medway and Thames and has enjoyed tours on the Continent.

Among the works of this prolific artist are a series of catastrophe paintings showing the fury of the elements which, he says, underline humanity's insignificance within nature's scheme; among these are *Burning of the Houses of Parliament* (1835) and *Snow Storm at Sea* (1842). *Rain Steam and Speed,* the rival painting to *The Fighting Temeraire* (1838) was painted last year.

Turner, now 70, likes to depict steamboats and railway trains and smoking chimneys. Unlike other painters of the present period he does not recoil in aesthetic horror at the sights and sounds of these modern-day creations. He believes they have a potential for beauty.

J.M.W.Turner was born in Covent Garden and sent to school in Margate. He returned to lodge with Mrs Sophia Booth and her husband on the seafront by the pier. Today he spends much time in thc town where he has many friends and admirers.

See page 131

Richard Barham dies aged 57

***June 17*: Richard Harris Barham who was born at No 61 Burgate in the heart of Canterbury and became an unrivalled humorist, poet, genealogist, antiquary and a clergyman greatly beloved, died today aged 57.**

He never really recovered from the death of his much-loved son earlier this year. Barham caught a chill, which laid the foundations of a fatal illness, at the Queen's opening of the Royal Exchange.

He wrote three series of the *Ingoldsby Legends* and they have taken, and held, a high place in humorous literature. His biographer says that, as a man, Barham was "exemplary, a pattern Englishman of the most distinctively national type.

"It has been said that he had an inexhaustible facility of grotesque rhyming but no English author, with the exception of Hood, has produced such a body of excellent rhymed mirth, and in that he excels his rival as a narrative poet."

Peel is back as PM

Robert Peel is back as Prime Minister determined to introduce a bill to abolish the iniquitous corn laws, despite the fact that the reform will split the Tory cabinet. Events came to a head this autumn with the disastrous failure of the Irish potato crop. Poor harvests in England meant there was no corn to send to Ireland raising the prospect of widespread famine. The import of cheap corn has caused great hardship to the poor in Kent. *See page 118*

This is the Middle Row (or Shambles), Sevenoaks, part of a market site and surrounded by many dilapidated medieval buildings. The old Sevenoaks workhouse was much further north, not far from the Otford and Maidstone crossroads.

Sevenoaks workhouse — the worst in England

October: With the opening of a handsome new edifice, three storeys high, which provides accommodation for 500 inmates, the Sevenoaks Union can no longer be accused of running the worst workhouse in the country. A long running controversy is over at last.

In March 1837 Sir Francis Head reported that management of the workhouse had been sadly neglected. He wrote: "The Itch prevails amongst all classes to a lamentable extent and many of the inmates are in a state of great uncleanliness...The presence of vermin is remarkable".

That such conditions prevailed were blamed entirely on the guardians who were loath to build a new, large, clean institution because they didn't believe one was necessary, they were indifferent to the needs of the poor and they opposed the new Poor Law system.

For years the Sevenoaks Union was overshadowed by Lord Stanhope, an inveterate anti-poor law campaigner and founder of the short-lived National Anti Poor Law Association. He was supported by Lord Amherst. Both men expressed regret that their tenants had become guardians and trusted no more would be elected.

In 1837 outdoor relief to the able bodied was prohibited and a workhouse test introduced. This led to pauper numbers outstripping the Sevenoaks workhouse capacity of 300 and there was terrible overcrowding.

The *Times* reported in November 1841 that between May and November the children had not been properly washed and 75 boys had been sleeping in 16 beds and 86 girls in 19 beds. Some time later it was reported that 57 men shared 31 beds and 40 women 20 beds.

Disease was rife. 75 boys and 91 girls suffered from goitre and glandular fever and five women, confined to bed were said to be "beastly beyond description"

At a bad tempered local inquiry the commissioners blamed the master, matron and medical officer and the anti poor law activists blamed the system. The *Kentish Gazette* wrote: No union house in England has been conducted with so little attention to the interests and comforts of the inmates".

To the chagrin of Messrs Stanhope and Amherst the outcome is the imposing new workhouse erected on a hill between Sundridge and Ide Hill at a cost of £12,000. Solidly built of Kentish brick it will stand for ever.

Other communities which badly need new workhouses are Chatham where, it is said, the straw is changed only monthly and blankets swarm with lice, and Chislehurst, where a pauper recently died. His diet was said to be "insufficient for the support and nourishment of an able bodied person".

The Workhouse at Brenchley (above) and (right) the Gothic-style chapel of Maidstone Union Workhouse.

Tragedy at the Royal Arsenal: five die

September 18: Seven men, employed at the Royal Arsenal, were killed yesterday in an explosion which shook all the buildings on the vast site at Woolwich.

The tragedy occurred in the laboratory department of the Arsenal where the men were breaking up unserviceable fuses.

First on the spot was Mr Carlisle, master turner who found the doors to the laboratory shut and it was only with great difficulty they were burst open.

He witnessed the horrible sight of seven dead bodies lying by the entrance. The doors opened inwards and all the men had perished in their attempt to escape.

50th Foot meets Sir Henry Hardinge

December 11: The stout hearted men of the 50th Foot Regiment, now fighting the Sikhs of the Punjab under the command of Lt-Col Ryan, were inspected today by Sir Henry Hardinge, the new Governor General of India who was born in Wrotham, went to school at Sevenoaks and has his country seat near Tunbridge Wells.

Having served at Vimeiro, Corunna and Vittoria and having succeeded Lowe as senior British liaison officer to Blücher, Hardinge knew the Regiment well. He told Ryan's men: "I hope you will serve your country like the old 50th did in the Peninsula". Replied the colonel: "We are anxious to be tried". *See page 136*

Overland mail to India on the Waghorn route

A CHATHAM-born former merchant seaman has startled London by finding an overland route to India, thereby reducing the time it takes mail to arrive in the sub-Continent to around 35-40 days instead of three months.

It took some years for Thomas Fletcher Waghorn, aged 45, to convince the government that mail could be shipped to Egypt, transferred to a regular transit across the desert and then by steamers down the Red Sea into the Indian Ocean.

To make such a journey possibleWaghorn had to make friends with the Egyptian Arabs, live in their tents and teach them that pay was better than plunder. He then established a regular service of caravans, built eight halting places between Cairo and Suez and made, what had been a dangerous path beset with robbers, into a secure highway.

In acknowledgement of the national importance of his work Thomas Waghorn was promoted to the rank of lieutenant in the navy but he never served. His connection with the navy had ended in 1817.

Waghorn's wife Elizabeth, whom he married in Calcutta in 1822, died in 1834 and he married Harriet Martin, daughter of a miller at Snodland. They lived in Rochester until a new home was built in the upper High Street, Snodland.

Despite his heroic status Thomas Waghorn has not had things all his way. Having set up a company in Cornhill for conveying people and mails to India via Egypt he found the Pacific and Orient company in competition with him. A further blow came when his stock of 300 horses were destroyed by a plague.

Earlier this year Waghorn turned his attention to speeding the mails through Europe to Egypt via the burgeoning railway system. His trials were successful — and faster by two days — but they have left him with great debts. The government had promised to reimburse his costs but instead they are supporting P and O.

Charles Dickens has 'the life and soul of 50 human beings'

October: Ten years ago Charles Dickens was well known in Kent for his talent at writing short stories. Today, many regard this popular novelist as a literary genius who works with extraordinary intensity.

In addition to his books and newspaper articles he has discovered that public speaking can be both enjoyable and lucrative. He has also written a story — The Cricket — that was dramatised at 12 London Theatres and, as if that has not been enough to fill his hours, he has started this year his own newspaper, *The Daily News.*

Charles Dickens found fame and fortune with *Pickwick Papers* in 1836. Since then he has written *Oliver Twist, Nicholas Nickleby, The Old Curiosity Shop, Barnaby Rudge, A Christmas Carol* and *Martin Chuzzlewit.* All but *A Christmas Carol* were published as serials in monthly or weekly parts and Dickens has confessed that in many cases he had no idea how the story would end.

Since 1837 he has made regular visits to Broadstairs for a summer vacation. At first the Dickens family took a little cottage at 12 High Street for a rent of £21 a month. He later moved to Albion Street where he put the finishing touches to *Nicholas Nickleby.* Today he likes to stay at a little castellated house called Fort House high above the harbour, where he loves the sunset and the "good, old, tarry, salt, little pier".

Not all his books have been successful. *Martin Chuzzlewit,* for example, proved a commercial flop but that hardly mattered because Dickens was becoming a social success and very much in demand to speak in public. A few weeks ago Leigh Hunt spoke of his impact on people: "What a face", he said, "to meet in a drawing room. It has the life and soul in it of 50 human beings".

Four years ago, in 1842, Dickens went to America to try his luck there as a public speaker. He came back exhausted and immediately went to Broadstairs to recuperate.

He is now 36 and in the prime of life. He will write more novels and enjoy more holidays at Broadstairs like the one in 1842 when he saw his young son Charley "digging up the sand on the shore with a very small spade and compressing it into a perfectly impossible wheelbarrow!".

Corn Laws repealed

July: The Corn Laws have been repealed and that is a triumph for the free-traders of the Anti-Corn Law League, whose campaign began more than eight years ago.

The League was started by a group of merchants who distrusted Tory landowners and wanted power moved from the landed classes to the "intelligent middle and industrious classes".

For the Prime Minister, Sir Robert Peel, who has led the Conservative Party since 1832 and wanted reform, the last five months have been a disaster.

Four months after the corn laws were repealed he resigned, his party in total disarray.

E.H.Baily, the man who sculpted Lord Nelson and placed him on top of his column in Trafalgar Square has now completed the busts of the sixth Lord Cornwallis and his wife. They can be seen in Linton church.

Butcher who stole sheep is bound for Australia

April: Edward Boswell, a former Sevenoaks town butcher, is on his way to Australia having been convicted of the most audacious theft.

A few weeks ago Boswell stole a whole flock of sheep from a field at Bradbourne Farm about a mile north of the town centre. The farmer discovered his loss the next morning and immediately guessed that his flock of 49 were being driven to London on the new turnpike road which runs close by.

In fact, that was exactly the plan Boswell had in mind but having travelled through Riverhead, Chipstead and Knockholt he opted for a more circuitous route to London hoping he would throw pursuers off his trail.

The sheep-stealer, however, had not bargained for the annual February fall of snow. The farmer and his posse were able to follow the tracks of the sheep until they reached Leaves Green where the frost had left the ground so hard there was no trace of prints. By now he had abandoned the idea of London and headed for Croydon. By the time he reached Beddington he (and the sheep) were extremely tired so he attempted to sell half for slaughter to a local butcher.

The butcher's suspicions were aroused and while engaging his customer in conversation he managed to send a message to a local constable. Boswell was questioned, arrested and later tried. He has told friends that he never wants to set eyes on another sheep.

He will find that difficult in New South Wales!

The smouldering ruins — this is all that is left of the riverside area of Gravesend

Great fire brings distress to Gravesend

November: The riverside locality of Gravesend is today a gaunt skeleton. Most of the houses in West Street from the Town Pier towards Rosherville Gardens have collapsed into a heap of charred, smouldering timbers. Nothing remains standing except clumps of chimneys, tottering in the wind; the Pier Hotel, the Talbot Inn, the Punch Bowl Tavern and all the intermediate wharves, houses and taverns are destroyed. It is a calamitous situation. There are scenes of great distress.

One eye witness said he first saw smoke hovering yesterday morning above the premises of Mr Garrett, the grocer, adjacent to the Pier Hotel."The inmates were taken out and corporation engines were soon on the spot but the defective state of the water mains allowed the flames to spread. The military at Tilbury Fort were mustered with promptitude."

The scene by the afternoon was dreadful. From the south side of West Street the fire raged upwards towards the centre of the town destroying a great number of low dwelling houses, tenanted by poor fishermen, hawkers and labourers. With the help of constables and soldiers they were dragged out of windows as the immense body of fire continued to consume the area.

This is Gravesend's second great fire. Two years ago, in June 1844, several warehouses and homes in the narrow thoroughfares which run off West Street were destroyed.

It is believed the first fire started in Mrs Susan Sandford's fish shop and extended westward towards Union Wharf which was used as a store for pitch, tar and timber. As the building burned furiously firemen and soldiers realised that barrels of gunpowder were stored nearby. Two were rolled into the Thames before that warehouse caught fire and then exploded with such great force that it blew off the roofs and walls of buildings to a considerable distance. In all four ale houses and 19 homes and shops were destroyed.

A fund will be re-opened for the victims of yesterday's fire which the magistrates believe has caused damage in excess of £100,000.

Ideal site found in Ashford for loco works

AN ideal site has been found in Kent to build steam locomotives.

The directors of South Eastern Railway have bought 185 acres of farmland in Ashford. Here, in time they hope to create a factory building the finest standard design locomotives.

With so many extensions to the great railway system now in place and more and more lines under construction it is intended that Ashford should grow into a railway town.

There is considerable opposition to the plans. The Archbishop is worried about the inadequacy of church provision for the large number of men likely to be employed.

SER reacted with the speed for which they are renowned. The Rev John Pughe has already been invited to minister to the spiritual needs of the workforce at Ashford and the company has awarded him a grant of £100. *See page 137*

New ground in Canterbury for the famous cricket week

AS the "good old Kent cricket eleven" goes from strength to strength with more successes against a full England team, strenuous efforts are being made in Canterbury to move the popular cricket week from the Beverley ground to a new field on Winter's Farm, Nackington, known locally as St Lawrence.

Since its introduction in 1842 the Week has been a great success. That is due to the success which the county team now enjoys, tremendous organisation by the officials and also a gap in the social life of the district following a falling off of interest in the race meeting at Barham Downs which used to attract thousands from across the county.

Instead these people now flock to the Canterbury Week where the programme will include, as usual, an evening performance by the Old Stagers — a body of former Cambridge friends who acted together at University.

The Old Stagers are good cricketers but also amateur actors and will be on stage at the Old Theatre in Orange Street. Last year their play was entitled "Othello Travestie", described on the billboard as "the most excruciating comic operatic-tragedy that was ever tragedized by any comical and pastoral company of Tragical Tragedians". It was a great success.

Although the Town Malling ground is no longer used by Kent, matches are played on The Common at Tunbridge Wells, Preston Park, Aylesford and the Bat and Ball, Gravesend.

The new ground at Canterbury is small with few seats and the wicket should suit the fierce slinging pace of Alfred Mynn. There is also a bank on one side of the ground where many catches are likely to be taken in the crowd. *See page 152*

South Eastern buys canal for railway route

THE Thames and Medway Canal — built partly under the North Downs to provide a navigable link via the River Medway and the Royal Military Canal to the coast and then abandoned — will soon be part of a railway route!

South Eastern Railway has bought the canal, drained it and are now in the process of laying rails on its bed. The idea is to provide a train service from Denton (Gravesend) to Strood. The work involves the digging of a 2° mile-long railway tunnel between Higham and Frindsbury which has been designed by the great railway engineer, William Tierney Clark.

The company building railway lines across much of Kent has frequently boasted that their trains provide the safest and most efficient form of travel. No longer is that the case. In recent years there have been several accidents involving injury and loss of life.

In July 1845, an evening train from Dover arrived at Tonbridge and a carriage was detached. Sadly the railwaymen forget to transfer the tail-lights so an engine was sent with the missing lamps to catch up. The inevitable happened. It was dark when the train had stopped at Penshurst and the chasing loco ran clean into the back injuring 30 people.

Last year the people of Chiddingstone Causeway, and particularly those who work for the cricket ball makers, Duke and Son, were spectators at another train accident. As a locomotive was negotiating the wooden bridge, which crosses the tiny River Eden, the supports gave way and the engine and much of the train plunged into the water. The driver was killed. *See page 123*

New churches completed this year are St John the Evangelist, Woolwich, Holy Trinity Church, Brompton and the new St Peter's, Upper Pembury.

Aftermath: John Hall and Son will now close its guncotton works at Oare following the disastrous explosion.

Gun-cotton explosion at Faversham kills 20

TWENTY people were killed and many injured in a disastrous explosion at the gun-cotton factory at Marsh Works, Oare, near Faversham. Two buildings at the western end of the works blew up in quick succession and the explosion was heard within two miles of Maidstone.

The Times today wrote: "The roofs of all the buildings within a quarter of a mile of the explosion are completely stripped of their tiles. Even in the town of Faversham, fully a mile distant from the scene of the disaster, windows are broken and houscs damaged."

The gunpowder works are owned by John Hall and Son of Dartford who bought the Home Works at an auction at the Ship Hotel, Faversham in 1825 for £17,935. Some years later they bought the Oare and Marsh Works.

It was in 1846 that Hall introduced gun cotton. His scientists, constantly seeking an explosive more powerful than gunpowder, mixed purified cotton with equal parts of nitric acid and sulphuric acid which was then dried. It had the appearance of cotton wool. John Hall and Son were quick to obtain a patent and built their guncotton factory — the first in the world — at the Marsh Works. Six months ago they claimed that guncotton was six times as powerful as gunpowder.

That claim has now been proved in the most tragic way. Hall and Son have agreed to close their guncotton factory and bury the remaining stocks.

Swell Mob preys on inebriated farmers

October: A highly organised and skilful gang of thieves, called the Swell Mob, are causing great consternation among the more affluent people of Kent.

The Swell Mob is not the name of a gang but a term applied to well-dressed, seemingly well-off 'gentlemen' who are attracted to special events in the county. They are, in fact, pickpockets.

Race meetings, cricket matches, public executions and markets are popular with gang members but the favourite venues are Maidstone Cattle Fair, where wealthy and highly inebriated farmers meet and the Pantiles, Tunbridge Wells where the frock-coated, top-hatted, fur collared gentlemen like to gather.

This week Swell Gang members were seen mingling with the jostling crowd in Maidstone High Street and several farmers found they had been relieved of their bulging wallets. A few weeks ago in Tunbridge Wells a shopkeeper was swindled out of £70 worth of cloth by two 'dandies'.

Newspapers say they are the "elite of the criminal world". They enjoy a highly comfortable life style and skilful planning helps them to avoid arrest.

His heart was set on a great history of Kent

FOR more than 50 years the Rev Thomas Streatfeild of Chart's Edge, Westerham has dreamt of writing a history of Kent with 'better prose' than Lambarde's famous 'Perambulation' and in 'greater detail than the works of Edward Hasted'.

Streatfeild found 300 subscribers for this colossal task, a support almost without parallel these days.

He examined thousands of documents, prepared hundreds of copper plates and book blocks, spent £3,000 on paintings, made exquisite drawings of his own and discussed the project with Henry George, a printer of Westerham.

This week, almost on the eve of the launch of "such a history of our county as prosperity will be unwilling to forget", Thomas Streatfeild was struck with paralysis. His work of half a century cannot be completed.

He has lived at Chart's Edge for 26 years. In his description of the house he says: "The house cheated me with its Elizabethan air because I thought I saw a row of ancestor portraits in flowing wigs and ample ruffles but these, in fact, were only cockneys and Kentish yeoman."

Streatfeild has published one book — a tragedy in five acts. He was a Fellow of the Society of Antiquaries , a curate at Tatsfield for many years and a very wealthy man having inherited a fortune from his first wife. He is giving the 50 volumes of manuscript to his friend, Lambert Larking, a well-known Kent antiquary.

A drawing of the proposed Margate Sands railway station which is currently served by a wooden shack. The railway reached the Thanet resort in December 1846 and provides an alternative to the Margate Hoy for day trippers from London.

From prison to president: Louis Napoleon is the toast of France

December 11: With the overthrow of the French king by a popular Paris uprising Louis Napoleon Bonaparte, nephew of the former emperor, has been elected as the President of France. It is an extraordinary about-turn for the man who left Gravesend only eight years ago with a handful of men and an eagle to invade his country and was then imprisoned for life.

The revolution that unseated King Louis Philippe was sudden and violent and travelled across the continent with the speed of a lightning bolt.

By March 13 much of Europe was in revolutionary turmoil. Prince Metternich, Chancellor of Austria, was driven off by rioters and the King of Prussia granted a free press, a constitution and a general reform. Many other German states and Hungary followed suit.

An attempt in England in April to bring about political reform fizzled out. It was organised by Chartists who took a giant petition, said to contain more than 5 million signatures, to parliament.

The Duke of Wellington, now 78, brought troops into the capital and enrolled 170,000 special constables, many from Kent. He advised the Queen to leave London. Heavy rain then thwarted those who planned to march on London.

Many of his friends in Kent are delighted that Louis Napoleon is President of his country at last. Before his escape from prison he wrote a popular book setting out his vision for the future of France. The voters like his vision and the security of the name Bonaparte. *See page 126*

New churches opened this year are: St Margaret's, Collier Street and St Margaret's, Yalding. Frittenden church has been rebuilt.

The railway swing bridge at Folkestone Harbour. Thanks to the railway this prosperous and gracious Kentish resort is flourishing like never before.

Tentacles proliferate in the Garden of England

IT has taken the South Eastern Railway Company just 10 years to cover much of Kent with its network of lines which now feel their way like the tentacles of an octopus across much of the Garden of England..

A short line from Tonbridge to Tunbridge Wells was opened in 1845. Then, a year later, came the long stretch north-east from Ashford to Canterbury and on to Ramsgate and Margate.

To avoid the North Downs the engineers found a course through the Stour Valley via Chilham and Chartham. From Canterbury they struck across the rich marshland to the Thanet resorts where everyone now expects railway travelling day trippers to proliferate; this to the regret of the genteel but perhaps to the prosperity of tradesmen.

The branch from Canterbury to Ramsgate was opened on April 13, 1846 and the terminus, initially known as Ramsgate SER, was located on the outskirts of the town. Within eight months four new miles of track had been laid and a temporary wooden station (Margate SER) was opened amid great excitement among islanders.

South Eastern Railway still hadn't finished. Encouraged by "railway mania" which extended to this part of East Kent a line was opened from Ramsgate to Deal giving Sandwich access to London in little more than two hours. This medieval town, once prosperous as the most important port in the country and now some two miles from the still-receding sea, is a backwoods no longer.

Finally, a railway line from London Bridge is due to reach Gravesend next year. The development of steam boat transport has already transformed Gravesend from a characterless, depressed, grimy slum into something of a trippers' paradise with nearly two million visitors a year. *See page 137*

It's called the Harbour of Refuge

WORK is well under way at Dover on the western arm of the Harbour of Refuge which has been designed by engineer James Walker and commissioned by the Admiralty. When completed it will be known as the Admiralty Pier and should solve the problem of shingle in the harbour mouth allowing cross channel steamers to berth alongside.

The first improvements to this tidal harbour took place soon after the outbreak of war with France when wet and dry docks, stone quays and north and south piers were built. Shingle remained a problem and it was the famous engineer Thomas Telford who submitted plans to improve the sluices and jets.

He proposed to increase the volume of water available with a tunnel between the Basin and the wet dock and increase the diameter of the pipes supplying the jets. He said that would clear the harbour mouth of shingle.

Telford died before he could work on the project but Walker carried on and the improvements went a long way towards solving the shingle problem.

It was the Royal Commission of 1840 which laid the ground for the modern harbour with the recommendation two years ago that Dover becomes a Harbour of Refuge "capable of receiving any class of vessels under all circumstances of the wind and tide".

Cholera kills 43 'strangers'

September 23: The Rev Henry Wilberforce, vicar of East Farleigh, today buried 43 "strangers" in a mass grave in his churchyard. They had suffered a terrible death in one of the worst outbreaks of cholera Kent has ever known.

The victims were hoppers working for Mr Ellis of Court Lodge, Barming, the largest grower in Kent. It is believed most of the dead were from Ireland and they lived in the most appalling insanitary conditions. 30 more died among hop pickers at nearby Yalding and Loose.

It was on September 12 that the epidemic broke out at East Farleigh and Dr Plomley of Maidstone, who arrived four days later, found a terrible scene. In his medical report he said: "Sixty two persons were suffering more or less from the disease. Four were in the agonies of death and eight more in the most profound collapse, all of whom died before the following morning....The melancholy was much heightened by the almost incessant wailings of the Irish in "waking" their lost friends.

East Farleigh school was hastily converted into a hospital and a cholera ward prepared at the union workhouse nearby. Dr Plomley was joined by the union surgeon and other doctors including some from Guy's Hospital. Despite the contagious nature of the disease ladies of the district bravely volunteered to form a nursing team. They included the wife of the vicar and Mrs Thomas Rider from Boughton Monchelsea Place.

Although the disease is not yet under control and its basic cause unknown miasmatists and contagionists are blaming Mr Ellis for allowing his itinerant pickers to live in such in such feculent conditions. Dr Plomley has pointed out that those who slept at home have avoided infection. "Cholera is linked to the accommodation with which the 'strangers' were provided".

He said: "The disease arose entirely from causes which are remediable and removable; namely impure air rising from overcrowded and ill-ventilated apartments, impure water derived from wells containing the soakage of cow yards and human filth and impure food sold at a cheap rate by unprincipled itinerant vendors of putrid fish and adulterated bread."

In one room of 700 cubic feet Dr Plomley found 14 persons including a child suffering from cholera. The 'effluvium' was so powerful that he could not enter. "Mortality for extra-metropolitan Kent is 1,208", he said, "which is much below that of London and ten other counties in England and Wales. Such precautions as had been taken quickly lapsed."

The memorial in East Farleigh churchyard dedicated to the 43 tragic 'strangers'

Some 15 years ago cholera killed 34 pickers on the same farm. It appears that no lessons have been learned. The lingering question is this: Does medical responsibility for "strangers" lie with the hop farmers or the Poor Law guardians? The debate will rage for many months. *See page 143*

Dead hoppers are refugees from a potato famine

Who are the 'strangers' who suffered such a cruel death in the village of East Farleigh? The survivors can tell us that these poor people had emigrated from Ireland to avoid the potato famine and, ironically, the cholera that was sweeping that country.

Rather than crowd into Irish workhouses where many unions were facing bankruptcy because farmers could no longer pay their rates these beleaguered people applied to the British treasury for financial help. It was refused so many gave up their stock and came to England to find work. Hop picking on the farms of Kent was early option.

They arrived at the peak of a cholera outbreak that has been ravaging the British Isles for two years. It had been taking as many as 2,000 lives a week and, in London alone had killed 12,847 in three months.

Despite the advances in transport and engineering Britain's sewage system remains primitive and Kent is no exception. The landed gentry living in their great houses have water closets but, in much of the county, open sewers still flow into rivers.

In the cholera outbreak last year only Deal, Folkestone and Tunbridge Wells remained untouched from an outbreak that began in cottages in Upper Rainham. There they found a 'black ditch' containing all sorts of abominable things. Nine persons died before the parish authorities began whitewashing with lime.

May: Following the cholera epidemic, which killed the East Farleigh hop pickers and thousands more in England, a medical officer is to be appointed in every major city and borough. The new Public Health Act says the Thames must be cleaned. *See page 151*

David Copperfield — 'my best book yet', says Dickens

October: Another book has materialised from the pen of Charles Dickens and this one has all the ingredients of being his best, if not most popular novel.

It is called *David Copperfield* and tells the poignant story of Dickens' boyhood in Chatham In fact, in an unintentional reversal of initials, CD becomes DC.

Apart from the self-revelation of Dickens, *David Copperfield* is notable for the derivation of the unforgettable Mr Micawber from the author's father.

The book was first published in instalments and a Mrs Seymour Hill recognised her own portrait in the character Miss Moucher and complained bitterly to the astounded author. By the 32nd chapter she was a lot happier!

Steerforth is almost certainly based on George Stroughill who lived in the same street in Chatham as the Dickens family.

Dickens said this week: "Of all my books I like this the best...It would concern the reader little, perhaps, to know how sorrowfully the pen is laid down at the close of two years' imaginitive task..." *See page 134*

Victoria meets her dying aunt in 'dear Tunbridge Wells'

June 23: The failing health of the Dowager Queen Adelaide has so concerned Queen Victoria that today she made a surprise visit to Tunbridge Wells where her favourite aunt has been staying in the Calverley House Hotel.

The necessary arrangements to convey the royal party by train from London were made at very short notice. The Queen had enjoyed her first rail journey only seven years earlier and she looked upon it as an exciting and modern thing to do "with just a whiff of danger to add relish to the adventure". She was accompanied by Prince Albert.

With a few minutes of their arrival at Calverley House, the two Queens and the Prince Consort drove through Calverley Park to the town centre with Earl Howe and Captain Somerset in attendance on horseback. Hundreds lined the route as the royal party passed over Mount Ephraim and crossed Rusthall Common to High Rocks. The return journey took them through the forest to the Eridge Road and then to Mr Nye's repository where Her Majesty made several purchases for the royal children.

The royal party dined at Calverley, said goodbye to Queen Adelaide and arrived at the station at precisely six-o-clock.

It is not the Queen's first visit to this popular spa town. As Princess Victoria she spent several holidays in Tunbridge Wells with her mother the Duchess of Kent in the 1820s and 1830s, usually staying in a grand house called Mount Pleasant.

On each occasion Tunbridge Wells was abuzz with excitement and each royal visit was marked by parades, illuminations, the presentation of loyal addresses, civic dinners, balls and fireworks. The Princess wrote in her diary: "The return from Tunbridge Wells to Kensington was generally a day of tears".

On her last visit in 1834 she noted: "At ° past nine we left Tunbridge Wells. I am so very sorry to leave the dear place. I am so very fond of it. I liked Boyne House better a good deal than old Mount Pleasant. We changed horses at Tunbridge Town, then at Sevenoaks and lastly at Bromley. We reached Kensington Palace at 2".

Louis Napoleon achieves his destiny at last

April 21 1855: Queen Victoria is flanked by Omar Pasha, Commander-in-Chief of the Ottoman Army and Charles Louis Napoleon during a visit to England by the two statesmen. Four years ago Louis — posing as the saviour of the French society from radical revolution — took the title of Napoleon III and later married the Spanish countess Eugenie de Montijo de Guzmán. At that time he had not quite achieved the destiny in which he so persistently believed. He was anxious to be received by the Queen of England.

That has now been resolved. The Emperor and Empress arrived in Dover on Monday (April 16) for a six-day state visit and, accompanied by Prince Albert, boarded a train for London with crowds of people cheering them all the way. They completed the journey to Windsor by carriage where the Queen with the Prince of Wales and the Princess Royal greeted them royally.

"That is is a very extraordinary man, with great qualities, there is no doubt", wrote the Queen in her diary. "He is possessed of indomitable courage, unflinching firmness of purpose and self reliance".

The state visit was a great success, the Queen being acutely aware of the beneficial effects of a meeting between a Queen of England with the nephew of Bonaparte.

Omar Pasha took command of the Turkish forces after the Hungarian Revolution of 1848. *See page 182.*

1850-1859

1850: July 2: Robert Peel, former Prime Minister, dies following a fall from his horse. He was 62.

November: Alfred Tennyson is appointed poet laureate in succession to William Wordsworth.

1851: February: Mary Shelley, best known for her novel, *Frankenstein*, dies.

Hundreds of Britons, including many from Kent, are flocking to New South Wales in search of gold. It is similar to the California gold rush of 1848.

December: To the delight of Queen Victoria, Lord Palmerston is dismissed as foreign secretary. Louis Napoleon was among those who supported the coup.

The national census completed this year shows that the majority of the population no longer lives in rural areas. The overall population of England is 17.9 million. London has doubled in size to reach 2.7 million.

1852: A public flushing lavatory for gentlemen is opened in Fleet Street.

September 14: The Duke of Wellington and Augustus Pugin die in Kent on the same day, one at Walmer Castle and the other at Ramsgate.

November: The post office introduces a pillar box for posting letters at St Helier on Jersey.

1853: February: James Andrew Ramsay, the Marquis of Dalhousie and former governor-general of India, is appointed warden of the Cinque Ports.

June 2: A British fleet is to sail to the Dardenelles as a warning to the Russians not to attack the Ottoman Empire.

A smallpox vaccination is made compulsory for all infants within four months of their birth.

1854: Britain and France, as allies of the Ottoman Empire, declare war on Russia.

Bartholomew Fair is closed because of "whoring, rowdiness and crime". It is the last of the great mediaeval fairs.

1855: February: Lord Palmerston, a Whig, forms a government after the collapse of Lord Aberdeen's administration.

April 16: Napoleon lll and Queen Eugenie land at Dover on a state visit to Britain. The East Kent Mounted Rifles forms a guard of honour.

August 9: Queen Victoria and Prince Albert review the troops at Shorncliffe.

New Kent churches dedicated this year are: St John's Deptford, Christchurch, Forest Hill, Christchurch, Milton, St James, Plumstead and Christchurch, Shooters Hill.

September: Sevastapol surrenders.

November 17: A huge waterfall is discovered by David Livingstone, the Scottish explorer, in Africa. He names it Victoria Falls.

1856: The Victoria Cross "for valour among all ranks" is instituted. Guns from the Crimea are melted down to make the crosses.

Queen Victoria's eldest daughter is to marry Frederick, the Crown Prince of Prussia.

A new-style prison, St Mary's, Chatham, is completed. It will take the place of prison hulks.

1857: Other Kentish recipients of the Victoria Cross in the Crimean War include Sergeant William McWheeney of the 44th Regiment, who lives at Dover and Joseph Kellaway, chief boatswain from Chatham.

February: The British Portrait Gallery is founded in Westminster.

July: Over 200 Britons are murdered at Cawnpore by Indian mutineers.

Tom Brown's Schooldays, a novel by Thomas Hughes, is published.

1858: January 25: East Kent Railway opens a line from Strood to Faversham.

February: Lord Derby follows Lord Palmerston as Prime Minister following the defeat of the latter's bill of conspiracy. He is accused of "truckling to France".

A London Omnibus Company is founded with nearly 600 buses and 6,000 horses. They take daily rail travellers from the termini to their City of London offices.

A museum opens at Maidstone.

The East India Company is abolished and India is to be ruled by the British government.

Fort Burgoyne, Dover is completed.

Ebony church is moved stone by stone from the Isle of Oxney and rebuilt. New churches are All Saints, Blackheath and St John's, Tunbridge Wells.

The clock tower at Westminster, nicknamed Big Ben, is completed for the new Houses of Parliament.

Dante Gabriel Rossetti, John Millais and William Holman Hunt are among the founders of the Pre-Raphaelite Brotherhood.

1859: Isambard Kingdom Brunel, the most famous of Britain's brilliant engineers dies aged 59.

A street railway (or tram) opens at Birkenhead with horses pulling carriages of 60 people along a two-mile route.

Age of church building shows no sign of fading

BUILD, build, build. That's the message from Christian bodies throughout Kent which are convinced that greater accommodation for worship will lead to an increase in churchgoing.

For some years now a widespread programme of church building and restoration has been carried out by all denominations, although the Church of England and the main branches of Protestant dissent account for 90% of them.

Since 1840, 21 new churches have been built in Kent, many of them in the style, detail and internal arrangements of the churches of the Middle Ages.

The most influential figure behind the 'ecclesiologist movement', as it is known, is the great architect A.W.Pugin. His disciples certainly seem prepared to sacrifice practicality.

The first Anglican churches to incorporate these principles were those of Kilndown and Rusthall. A new church at Canterbury, St Gregory's, is currently under construction and that will be a memorial to the late Archbishop Howley. All the seats are free and face east in the nave and north aisle.

The more traditional have included East Peckham, Platt, Hildenborough, Pembury, Collier Street and Fordcombe. There have been modern restorations at All Saints, Maidstone and Stockbury.

An approximate guide to church building shows the Church of England is leading the way followed by Wesleyan Methodists, Congregationalists and General Baptists. Other groups who have built places of worship include Roman Catholics, Particular Baptists, Presbyterians, Bible Christians and Calvinists. *See page 130*

Paxton's crystal palace rises in the park

November: Thousands of people from Kent are booking tickets for the Great Exhibition in Hyde Park which is due to be opened on May I next year by the Queen.

Devised by Prince Albert and planned by a specially created royal commission it will be housed in a fairytale structure of glass which the people are calling the "Crystal Palace".

Described as the world's most remarkable demonstration of human ingenuity and resourcefulness the exhibition building will almost certainly be the most striking artefact because it is constructed of glass and iron to a remarkable design submitted by Joseph Paxton, head gardener on the Duke of Devonshire's estate at Chatsworth.

This week Charles Dickens wrote in *Household Worlds*: "Two parties in London, relying on the accuracy and goodwill of a single ironmaster, the owners of a single glassworks and of one master carpenter, bound themselves for a certain sum of money and in the course of some months to cover 18 acres of ground with a building upwards of a third of a mile long".

The Crystal Palace is a wonderful example of English manufacturing enterprise because Paxton's plans — apart from the iron — demand 900,000 square feet of glass comprising 293,655 panes and 600,000 cubic feet of timber. The contractors, Messrs Fox and Henderson took possession of the site on July 30 and promise to complete the building before the end of this year.

Had this enterprise been considered some 100 years ago then the great ironmasters of Lamberhurst and the Weald would have certainly been employed to help with the construction of 205 miles of sash bars, 33,000 iron columns and 2,150 girders. But the Kentish iron industry has been long silenced and the heavy industrial production centres are now in the Midlands. *See page 140*

Joseph Paxton designed the Great Conservatory at Chatsworth making possible his sudden leap to fame with the Crystal Palace. He is to receive a knighthood.

Send for the Duke...

April: Lord Wellington has found the solution to a crisis which threatens to ruin the Great Exhibition at Hyde Park, just two weeks before the official opening by Queen Victoria.

A few weeks ago a flock of sparrows, escaping from the chilly March winds, made their nests in the tall elm trees which are protected in an arched transept in the middle of the Crystal Palace.

Enjoying the warmth of the glasshouse, the birds perched on the trusses and girders but showed no consideration concerning their natural functions.

The great engineers on the building committee including George Stephenson, Isambard Brunel and Joseph Paxton racked their brains to find a way of emptying this giant aviary. They tried poison but that failed and they knew that guns were out of the question.

This week Queen Victoria applied her mind to the problem and quickly came up with the answer — "send for the Duke".

Wellington, summoned from Walmer, studied the dilemma with the efficiency of a general plotting the downfall of the enemy at Waterloo.

"Simple", he told the building committee. "Bring in the sparrow-hawks". The crisis has been solved.

In this painting by George Childs a steam locomotive, hauling passenger carriages, approaches the tunnel below the Shakespeare Cliff, Dover.

Theatre Royal Maidstone — a warehouse!

THE curtain has finally fallen on the Theatre Royal in Maidstone. Famous for its comedies and for attracting some of the greatest actors, the building is to be converted into a warehouse — a sad finale after more than 50 glorious years.

The virtuoso behind the success of the Theatre Royal was Sarah Baker, the first theatrical woman manager in England once better known as the governor general of Kentish drama. She built the theatre in the High Street in1796 entirely at her own expense. It could seat 700 patrons.

In 1844 the set design and scenery were improved and gas lighting was introduced. The plays of Sheridan and Shakespeare were presented and customers travelled from outlying areas to see such stars as Kean, Grimaldi, William Dowton, Miss Foote and Miss O'Neill.

Riots in Maidstone as Rev Wilberforce becomes a Catholic

August 29: Feelings are running dangerously high in the long running dispute between Kent's Protestants and Catholics.

This week, following the passing of the Ecclesiastical Titles Act prohibiting Catholic clergy from assuming territorial titles, a Catholic Defence Association has been formed.

Nowhere is the situation worse than in Maidstone where controversy has been bubbling since the great mass protest against emancipation on Penenden Heath 22 years ago.

This week it reached boiling point when Henry Wilberforce, the former Anglican priest of East Farleigh and now a member of the Catholic Association attempted to buy property in the town. There were riots in several quarters of the town.

Wilberforce, son of the anti-slavery campaigner William Wilberforce, has encouraged so many local people to convert to Catholicism that he wants to establish a regular meeting place rather than have mass in various lodgings.

He is not the only influential convert. Many former well known members of the Church of England have changed direction encouraging Pope Pius IX to restore a Roman Catholic diocesan hierarchy in Britain by appointing Cardinal Wiseman as Archbishop of Westminster.

This has not pleased Maidstone Protestants who have a deep-seated dislike of Catholics. The feeling, however, is mutual because Catholics — like the town's Quakers — refuse to pay the church rate levied on all ratepayers for the upkeep of Anglican churches.

This has developed into a major battle with regular seizures of nonconformist property.

Wilberforce will not give up. He will continue to look for a priest who can give instruction to local children in an established Roman Catholic Church. Meanwhile an appeal for funds will be made within the local Catholic community.

See page 202

RESULTS OF CENSUS SUNDAY

The government has attempted to estimate the number of people attending religious services in England and Wales and the table below shows the figures for Kent. The total population for the county this year, including the metropolitan areas, is 615,766 and the returns show there is sitting accommodation in places of worship for just under half the population.

Census Sunday, as it was known, took place on March 30 and the results are interesting. It shows that fewer than 40% of the population of Kent are regular churchgoers. Very few churches were full at every service and some were almost empty.

The most encouraging news is the progress of the Sunday School movement with two thirds of all churches in Kent making such provision.

Denomination	Places of Worship	Sittings	Attendances	Sunday Schools
Church of England	479	194,443	219,880	301
Old Dissent				
Presbyterians	3	1,738	1,738	1
Independents	86	27,091	32,054	77
Baptists	107	25,668	33,063	60
Society of Friends	10	1,753	342	-
Unitarians	2	662	456	2
New Dissent				
Weslyan Methodists	184	33,759	41,701	138
Primitive Methodists	26	2,877	3,027	6
Bible Christians	27	3,298	3,286	18
Other Methodists	13	1,690	1,763	10
Lady Huntingdon's	5		3,202	5
Other Groups				
Roman Catholics	13	3,337	4,636	-
Latter Day Saints	7	592	1,277	1
Jews	5	315	345	-
Irvingites	2	288	197	-
Brethren	2	105	90	-
Swedenborgians	1	70	60	-
French Protestants	1	30	21	-
Isolated Congregations	24	2,897	3,589	19
TOTAL	**997**	**302,948**	**350,526**	**638**

The census shows that the Anglican church in Kent is still attracting two thirds or more of the regular churchgoers in most parts of the county. However, they are outnumbered by the main branches of Protestant dissent in Chatham, Margate and Sheerness. Methodism is strong in the Medway towns and the Hoo Peninsula, where it first began.

See page 195

Kent plays its part in Britain's supremacy

AS we reach the middle of the century, the people of Kent can be proud of the role they are playing in Britain's undoubted world supremacy.

Many of the 129 Royal Navy vessels stationed in the Mediterranean, guarding the newly acquired treaty ports in China or hunting pirates in the East Indies, were built in the historic Kent dockyards at Chatham, Sheerness, Woolwich and Deptford.

Some are still engaged in stamping out the Atlantic slave trade and others are in the far Pacific carrying out Lord Palmerston's brand of gunboat diplomacy.

Currently there are only 50,856 men under arms but our home based forces — the Buffs at Canterbury, the 50th Foot at Maidstone, the Royal Engineers and Sappers at Brompton are still recruiting with the knowledge that frontier skirmishes can break out at any time.

Woolwich is the home of the Royal Artillery which derived from the Board of Ordnance as long ago as 1485. In those days they were known as the King's Gunners.

The first association of artillery with Woolwich began with the setting up of a gun depot in the reign of Elizabeth. Later a Royal Carriage Department was opened and in 1695 a laboratory was established for the manufacture of ammunitions and pyrotechnics at The Warren in Tower Place. Together with a foundry for casting brass guns this formed the nucleus of the Royal Gun Factory.

When the Royal Artillery was formed in 1716 Woolwich became its headquarters. The first block of barracks was put up in 1719 and the Regiment grew in step with the expansion of Britain's overseas interests and exerted considerable influence on the manufacture of guns and ammunition.

In 1721 the Royal Military Academy was founded. It was the first in Britain.

The establishment at The Warren, which was christened Royal Arsenal by George III in 1805, led the way for the building of more departments and establishments.

Today the Woolwich Arsenal is Britain's chief arms factory and is showing off some of its technological excellence in the Great Exhibition at Hyde Park.

The exhibition is a showcase of the country's economic strength. It was opened by Queen Victoria on May 1 and during its five month existence is expected to attract at least six million visitors.

Most will travel by the railway. On arriving in Paxton's amazing glasshouse they will find 14,000 separate exhibitors keen to demonstrate their achievements in engineering, manufacture or fine art.

Turner dies in hiding

December 19: His few friends in Margate were saddened today to hear of the death of Joseph Turner, the brilliant but quite eccentric land and seascape artist who has been exhibiting at the Royal Academy since he was 15.

Kent was the inspiration for some of Turner's finest work and from his base in Margate he studied the effects of sea and sky in every kind of weather and developed a painting technique all of his own. He also travelled widely in Europe.

As he grew older Turner became an eccentric and gradually lost contact with all but a few. He allowed no one to watch him while he painted, gave up attending meetings of the Academy and always travelled alone. Sometimes his friends never saw him for months, perhaps years at a time.

Last year he exhibited for the last time and then disappeared. His housekeeper, after a search of many months, found him hiding in a house in Chelsea. He had been ill for a long time and he died the following day. Turner has left a large fortune which he wants to be used to support what he calls "decaying artists". He has requested to be buried at St Paul's Cathedral. He was 76.

New churches opened last year were: St Andrew's, Deal, St John's, Kingsdown (Dover), St Paul's, Rusthall, St Mary's, Woodlands and St Thomas, Woolwich.

Over 7,000 miles of railway track will be in use in Britain next year; 3,000 more are sanctioned by parliament.

May 17: *RMSP Orinoco*, built at Pitcher's Yard, Northfleet was launched today. It is the largest vessel to sail on the Thames.

Turner is not the only great national figure to die in recent months. The country is still mourning the death of William Wordsworth, poet laureate, Mary Shelley, author of *Frankenstein* and Sir Robert Peel, former Prime Minister who died after falling from his horse.

Preston Hall near Maidstone has been rebuilt.

A contemporary colour washed engraving showing the death of the Duke of Wellington. The Duke is surrounded by his family, doctors and servants at Walmer Castle.

(picture courtesy of English Heritage)

See story page 135

An oil on canvas painting by Pierre Justin Ouvrie which depicts the new Palace of Westminster during the final stages of construction with Westminster Bridge in the background. The clock tower and the Victoria tower are still crowned with scaffolding. This painting was exhibited at the Paris Salon two years ago.

Architect dies before Westminster is completed

October: When Queen Victoria opened the newly-built Houses of Parliament in February one of the two men most responsible for the building was not present. Sadly, Augustus Pugin was ill and he died on September 14 before the great work was finished.

The magnificent Victorian Gothic structure standing on the bank of the Thames by Westminster Bridge, with an unfinished clock tower at its northern end, was made possible by the fire of 1834 which destroyed most of the Palace of Westminster.

Charles Barry's design was selected from 97 submitted for a new building in the Gothic (or Elizabethan) style to contain both the House of Commons and the House of Lords. The building with its delicately ribbed facades is his but he brought in Pugin to provide the Gothic interiors— the paintings, mosaics, and stained-glass as well as fittings and furniture.

Pugin, exhausted both mentally and physically from the work, died, aged just 40, a few weeks after his third wife, Mary, had rescued him from Bedlam. He lived at The Grange, a house with a battlemented tower next to the West Cliff at Ramsgate, where he once lodged out shipwreck survivors at his own expense. He had planned

continued on next page

Augustus Pugin

(continued)

to add a tall spire as a landmark warning of the dangerous Goodwin Sands but, by this time, he had become entirely devoted to the new Westminster.

The great architect was a protagonist and theorist of the Gothic Revival and wrote profusely on architectural and ecclesiastical matters. He believed that in medieval days great church architecture to the Glory of God had been achieved only by men who lived good lives.

Pugin worked on many Roman Catholic churches in Kent including Greenwich (Our Ladye Star of the Sea) and Woolwich, while his son Edward Welby Pugin, who is also an architect, is helping to complete St Augustine's, Ramsgate following the death of his father.

Sailing down the pier on a Saturday afternoon. This is Herne Bay, now a classic seaside watering hole with broad promenades, bandstands, pavilion and a clock tower erected to celebrate Queen Victoria's coronation in 1837.

Many consider St Augustine's to be Augustus Pugin's greatest achievement. He supervised the building himself and was able to avoid the features he most despised — sham facade and non-functional ornament. Sadly, the spire, which delighted him most of all, was never erected.

He once said: "I can truly say that I have been compelled to commit suicide with every building in which I have been engaged, and I have good proof that they are built little better than ghosts of what they were designed; indeed, had I not been permitted by the providence of God to have raised the church at St Augustine's, I must have appeared as a man whose principles and works were strangely at variance."

The past few years have not been easy for Augustus Pugin. Working to a deadline and suffering from financial troubles and a fear of failure he has also been troubled by the acrimonious dispute as to whether his or Barry's has been the finer work.

Dickens draws upon his own life experiences

THE mental exhaustion which has afflicted Charles Dickens in recent years has not affected his literary output. This year he published *Bleak House* — in which he assails the abuses of the Court of Chancery— and is already busy with another book under the working title of *Little Dorrit.*

In *Bleak House* Dickens draws upon his own experiences, first as a boy-clerk to an attorney and then as a reporter. *Little Dorrit* also concerns those formative years but takes a different course.

When Charles Dickens was a young solicitor's clerk he courted and fell in love with Maria Beadnell, daughter of a wealthy baker who "was more beautiful than the flowers I gave her".

Maria, with heartless indifference, left the 19-year-old clerk and, on the rebound, he met and married plump and placid Kate Hogarth.

By the time Maria had become Mrs Winter, Dickens (through the eyes of David Copperfield) once again bumped into the object of his youthful passion. But, what a change! She was fat, giggling and garrulous "a caricature of her girlish manner".

Much of *Little Dorritt* was written while Dickens was staying at Waite's Hotel, Gravesend. It is a double portrait of Maria.

See page 150

Iron Duke dies at Walmer: the nation mourns

September 14: The Duke of Wellington, statesman, diplomat and Commander-in-Chief of the British Army died today at Walmer Castle plunging the nation into mourning. He was 83.

The Iron Duke had spend the last few days of his life visiting friends, writing letters and playing with his grandchildren at Walmer.

On September 1 he travelled by train to Tunbridge Wells to visit the Salisburys at Buckhurst Park. Two days later he spent a pleasant few hours with John Croker at Radnor Place, near Folkestone. Returning to Dover by train a tipsy Irishman sporting a Peninsular medal begged for a sovereign. The Duke obliged.

Back at Walmer there were more requests from total strangers asking for money. An officer's widow, stranded in Boulogne, pleaded for her fare home. Wellington sent five pounds.

On Saturday September 11 he rode unannounced to Dover to inspect the partly constructed Admiralty Pier in company with the harbourmaster and on Sunday he went as usual to Walmer Church.

Monday September 13 was his last full day. He rode out to view the coastline and inspect the defences, played with his grandchildren and ate heartily in the evening — mock turtle soup, turbot and venison. At 8.30 pm he retired to bed carrying his saveall with flickering candle down the long dark passage to his study.

He was woken the next morning by his valet, Kendall who said: "It's getting quite late your Grace. It's past seven o'clock".

"It is", replied the Duke. "Do you know where the apothecary lives?".

"Yes, your Grace".

"Then send for him and let him know that I should like to see him. I don't feel quite well".

The apothecary, Mr Hulke, arrived at nine o'clock from his home in the High Street at Deal and pronounced the Duke was suffering from indigestion. He ordered tea and toast for the patient to be followed by ammonia stimulant. As soon as he had gone Kendall asked the Duke if he would take some tea.

"Yes, if you please". They were the last words spoken by the Duke of Wellington. Tea was followed by a series of violent fits and he slipped into unconsciousness. He died surrounded by his family.

As Arthur Wellesley, the fifth son of an Irish peer, he transformed the British army from, in his own words: "the scum of the earth" into "worthy fellows".

As Prime Minister in 1828 he avoided revolution in Ireland by conceding Roman Catholic emancipation — the right of Catholics to sit in parliament.

Thousands line the route to St Paul's

November 18: The Duke of Wellington has joined Lord Nelson as only the second commoner this century to be given a state funeral. The elaborate plans, believed to cost more than £30,000, were made while his body lay at Walmer Castle. After travelling from Walmer by train his coffin lay in state in the Great Hall of Chelsea Hospital. On the night before his funeral it was moved to the Audience Hall of Horseguards in Whitehall where men were still working to complete the massive funeral car.

By dawn on November 18 the crowds which were to number well over one million were starting to fill the route between the Horseguards and St Paul's. The funeral car drew out of Horseguards led by military bands playing the Dead March from Saul. The procession included representatives of all areas of church and state but the most moving sight was the Duke's horse which was led through the street saddled and riderless with the Duke's own boots in the stirrups.

For more than two hours tens of thousands lined the route to St Paul's to see the cortège pass by.

Former Sevenoaks pupil is commander of British Army

Henry Hardinge — a pupil at Sevenoaks.

GENERAL Sir Henry Hardinge, who served as Wellington's divisional commander in the Peninsular War and lost a hand during the battle at Quatre Bras a week before Waterloo, has become Commander-in-Chief of the British Army.

The news confirmed by the Horse Guards this week has brought great honour to Sevenoaks School where Henry was a pupil at the turn of the century. One story about him, recently related by the present headmaster, concerns his early friendship with John Woodgate of Riverhill House, Sevenoaks.

On his first day at Sevenoaks, John noticed that some boys had got hold of young Hardinge and were "roasting him before the fire" according to the genial custom of the times. Though only a 'new boy', John made such a fuss that Hardinge was released. In gratitude he carved a small wooden boat for his 'rescuer'.

Both boys joined the army, Woodgate with Sir John Moore's forces in which he served in many engagements in the Peninsular War. He was severely wounded several times.

Henry was no less brave. When a cannon ball shattered his hand on June 16, 1815 he ordered it to be amputated. Improper treatment of the wound and the necessity of retiring with the Prussians to avoid falling into the hands of the French, caused intense suffering but Hardinge was back with Blücher within a fortnight, having just missed the Battle of Waterloo.

He went on to become Secretary of State for War in 1828 and Governor General of India in 1848. He returned to England as Viscount Hardinge of Lahore.

His parents, who died some years ago, were proud of their soldier son. His father, a former rector at Stanhope in County Durham, and his mother, of Park House, Boxley, lived at Wrotham where Henry was born. Henry's seat today is at South Park near Tunbridge Wells. *See page 146*

Life at the seaside— its fun for the famous

SCORES of artists, poets, authors have chosen to enjoy their summer breaks in Ramsgate with its fine sand, excellent harbour and commodious bathing machines. Among them is the artist William Powell Frith, a friend of Charles Dickens and a great favourite of Queen Victoria.

Inspired by his holiday this year, he has painted *Ramsgate Sands: Life at the Seaside*, which sold for 1,000 guineas and is now in the possession of the Queen. Like most of his paintings it shows lively crowd scenes in a setting well chosen for its significance in English life. *The Railway Station* and *Derby Day* are two other great examples.

Another artist seen on the Sands this summer is Samuel Luke Fildes who lives at Holland House in Kingsgate. Well known for his portraits, Fildes has been commissioned to illustrate Dickens' novels.

William Makepeace Thackeray, journalist and novelist has holidayed in Ramsgate and Margate and so has Hans Christian Andersen, who has spent some months in Thanet working on the English translation of his fairy stories.

Whitstable: the home of the oysters

THE oyster industry at Whitstable, believed to be about 2,000 years old, is flourishing. This year there are some 300 members and 80 smacks in the fleet producing more than 50 million oysters a year, mainly for the London market and priced at two a penny.

The private oyster beds, or layings, start about two miles off shore and extend to some seven miles out, covering about 5,000 acres. They are dredged by the distinctive yawls of the Company of Free Fishers and Dredgers.

Whitstable is, in some degree, the port of Canterbury and near the mouth of the Swale connecting the Medway with the Thames. The harbour was completed 18 years ago and ships call here from Scandinavia and the Low Countries with coal. It has a small but lively shipbuilding industry.

Railway town rises from the Ashford marshes

July : A new Kentish town has been built on 185 acres of the Ashford Marshes by the South-Eastern Railway Company. It has a school, a church, long terraces of new cottages, shops, a tavern and even a newspaper. As a company town it is unique in south-east England.

The new Ashford, or Alfred as the town is known, has been built around the Locomotive Establishment where hundreds of new inhabitants are already working on the construction, maintenance and repair of steam locos. It is an impressive sight built on a scale never before seen in this part of Kent.

It was a few years ago that the South Eastern Railway Co. decided to construct new works but the company needed a site that gave easy access to the network of railway lines appearing across Kent. Tonbridge and Maidstone were considered but when a local landowner consented to sell a large tract of land south of Ashford, the decision was quickly made. Ashford was to be the Railway Town.

Parliamentary approval was secured with the authority to spend up to £500,000. Farmhouses and farmland were purchased and a small hamlet called Aylesford Green taken over by the developers, Golder and Lucas. The architect Samuel Beazley, well-known for building the Lord Warden Hotel at Dover, meticulously planned every detail. He arranged the cottages around a large open green with shops and a tavern. He built a great bath house with pumps at each of the three corners of the green to provide fresh drinking water.

The work started in 1847 and by 1850 almost 140 houses had been erected. Divided into ground floor and first floor flats they are believed to be the only back-to-back cottages of their type in Southern England. Gasworks were erected, street lamps introduced and a Mechanics Institute opened for adult education. "It was", said the Maidstone Journal, " a little community of industrious artisans and their families, giving promise to become very flourishing..."

The South Eastern Railway Company decided to call its new town 'Alfred' and welcomed new inhabitants from all over the country. One fifth came from Kent, another fifth from Northumberland and Durham and the rest from areas of high unemployment. The 'migrants' were young, healthy and their earnings gave them a better-than-average life style.

The most impressive buildings are the Railway Works. The main workshop is 396 feet in length and houses the machine shop, the tender shop and a smith's shop with 20 furnaces. There is a wheel hooping and boiler shop, an hydraulic press, an engine repairing shop and a crane capable of lifting 20 tons. Alongside is an engine shed, water tank and store rooms.

A more recent addition is the carriage and wagon department, 645 feet in length, capable of housing 50 carriages and 80 trucks. Forges and foundries are also in place.

The school, commissioned last year, after much campaigning by the railway company chaplain, the Rev John Pughe, was built by Albert Smith who was an enthusiast for Gothic styling. It was completed this year and to celebrate the occasion 350 pupils set out on a railway excursion to Dover last week with all costs borne by the company. It is hoped the seaside treat will become an annual feature of life in Alfred. *See page 155.*

Return of the Oystermen. Dredging is over for another day.

30 hoppers die as wagon falls into river

October 26: Thirty hop pickers, including 16 from one family, were drowned yesterday evening when the wagon in which they were returning from a day's work in the hop gardens toppled over the side of a bridge into the River Medway at Hartlake near Tudeley. They were swept into the murky torrent, running exceptionally fast at the time because of heavy rains.

The wagon, drawn by two horses — one in front of the other — was fully loaded with pickers from London and Ireland. Some were sitting on the sides and back and others supported each other as it jolted towards the bridge in gathering gloom around 6pm.

The lead horse went over the crest of the bridge and was nearing the steep gradient on the other side when the horse behind stumbled, causing a wagon wheel to swerve against the boarded side of the bridge. As the bridge gave way those sitting on the sides and back were able to jump off. The others, screaming frantically, were thrown into the river and swept downstream.

Customers at the Bell Inn, Golden Green, some distance away heard the cries for help and joined those who were already trying to rescue the victims with their hop poles. A few were saved in this way but of the 41 on the wagon there were only 11 survivors.

All of those who died were 'strangers' — people who come 'hopping down in Kent' every year and take advantage of the cheap fares which are offered by the railway companies. They had been working at Cox's Farm on the Hadlow side of the Medway and after a long working day — it had begun at dawn — were returning to their seasonal camp on the Tudeley side.

The waggoner on this fateful journey was John Waghorn. Having collected up the ten-bushel sacks of hops and taken them to the oast house to be dried, he returned for the pickers. First to travel were villagers who lived on the other side of the river; men who worked on the farm and those who enjoyed earning extra money during the picking season.

He returned for the 'strangers'. As they reached the approach to the timber bridge at Hartlake, Waghorn knew that flood water lay some two feet deep so he climbed onto the back of the lead horse. The bridge, belonging to the Medway Navigation Company, had a three-feet close-board fence on either side and metal rungs on the decking. It was in poor condition but nobody had bothered to report this to the Company.

The second horse slipped on the decking and the bridge just collapsed. All last night people with lanterns looked in vain for more survivors. By first light this morning they realised that 30 had died including 16 members of the Leatherland family from the Rosemary Lane area of London. Several others were Irish gipsies.

They will be buried in one common grave, possibly in Hadlow churchyard. *See page 139*

Australia says 'no more poms' (prisoners of motherland)

Prisoners on the Medway and Thames hulks, awaiting transportation to Australia and a life of hard labour will not be leaving their redundant warships. Sydney and Melbourne are refusing to accept any more convicts.

As a result of this ruling the British Government will introduce the Penal Servitude Act as an alternative to transportation. Future convicts will now receive longer sentences with hard labour.

More and more 'model' prisons are being built to relieve the overcrowding at Maidstone and Chatham. They include penitentiaries at Millbank and Pentonville where prisoners will receive solitary confinement and religious instruction in an attempt to reform them.

Catherine Marsh — the saint of Beckenham

CATHERINE Marsh is a name unknown to those who live outside Beckenham. But, for the hundreds of navvies who have found lodgings while employed on the building of the Crystal Palace, Catherine is a saint.

Some months ago this daughter of the rector of Beckenham decided these poor, unkempt, footsore men needed spiritual guidance. She gained entry to their lodgings on a Sunday evening and now conducts Bible classes three times a week.

"Many of the navvies now go to church", she said, "and the 'cottages' where readings are given are thronged. ...I hope their example will shame a few more wilder young men into attendance at public worship".

With war now imminent in the Baltic many of the navvies hope to become soldiers. Catherine says she will fortify them with prayers and testaments to go in their kit bags.

October 28: The Upper Great Hartlake Bridge over the River Medway where 30 hop pickers were thrown downstream and drowned. On Sunday, the day after the accident, the neighbourhood was visited by thousands of the curious, some of them from remote distances. Today, Monday, eight bodies were interred at Hadlow churchyard, the melancholy ceremony again attracting a great number of spectators.

Faversham Brewery is the oldest in England

March: Despite the growing temperance movement, whose principal supporters wish to control drinking habits, more and more breweries are opening in Kent. The current total is 124 with Maidstone firmly established as the major Kentish brewing centre.

With the proximity of the hop gardens and with water especially suitable for pale ales Maidstone's position is ideal. Apart from the breweries of which A.E.Style and Frank Fremlin are dominant Maidstone also produces Grant's Morello cherry brandy. But gin distilling has now ceased.

In Ashford there are two major breweries — the Original and the Lion — who both thrive on the support generated by the influx of railway workers from Northumberland and Durham. A casualty of the growth of Ashford is the small town of Lenham which, by-passed by the railway, has lost both its brewery and its seed-crushing mill.

There are five important brewing centres in the Medway towns and two at Faversham — Edward Rigden and Shepherd and Hilton.

The latter has the reputation of being the oldest brewery in England dating back to 1698 when Captain Richard Marsh, a militiaman, set up his business in Court Street West.

When Marsh died in 1727 his daughter sold the Faversham Brewery to Samuel Shepherd whose family owned land at Great Mongeham near Deal. Shepherd made good use of the underground sources of water which contained the appropriate quantities of calcium needed for making good beer.

Edward Rigden also started brewing in the town around this time and moved from Preston Street to a site in Court Street right opposite the Faversham Brewery. Competition between the two is as fierce as ever.

Crystal Palace rises again — on a green hill in Kent

Crystal Palace wallpaper, designed for the Great Exhibition of 1851 and now a feature of many homes.

May 24: The Crystal Palace has been transferred from Hyde Park to a new 200-acre site on the summit of Sydenham Hill, near Beckenham. Building began in 1852 and has taken nearly two years to complete. The final cost of the undertaking is in excess of £1,300,000 and it will be opened by the Queen on June 10.

The Sydenham Crystal Palace is much larger than the Hyde Park structure. Sir William Paxton, who was knighted shortly before the doors of the Great Exhibition finally closed, has added two more storeys and greatly enlarged the building. In fact it has doubled in width.

Paxton always wanted the Palace to remain at Hyde Park and put a proposal before Parliament. But the opposition led by Col Sibthorpe was too great and Fox and Henderson, the constructors were served with notice to remove the building. In the House of Commons debate Sibthorpe reached inspired heights of eloquence: "Nothing would have given me greater pleasure", he said, " than if, by some superior power, it was annihilated at one fell swoop, and no trace left of the gross delusion.

"Who benefited from it?", he asked. "Not one...Foreigners and contractors were the gainers. The poor people were drawn from their distant homes and from their honest occupations, to see this big bauble. They were trapanned, seduced, ensnared and humbugged out of their hard earnings...By their (the Government's) fraudulent insinuations they have wrung the shillings out of the hands of the poor and sent them back to their families penniless. The Crystal Palace is a transparent humbug."

Paxton, already busy with an alternative scheme, raised £500,000 to form a company to buy the building. This was achieved and the great architect set to work to create a system of fountains that would rival Versailles. He commissioned Brunel to build two water towers, 284 feet high which each contains a tank holding 300,000 gallons of water to feed the fountains. He has laid out water temples and waterfalls with 7,000 jets using 7,000,000 gallons of water an hour. He has created lakes, islands, a maze, a grotto, temples and sweeping lawns.

As the new site sloped steeply Paxton had to add a basement storey and then two more storeys above and two transepts with wings to balance them. By then the Crystal Palace Company issue had been well oversubscribed and had no difficulty in raising more money.

Inside the Palace, Paxton has created a series of Fine Art Courts each illustrating a particular period in the history of art. Pugin's Medieval Court has been transferred from Hyde Park and joined by the Grecian, Roman, Byzantine, Romanesque, Pompeian, Chinese, Renaissance and Egyptian Courts.

The whole enterprise is planned to give Londoners the opportunity to expand their knowledge of the world on a site that gives stunning views across rural Kent. For children there is a boating lake and monsters are appearing among the trees.

There have been many set backs including the disaster in August last year when the scaffolding for the Great Transept collapsed and 12 workmen died. *See page 171*

The Relief of the Light Brigade at the Battle of Balaclava on October 25, 1854. Oil on canvas by Richard Caton Woodville. National Army Museum

Crimean War — just a craving for military adventure?

November 12: Kent's soldiers are continuing to distinguish themselves in the Crimean War which began in March this year when Britain and France, as allies of the Ottoman Empire, declared war on Russia. The 50th, newly equipped with Minie rifles to replace their muskets, arrived in September, advanced along the coast towards Sevastopol, crossed the Alma and, with fixed bayonets, sent the Russians into full retreat.

That was comparatively simple but the battle which began on November 5 was a different story. The Russians launched a furious attack on the British lines outside Sevastopol close to the ruins of Inkerman. Col Fyler, a young officer who was present throughout the campaign has written: "Before dawn the camp was aroused by the distant sound of heavy musketry, away to our right towards the Inkerman Valley. That day broke dull and foggy, with a misty rain, and before it was fully light the bugles had sounded the alarm and the Regiment was under arms".

So followed the Battle of Inkerman. When their ammunition had gone the 50th used their bayonets against equally determined Russians. For three long hours 8,500 British held off four times that number and Lt-Col Waddy, commanding the left wing of the 50th, held off four Russian battalions, 3,000 strong. He was eventually wounded and had to withdraw under heavy fire.

Lord Raglan, who lost an arm at Waterloo, is the Commander-in-Chief of the British forces in the Crimea. It began, not because of the 'monkish' dispute over the jurisdiction of Holy Places, not because of the hatred for the Tsar of Russia but because, after nearly 40 years of peace in Europe, there has been a widespread and unworthy craving for military adventure. *See page 142*

Kentish men survive as Light Brigade charges into the 'Valley of Death'

November 1: News is reaching Kent this week of an astonishing (some say reckless) feat of arms by the Light Brigade of the British cavalry near Balaclava in the Crimea. On October 26 Lord Lucan, the divisional commander, was told that he must prevent the Russians from carrying off some captured guns but mistakenly ordered Lord Cardigan, commanding the Light Brigade to attack well-defended Russian guns at the end of a long valley.

The Light Brigade, which included several Kentish officers and men, set off as if it were in review but ran into a maelstrom of shot and shell fired from all sides. Having reached the guns and sabred the gunners the brigade then turned round to fight its way out of this 'valley of death'. Of the 673 men only 426 returned unhurt. It was a murderous encounter but, for discipline and red-blooded courage, stands out as a military feat perhaps never to be surpassed.

One of the young lieutenants in the 4th Light Dragoons who survived the charge is Fiennes Wykeham Martin of Hextall Court, Peckham Bush. His charger Toby also survived but 198 horsemen were killed and 80 badly wounded. Wykeham Martin, grandson of the fifth Earl of Cornwallis, has described the "gallant disaster" in a letter to his brother. "We charged for about a mile and a quarter down a valley flanked on both sides by artillery and infantry and with a tremendous force of cavalry at the bottom", he writes. "They bowled us over right and left with grape shot, balls and round shot.

"Of the 700 men who went into action only 190 (sic) came out — all for no good as we were not backed up. We have twice heard from a Russian officer who was taken prisoner that our little brigade charged 20,000 — rather long odds!"

Wykeham Martin and about 90 men somehow managed to escape between two forces of Russian cavalry. He told his brother: "We charged at them with all our might...and succeeded. The sword you got at Wilkinson's had very bad edge as it turned quite blunt with one cut I gave a Russian at Balaclava".

The Times correspondent in the Crimea, William Howard Russell, has also sent back vivid despatches from Balaclava. "When at last the guns went silent and the smoke was drifting from the valley", he wrote, "all that could be heard was the melancholy thud of the farriers' pistols as they went around despatching wounded horses".

Another Kentish man who took part in the Charge is Private Albert Mitchell of Norton Road, Southborough who rode with the 13th Lancers and was right in the first line of attack. "One of the first to be hit", he said, "was Captain Nolan who was galloping to the head of the line shouting and gesticulating as if trying to tell Lord Cardigan that he was never meant to charge up the valley. No-one heard him in the noise and Cardigan, in any case, was in no mood to listen. We all heard Nolan's fearful cry as he was hit. His charger galloped back through the ranks as Nolan fell dead from the saddle."

Mitchell wrote: "We were now very close to the guns for we were entering the smoke and I could see some of the gunners running from the front to the rear when a shell struck my horse...On my recovery I found my horse was lying on his left side. My left leg was beneath him but after a while I managed to free myself and stood up sword in hand. Lord Cardigan who had galloped clean through the Russian guns with his sabre held high came across me. "Where is your horse?", he asked. "Killed my lord", I replied. "Hurry back down the valley", he urged me. "Avoid being taken prisoner".

Private Mitchell escaped but Trooper Henry Boxall of the 4th Light Dragoons who rode alongside Wykeham Martin has been badly crippled. His horse was shot from under him and he was stabbed 14 times while he lay on the ground. He was left for dead but somehow his life clung to him and the Russians say he is now one of their prisoners of war. However, he was still breathing when the Russian Red Cross came onto the battlefield. They commendably dressed his wounds, set his leg and placed him on a baggage waggon with other British survivors.

Other Kentish men who somehow survived that terrible day include Trooper Sgt Edwin Leaney and Trooper Sgt Major John Mulcahy both of Maidstone. The military adventure in the Crimea is now seen as futile. Britain has blundered into a war with the Russians with the old enemy France as the most unlikely ally. The Charge of the Light Brigade is best summed up by General Boisquet who said: "C'est magnifique, mais ce n'est pas la guerre".

See page 145

The name of East Kent Yeomanry Cavalry has been changed to East Kent Mounted Rifles.

Lord Hardinge and William Gladstone have each planted a new yew tree at Betteshanger church.

Ship's Mate hurls live shell into sea

December: As Kent continues to play a key role in the war against Russia, news is reaching the county of an unbelievable act of courage in the Baltic by a 20-year-old ship's officer, Charles David Lucas.

On June 21 his ship, *HMS Hecla*, captained by William Hall of Mereworth found itself engaged in the bombardment of Bomarsund, a fort in the Aland Islands off Finland.

The fire was returned from the shore and at the height of the action, with a roar and a scream, a great live shell crashed onto the *Hecla's* quarter deck where young Mr Lucas stood directing his men. All hands were ordered to fling themselves flat on the deck but, as they did so and in the twinkling of an eye, the brave young mate seized the shell with both hands. With the fuse hissing in his face he hurled it into the sea.

England expects...The shell is hissing as young Charles Lucas picks it up and throws it into the sea. ***See page 149***

Almost before reaching the water the shell exploded with a terrific roar but its destructiveness was harmlessly spent on the dancing, sunlit waves. A trembling Lucas was immediately congratulated for his great presence of mind. No-one was wounded.

Among those which sailed to the Baltic and the Black Sea earlier this year were 156 wooden gunboats, 54 of which were built at Gravesend by the celebrated ship builders W and H Pitcher.

The *Prince Albert* is also on her way to join the Royal Navy fleet. She was launched by Queen Victoria on Saturday May 13 at Woolwich dockyard in front of 60,000 cheering spectators. The Queen and her consort were accompanied by the Princess Royal, the Prince of Wales and the Duchess of Kent and there were 60,000 spectators.

The royal party were given a guard of honour composed of cadets from the Royal Military Academy.

Action at sea in the Crimean War has been sporadic and Royal Navy commanders have been accused of lacking the Nelson touch.

Cholera now penetrates into 'deepest' Kent

December: The 'terrifying visitor' has returned to Kent with a vengeance. Cholera, which is killing so many soldiers in the Crimea, is also sweeping through Canterbury, Greenwich, Sheerness, Maidstone, Sevenoaks, Milton and Tunbridge Wells.

During the last two months 2,914 diarrhoea cases have been treated by Chatham dispensary and there are almost 2,000 cases in the 30 parishes of the Eastry Union.

A London physician, Dr John Snow, believes cholera is spread by contaminated water and to prove his point he has removed the handle from a public pump in Soho. No-one can now drink from that source and there are fewer fatalities in this area of London.

Not everyone accepts his ideas. Most people believe that the disease has spread from the Orient killing tens of thousands in Europe alone.

The most telling outbreak in Kent is at Sandgate where, to the consternation of all inhabitants, improvements have been made in drainage and water supply. Sanitary reformers have now discovered that the new drainage system is deficient and drains are blocked and leaking. It appears that all private water supplies are polluted.

Meanwhile, there are reports of more and more cases across Kent, including 170 in Tonbridge, which has co-incided with 900 cases of dysentery.Cholera has also penetrated far into the Kent countryside to places as remote as High Halden and Staplehurst.

The Canterbury dispensary has taken a lead by supplying free medicines. Folkestone is handing out handbills to the poor urging them to accept free treatment. *See page 171*

Corporal Harris meets 'the lady with the lamp'

January: Villagers of Harrietsham are mourning the death of Corporal William Harris who has died of cholera in the makeshift Crimean hospital at Scutari.

Harris fought at Balaclava with the Light Brigade, came through the Battle of Inkerman but suffered unspeakable agony late in November as the British force lost most of its winter supplies in a great snowstorm. Food was short, shelter almost non existent and, other than greatcoats there was no winter clothing.

Cholera raged and Harris was among the first to succumb. As men began dying like flies a British nurse, Florence Nightingale, who had arrived in Scutari in October last year with a team of 38 other nurses, began to perform her miracles. She found men dying, not only of cholera, but also of their wounds, dysentery and typhus. The sanitation was appalling.

As Harris lay in his hospital bed he would have seen Miss Nightingale at work in the daylight hours tending to the dying men and, at night, carrying her lamp through the disease ridden wards.

Miss Nightingale, escorted by a chaplain, a doctor, a Sergeant guard and eight Croats carrying baggage, climbs the steep path to the hut hospital at Balaclava. There are 12 hospital huts which stand against the limestone cliffs.

Buffs colours fly in Sevastopol

September 9: The allies are today in possession of Sevastopol following a British assault on the beseiged city in which the Buffs, the 97th (the Earl of Ulster's) Regiment and the Corps of the Royal Engineers played a crucial part.

The three parties provided the ladder party which was to force the way up the walls of the Redan and into the great fortress under a barrage of Russian bombs. The Buffs entered the city, quenched the fires and forced the enemy to evacuate. Theirs were the only British colours to fly in Sevastopol. With 260 ordered into the battle the Buffs lost 32 killed and 106 wounded.

Among the heroes are Major Maude, commanding the Buffs, who performed prodigies of valour from an advanced position and Private Connors who fought his way single handed through a ring of Russians to rescue an officer. A few days later he fell down an ancient rampart and was killed.

It was the 97th which met the full force of the Russian fire. Of 360 officers and men, 212 became casualties and there have been many acts of great gallantry. Sgt John Coleman remained in the open under sustained Russian fire until all around him had been killed or wounded. It was a episode of sustained and obstinate heroism. During the attack on the Redan, Captain Charles Lumley was among the first inside the fortress where he was immediately attacked by three Russian gunners. He shot two of them and was knocked down by a stone. Drawing his sword he vigorously urged his men forward until he collapsed from his wounds.

Royal Engineers win awards for gallantry

January 29: As the Crimean War draws to an end following the loss of Sevastopol and an an ultimatum from Austria, Queen Victoria has announced that she will institute an award for courage and bravery for all ranks of the armed services. Among those recommended to receive the Victoria Cross, alongside those from the Buffs and other units, are eight men of the Corps of the Royal Engineers, based at Brompton Barracks in Chatham. They are:

Corporal William James Lendrim, 25, who on February 14 last year superintended 150 French Chasseurs in building a new battery and replacing the gabions which had capsized. He worked under heavy fire.

Two months later Corporal Lendrim extinguished burning sandbags and was later one of four volunteers who destroyed the screen which the Russians had erected to conceal their advance rifle-pits.

Colour Sergeant Henry McDonald, a 31-year-old Scotsman, who took command at Sevastopol when eight of his fellow officers were wounded on April 19. He continued carrying on the sap notwithstanding the repeated attacks of the enemy.

Colour Sergeant Peter Leitch, 35, who on June 18 approached the redan with the leading ladders and formed a caponiére across the ditch as well as a ramp by fearlessly tearing down gabions from the parapet and placing and filling them until he was disabled from wounds.

The Engineers performed two more acts of bravery on the same day. **Lieutenant Howard Elphinstone** commanded a party of volunteers, who searched for the scaling ladders left behind after the repulse. He also conducted a search close to the enemy for wounded men.

While Lt Elphinstone was taking 20 wounded men back to the trenches, **Lieutenant Gerald Graham** and **Sapper John Perie** led a ladder party at the assault on the Redan. The two men also brought in the wounded, Perie suffering from a musket wound in the side.

By now the soldiers had learned that Lord Raglan, the Commander of the British forces, had succumbed to cholera, like many of his men. The Engineers, too, suffered their losses, but the acts of gallantry continued. On July 21 **Corporal John Ross**, 33, took a working party of 200 out at night. Each carried an entrenching tool. By morning they had connected the 4th parallel right attack with an old Russian rifle pit in front.

Finally, on November 20, **Lieutenant Wilbraham Lennox,** 24, entrenched his party of 100 men in rifle pits, which had just been captured from the enemy. Despite extreme exposure to attack they successfully repulsed all attempts to dislodge them during the night.

See page 149

Alfred, Lord Tennyson, Poet Laureate since 1850 and a favourite with both Victoria and Albert captured the national mood once again with his ode on the death of Wellington two years ago. His latest popular poem is called *The Charge of the Light Brigade* and it appeared in the *London Examiner* just six weeks after that epic feat near Balaclava.

Half a league, half a league,
Half a league onward,
All in the valley of Death
Rode the six hundred.
"Forward, the Light Brigade!
"Charge for the guns", he said:
Into the valley of Death
Rode the six hundred

"Forward the Light Brigade!"
Was there a man dismay'd?
Not tho' the soldier knew
Someone had blundered:
Their's not to make reply,
Their's not to reason why,
Their's but to do and die:
Into the Valley of Death
Rode the six hundred.

Cannon to the right of them,
Cannon to the left of them,
Cannon in front of them
Volley'd and thunder'd;
Storm'd at with shot and shell,
Boldly they rode and well,
Into the jaws of Death,
Into the mouth of Hell
Rode the six hundred.

Flash'd all their sabres bare,
Flash'd as they turn'd in air,
Sabring the gunners there,
Charging an army, while
All the world wonder'd:
Plunged in the battery smoke
Right thro' the line they broke:
Cossack and Russian
Reel'd from the sabre stroke
Shatter'd and sunder'd.
Then they rode back, but not
Not the six hundred

Cannon to the right of them,
Cannon to the left of them,
Cannon behind them
Volley'd and thunder'd;
Stormed at with shot and shell,
While horse and hero fell,
They that had fought so well,
Came thro' the jaws of Death
Back from the mouth of Hell,
All that was left of them,
Left of six hundred

When can their glory fade?
O the wild charge they made!
All the world wondered.
Honour the charge they made,
Honour the Light Brigade,
Noble six hundred.

Alfred Lord Tennyson

Henry Hardinge dies at Tunbridge Wells

September 24: Field Marshal Sir Henry Hardinge, former commander-in-chief of the British Army has died at South Park, his seat in Tunbridge Wells, aged 71. He will be buried in the neighbouring church of Fordcombe, the foundation stone of which he laid on his return from India and for which he had contributed the greater part of the building fund.

Sir Henry has been unwell for many months. He took much of the blame for the disasters of the Crimean War and, soon after attending the Queen at Aldershot to present the report of the Crimean Inquiry, he was stricken with paralysis and unable to retain his post.

He leaves a wife, Lady Emily, two sons and two daughters.

The 44th and 49th Regiments encamped at Archcliffe, Dover where an 18th century fort has been restored.

Three penny newspapers launched in Kent

May: Three growing communities now have new weekly newspapers thanks to the abolition of stamp duty on newspapers and the determination of radicals to encourage the provincial press. *The Sittingbourne and Faversham Gazette, The Ashford and Alfred News* and the *The Gravesend Reporter* are the pioneers of the penny papers in Kent and each one promises to "exert themselves for the benefit of ratepayers and inhabitants".

The lifting of the stamp duty has led to many arguments in Parliament. Many ministers want to suppress the "vile tyranny" of *The Times*, as Lord John Russell describes it. *The Times*, at 5d, sells 60,000 copies a day, four times all its serious rivals put together.

It has certainly angered the Government by its reporting in the Crimea. Since the stamp duty ended *The Manchester Guardian* has been made into a daily and *The Daily Telegraph* has been launched in London at 1d.

Proprietor of the *The Gravesend Reporter* is Thomas Morrel Blackie who believes the population of the town, currently 16,000, will continue to grow now the railway is so well established. In his first leading article he says his paper will be "conducted with spirit and independence and at a low price which will secure a large patronage".

He also says he will launch campaigns for the benefit of the community. He calls for a better drainage system and says he will give vehement support to the campaign to have early closing of shops one day a week.

A newspaper launched last year to serve the twin towns of Ashford and Alfred follows the opening of the Locomotive Establishment and the building of a new town to house its workpeople.

The same applies to Sittingbourne where great paper mills, cement and brick works and fruit preserving factories are well established. The railway has not yet arrived in this north Kent staging post.

See page 160

The bugler gives the signal and the Royal Engineers blow up the old bridge at Rochester.

Old Rochester bridge demolished by gunpowder

November : A new bridge at last spans the River Medway at Rochester. Designed and built by William Cubitt it was opened on August 13 when a procession of mayors and wardens walked across the new superstructure accompanied by a Royal Marine band. This was followed by a dinner at the Corn Exchange when plans were outlined for the removal of the old bridge which has stood for hundreds of years.

This has now been achieved in the most dramatic fashion — not by time but by gunpowder. Colonel Sandham, commanding officer of the Royal Engineers, decided he would assist in the demolition by experimenting with his mining and blasting techniques. After much preliminary work by Sappers and Miners, 500 pounds of powder was deposited at the base of each pier, arch and abutment and, with a bugler sounding the signal, several thousand tons of masonry came crashing into the river. Barges were on hand to remove the surplus stone and material.

The magnificent new road bridge completes the second instalment of Cubitt's contract for it sits alongside a separate railway bridge of iron construction on masonry piers which takes rail traffic through St Nicholas, Rochester, over the Medway to join the North Kent line in Strood.

A police force for Kent

January: Kent has responded positively to the new Act of Parliament which requires every borough and county in the kingdom to set up a local police force. This month a house in Maidstone, not far from All Saints' Church, has been taken over as police headquarters and Captain John Henry Ruxton appointed as Chief Constable. In his great task to bring law and order to the county, he will have the help of 222 officers and men.

There has been opposition to the new act. For those who live in villages and small towns, where everyone knows his or her neighbour, crime seems a less urgent problem compared to the city dwellers. London led the way with the Bow Street Runners in 1748 and the Metropolitan Police in 1829 and other cities slowly followed London's example.

Now the principle is to be extended and local authorities must provide professional forces.

For years the village constable has been responsible for law and order but until now he has been able to interpret the law according to the ideas of the local squire who was almost invariably the local magistrate and administration and penalties have varied from parish to parish.

This is no longer the case. Individualism is no longer encouraged but initiative is and in these days of great railway building people are moving out of their parishes for the first time. Travel is ceasing to be the privilege of the wealthy; but crime is also increasing and there needs to be a centralised police force.

The HQ in Maidstone is called Wren's Cross and is set in one acre of ground. There will be offices for administration and criminal investigation, barracks and training school, tailor's shop and stores and a few cells for local prisoners. There is also a parade ground and a paddock for the horses.

Captain Ruxton, a former army officer will be paid a salary of £400 a year. His force will be largely illiterate but he insists that his senior officers must be able to read and write. The training will be tough. The recruits include soldiers, sailors, clerks, mechanics and even mother's boys but for three months they will be drilled daily, take physical education, learn ju jitsu, attend divine service on a Sunday, learn how to dress smartly, drink only off duty and learn how to cook on the coal range. Of course they must be able to ride a horse. The doubtful ones will be sifted out early.

Difficult recruits will be hung out of one of the top windows at Wren's House until they have promised to mend their erring ways. Capt Ruxton says there will be no privacy but great fun. After three months he expects to have a fit and happy team of police officers who will carry a pocket guide full of practical advice.

Captain John Henry Ruxton, who lives at Broad Oak, Brenchley and travels to Wren's Cross from Paddock Wood railway station.

Ruxton appoints his supers

March 10: Alongside 12 superintendents, each to be in charge of a petty sessional division of Kent, Captain Ruxton has now appointed 17 sergeants and 185 constables. The constables will wear a blue frock coat with embroidery, sergeants will have the distinction of mohair lace on their braided collars and a superior quality greatcoat. Accommodation is provided for all men, the cost of which will be deducted from their wages.

For these physically sound and honest men the greatest attraction of the new force is that it offers economic security. However, there are no meal breaks, no such thing as regular hours and each recruit may be on duty for 24 hours a day.

The 12 superintendents are as follows: Bearsted: William Turrall, Rochester: Thomas Everist, Faversham: Thomas Maplestone Green, Wingham: William Stokes, Ashford: David Dewar, Tonbridge: Richard Dance, Malling: George Hilton, Cranbrook: Thomas Hazle, Home: William Walker, Sevenoaks: James Handley, Dartford: Christopher Brandon, Elham: Edwin Robins

See page 187

June 26: Charles Davis Lucas, a 26-year-old Mate on **HMS Hecla** *has become the first man to be awarded the Victoria Cross. He received his medal at Hyde Park in the presence of the Queen. Meanwhile, at Chatham, it has been announced that a Memorial Arch will be erected at Brompton Barracks to the officers and Sappers of the Royal Engineers who fell in the Russian War.*

Fire destroys last prison hulk

July 15th: The last of the English prison hulks has been destroyed by fire. Moored in the Thames off Woolwich Arsenal the conflagration occurred so suddenly that the convicts were lucky to escape with their lives. They have been transferred to an invalid ship alongside and will shortly be removed to the newly-built gaols at St Mary's Chatham and Woking.

The fire was reported by *The Times*: "It originated in the fore part of the ship where about 200 or 300 tons of coal were housed...Every part of the huge vessel was soon filled with smoke and the whole of the inmates were hastily removed...either from want of ventilation or some other cause, the entire body of fuel had become ignited, it is supposed by spontaneous combustion caused by the confinement of gas.

"The united fire brigades at the Royal Arsenal and the dockyard were promptly in attendance...It was not, however, extinguished for some hours. There's a probability of the fire having been occasioned by a spark from the pipe of one of the convicts picking oakum, although the regulations strictly forbid the use of tobacco..."

The *Defence* was the last prison hulk left in England. Its demise brings the end of a government penal system introduced about 75 years ago, the evils of which will echo around the country for many years to come.

About 10 years ago an anonymous writer on a visit to Woolwich Dockyard gave this description of a convict he saw brought from one of the hulks: "This grey old man, with sunken eye and dejected visage and form still portly, though stooping was once the Reverend Minister of a pious flock, the adviser and comforter of the aged. He is now a suborner of perjury, a forger and a convict...His father was a soldier who died of sickness without glory in some foreign land...His mother nursed him and starved herself to feed him. And this is her reward. The story may not be told, you can read it any day in the newspapers...."

A time ball at Deal for ships in the Downs

October: The Semaphore at Victoria Parade, Deal, which was built as part of an anti-smuggling campaign to pass signals to Customs patrols, has been converted into a Time Ball Tower. The ball drops at precisely 1 pm each day to indicate Greenwich Mean Time to ships in the Downs.

The introduction of the Time Ball is a great talking point in Deal and so is the renewal of the Pavement Act which gives new instructions to carriers of sedan chairs plying for hire and warns against the furious driving of horses, mares and geldings. Inhabitants have also been advised not to beat carpets in the streets and lanes after seven in the morning .

Deal prospered during the Napoleonic Wars when the streets thronged with soldiers and sailors and activities in the corn mills, warehouses and breweries prospered. Today rope making and sail making are the most successful occupations and a few straw hat makers are busy in the maze of small streets leading off from the beach.

In his book *Bleak House* published three years ago Dickens gave this description of Deal: "The long flat beach with its irregular houses, wooden and brick, its litter of capstans and great boats and sheds and upright poles with tackle and blocks— nothing else was moving but a few early rope-makers, who with the yarn twisted around their bodies, looked as if they were spinning themselves into cordage."

Dickens finds a new home — and a mistress

October: Charles Dickens and his wife Kate have agreed to separate after 21 years of a loveless marriage. Friends say he considers her "uninterested and uninteresting" and she is "hopelessly outgunned by his own dynamic personality".

It is believed that it was the birth of the couple's tenth child — "a compliment", said Dickens, "that I could well have dispensed with" — that settled the issue.

The author says the separation was more Kate's wish than his and he is hurt by "the most false, most monstrous, most cruel accusations" that an 18-year-old actress called Ellen Ternan is the object of his affections.

Ellen 'Nelly' Ternan came into the hardworking life of Charles Dickens like a breath of spring. She flattered him and enslaved him. He was 44 and she was 18.

Those close to Dickens believe his affair with Ellen was influenced by Wilkie Collins, the writer of mysteries, who has a reputation as a compulsive philanderer.

When Ellen was 16 and a struggling actress Dickens found her crying because she was being made to wear a costume she considered too revealing. Cynics say the tears were for the benefit of Dickens since she had worn the costume before.

The ruse worked. Dickens bought Ellen a house in Peckham and then wondered what he should do with Kate. Eventually it was decided that she should live in London with only restricted access to the children.

Two years ago the wealthy author moved back to the Rochester area, to a large house he had coveted as a boy. In a letter to a friend he has described that moment.

"Down at Gads Hill near Rochester is a quaint little country house of Queen Anne's time. I happened to be walking past a year and a half or so ago with my sub editor of *Household Words* when I said: 'You see that house. It has a curious interest for me because when I was a small boy down these parts I thought it the most beautiful house ever seen. And my poor father used to bring me to look at it and used to say that if ever I grew up to be a clever man perhaps I might own the house.

"We came back to town and my friend went out to dinner. Next morning he came in greatly excited and said 'It is written that you are to have Gads Hill Place. A lady had told me that her father was the rector and lived there for many years. He has just died and left it to me but I want to sell it' ".

Charles Dickens bought the house for £1,790 and knew he had found his spiritual home. He enjoys long walks in the countryside and likes to arrange weekend parties for his literary friends. Wilkie Collins is a frequent visitor and so is Hans Christian Andersen who stayed for several weeks.

Gads Hill Place which cost Dickens £1,790.

The author has acquired a wooden chalet and bought a travelling carriage, so heavy that its top speed is under 10 miles an hour. In this he has travelled through France and Italy, particularly enjoying Pisa ("unforgettably lovely") and Venice ("Venice is The Magnificent").

Having completed three more books — *Little Dorrit, Bleak House* and *The Tale of Two Cities* — Dickens has put his pen down to spend more time on the stage. He gives readings of his most famous passages, acting each part with great drama and hypnotises his audiences with his enthusiasm and energy. "I am", he says, "incapable of rest". *See page 168*

Kent mourns heroes of the Indian mutiny

November 24: General Henry Havelock, acting commander of the British army in India, may have quelled a series of uprisings and riots in India but he has been unable to defeat an attack of diarrhoea.

The hero of the long seige of Lucknow and a man whose name is on every English tongue was buried today at the Alumbagh. On the day of his death he told his soldier son: "See how a Christian can die".

As a young boy the general spent his boyhood years at Ingress Abbey, Greenhithe — a gothic manor house rebuilt in 1838 with masonry from the old London Bridge.

The sweeping lawns that led down to the river at Greenhithe must have seemed a long way off for General Havelock as he and a handful of troops held out at Lucknow from September last year until March when reinforcements finally arrived. Today, peace has been restored and Queen Victoria once again rules this vast, unsettled, undisciplined country.

The uprising began in May last year when Indian soldiers mutineered against their British officers. The mutiny spread widely among the 250,000 Indian troops. Hundreds of British soldiers were hacked to pieces and many taken prisoner. Lucknow and Cawnpore were among the garrisons under seige. One of those slain at Cawnpore was a 20-year-old Kentish man from Squerryes House, Westerham, Henry John Warde. He was just 20.

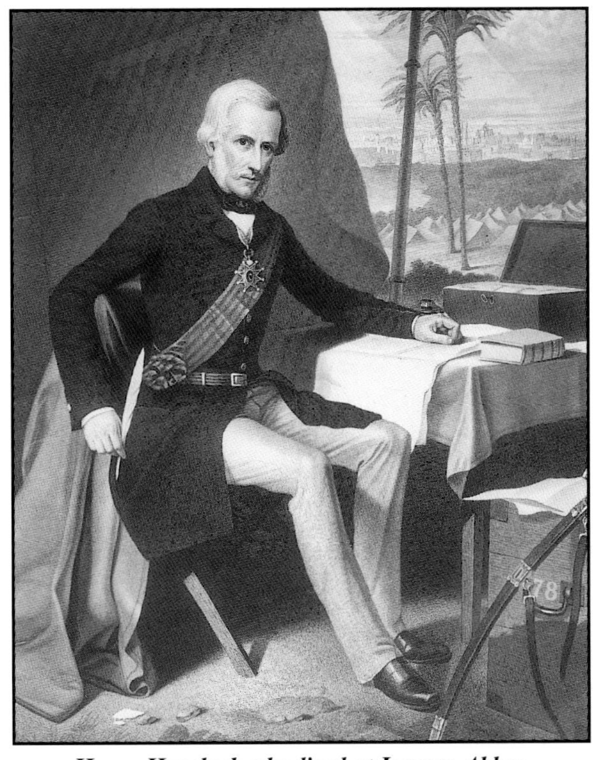

Henry Havelock who lived at Ingress Abbey.

Survivors of Cawnpore are full of admiration for young Warde. He never left his post during the three-month siege and, regardless of his own wounds, insisted on rescuing women and children and many of the wounded from the burning barracks. It was an Indian prince, Nana Sahib — blamed for the worst atrocities— who ordered the massacre of Warde and about 200 other prisoners. Their bodies were tossed into a well.

For many days the British public were unaware of Havelock's death. During this period parliament promoted him to the rank of major-general and he was created a baron. Then came news of his death. It plunged the nation into mourning and money is being collected by public subscription for a statue in Trafalgar Square.

Henry John Warde is the second Westerham soldier to die a hero's death on the battlefield. In 1759 General James Wolfe was killed as he led his troops up the heights of Abraham and captured Quebec.

Corporal Michael Sleavon, 31, of the Corps of the Royal Engineers has been awarded the Victoria Cross for maintaining his position at the head of a sap and working under heavy fire with cool determination during an attack on the fort at Jhansi.

Parliament polluted by the Great Stink

June 18: Yesterday afternoon, on one of the hottest days of a sweltering summer, the stink of sewage from the polluted Thames was so obnoxious that it drove Members of Parliament from the chamber of the House of Commons.

The Times describes it as "The Great Stink" and in a leading article today said: "A few members bent upon investigating the matter to its very depth, ventured into the library, but they were instantly driven to retreat, each man with a hankerchief to his nose. We are heartily glad of it."

For many years now sewage from two million Londoners has been pouring into the river where it is carried to and fro by the ebb and flow of the tides. Even those who live near the banks of the Thames in Woolwich, Erith and Dartford find the smell offensive and have repeatedly called upon Parliament to improve London's primitive system of sanitation. *See page 161*

Alfred Mynn, who retired this year after playing 99 matches for Kent, is pictured here with Nicholas Felix, whose real name was Wanostrocht. A brilliant batsman who once scored 1095 for England he was also a brilliant musician, artist and band leader. Last year a testimonial match was played in his honour.

Three Derby winners for the 'lucky baronet'

NO patron of the turf has ever matched the extraordinary feats of Sir Joseph Hawley of Leybourne Grange, near Maidstone. This year he has won the Derby Stakes for the third time in eight years and is on course to become the most successful horse breeder in the history of the sport.

Hawley, born at Harley Street in 1813, served in the army and devoted himself to yachting before taking an interest in horses.

While living in Florence he imported some horses from England and ran them at various meetings in Italy with some success. On his return to England he registered his famous black and white cap in the 'Calendar'and, in 1844, served as High Sheriff for Kent.

His turf career took off in 1847 when Sim Templeman won the Oaks for him on *Miami.* Four years later *Teddington* won the Derby. About this time he purchased *Mendicant* for 3,000 guineas and last year saw her son *Beadsman* win the Derby.

By this time Hawley had gained the nickname of the 'lucky baronet'. His filly *Aphrodite* romped home in the One Thousand Guineas and *Fitzroland* added the Two Thousand Guineas. This week he was a Derby winner again when *Musjid* was the triumphant horse.

Hawley spares no pains in the selection of his stud and from his vast stables in Leybourne has done much to improve the breed of horses.

Glory days over: Kent seek players for a new club

March 19: A new Kent Cricket Club has been formed, not in opposition to the existing one but to supplement it and look after cricket in general. Lord Darnley is President and of the seven committee members six have played for Kent.

The reason for the new club is twofold. The glory days of Fuller Pilch and Alfred Mynn have passed and Kent is in the doldrums. Many skilful amateur cricketers prefer to play for I Zingari or West Kent and turn out for the full county side only during the Canterbury Week which stands on a footing of its own.

C.J.Ottaway who has played five times for the Gentlemen but only twice for Kent said: "There is no great honour in representing a side that was scouring the highways and hedges for players and was constantly defeated".

The new club has been formed on the initiative of brothers Edward and Henry Bligh. The meeting at the Mitre Hotel, Maidstone resolved that matches should not be confined to any particular locality and will be played without the assistance of 'given men'.

The second reason for the new club is that the county, as its stands, is no longer a sufficient draw in Canterbury Week. In matches against England, Kent play with 13, 14 or even 15 men and spectators prefer I Zingari v Gentlemen or North v South.

The county sank so low in popular estimation that the Week was in danger of being dissolved and Canterbury foresaw a considerable loss of trade.

They supported the move to sack the committee, start again and attract, as players, some of the outstanding amateurs and a few lively professionals — from both halves of the county.

See page 163

Life has evolved over millions of years, says Darwin

December 24: Charles Darwin knew it would be controversial and he is not mistaken. His book *On the Origin of Species by Means of Natural Selection*, published one month ago, has had such a tremendous impact on religious thought that Christians throughout the country are saying that it contradicts the *Book of Genesis* and should be banned from the bookshops.

It is a little late for that. All 1,250 copies of the book, published by John Murray, sold out in advance and hundreds of people are waiting anxiously for a reprint.

Darwin has been working on his book ever since he returned as a naturalist from the British Science expedition, aboard *HMS Beagle*, in 1836.

Like a few intellectuals before him he believes that all the life on earth evolved over millions of years from a few common ancestors.

Many of today's scientists agree. They believe Darwin's work constitutes probably the most coherent theory of evolution yet developed. They refuse to agree with conservative clerics that it undermines religious belief.

Darwin refuses to talk about the theological and sociological aspects of his work except to say that his research has been thorough and he has collected many specimens to help prove his several related theories.

He said recently. "One, evolution did occur; two, evolutionary change was gradual, requiring thousands to millions of years; three, the primary mechanism for evolution was a process called natural selection; and four, the millions of species alive today rose from a single original life form through a branching process called 'specialisation' ". The arguments rage on.

See page 159

HMS Beagle, ***the three-masted brig which took Darwin around the southern oceans between 1831 and 1836. The brig was 100 feet long and carried ten cannons and 74 people. There was very little space.***

Wilkie and the Woman in White

October: Encouraged by his great friend, Charles Dickens — who likes to serialise good detective stories in his magazine *Household Words* — Wilkie Collins has now written a book which has all the ingredients of being a monumental best seller. It is entitled *The Woman in White* and is hailed as an admirable though melodramatic tale.

Collins has been working on the book for many months while staying at Church Hill Cottage, an isolated cottage on the Ramsgate Road near Broadstairs. Not far away is the North Foreland lighthouse and it is known that the visual effects of the lighthouse on a foggy night has much to do with the spine-chilling appearance of *The Woman in White.*

The author, now 35, first came to Ramsgate as a small child with his parents in 1929 when they stayed at Sion Row. On their next visit some years later the family stayed at Albion Street but Mr William Collins was so appalled by the state of the lodgings that he hired a wheelbarrow and pushed all their belongings to another house round the corner at 4 Plains of Waterloo.

See page 177.

After the terrible massacres by Indian mutineers and equally bloody reprisals by British troops, peace has returned to India and the soldiers are coming home. Here, they are seen disembarking at the port of Gravesend last year.

The Tunbridge Wells and Hastings railway as it enters the spa town of Tunbridge Wells.

Railway rivalry intense as the London Chatham and Dover Company is born

September: The East Kent Railway Company, which was formed six years ago to build a line from Strood, through the fertile orchards of North Kent to the ancient town of Faversham, has now changed its name to the London Chatham and Dover Railway and promises to provide a service to Dover — faster and more efficient than SER's Weald of Kent route.

Here, say the LCDR directors, a new steamer service to Calais will be opened — enabling them to undercut the SER's journey time between London and Dover and give them a chance of obtaining the lucrative European mail contract. The South Eastern directors are bitter; the rivalry intense.

The architects behind the LCDR's ambitious plans are the railway speculators, Sir Morton Peto and Sir Charles Fox. Peto has already built many fine lines for the SER including Paddock Wood to Maidstone. He, more than anyone, was the man responsible for bringing prosperity to Folkestone and the towering Foord Viaduct stands as a fitting memorial.

Morton Peto has now offered his great benevolence to the "opposition". Skilful in turning the most rugged and pugnacious Irish navvies into an efficient working party he has already encouraged the LCDR directors to link Strood with Bromley via Swanley where it will join the Mid Kent Railway, terminating at Pimlico via Crystal Palace.

The London connection gave the East Kent Railway Company the impetus to find a new name. Hence the birth of the London Chatham and Dover.

For years now Navigators' Camps have been a feature of life throughout Kent. Stories of squalor and sickness, of violence and debauchery abound and questions have been raised in Parliament about the terrible conditions under which the men work. "This", says Morton Peto, "will not be allowed in my camps".

The railway mogul promises to outlaw "Tommy shops" where work vouchers have been exchanged for low standard food sold at exorbitant prices. He wants to control the availability of alcohol and, in return, promises fair pay and comfortable accommodation.

As the frenzy to acquire railway shares continues,

continued on page 156

Volunteer Corps reborn in Kent

December: Kent's civilian army is being raised once more. Napoleon III's sudden antagonism towards England, the helpless state of the nation (should he decide to invade) and the patriotism, which remains as strong as ever, has rekindled a new determination to defend our shores. The Volunteer Movement is being reborn.

In the last few months meetings have been held throughout Kent with Rifle or Artillery Corps raised independently in almost every town. The county is determined to give practical evidence of its loyalty although the military authorities are treating this new-found enthusiasm with much contempt.

The leaders mean business. Each Corps has been formed with the help of local subscriptions with the members themselves contributing towards the funds. These patriots have promised to devote time, fortune, energy and even their lives to protect their country. They know the French cannot be trusted.

The Volunteers were active during the Napoleonic Wars but after Waterloo they disbanded and drifted into civilian life. As the French threaten again, leading inhabitants of most towns are determined to take active steps in reviving the movement.

Sevenoaks has been one of the first towns to act. Three months ago Earl Amherst called a public meeting at the Crown Hotel and invited young, active men of the district to come along. Among the 40 who signed in was Bill Bass, a fishmonger aged 52.

The first officer is Multon Lambarde, the first Lieutenant Nelson Rycroft and the Ensign is the Earl of Brecknock whose family resides at the Wildernesse, a large mansion near Seal. Mr John Bligh, a brewer, has given use of his drying house in the High Street for drills.

Farnborough has also raised a company. So has Tonbridge, Tunbridge Wells, Penshurst and Westerham. These, it is hoped, will form a battalion with a commanding officer to be elected. Field officers and adjutants need to be appointed and rules laid down. There is much work to do. *See page 160*

Railway mania here to stay *(continued)*

Parliament is busy passing more and more Railway Acts. In one year alone — between 1845-6 — 280 Acts were passed allowing the construction of 4,450 miles of track in England. Fortunes are being made across the country and wealth is arriving in small communities that were once little more than forgotten backwaters. Little wonder they call it railway mania.

Tonbridge, the first town in Kent to get a railway station, has already become a thriving market town offering a diverse range of employment such as tar distilling, printing, sheepskin rug making and even cricket ball production.

Maidstone Road (now called Paddock Wood) is a centre for canning and the storage and packing of fruit. Hop pickers, who take advantage of the cheap fares, have adopted this community as their main hopping outpost.

In the county town of Maidstone — which remained "anti-railway" for so many years and where the mayor once warned that the "iron road" would ruin trade — brewing, paper making and engineering companies are thriving and new factories are being built along the banks of the Medway. Ashford is growing, thanks to its new town and the great loco works and the Thanet resorts are growing in popularity.

One sad note. Isambard Kingdom Brunel, perhaps the greatest engineer in history, has died at the age of 53. He worked with his father Sir Marc Brunel on the Thames Tunnel which opened in 1843 and later became chief engineer to the Great Western Railway. He designed many stations and bridges including Paddington and the spectacular suspension bridge over the River Avon at Clifton.

His ships included the *Great Britain, The Great Eastern and the Great Western.* Brunel revolutionised iron-clad construction, screw propulsion and the use of steam power. *See page 163*

Railway lines now open in Kent with the completion dates are:

1830 Canterbury to Whitstable
1836 London to Greenwich
1842 Redhill to Ashford
1843 Ashford to Folkestone
1844 Folkestone to Dover
1844 Paddock Wood to Maidstone
1845 Tonbridge to Tunbridge Wells
1846 Rochester to Gravesend
1846 Ashford to Canterbury
1846 Canterbury to Ramsgate
1846 Broadstairs to Margate
1847 Deal to Sandwich and Richborough
1849 Greenwich to Dartford and Gravesend
1851 Ashford to Hastings via Rye
1851 Tunbridge Wells to Robertsbridge
1856 Maidstone to Rochester
1858 Strood, Rochester, Chatham and Gillingham to Faversham.

Under construction

Faversham to Canterbury via Whitstable
London to Chatham via Swanley
Canterbury to Dover
Swanley to Sevenoaks

1860-1869

1860: Beijing surrenders to an Anglo-French expeditionary force following more than 20 years of intermittent hostilities over the exclusion of Europeans from Chinese soil.

June 17: *The Great Eastern*, the largest ship afloat, designed by the late Isambard Kingdom Brunel sets off on the first transatlantic voyage to New York.

A rugby club is founded at Blackheath.

1861: Charles Blondin, the tightrope walker, who walked across Niagara Falls, gives a performance of dare-devil stunts at the Crystal Palace.

Earl Russell, the Foreign Secretary, says Britain will follow a policy of neutrality as civil war divides the United States between North and South.

1862: Earl Stanhope of Chevening erects a seat in grounds of Holwood House, Keston telling of the meeting between Wilberforce and Pitt which led to the abolition of slavery.

The people of Kent are divided in their support of the civil war in America. The anti-slave supporters sympathise with the Yankies but many others support the Confederate cause because of the importance of cotton.

September 5: Henry Coxwell, an aeronaut and James Glaisher, a meteorologist achieve a record height of 29,000 feet in a balloon flight.

See page 171

September 6: Archbishop John Bird Sumner dies at Addington. He will be succeeded by Charles Thomas Langley.

A new bridge over the Thames opens at Westminster.

Gilbert Scott designs a memorial to Prince Albert who died in December last year. It will stand opposite the Albert Hall which is under construction.

New churches consecrated this year are St John's, Blackheath, St James, Gravesend and Holy Trinity, Mark Beech.

1863: March: The Prince of Wales marries Princess Alexandra, 18-year-old daughter of Prince Christian of Denmark.

An asylum for the criminally insane opens at Broadmoor, Crowthorne, Berkshire.

December: William Makepeace Thackeray dies aged 53. He has rivalled Charles Dickens for popularity for many years.

1864: January 11: A railway station opens at Charing Cross.

Karl Marx, the exiled German philosopher helps to form the International Working Mens' Association in London.

1865: Lord Palmerston dies in his 81st year. Queen Victoria writes: "Strange, and solemn to think of that strong, determined man, with so much worldly ambition, gone." The new premier is John, Lord Russell.

February 6: Isabella Beeton, the author of the sensational book on household management, dies at Greenhithe from puerperal fever, six days after the birth of her fourth child.

July: The Matterhorn in Switzerland is conquered by a British team. Tragically three of them and one Alpine guide are killed during the descent.

Work on the Western Heights at Dover is completed with casemated barracks built into the walls of the moats and galleries and bridges of communication constructed. These strategic modifications are introduced to combat technological advances in heavier artillery which the French now possess.

1866: *The Great Eastern* successfully lays a transatlantic telegraph cable under the Atlantic Ocean.

A mass protest of several thousand marchers, calling for electoral reform, advances on Hyde Park. The issue has already led to the resignation of Lord Russell as Prime Minister.

September: A new railway station opens at Cannon Street.

Queen Victoria creates her second son Duke of Kent.

1867: July: British working men with an established place of residence receive the right to vote in a second Reform Bill passed under a minority Tory administration led by Lord Derby. It is no longer necessary to be a significant property holder.

July 1: The new Dominion of Canada came into being today. Four provinces will form a self-governing administration.

August: Michael Faraday, 75, pioneer of electricity, dies at Hampton Court in a house provided by Queen Victoria.

1868: May: The last public execution takes place at the Old Bailey. Michael Barratt is hanged for his part in a Fenian explosion at Clerkenwell in which 12 people died.

Archbishop Charles Thomas Langley dies at Addington. He is suceeded by Archibald Campbell Tait,Bishop of London.

New churches are consecrated at St Mary's, Shortlands, Bromley and St Marks, New Brompton.

Geraldine Jewsbury, a novelist famous the the book, *Zoe,* moves to Walnut Tree House, Sevenoaks.

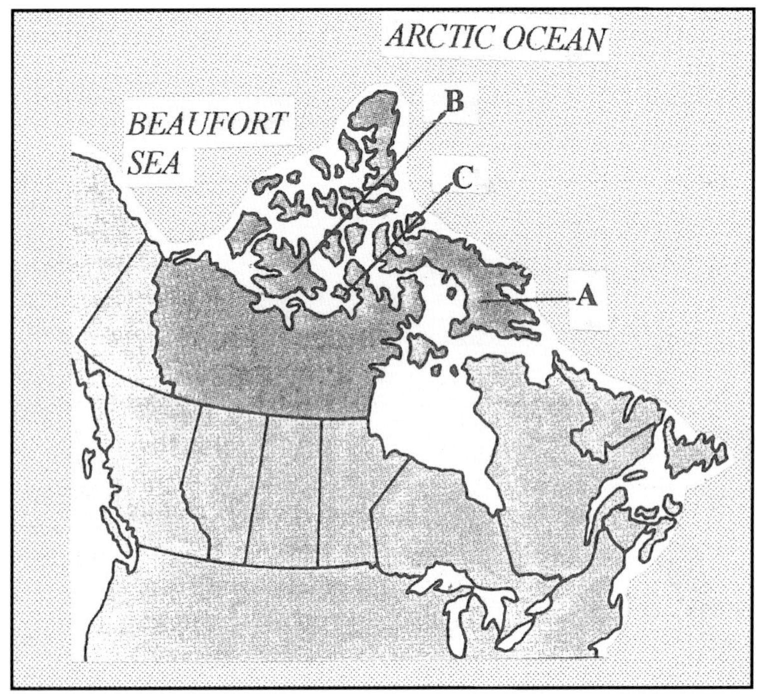

It is through this labyrinth of islands between the mainland of Canada and the North Pole that Franklin and his crew sailed in their tragic yet victorious mission to find the elusive North-West Passage. Baffin Island (A), twice the size of Great Britain, is the largest, Victoria Island (B) is above the mainland and King William's Land (C) is where many of the party perished

Rail goes underground

AN underground railway, called the Metropolitan line, is under construction in London. It will run for four miles linking Paddington, Euston and King's Cross stations with a terminus near Smithfield. No buildings will be demolished; the railway will be built mainly underground.

Franklin perished with crew after finding the North-West Passage

January: It has now been confirmed that Rear Admiral Sir John Franklin discovered the North-West Passage but died in the course of the exploration.

The Arctic explorer, who left Greenhithe in May 1845, was last seen in Baffin Bay on July 25 or 26 of that year. When nothing more was heard of the party no less than 40 expeditions were sent to find him.

Last year a search vessel fitted out by Lady Franklin under the command of Captain Leopold McClintock came upon distinct traces of the lost expedition. Numerous relics were then found — a boat, a few skeletons, chronometers, clothing and instruments.

Also discovered in a cairn was a written paper confirming Franklin's death and the fact that he had found the strait separating King William's Land from Victoria Land but was unable to sail right through it.

McClintock, now back in London, has been able to put together the incredible story. Twelve miles off the northern extremity of King William's Land, Franklin's progress was halted by ice and his ships *Erebus* and *Terror* wintered at Beechey Island.

From the Eskimos, McClintock learned that one of the ships sank in deep water and the other, much broken, was forced on shore. There was no further news of the men and it became clear that every soul of the party had perished miserably, some earlier on King William's Land, some "falling down and dying as they walked" — as an old woman Eskimo told McClintock — many on the mainland by the Great Fish River.

Franklin, to the delight of his proud but grieving family, has been officially recognised as the discoverer of the North-West passage and that will be styled on the pedestal of the statue in his memory which is being erected at public cost in Waterloo Place, London.

The explorer has been described as a man of iron resolve, indomitable courage and a simplicity which kindled the warmest affection in his comrades and subordinates. He leaves a wife and a daughter by his first marriage.

Advent Sunday: A unified hymn book has been used by the Church of England for the first time. Called Hymns Ancient and Modern it arose from the efforts of Canon Francis Murray, rector of Chislehurst.

July 9: The London, Chatham and Dover railway is extended to Sheerness and then on to Canterbury East.

The Northfleet shipyard of William Pitcher has closed. The dry docks will be filled and the site occupied eventually by an industrial unit. The castellated gateway built from the stones of London Bridge will remain.

New churches opened this year are St Thomas, Southborough and St Paul's, Swanley.

The Red House — superb views over the Cray Valley.

Bexleyheath welcomes poet-socialist with a vision

William Morris, the renowned designer, poet, entrepreneur and socialist, has moved into a magnificent new house at Bexleyheath which has been specially built in a simple, medieval-based style and commands superb views over the Cray Valley.

There with Jane Burden, his wife of two years, and his new company Morris and Co he will continue to produce embroideries, wallpapers, stained glass, textiles of all kinds and furniture all made to his high standard of craftsmanship.

Morris is a leading member of the Pre-Raphaelite Brotherhood who have set themselves up to create art which expresses important ideas and derives from a direct study of nature. His vision of a pre-industrial Utopia owes much to the influence of his friend John Ruskin, the art critic.

He is also a socialist and believes that all men should be living in equality of condition and should manage their affairs unwastefully, and with the full consciousness that harm to one would mean harm to all. Morris calls this "commonwealth". Only recently he wrote: "What I mean by socialism is a condition of society in which there should be neither rich, nor poor, neither master nor master's man, neither idle nor overworked...."

Meanwhile Morris and his pre-Raphaelite circle are busy decorating his new home in a style which one has described as "more of a poem than a house". The floors are of plain tile and the staircase is simple. Burne-Jones paintings of medieval scenes are on the drawing room walls and Morris' own stained-glass windows are in evidence.

Morris has given each member of the Pre-Raphaelite circle a share in his new company which aims to foster an appreciation of the fine arts.

See page 200

Bishop attacks Darwin's theory of evolution

CHURCHMEN all over England are attacking the theory of evolution as advocated by Charles Darwin in his book, the *Origin of Species.*

Soon after it was published Samuel Wilberforce, the Bishop of Oxford, attacked Darwin's "atheistic" principles and challenged those who believed in evolution to join him in debate.

That debate has now been held, polarising public opinion between science and religion. Darwin's views contradict many established patterns of thought.

During the debate at Oxford the scientist found one outspoken champion in Thomas Huxley who told Bishop Wilberforce that many years of detailed study had preceded Darwin's findings. "Contrast these", he said, "to the lack of evidence which you offer".

The Bishop, seemingly undaunted by this criticism replied to Huxley: "Are you descended from a monkey on your grandmother's or grandfather's side?".

As science and religion battle it out, more and more people are coming to the conclusion that humans are one species among many that have evolved from a more primitive one.

See page 208

Iron ship is launched on the Thames: the first of many

December 29: A new ship, launched on the Thames at Blackwall today, has a hull made — not just of wood — but iron as well.

HMS Warrior is the Royal Navy's first "iron ship". Classified as a steam frigate, she displaces 9,200 tonnes and is 65 metres long.

During the Crimean War it was discovered that wooden warships could not stand up to the modern high explosive shell but it was the French who took the lead two years ago by launching the ironclad frigate *Gloire* and then laid down four more similar vessels. The hull of the *Warrior* is teak with 4.5inch iron plates bolted to it.

See page 165

Kent beware — the French are restless

Almost ready: The new barracks at Western Heights, Dover.

March: All seven battalions of the Kent Volunteer Corps are now in place thanks to meticulous planning by the leading spirits throughout the county. Each battalion is divided into several companies with a Lieutenant-Colonel as commanding officer.

Among them is Lt-Col Viscount Hardinge who says the men will prove themselves capable of manoeuvring with the precision of regulars. "In time they will develop into a great national institution".

Meanwhile concern about a French invasion continues to grow. Several iron-clad warships are lying at anchor in Cherbourg Harbour and they bring the question of English defence sharply into focus.

Last year, under the direction of Lord Palmerston, a Royal Commission found the existing defences at Dover were "imperfect".

Within months of the publication of the commission's report a new building project was under way on the Western Heights.

Unemployed men from all parts of the United Kingdom have been encouraged to migrate to Dover to excavate deep dry moats at the North and South Lines and the land between the Citadel and the Redoubt.

The work will take many months, perhaps years, but it will include casemented barracks, built into the walls of the moats and the construction of galleries and bridges of communication.

One of the principle features of the fortifications is the Citadel which is situated 100 feet higher than the Drop Redoubt and will serve the same function as the Keep in a Norman Castle.

The activity on the Heights is impressive. Up to a 1,000 additional barracks have already been erected to help accommodate the five regiments, who were required to live under canvas when they returned from the Crimea War some five years ago. The barracks have been built in a huge ditch excavated out of the side of the hill overlooking the sea. The bombproof buildings are connected to the hill behind by a cast iron bridge.

For the married soldiers it is proposed to erect a crescent of detached cottages in Hospital Meadow.

More local newspapers as excise duty is abolished

October 1: Thousands of people in Kent will soon be able to read daily and weekly newspapers now that the excise duty on paper — or "tax on knowledge"— has been abolished.

With effect from today all newspaper prices are expected to fall, including *The Times* and that means they will no longer be the preserve of the privileged few.

Two new newspapers in Kent, both founded last year, are *The Maidstone Telegraph* and *The Chatham News.* Available each week on a Thursday morning they are a mix of local and national news together with many interesting letters from readers. It was eight years ago that duty on advertisements was abolished followed two years later by the abolition of the stamp duty.

Bryan Donkin, who set up a canning factory for preserving foodstuff with his father-in-law John Hall, is now leading the way in the manufacture of paper. The former Dartford apprentice has now installed 191 papermaking machines in Britain and Northern Ireland.

In Kent the papermaking industry is expanding on a large scale at Dartford, Northfleet and Sittingbourne — all conveniently placed for the import of logs and wood pulp from the Baltic and from Canada.

6,500 Crimean patients pass through St Mary's

November: Florence Nightingale, a national heroine since her selfless work tending the wounded during the Crimean War, has set up a training school for nurses in St Thomas's hospital. The public has contributed thousands of pounds.

As a government adviser on hospital reform, she plans to lay down strict rules for her nurses. She said "They must be fully literate, sober, honest, orderly, clean and neat".

Many hospitals in Britain are still bleak and unhealthy institutions and Miss Nightingale who comes from a wealthy family is contributing generously to all those planning to improve sanitation and hygiene.

The great lady this week sent money to a relief fund which has been set up in Gillingham to help the sick and wounded of the Crimean War.

Since January this year more than 6,500 men have passed through St Mary's Invalid Depot.

Many have no supplementary assistance and some of the married men have been left with about 3d a day to support themselves and their families.

Prince Albert dies of typhoid — aged 42

December 15:* *A few months ago Queen Victoria and Prince Albert visited the wounded and dying at St Mary's Hospital, Chatham and then went on to comfort those at Fort Pitt. Yesterday evening, with his family at his bedside, the 42-year-old Prince Albert himself died of typhoid. Queen Victoria is inconsolable. When Prince Albert married Victoria in 1839 he was mocked by* **Punch** *and treated with suspicion by Parliament but he earned the respect of the nation by hard work, modernising the Army and improving conditions in working class homes. He worked closely with Augustus Pugin, who designed the interior of the Houses of Parliament and encouraged museums, colleges and art galleries to open in South Kensington.

His greatest triumph was the creation of the1851 Exhibition.

Engineer's plan to clean the Thames

JOSEPH Bazalgette, chief engineer to the Metropolitan Board of Works, has been entrusted by Parliament with the task of building a system of intersecting sewers, pumping stations and treatment works in an effort to prevent London's sewage from polluting the Thames.

It is a massive project that will cost in excess of £2million and he wants to build with Portland cement from Northfleet.

If he, in the process of this task, can cleanse the River Thames and banish cholera which has already carried off approximately 40,000 Londoners in the last 15 years, then he will transform the standard of living in the capital. *See page 170*

Although Earl Russell, the Foreign Secretary, has said that Britain will follow a policy of neutrality, many people from Kent are privately supporting the Yankies in the civil war which divides the United States between north and south.

British sympathies are with the slaves. *Uncle Tom's Cabin* has sold more books in Britain than in America.

New churches are All Saints, Higham, Highgate and Hawkhurst and St Paul's, Maidstone. The churches of St Mary-in-the-Castle, Dover and St Margaret's, Canterbury have been restored.

The latest novel from the prolific pen of Charles Dickens is *Great Expectations*. It is being published in instalments in the periodical, *All The Year Round.*

A Royal Marines Depot has been established at Deal.

A daughter for the diplomat and Spanish dancing queen

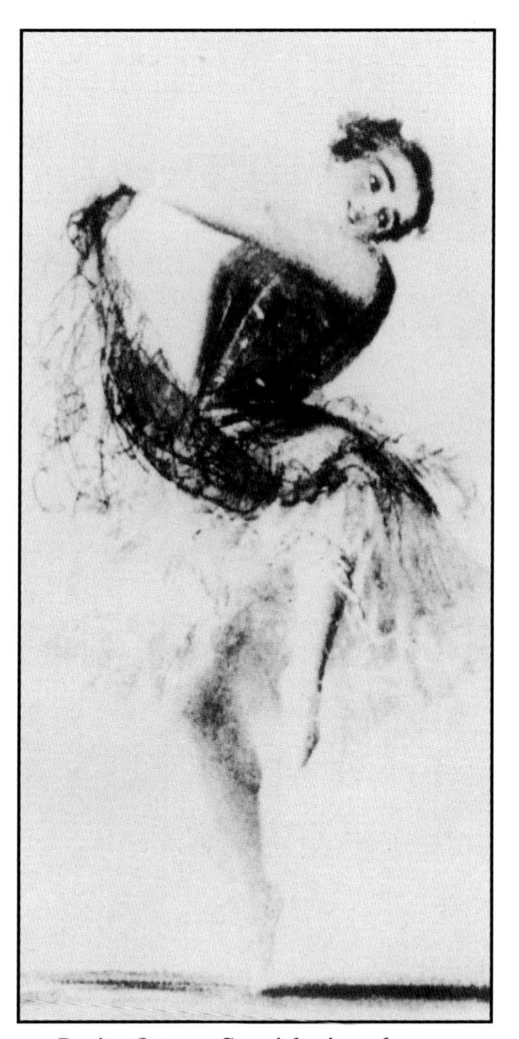

Pepita Ortega, Spanish gipsy dancer.

September 23: Miss Pepita Ortega, a beautiful Spanish gipsy dancer, gave birth in Paris today to a daughter, Victoria. Nothing really surprising about that except that Pepita is the mistress of a British diplomat, who is heir to one of the largest and most historic English country houses — Knole at Sevenoaks in Kent.

How the young aristocratic attaché serving Her Majesty's Government at the British Legation in Stuttgart and the internationally-acclaimed dancer have managed a private life together has been the subject of gossip in blue-blooded European circles for more than 10 years.

It was in 1852 that the Hon Lionel Sackville-West came to Paris for a week's leave and went to the theatre. There he met and fell instantly in love with Pepita, a beautiful girl with long chestnut hair who had already packed the theatres in Germany, Austria, Denmark and Spain. Lionel said she danced like "a bird in the air".

She was the 22-year-old daughter of a stage-struck washerwoman from Malaga who wanted something better in life and encouraged Pepita to train as a ballet dancer. In time she became known as the 'Star of Andalusia'.

He was the 25-year-old son of the fifth Earl de la Warr of Buckhurst, Withyham but on course to become Baron Sackville of Knole. Of medium build, with deeply hooded blue eyes, he is reticent, cautious and outwardly conventional.

The couple spent every night of that intoxicating first week together and have been together ever since. When Lionel was moved to another post he took Pepita with him — to Heidelberg, Hackenfeldt, Como, Genoa and Arona on Lake Maggiore.

Sadly, Lionel cannot marry Pepita because she already has a husband, Juan Antonio de Oliva. Their Catholic marriage had lasted only a few months but under Spanish law divorce is not an option.

Somehow the Foreign Office turns a blind eye to Lionel's double life. He is a conscientious diplomat who carries out his official duties with great skill. In London his liaison remains undiscovered.

Victoria is the second child to be born illegitimately to Lionel and Pepita. The first, Max was born in 1858. *See page 212*

Good news for Kent's hop farmers. The duty on hops has been abolished. *See page 172*

Wingham mourns a 'freedom fighter'

NEWS has reached Canterbury that William Miller has died at sea under the British flag. He was 67 and will always be remembered for the part he played in the liberation of the British colonies in South America.

Born in Wingham in 1795, William Miller joined the army at 16, took part in all the great battles of the Peninsular War and sailed to South America. In Peru he fought alongside Bolivar the Liberator and helped to free the country from Spanish control.

Bolivar, in gratitude, made him general of all the Peruvian cavalry and commander of the entire army. Miller gained many astounding victories.

His military work done, Miller returned home to Canterbury, received a hero's welcome and was given the freedom of the city. It was an appropriate honour for a great and famous warrior. Sadly, political differences drove him away again and he returned to Callao as a representative of the British Government.

Canterbury learned this week that William Miller's body was borne ashore at Bella Vista while the bells of the churches tolled requiem.

Cricketers mourn the 'lion of Kent'

June: Future Kent cricketers who need financial help may be able to benefit from a new charity established this month in honour of the greatest all rounder to have graced the playing fields of England.

The Mynn Memorial Benevolent Institution has been set up with the help of donations from admirers of Alfred Mynn. The celebrated cricketer died last year aged 54.

The money — more than £138 — will also be used to erect a tombstone at Thurnham, near Maidstone, where Mynn was buried with full military honours.

Born at Twisden Lodge, Goudhurst in 1807 he was taught the game by Mr John Willes and appeared in 99 matches for Kent between 1834 and 1859 as an all rounder.

Known as the 'Lion of Kent', Alfred Mynn stood six foot one inches high, weighed between 17 and 20 stone and declared his sustenance to be 'beer and beef'. His hitting, especially in front of the wicket and to the leg side, was brilliant and his bowling was fast and ripping.

One newspaper wrote this week: "Alfred Mynn walked six steps exactly, in the last step accelerating his pace and landing so heavily on his left foot that he dug a small grave in the turf."

In first class matches he scored over 50 in an innings on 15 occasions and, in a match at Leicester for South versus North scored 125 before retiring injured. In fact, so serious was the injury that he was carried off the field and placed on the roof of a stage coach for London. He was examined by surgeons at St Bartholomew's Hospital who decided they should amputate the thigh at the hip joint.

Mynn refused to allow them to do so and, after an absence of two years reappeared on the cricket field playing as well as ever. *See page 190*

Work on the great viaduct at Eynsford was stopped last year because a director of South Eastern Railway Company, Mr Percy Hart-Dyke found inferior bricks were being supplied. That was resolved and so was the difficulty in purchasing land from Mr Mildmay of Shoreham who declined to be paid in shares and even rejected an offer to stop express trains when required by his family. After protracted talks he settled eventually for £1,000.

Tale of love underneath the arches

June: Another great viaduct has been completed on the London, Chatham and Dover's newly-opened railway route between Swanley and Bat and Ball, Sevenoaks.

The viaduct at Eynsford, which has taken two years to build, is impressive. It consists of nine 30-foot spans which rise to a height of 64 feet. Bricks were made on the site and the construction work was carried out by Mr Thomas Crampton.

One of the young bricklayers working on the viaduct managed to find accommodation in the small timbered cottage which stands today in the shadow of the handsome arches. He fell in love with the blind daughter of the family who sat at the window day after day listening to the hustle and bustle of the navvies outside. On completion of the bridge this month the bricklayer and his love were married and continue to live in the cottage which brought them together. *See page 164*

Mrs Beeton's cook book is a publishing sensation

May: The village of Greenhithe, on the banks of the Thames, set among the undulating hills in North Kent and conveniently connected to London by a railway line, is set to welcome one of the county's most famous women.

Her name is Isabella Beeton — better known as Mrs Beeton author of *The Book of Household Management.*

The book published last year by her husband and a big best seller opens with the words: "As with the commander of an army, or the leader of any enterprise, so it is with the mistress of a house".

It took four years to compile and edit, has more than 1,000 pages and contains everything a middle-class married woman and housewife would need to know.

For example, she writes: "Rise early, bath daily (in cold or tepid water), form friendships slowly, invite guests who are amusing, never speak an unrefined word, keep your servants discreet, see your nurses dispense no dangerous drugs and pay rigorous attention to the right way of frying a cow's heel".

Isabella Mary Mayson was born in March 1836 in Milk Street, London, the eldest of 20 brothers and sisters.

In 1856, aged 20, she married Sam Orchart Beeton, a journalist and a publisher who had ambitiously bought the English rights of *Uncle Tom's Cabin* and earned a fortune from its sales.

Sam also launched a monthly *English Woman's Domestic Magazine* to which Isabella contributed. The book followed, providing not only an invaluable guide to the domestic services women provide such as shopping, caring for children and running an orderly home, but more than 3,000 recipes.

At the time the couple were living in a rented house in Pinner but after the success of *Household Management* they could afford a house of their own and are moving into a low rambling farmhouse at Greenhithe.

From there, Sam travels daily to his offices in The Strand while Isabella is forming new friendships — (slowly?)

Isabella Beeton — mistress of her house.

South Eastern loses railway monopoly in Thanet

October 5: With the opening today of the London Chatham and Dover railway line to Margate and Ramsgate, passengers from London can now enjoy a shorter journey to the Thanet resorts than the circuitous route offered by the South Eastern.

The civic fathers are delighted with the new stations and the increased trade and prosperity which is certain to follow.

Margate has been popular for many years thanks to the hoys carrying hundreds of passengers from London every week. So has Ramsgate with its donkey rides to Pegwell, tea parties at Drapers and rows of bathing machines on the sands.

Last year a trader remarked that whereas "Margate is pronounced Margitt and the same applies to Ramsgate, Broadstairs is frequently pronounced "Dull".

This is not really fair. Broadstairs has a life and tranquility of its own and the fishermen have more entertaining stories to tell than those heard in Margate or Ramsgate.

The South Eastern has not enjoyed losing its monopoly in Thanet. When opposition trains reached Herne Bay two years ago, the company attempted to delay the opening on the grounds that the bridge under the Canterbury and Whitstable line was unsafe. That claim was unjustified and the line went ahead. *See page 170*

The Achilles, largest sail and steam-powered iron-clad battleship to be assembled.

1,200 men are building Chatham's first iron ship

March: The Royal Dockyard at Chatham has built many remarkable ships but none can compare with the mammoth vessel currently under construction.

The *Achilles* is 380 feet long and is the largest sail and steam-powered iron-clad battleship to be assembled. It marks the dawn of a new era, not only for the dockyard but also for the Royal Navy.

Last week Charles Dickens visited the Dockyard to report on the progress of the *Achilles. T*his is what he wrote:

"Ding, clash, dong, bang, boom, rattle, clash, clink, bang, clatter, bang, bang BANG. What on earth is this? This is, or soon will be, the *Achilles*, iron armour-plated ship. Twelve hundred men are working at her now; twelve hundred men working on stages over her sides, over her bows, over her stern, under her keel, between her decks, down in her hold, within her and without, crawling and creeping into the finest curves of her lines..."

It was two years ago that Chatham received its first orders to construct two iron clad warships, *Achilles* and *Royal Oak.* At the time the royal dockyards had no experience of iron working but the private yards like those on the Thames at Blackwall and Woolwich had attempted to keep up with the French.

The pioneer of these heavily armoured, all-iron ships is the French designer, Dupuy de Lome who put forward plans for an iron fighting ship of 2,400 tons in 1845. This was so ahead of its time that the French authorities dismissed it with some disdain. Thirteen years later, however, in 1858 the French navy ordered four steam powered iron clads.

The launching of *Achilles* and the *Royal Oak* signals a new race against the French for supremacy at sea.

See page 167

The old buildings of Tonbridge School have been taken down and a new school erected. The money was made available from lands held by the Skinner's Company in London which were compulsory acquired for the building of St Pancras Railway Station.

New churches completed this year are All Saints, Langton Green, St George's Garrison Church, Woolwich and St Michael's, Tenterden.

Sandown Castle, near Deal, has been demolished.

Thomas Aveling's patent locomotive built to a Clayton and Shuttleworth design. The cylinder was steam jacketed and mounted in the smokebox.

Thomas Aveling — an industrial pioneer

October: As the industrial age gathers momentum, more and more inventors and entrepreneurs are rising from humble beginnings to reap the rewards of their energies.

An outstanding example is 39-year-old Thomas Aveling whose small engineering factory in Rochester is producing traction engines capable of hauling six strongly built oak wagons.

At this year's Smithfield show at Islington it was stated that Aveling had completed 97 engines under contract and was selling to companies as far away as Buenos Aires.

Thomas Aveling was born in Cambridge in 1824 and moved to Kent with his mother on the death of her husband. In Rochester she married a clergyman who "held a bible in one hand and a birch in the other" and completely dominated the terrified boy.

Apprenticed to a farmer, Thomas moved to Canterbury, married his master's niece and later began farming on his own on Romney Marsh.

What Thomas lacked in formal education he made up with his mechanical abilities and made a name for himself by repairing agricultural implements with impressive efficiency.

Thomas, believing he could apply mechanical power to agriculture, set up his engineering shop at Rochester and, in 1856, produced a steam plough. The Association representing Kentish farmers was delighted and presented him with a cheque for 300 guineas.

He went from strength to strength by making portable engines self-propelling. By 1858 he was adapting Clayton and Shuttleworth portables by driving one hind wheel by pitch chain, with an intermediate reduction gear. The pinion slid on splines on the crankshaft so it could be engaged or disengaged at will.

A year later Aveling took out a traction engine patent and the following year successfully applied for a patent for a steam-jacketed cylinder.

Today he is building his own engines and finding a ready made economic advantage in Britain's available market. He is one of our greatest industrial pioneers.

See page 209

Three new basins for Chatham Dockyard

THE order to build the *Achilles* and the *Royal Oak* marks the beginning of a new era in the long history of Chatham Dockyard. It has also generated many industrial problems.

This year the Admiralty decided the yard is not big enough for the building of new warships while others are being refitted. It is now planning a massive extension — in fact the yard will more than triple in size.

Three huge basins, built along the line of St Mary's Creek, will be accompanied by the construction of numerous docks, factory buildings, a pumping station and hydraulic cranes — adding 380 acres to the existing yard.

It means that St Mary's Island will be totally absorbed and the dockyard will extend into the parish of Gillingham. Convicts from the nearby prisons will be conscripted for the work.

Meanwhile, both ships have now been launched with the *Royal Oak*, a 50-gun iron clad, winning the race. At her launch *The Rochester Gazette* reported: "As this was the first launch of a vessel of this kind from Chatham — and in fact from any of the royal dockyards — great interest has been excited by the event. An immense staging was erected at the head of the slip...and admission was only to be gained by ticket. At half past one o'clock labour was suspended in the yard and a large crowd was greatly increased by the flocking to the spot of hundreds of workmen".

With the *Royal Oak* on the high seas the 1,300 workforce was transferred to the *Achilles* and the Admiralty required to engage ironsmiths and boilermakers from outside Kent. These outsiders did not take kindly to working alongside the skilled and better paid shipwrights and went on strike for increased pay. They were all dismissed.

Shipwrights will now be trained at the dockyard in the art of iron construction.

Achilles, 9,500 tons, was launched in December. Supplied with a canvas to cover a total area of 50,000 square feet she also has 750 tons of coal in her bunkers. With three masts and two funnels her guns are mounted in the broadside pattern. She has 30 miles of rigging cordage and a 12°-ton screw propeller is fitted to her stern. *See page 219.*

The scene today after the Erith explosion. More than 400 navvies from the Crossness sewer works helped in a race against the tide to repair a breach in the river.

'Earthquake' — by gunpowder

***October 1:* Fifteen people were killed today when two gunpowder magazines on the Erith marshes exploded with such violence that it could be heard 50 miles away.**

For a time inhabitants thought they had experienced an earthquake such was the nature of the explosion. Window panes shattered for miles around and the Crystal Palace shivered with the vibration. Erith church had its roof blown in and a clock that stopped at South Darenth timed the catastrophe precisely: 6.40 am.

Many thought the explosion had occurred at the Woolwich Arsenal; in fact the detonation erupted on one of two barges each containing 1,000 barrels of gunpowder. A huge pillar of black smoke spread to form a mushroom shape that obscured the sky. The barge, the jetty, the two magazines, three cottages and all the men, working for John Hall, had disappeared .

July: A Herne Bay, Reculver and Hampton Oyster Fishery Company has been created.

July: The iron age is truly here. A second Deal pier has been opened and built of iron to withstand the Channel storms.

August: The second phase of the building of Admiralty pier, Dover has begun. The pier is now connected to rail traffic. *See page 233.*

September: The name of West Kent Yeomanry has been changed to The Queen's Own Royal West Kent Yeomanry.

December: New churches opened this year in Kent are: St Paul's, Beckenham; St George's, Bickley; St Mary's, Plaistow; St Mary's, Bromley and Christchurch, Deptford.

Scene of the fatal accident at Staplehurst, on the South Eastern Railway — from a sketch taken next day.

Charles Dickens survives as carriages tumble over railway bridge: 10 killed

June 9: Ten passengers were killed and more than 50 injured today when a boat train from Paris to London, via Folkestone, was derailed on the Beult Viaduct near Staplehurst.

Eight of the 14 carriages toppled over the timber bridge and into the muddy water below, which was swollen by many days of heavy rain. The accident occurred at a lonely spot, known locally as Hockenbury Bridge, surrounded by open fields and just a few cottages.

Among the passengers on the train was Charles Dickens who was returning from a holiday in France with Ellen Ternan and her mother. Flung together into a corner of the compartment, they discovered they were in one of the two undamaged carriages. It was hanging precariously over the edge of the bridge.

Mr Crombie, driver of the train, described the drama: "I was travelling about 50 miles an hour when I saw a flagman waving furiously on the line ahead. I applied all five brakes and the tender brake and shut off the steam.

"I was still travelling about 30mph when I reached the bridge and the impetus carried me over together with the tender behind, the brake van and two first-class carriages".

Unbeknown to the driver, the track over the bridge was actually being repaired and the platelayers had removed a section of rail in order to insert a new wooden sleeper. Naturally they had timed this to coincide with an interval between scheduled trains but had forgotten the boat train. Its departure time from Folkestone was governed by the arrival of the cross Channel ferry and also by the tides.

Henry Benge, in charge of the repair gang, said: "I watched the 2.50 steam past and then looked in the South Eastern Railway Company's time book to see the time of the next train. It told me the boat train was due at 4.15. I then sent the flagman the usual ten telegraph poles up the line".

The foreman and his men stood by the bridge in sheer terror as the train skidded towards the gap in the rails, snapping off one of the bridge girders. As the eight carriages toppled into the water, escaping steam added to the drama.

Five killed at the hands of a man consumed with anger

December 19: Stephen Forwood, a Ramsgate-born former baker and later Jack-of-all-trades was hanged at Maidstone gaol today for the murder of his wife, Mary and daughter, Emily. During last week's trial he also admitted killing three boys aged nine, 11 and 13 with a spoonful of prussic acid. They were the sons of his lover, Mrs White.

The case received massive publicity because Forwood — also known as Stephen Southey — was consumed with anger over a sum of £1,700 which he had won in a game of billiards against the Hon Dudley Ward, brother of the Earl of Dudley, some years earlier.

When Ward refused to pay Forwood made desperate bids to collect the money he was owed. On one occasion he told a national newspaper that he would sacrifice himself, Mrs White and her children, his own wife and children and the Earl of Dudley so as to draw public recognition to the debt.

Forwood blamed all kinds of people for what had happened including Palmerston, Gladstone, Disraeli and the Earl of Shaftesbury because they all failed to reply to his letters. "I charge back the guilt of these crimes", he said, "on those high dignitaries of the church and state and justice who have turned a deaf ear to my heart-broken appeals..."

A *Maidstone Journal* reporter was among the crowd present at the execution. "The body after hanging for an hour", he wrote, "was cut down and a cast of the head taken. Forwood was buried within the precincts of Maidstone Gaol".

Staplehurst tragedy

continued from previous page

Then there was a momentary stillness followed by the cries of the injured.

Dickens waited until the carriages had settled, climbed out of the window and made his way to the guard's van. He obtained the key, opened his carriage door and helped the two ladies out. He then turned his attention to the injured, extricating a Mr Dickenson from the wreckage and possibly saving his life.

The author then remembered that he had left a precious manuscript on the train along with his luggage. He calmly returned to the still-tilted carriage and rescued the papers of his unfinished book, *Our Mutual Friend.* He then took a special train back to London.

Earlier this evening Dickens said he had suffered from an "attack of the shakes". He said: "I had to cling tightly to the seat to prevent myself falling off. I felt pale and sweaty and was unable to look at anyone directly. The doctor tells me I may be suffering from nystagmus.

An inquest into this lamentable accident will be held at the Railway Hotel, Staplehurst tomorrow, Saturday.

See page 181

New Kent churches this year are St Stephen's, Lewisham and (left) St Mary's, Ide Hill (pop 250) which replaces a small hut converted into a church earlier in the century. With its tall spire, Ide Hill now boasts 'the highest church in Kent'.

Hard labour for railway foreman

HENRY Benge, foreman responsible for the repairs to the bridge over the River Beult, has been found guilty of the manslaughter of 10 railway passengers and sentenced to nine months' hard labour. Joseph Gallimore, district inspector of the permanent way, has been acquitted.

The jury at the Kent Summer Assizes was told that Benge read the details of train arrivals in his time book for Saturday instead of Friday. He had no watch.

The flagman, Wiles and driver Crombie have both been exonerated from blame.

Mark Beech riot comes to a peaceful end

August 6: Kent police, led by the Chief Constable, Commander William Ruxton averted a potentially explosive situation today when some 60 or 70 aggressive and drunken English railway navvies chased and cornered their French-speaking counterparts at a site near the new Edenbridge town station.

The inhabitants bolted their doors and boarded up windows as frantic foreigners ran up and down the High Street desperately seeking sanctuary. As the mob closed in for the final reckoning they came face to face with almost 100 policemen and the riot petered out to a tame, anti-climactic conclusion.

The English navvies were enraged by the railway company's decision to hire cheap foreign labourers on the construction of the line and the digging of the mile-long tunnel through the escarpment of the High Weald between Hever and Cowden.

Of the 800 men employed, some four to 500 were a mixture of French, Belgians and Luxemburgers and they were being paid between a third to a half less than the English navvies. It created an explosive, xenophobic situation, likely to boil over at any time.

Yesterday, Sunday, a sergeant and several constables from Tonbridge saw the English navvies engaged in heavy drinking in the two public houses, the *Kentish Horse* at Mark Beech and the *Victoria Arms* at Horseshoe Green. Threatening language was heard; a conspiracy was brewing.

That night in the Mark Beech tunnel English workers started to smash windows and assault Frenchmen who escaped to Brook Farm. The farmer alerted the police who quickly summoned reinforcements. Commander Ruxton took control, put a company of infantry on standby at Shorncliffe Barracks and proceeded to Mark Beech in his fly.

His actions proved a sobering influence. The men eventually dispersed.

Sir Morton Peto goes bankrupt

October: Trouble looms for the future of the London Chatham and Dover Railway Company with the news this week that its ambitious contractor and speculator, Sir Morton Peto has been bankrupted.

Peto, once a builder's labourer who learned to lay 800 bricks a day, has been a giant figure in this heady era of railway mania. To him Kent owes many of its successful lines and he has turned seaside villages into thriving resorts.

The people of Folkestone see him as a kind of Messiah; by building the long Sandling tunnel and the towering Foord Viaduct he has brought great prosperity to the area.

Sir Morton had hoped to bring that same prosperity to the LCDR but too-rapid expansion, a lack of capital and numerous accidents led to a decline in its fortunes. Then came 'Black Friday' — May 11 this year — when Overend, Gurney and Co stopped trading and the Stock Market collapsed, sending shock waves throughout the railway industry.

Clean water and no smells thanks to Crossness engines

WITH the opening of the Crossness engines and pumping house on what used to be marshland at Erith, a brand new sewerage system is now in full operation and the Thames is no longer an open sewer.

Already the quality of life is changing. Clean drinking water is now supplied to many London homes by newly-formed water companies and the city has been rid of foul smells and filthy streets. Cholera has almost been eliminated.

Sir Joseph Bazalgette, chief engineer for the Metropolitan Board of Works, is the mastermind behind this civil engineering project. His system encompasses a network of drains running into vast sewers made of engineering bricks and using Portland cement as a mortar. Sewage now runs through these tunnels with the aid of gravity along both banks of the Thames, travelling to Crossness on the south and to Barking on the north.

At Crossness, sewage is pumped into a covered reservoir and held until an ebb tide when it is released into the Thames to be taken away towards the North Sea. Four massive pumping engines have been constructed together with a magnificent new building to house them. *See page 223.*

Tonbridge Liberal stampede

August 6: Election day rioters, armed with stones, eggs and rotten tomatoes caused such a disturbance in Tonbridge yesterday that the town resembled the aftermath of an earthquake. The streets were littered with debris, windows were broken and people lay injured in great numbers.

The rioters — supporters of the Liberal Party — were angered by the success of the Conservatives in the recent general election and decided to lie in wait for those who had gone to Maidstone to hear the declaration of the poll. Four rioters were arrested.

'Black illness' returns to the hop gardens

October: The 'black illness' is back in Kent. Despite the efforts of specially appointed inspectors to seize bad food from itinerant vendors, cholera has appeared in Mid Kent and is particularly rampant in the 'hopping' villages of Yalding, Hunton, Nettlestead, Teston, Marden, Staplehurst, Otham, Bearsted and Barming.

The disease was first reported in London and aboard the *Queen of the Colonials* at Gravesend. From London it was carried by barge to Faversham, Sittingbourne, Maidstone, Sheerness and Aylesford.

In Chatham, three dispensaries were opened and the roads watered with diluted carbolic acid. It was to no avail.

In September the Maidstone guardians persuaded the South Eastern Railway to take as many hop pickers as possible directly to the hop gardens to protect the town.

They did, but the workers were idle for some time because of heavy rains and spent many hours sitting in their hovels or old Crimean tents. The rain came in and so did the 'black illness'. *See page 172*

Four miles high in a balloon

January 12: Professor James Glaisher, an eminent scientist at the Royal Observatory, Greenwich but better known as a pioneer balloonist today delivered the opening address at the inaugural meeting of the Royal Aeronautical Society of Great Britain.

He said progress made in aeronautics had been for any useful object almost nil. "Our flights", he said, " have pandered to the public taste for the grotesque and hazardous which has tended to degrade the subject which, until recently, was looked upon with contempt by scientific classes".

Prof Glaisher and his colleague Henry Coxwell have made more than 28 balloon ascents from the grounds of Crystal Palace. In April 1963 they rose to a height of 24,163 feet (more than four miles high) and on the descent discovered they had drifted towards Beachy Head. They struck the earth at Newhaven with a heavy bump.

More flights will be made for the purpose of scientific and meteorological observations.

The Prince of Wales and Princess Alexandra were guests this week of Elizabeth Sackville — who inherited Knole on the death of her sister Mary two years ago — and her husband George West, the 5th Earl de la Warr.

Although it was a private visit the residents of Sevenoaks had the opportunity of giving the royal couple an enthusiastic welcome as they drove through the town and onto Knole. Edward and Alexandra brought a large party of friends with them who enjoyed croquet and tea on the lawn.

1867

When the 'dregs of London' pour into Kent

April: No longer can hop pickers travel to Kent and hire themselves out to local farmers on a first-come-first-served basis.

In the last of many great reforms, introduced by the growers, London hiring agents will make a list of those who wish to register themselves for hopping. They will pass the information on to an agent in Maidstone and thus help to control the enormous burden on county services.

'Opping down in Kent. The Cockneys are on their way.

For many years now thousands of Londoners have come to Kent each year in search of work in the hop gardens and discovered they are not required.

Hungry and destitute they have either thrown themselves on the mercy of the union house keepers or made their way home again on foot, with no money, no food and no lodgings.

Last year thousands came from London, sleeping rough under hedges or in open fields. As they got nearer to the farms hundreds applied to the relieving officers for lodgings but others slept on the doorsteps in the towns of North and Mid Kent. The Coxheath Union, four miles from Maidstone, was taking 600-700 people every night but 1,200 slept rough in Gravesend town centre.

From now on each picker recruited will be given a Hopper's Letter which contains a registration number, the picker's destination, train times and the name of his employer. At the end of the picking season the farmer must endorse the letter with his comments about the suitability of the picker. This will be delivered to a London agent who will be in a position to draw up a 'black list' of pickers.

And there will be a 'black list' because bad feeling has existed for many years. Militancy has been rife and it is not unknown for pickers, led by bully-boys, to threaten farmers or set fire to their houses. Mob rioting has broken out frequently and local pickers have been terrorised by their visitors.

The Rev J.J.Kendon from Curtisden Green, Goudhurst has been undertaking missionary work in an attempt to 'save the souls' of the unsavoury characters and improve conditions for the hoppers. In his first report last year this is what he wrote:

"Here may be seen the dregs of many of our larger towns, and of London. They sleep in stables, lodges, barns, hoppers' houses, straw huts etc, almost like the cattle of the fields. To mingle among these poor creatures, to see their habits and hear their language to witness the awful lengths in wickedness to which they go, makes it seem almost impossible that we can be living in England in the latter part of the 19th century".

Mr Kendon intends to send missionaries into the hop gardens and hand out tickets for free teas at Curtisden Green. He wants to introduce prayer meetings and hymn singing, recognising they will "probably hear more of the gospel during hop-picking than they will during the rest of the year".

The Reverend J.Y.Stratton is also concerned about the seamier side of life in the Kentish farms during hop picking time and is delighted that the need for great improvement has been recognised by the growers themselves.

Two years ago a group of land-owners and tenant hop farmers formed the Society for the Employment and Improved Lodgings of Hop Pickers. They said the huts should be wind and rain proof, that adequate latrines be provided and that an inspector be appointed by the Board of Guardians of each district to inspect food and water supplied to the hoppers. There must be sufficient floor space and screens between the beds. Even more revolutionary, they recommended that hopper huts should, in future, be brick built.

With tighter controls over the numbers arriving in Kent it should be easier to provide better conditions when they arrive.

See page 226

The steamship Great Eastern which sailed from Sheerness with the transatlantic telegraph cable.

The town that was a village

THE once quiet market town of Bromley, — ('the glade among the broom') — favourably situated on the London to Hastings turnpike road and always a busy and important coaching stop, is undergoing such an amazing metamorphosis that it now needs a Local Board to administer its affairs.

The Board was elected this year to look after all the problems associated with progress — drainage, sewage disposal, water supply and the provision of new roads and schools.

Like most Kentish towns the change has been brought about by the arrival of the Iron Horse. When Bromley railway station was opened on Mason's Hill less than 10 years ago the impact was immediate. New families arrived from London and some moved up from rural Kent. To them, the lure of residing in a small country town, surrounded by woods and fields, was far too compelling.

The population of Bromley is now approaching 7,000. Many are living in new homes built on the site of Bromley Palace and Bickley Park. Both estates were sold off for development.

One man who has a small shop in Bromley High Street is the Kent cricketer Joseph Wells. It is a kind of pottery emporium and is called Atlas House. Wells is better known for a remarkable feat of bowling than the world of small-time commerce. In his second county match against Hove five years ago he took four wickets in successive balls — all bowled. He became the first man in first class cricket to accomplish this feat.

Anothern northern parish showing signs of growing is the village of Sidcup which welcomed the railway last year. The Sidcup line follows a route to rejoin the same line just west of Dartford.

Telegraph cable under the sea

A 2,300-mile transatlantic telegraph cable has been laid under the sea between Sheerness and Newfoundland by the 12,000-tonne steamship *Great Eastern.*

The ship — built by Brunel — has taken 15 months to complete this ambitious and costly exercise.

A few weeks ago the *Great Eastern* steamed into Heart's Content Bay, Newfoundland with the final length of the cable. The first message was transmitted immediately.

The cable has been funded by the governments on both sides of the Atlantic and by Mr Cyprus Field, an American millionaire.

New churches completed this year are St Peter's, Brockley, St Peter's, Eltham, St Peter's, Greenwich, St James, Kidbrook, St Lawrence, Seal, and St Margaret's, Underriver.

Lone sailor rescued by the vicar of Dymchurch

October: The vicar of Dymchurch, the Rev Charles Cobb, has been presented with the Albert Medal in gold for helping to save a sailor whom he spotted hanging on to the rigging of his shipwrecked lugger.

Mr Cobb knew there had been a terrific storm in the Channel but was unaware that a French ship had been blown off course and was wrecked on Dymchurch Sands until he rose for breakfast on a recent Sunday morning and heard the sound of gunfire through the vicarage windows.

Four men were clinging to the rigging and the coastguards were trying to fire a lifeline to the wreck but it continually fell short. As John Batist, one of the coastguards tied a lifeline round his waist and tried to swim out to the wreck, three of the four Frenchmen were washed away, but one hung on grimly.

Mr Cobb appeared on the scene, ran down to the water's edge, took off his coat and plunged into the brine. His parishioners, gathered on the shore, begged him to return but he swam strongly through the waves, briefly disappeared and was then seen clambering on to the wreck.

John Batist was now making another effort to reach the wreck. He succeeded and, with the help of Mr Cobb, grabbed the survivor and brought him safely to shore. Mr Batist has been given the Albert Medal in bronze.

Last person in Britain to be publicly hanged

April 29: Frances Kidder, a 25-year-old housewife from Hythe — who murdered her step daughter Louise — yesterday became the last person in Britain to be publicly hanged.

At her Maidstone trial the jury heard that Frances married William Kidder in 1865 but took an instant dislike to his two children by his previous marriage and frequently abused them. In August last year she took Louise,11, for a walk and at Cobbs Bridge, New Romney drowned the girl in a stream.

Frances Kidder was in prison for three weeks before her execution at Maidstone where gallows were erected on the western side of the main gates in County Road. Massive beams supported the platform. There were cross beams, ropes and table and the drop was a trap door in the centre. More than 2,000 people were present. They saw Kidder walk falteringly to the scaffold and then become hysterical, asking Jesus to forgive her.

As the bolt on the trap door was drawn she fell three feet and struggled violently. One woman in the crowd screamed, others almost fainted. It took several minutes for Kidder to die.The hangman was William Calcraft who liked to use a small drop because it caused victims to strangle slowly.

This morning Charles Dickens said that he and Thomas Hardy had both witnessed a Calcraft hanging and were angered not only by his cruel methods but also by his heavy drinking and abusing ways.

"He can be very abusive", said Hardy. "I once saw a girl of 16 being hanged by Calcraft and was greatly affected. I based my book *Tess of the d'Urbervilles* on this poor woman's circumstances". *See page 187*

Boy executed 'in private'

***August 13*: Only 16 journalists, a priest and a few prison officers were present at Maidstone Prison scaffold today as 19-year-old Thomas Wells became the first person in Britain to be executed 'in private'.**

The boy, a carriage cleaner for London Chatham and Dover Railway, had shot and killed his employer, stationmaster Edward Walshe, at Dover in a fit of bad temper.

Convicted of murder after the Act of Parliament banning public executions, he was unlucky not to win a reprieve.

The Police Gazette said last week that the authorities needed "to test the new law". As he died a black flag was raised at the entrance to Maidstone Prison.

January 1: During an aeronautical show at Crystal Palace today John Stringfellow exhibited a steam-powered triplane. It is, as yet, untested.

February 27: Benjamin Disraeli, former MP for Maidstone and a favourite of Queen Victoria, is the new Prime Minister, taking over from Lord Derby. As a parliamentary veteran Disraeli has revitalised the Conservatives with the passage of the Reform Act by adding more than one million voters to the electorate.

Today he told newspapers: "Yes, I have climbed to the top of the greasy pole".

Yesterday was the hottest day Britain has ever known

July 23: When Dr George Hunsley Fielding stepped into his garden at Grove House, Mill Lane, Tonbridge yesterday evening to check his weather instruments he could not believe his eyes. The shade temperature was giving a reading of 100.5 deg F (38.1C) — it was the hottest day Britain has ever recorded.

Dr Fielding works for the Royal Observatory and faithfully submits his findings each day to the superintendent, Mr James Glaisher FRS.

Today the staff of the magnetic and meteorologiocal department would be dancing around in a state of great excitement, if it wasn't so warm. The heat is suffocating, the sky cloudless and there is scarcely a breath of wind. Those outside feel as if they are passing through an oven.

Dr Fielding, who will be writing to the Meteorological Society with his report, said: "Tonbridge, like every town in Kent, has wilted in the heat since May. Food has been thrown away, people are choosing to walk on the shady side of the street and cattle are dying through lack of water".

He is right. People are struggling to keep cool and can hardly wait to get into the privacy of their own homes where they can shed a few layers of clothing.

1,500 navvies take six years to build Kent's longest railway tunnel

May 1: The longest railway tunnel in Kent has been completed at last. It runs for one mile 1,693 yards under the lower greendsand ridge between Sevenoaks and the Liberty of Weald. It is the fifth longest in Britain and stands as a masterpiece of engineering.

The tunnel has taken more than 1,500 men — using five locomotives, 16 pumping and winding engines, 500 earth wagons and 150 horses — six years to complete.

Thirteen shafts were sunk and at the shaft in Flood Lane, the contractors tapped an underground stream which caused a serious delay. So great was the flow of water that it completely drowned the workings and an underground reservoir had to be constructed. This now provides the town of Sevenoaks with all of its drinking water.

There were many accidents during construction. In November 1863 the water rose seven feet in two hours and a number of navvies just managed to escape with their lives. During the same month William Leaver fell down one of the shafts and drowned.

Two years ago four men fell 250 feet to the bottom of a shaft and died. The badly injured were taken to Guy's Hospital in London.

The tunnel passes through layers of rock strata which were removed by blasting with gunpowder. Otherwise the construction tools were hand drills, picks, shovels, crowbars and much human and horse power. Behind the miners came the bricklayers using stock bricks and five courses in most places.

The navvies were given accommodation in White Hart Wood, provided with a medical officer, Dr Browne while a tin church was erected to look after their spiritual welfare.

John Jay was the main contracter whose estimate for the overall cost was £901,849. That included the value of the land under which the tunnel passed which was owned by three estates — Kippington, Knole and Beechmont.

May 2: Railway passengers from Tonbridge today travelled to London through the Sevenoaks and Polhill tunnels. There was no ceremony to mark the occasion.

Hops in abundance after a long hot summer. Here is the September scene at Marden.

North Kent — natural home for Portland cement

WHEN William Aspdin first began to make Portland cement 30 years ago, Northfleet and Swanscombe were small agricultural riverside villages. Today, they are industrial townships and will continue to grow as long as chalk and clay, the main ingredients of the cement industry, continues to be quarried in abundance in this area of Thames-side.

William, youngest son of Joseph Aspdin — who claims to have invented Portland cement in 1824 — has revolutionised the construction industry. With two colleagues, Messrs Robins and Maude he set up his works at Northfleet Creek in 1834 and used a 'beehive' kiln to make Portland cement, so called because its colour resembles that of Portland stone.

It was first used in civil engineering in 1843 when Sir Marc Brunel and his son Isambard were building the Rotherhithe Tunnel and the roof collapsed. Brunel dumped tons and tons of Aspdin's cement into the river. This sealed the break in the tunnel roof and the engineer was able to pump the tunnel dry. He rebuilt it using Portland cement for the relining and today the tunnel remains as strong as ever.

As rival companies spring up to take advantage of the growing demand, North Kent continues to be the cradle of the cement industry. Chalk is dug with shovels, picks and crowbars, grinding is completed in the windmills and Thames barges stand by to transport the finished product.

Above: Portland Hall, Gravesend, built by William Aspdin in 1855. Left: His original kiln at Northfleet.

Woe betide those who attack fortress Kent

TEN years ago a Royal Commission, concerned about France's growing hostility, and remarkable powers of recovery, recommended massive new fortifications for Kent.

They included three new forts at the eastern end of Gravesend Reach, the demolition and reconstruction of the polygonal fort at Shornmead, a mammoth fort at Garrison Point, Sheerness and two circular strongholds upstream on Hoo and Darnet islands.

In addition the Commission proposed a ring fortress for the land defence of Chatham, a connecting line of forts from the western bank of the Medway to the Thames at Shornmead and improved seaward defences at Dover Castle for protecting the harbour.

Since those worrying days frantic activity has been taking place in the county and no expense has been spared in providing all the latest technology such as all-metal traversing platforms for the guns and hand-geared machinery for elevating and turning them on to their targets.

The engineers who supervised the building of these impressive citadels have learned much from the American Civil War in which brick and masonry forts were reduced to rubble by the rifled guns.

These Kentish fortifications represent a great industrial age. No invader can march through Kent in comfort for the new fortifications house guns that can fire projectiles weighing more than 200 lbs over a range of three miles.

One leading engineer said recently: "We can now compete on equal terms with any warship in service. At Dover Castle we have 15 heavy, rifled muzzle-loaders. At Archcliffe Fort we have built a counterweighted carriage which rises up to fire and on recoil disappears below the parapet for reloading. It is ingenious".

Whitstable Bay like a 'sea of molten gold'

November 16: When a disastrous fire destroyed Whitstable's two popular public houses, *The Duke of Cumberland* and the *Red Lion* three years ago, the town had no fire engine of its own. However, the Norwich Union generously offered to provide one if a building to house it could be found.

A year later, in July 1867, a volunteer brigade was formed and the 26 Whitstable firefighters looked forward to their first serious battle with the flames.

It came this week when a blaze from a shop roof in Marine Street quickly spread through the town under the influence of a brisk north-east wind. The firemen quickly made their appearance, drew seawater from the beach but then, to their horror, heard the engine stop — choked by sand and weed.

An onlooker had this to say about the fire: "The flames now had all their own way and they devoured the inflammable dry timber and tarred buildings with a terrible avidity. The excitement among the crowds every moment increased, the confusion and distress being heightened by the terrors of those whose dwellings were being consumed.

"At length the engines arrived, the 'Kent' and 'Phoenix' from Canterbury and the 'Kent' and 'Norwich' from Faversham but the fire was now raging furiously. The spectacle presented by the great mass of blazing buildings was magnificently terrible...it lit up luridly the surrounding country and reflected itself in the waters of the Bay that lay beneath the gloomy reddening clouds like a sea of molten gold".

In all 71 buildings, of which 25 were inhabited houses, were destroyed. This included 36 stores, 16 cottages, three sail lofts, one blacksmith's forge and one ship chandlers shop. Whitable also lost two more inns — the *Victoria* and the *Spread Eagle*

Archbishop Archibald Campbell Tait.

With the death at Addington of Archbishop Charles Thomas Langley, Bishop Archibald Campbell Tait 57, Bishop of London, is to be the new Archbishop of Canterbury. A favourite of Queen Victoria, he was formerly bishop in the Deanery of Carlisle where he tragically lost five daughters from scarlet fever. In London he was favourable to the Evangelicals and enjoyed preaching in the open air. One extravagant claim from a minister suggests Tait will be "the greatest primate since Augustine".

At last: rules for the game of football

March: A football team which calls itself *The Alligators* is enjoying some success in Maidstone under the rules laid down by the recently formed Football Association.

This means that no team member other than the goalkeeper can pick up the ball and run with it. Also he cannot punch or harm the opposition.Football has been played in Kent for centuries, usually between neighbouring parishes in fields or even streets but there were no rules governing the number of players per side and how big the goals should be.The Football Association was formed six years ago in a Holborn tavern.

Wilkie Collins, who is probably Charles Dickens' best friend, has published a sensational new mystery novel called *The Moonstone.* Many believe that Dickens has emulated this kind of 'detective story writing' in his new book *The Mystery of Edwin Drood.* *See page 223*

Two new Kent churches have opened this year. They are Holy Trinity, Eltham and St Mary's, Strood.

To make them stand out from soldiers, naval officers are to be clean shaven or wear beards (but no moustaches) as soldiers favour hair on the upper lip. There are also new uniforms to replace the infamous 'bluejackets', bell-bottom trousers and wide straw-beribboned hats. The Queen approves of the new dress code.

ANOTHER KENT NEWSPAPER: ***William Blair, an enterprising 23-year-old from Canterbury, has bought a hand operated printing press and set up his own newspaper next door to a wool shop in Tonbridge. The*** **Tonbridge Free Press** ***sells at three halfpence and has four pages packed with news.***

Woolwich Dockyard closes in 'the crime of the century'

September 18: When William Ewart Gladstone, leader of the Liberal Party and MP for Greenwich, became Prime Minister in December last year; he promised a vast legislative programme of far-reaching economic reforms which included the closure of Woolwich Dockyard.

He has been as good as his word. Today, the bell rang the workmen out for the last time and the gates closed on this historic yard where more than 100 great ships have been built. It has been described as the "crime of the century".

The Government has also abolished the Woolwich Division of the Royal Marines, moved the Army Clothing Factory to Pimlico and, as a further economy measure, dismissed many of the workers of the Royal Arsenal.

Among them is William Rose who only last year founded a most successful co-operative society by writing to his colleagues and inviting them to a meeting at the *Lord Raglan* public house in Plumstead.

There, on November 28, 20 of them agreed to take up a £1 share. Rose was elected secretary, Alexander McLeod, chairman and the Royal Arsenal Co-operative Society was born.

The shop was set up in Rose's house at 11 Eleanor Road, Woolwich with a counter formed from a small vice bench. Two weeks later a chest of tea, 100 lbs of sugar and two crocks of butter were bought and the store opened. Gradually other goods — bacon, coffee and spices — were stocked, the managers gave their services free and new members from the Arsenal came along each week.

Rose, now out of work, is planning to emigrate to Canada with 2,000 unemployed men. He has become the first to surrender his share in the RACS.

Meanwhile machinery and some of the buildings will be removed to Chatham, where work has been offered to some of the men.

The Thalia, launched on July 13th, will now go down in history as the last ship launched from Woolwich. Deptford Dockyard has also closed.

May: A fine smock windmill, powerful enough to turn four millstones, has been built at Willesborough village near Ashford. The octagonal wooden tower stands on a brick base and it is hoped to add a steam engine to allow the windmill to continue working even when the wind drops.

1870-1879

1870: Britain declares its neutrality in the Franco-Prussian war despite the divided loyalties of the royal family.

Dr Thomas Barnardo, a physician, opens a home for destitute boys at Stepney.

The telegraph cable between Britain and India is opened.

1871: The Royal Albert Hall opens as a memorial to Prince Albert.

The discovery of diamonds at Kimberley, Southern Africa precipitates a diamond rush.

Admiralty Pier, Dover is completed. A repair basin and four dry docks are opened at Chatham.

Smallpox strikes again. The death toll in extra-Kent rises to 537, one of the worst epidemics ever known.

1872 New churches completed this year are: Christ Church, Chislehurst, St Luke's, Deptford, All Saints, Hatcham Park, St John the Evangelist, North Woolwich and St Paul's, Sheerness.

An international football match takes place between England and Scotland. No goals are scored.

Drinking fountains and horse troughs are to be erected in all Kent towns for the welfare of travellers — human and animal.

A new newspaper, the Kent and Sussex Courier is launched in Tunbridge Wells in opposition to the long-established *Tunbridge Wells Gazette*. The enterprising journalist proprietor is Matthew Andrew Harris Edwardes.

The Royal Cinque Ports yacht club is founded.

1873: Livingstone dies. Among those who accompanied him on his African journeys is William Cotton Oswell of Groombridge.

June 21: The Shah of Persia visits Woolwich Arsenal.

The Royal Naval Hospital at Greenwich becomes the Royal Naval College.

New churches consecrated in Kent are: St Mark's, Monk Cross, Eridge, Holy Trinity, Penge, All Saints, Shooters Hill. Otham parish church is restored.

A woman in dispute with her husband has the right to claim custody of any child below the age of 16.

1874: Lieutenant Mark Sever Bell, a Corporal with the Corps of the Royal Engineers and Australian by birth, has been awarded the Victoria Cross for his bravery at Ordashu during the First Ashanti Expedition on February 4.

Conservative leader Benjamin Disraeli becomes Prime Minister for the second time at the age of 70

1875: Edward Welby Pugin, eldest son of Augustus dies aged 41. He designed the Roman Catholic churches at Ashford, Dover and Sheerness and the Anglican church at St. Catherine Kingsdown.

The Factory Act decrees that no women, girls or adolescent boys will be allowed to work more than 10 hours a day. No child below 10 can be employed at all.

Gladstone resigns as leader of the Liberal party. His wife opposes his resignation.

Britain buys a controlling interest in the Suez Canal.

December 22: The training ship, *Goliath* is destroyed by fire off Gravesend.

1876: William Gladstone, MP for Greenwich since 1868, visits Blackheath on a rare visit to his constituency. A crowd of 10,000 are present. Queen Victoria has offered him a 'grace and favour' house at Greenwich so that he can discharge his constituency duties, but he has declined the offer.

HMS Worcester II, a training ship, has been established at Greenhithe.

Queen Victoria is appointed Empress of India.

Alexander Graham Bell, a Scotsman who emigrated to the USA, tests a new device for sending sounds down a length of wire. The 'telephone' is believed to have extraordinary potential.

1877: Britain annexes the Boer republic of Transvaal to protect its interests there.

The Australian cricket team wins the first cricket test match against England by 45 runs.

1878: The Christian Mission founded by William Booth is now called the Salvation Army.

John Ruskin, the art critic, is found guilty of libelling the artist James McNeill Whistler by saying he asks "200 guineas for flinging a pot of paint in the public's face". He is ordered to pay damages of one farthing!

1879: Joseph Swan, a member of the Newcastle Chemical Society, demonstrates his system of 'electric lighting'. His opponent in America, Thomas Edison has designed an alternative system.

Charles Parnell is appointed head of a Irish National Land League for the rights of tenants.

Much to the dismay of the Queen, Gladstone says he will fight the next general election as leader of the Liberal party.

Horsmonden School was built in 1853 for 140 children through the benevolence of the Rev William Smith-Marriott and John Smith. In many villages patrons have come forward and, in others, parents have been invited to contribute towards the cost.

Now all Kent villages will have a school

November: Less than 40 years ago only eleven Kentish villages possessed an elementary school — Benenden, Biddenden, Molash, Nonnington, Petham, Sheldwich, Southfleet, Stelling, Ulcombe, Waldershare and Hosey Common, Westerham.

Today, schools exist in 170 rural parishes and with the passing of the Education Act more and more are being built. This reflects the growing prosperity among those who live in the country and the desire to introduce education to the poorer classes.

The Education Act, designed by its proposer, William Forster, to "supplement the present voluntary system" was passed in August last year. It allows churches to continue running their own schools and has increased their grants. But in districts where churches have failed to establish "efficient and suitable schools", Local Boards are to be established to build and run additional schools.

The Act has certainly exposed the enthusiasm and energy, or otherwise, of those who run the church schools — usually a vicar or rector who relies on the generosity of local landowners. Many would like attendance to be compulsory but that is not the case.

Some towns are also benefiting from the Education Act. Canterbury's "bluecoat school" which has existed since the reign of Elizabeth and is run with funds provided from the revenues of the Poor Priests' Hospital in Stour Street, has closed.

The Charity Commissioners have now applied these funds to the building of a new school for boys and girls named after Archdeacon Simon Langton, the founder of the Priests' Hospital. It will be built in the heart of the city on the site of the old Austin Friars.

Also this year, on September 12, Dover College opened on the site of the former priory and, a month later, Maidstone Grammar School moved to new buildings on Tonbridge Road.

Many Kentish villages today are self sufficient thanks to intensive farming which gives employment to more men than the Poor Law Commissioners had ever believed possible. In this period of 'high farming' parents have the means to help finance their children's education.

See page 216

Charles Dickens, England's greatest novelist who died at Gad's Hill on June 9, said he would like to be buried near his home.

May 6: The rebuilt church of St Mary's, Speldhurst was consecrated today with a series of stained-glass windows designed by Edward Burne-Jones, who is a friend of William Morris and works in the "art nouveau" style.

Joseph Bancroft Reade has died in Barfreston after a life of scientific pioneering. He was the first man to separate heat rays from light rays, he sensitised paper for photography and he discovered a solution which made his pictures permanent.

Bayham Abbey near Lamberhurst, residence of the Marquess of Camden, has been built with stone from the nearby ruined abbey.

New churches consecrated this year are: Annunciation, Chislehurst, St Peter's, Fordcombe, St Mark's, Lewisham, All Saints, Perry Street, Northfleet. St Mary and St Eanswith, Folkestone has been restored.

Charles Dickens dies, exhausted by fame

June 9: Charles Dickens died suddenly tonight in his home at Gad's Hill, Higham, aged 58. He suffered a seizure while writing the 24th chapter of *The Mystery of Edwin Drood* which is set in Rochester. With his passing, England has lost her greatest novelist.

It is believed his recent strenuous programme of public readings here and in America may have contributed to his untimely death.

After the shock caused by the railway disaster near Staplehurst in which he worked tirelessly among the injured, Dickens pleaded with his doctors for one last tour. He returned home in very poor health. In America he was fêted wherever he went although he was appalled by the country's piracy of his books with their refusal to accept copyright. He addressed the Senate and the House of Representatives and was fiercely critical of slavery.

It was in 1858, following the publication of *Bleak House, Little Dorrit* and *The Tale of Two Cities*, that the stage took prominence over the pen. As he gave readings of favourite passages from his books he acted each part dramatically. The effort drained him physically and emotionally and he said: "I am incapable of rest".

On March 15 this year he gave his last reading and then looked forward to his meeting with Queen Victoria who was to award him a baronetcy. The Queen and Sir Charles stood and chatted for two hours; in return for a full set of his works she gave him a copy of her book on the Scottish highlands.

Dickens spent his last day in the chalet at Gad's Hill and then suffered a stroke during dinner. As he was dying the French artist Millais sketched him.

He has requested to be buried near Gad's Hill with its view "over the pensive Cobham Woods" but it is more likely to be Rochester Cathedral where he has been offered a resting place.

Empress Eugenie and Prince Imperial escape to a new home at Chislehurst

November 18: A new home at Camden Place, Chislehurst — a healthy village just 30 minutes distance by train from London — has been acquired for Empress Eugenie and her son, the Prince Imperial following the capitulation of France in the Franco-Prussian War.

The Emperor, Napoleon III, cannot join them. He is incarcerated at Wilhelmshöhe as the King of Prussia's prisoner and will remain there until an armistice is signed.

Louis Napoleon has been a popular yet authoritarian Emperor since 1852. He presided over the completion of France's railway network, encouraged the formation of modern credit institutions and transformed Paris into a modern city.

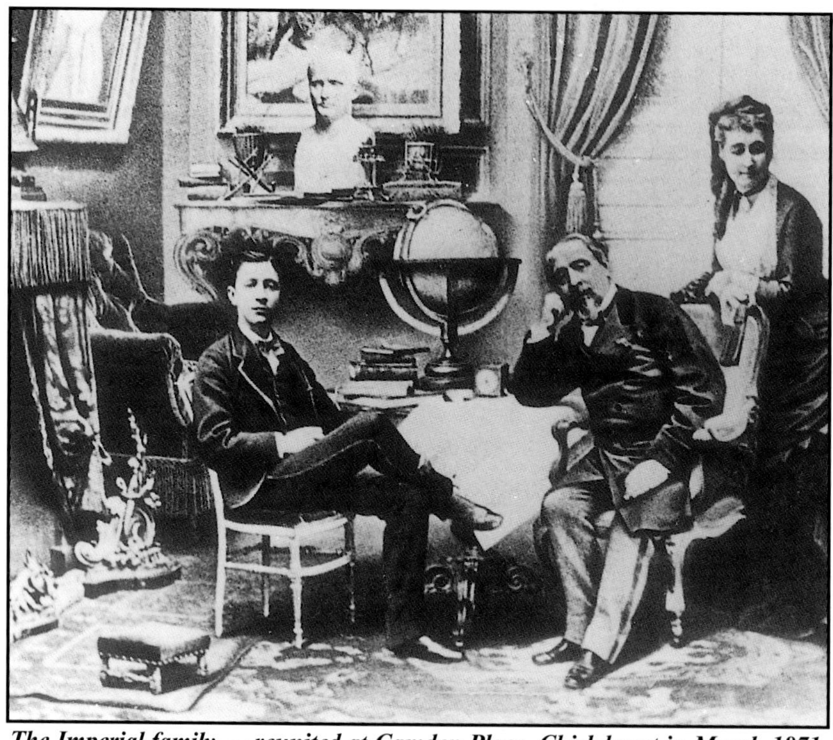

The Imperial family — reunited at Camden Place, Chislehurst in March 1871.

Foreign policy proved to be his undoing and as Prussia became more and more powerful France slid into a war that led to one disaster after another.

At the Battle of Sedan on September 3, Louis Napoleon's army of 80,000 men laid down their arms and France was declared a Republic.

The Prince Imperial was the first to reach England after the catastrophe. He landed at Dover on September 6, hurried past about 100 people who had gathered by the pier and was ushered into the Lord Warden Hotel. The next day Empress Eugenie landed secretly at Ryde on the Isle of Wight after a terrifying journey by sea in a small cutter-yacht. They were reunited a few days later.

It was Dr T.W.Evans, the Emperor's American dentist and a great friend of the Imperial family, who made almost daily excursions looking for a suitable country residence. He had planned to take a house at Tunbridge Wells until someone mentioned Camden Place. This was owned by Mr Nathaniel Strode who had foreseen the fall of the Second Empire and had prepared the great house as a refuge for his friends, decorating and furnishing it in French style.

The Empress travelled to Chislehurst with the Prince Imperial late on September 20 where two four-wheelers were waiting at the station to take them up the hill to Camden Place. The next morning, accompanied by Dr and Mrs Evans, they strolled over the Common to the Roman Catholic Church of St Mary for High Mass. No-one recognised them.

Empress Eugenie says she feels comfortable in Camden Place, a three storey Georgian building which is approached through an avenue of elms. There is a small balustraded balcony over the front door and above it a clock and a motto inscribed in the stonework: "Malo mori quam feodari" — Death rather than desertion.

As friends and servants of the Imperial family arrive to offer their services a small court is forming at Camden Place. French tenants are also taking occupancy of several houses in the vicinity. Meanwhile the Empress continues to show great concern for both her husband and her country.

"Morally I am at the end of my tether", she wrote to her mother this week. "........I cannot get used to the idea of seeing France ruined and unhappy and still less of thinking that I am far away in these days of trial"....What matters is that France must be saved, no matter by whom or how".

See page 183

The French exiles are reunited at Camden Place

March 21: Louis Napoleon, the now-exiled Emperor of France, has been reunited with his family at Camden Place. He arrived at Dover yesterday morning where the Empress was waiting to meet his boat train. After a tender reunion in front of hundreds of cheering onlookers the couple journeyed to Chislehurst in a special train.

A bedroom has been prepared for the Emperor overlooking the park with a small study next door. With him from Wilhelmshöhe he brought his equerry, Franceschini Pietri, his secretary, Baron Corvisart and Alexander Gamble, the *chef des piqeurs.*

Camden Place, a country house of modest size accommodated as many as it possibly could while 25, mostly French servants, were housed in the servants' quarters.

It was only two months ago that the Franco-German war drew to a close with the fall of Paris and the signing of an armistice. German troops marched down the Champs Elysées to the Place de la Concorde and a few days later marched out again.

Queen Victoria is delighted that her old friend is free and has already arranged for him to visit her at Windsor on March 27. *See page 186*

Four bank holidays — and 4m bank notes

JOHN Lubbock, the Liberal MP for Maidstone, has sponsored an Act that will make him the darling of the lower middle classes. He wants to provide the public with four more bank holidays — Easter Monday, Whit Monday, the first Monday in August which will be called Lubbock's Day and Boxing Day. The benefit of these extra days will be especially welcomed by those whose leisure hours are restricted to two days off each year — Christmas Day and Good Friday. Workers in industry have unpaid holiday each year when the works are closed for maintenance.

John Lubbock lives at High Elms, Keston just a couple of miles from the home of Charles Darwin with whom he shares an interest in ethnoarchaeology. In his book on the *Origins of Civilisation and Prehistoric Times* he has coined the terms paleolithic and neolithic.

John Lubbock became fourth baronet on the death of his father six years ago. Before he won the Maidstone seat at his second attempt last year, he had worked in his father's bank, rising to chairman.

John Lubbock

WITH the death this week of Augustus Applegarth, England has lost a man known in London City circles as the "banknote boffin".

A genius of an inventor, Applegarth lived in Dartford for more than 40 years and was proprietor of the silk and calico printing works established at Crayford in 1843. The company later moved to Dartford.

In 1818 he persuaded the Bank of England to allow him to print £1 and £5 paper bank notes which, he said, should go immediately into circulation.

Applegarth printed millions of quality notes at the Bank of England. They were in a variety of colours, of perfect register and said to be forgery proof.They were never issued because the superintendent of the printing office at the Bank of England, William Bawtree, was able to produce imitations of Applegarth's printed notes.

Applegarth had worked on the project for three years and wanted remuneration. He was granted £4,000. The Bank of England spent £40,000 and found themselves stuck with four million 'useless' bank notes.

Applegarth also invented the rotary press. In 1846 his 'four-feeders' had enabled *The Times* to increase its daily circulation to a massive 28,000.

February: More than 1,500 tons of provisions have been despatched from the Royal Navy Victualling Yard at Deptford to the starving inhabitants of Paris following the capitulation of the city to the Germans.

December: New churches in Kent this year are St Faith's, Maidstone (on the site of the old Medway Chapel) and St Andrew's Waterside Mission, Gravesend. The church at North Cray has been rebuilt.

Man 'descended from a hairy-tailed quadruped'

CHARLES Darwin has set the world arguing again by publishing *The Descent of Man,* which is the major statement of his theory of evolution.

In it, he claims man is descended from some less highly organised form. He writes:

"He who is not content to look, like a savage, at the phenomena of nature as disconnected, cannot any longer believe that man was a separate act of creation. Man is descended from a hairy, tailed, quadruped, probably arboreal in its habits".

Darwin goes on to say that his conclusions will be denounced by some as highly irreligious. In that theory he is certainly correct. *See page 208*

Victims of the Goodwin Sands live to tell the tale

December 18: The entire crew of a screw steamer, *Sorrento* was saved by the Walmer and Kingsdown lifeboats yesterday after the ship had gone aground on the notorious Goodwin Sands, laden with grain. Not only was it was one of the most daring rescues ever known but the grateful crew know they are among a rare group of mariners who have run into the Sands and lived to tell the tale.

And what a tale it was. The *Sorrento*, from Newcastle, ran aground in heavy seas and, with her back broken, the tide rising and the sea pouring in, she seemed on course to be another victim of an area known as the 'old shippe swallower'.

She was rescued by the crew of the lifeboats *Sabrina* and *Centurion* who somehow managed to pull alongside in heaving waters and then faced the most perilous return journey. Too heavy to go broadside to the waves Coxwain Arnold made the decision to go straight ahead, across four miles of dangerously broken water over the Sands themselves. Somehow, miraculously, they all survived.

The Goodwins, 10 miles long and four miles wide lie six miles off Deal and have a reputation among seafarers unrivalled anywhere in the world.

Authoritive estimates of ships lost in stormy weather on the Goodwin Sands vary between 1,500 and 5,000. At least one ship of the Spanish Armada lies there. In the great storm of 1703, 13 men-of-war were wrecked with the loss of 1,300 lives.

Despite the lifeboatmen's wonders of seamanship more lives have been lost than saved — little wonder the Newcastle sailors are so grateful. *See page 187*

'Drinking' riot in Maidstone

THE new Licensing Act, introduced this year by the Liberal Government, has provoked riots and protests all over Kent as liquor retailers, including those who run beer shops, are placed under the control of local magistrates. They will now be responsible for regulating opening hours in an attempt to limit drunkeness.

No-one is more opposed to the Act than the working class man of Maidstone. Last Saturday, on the first night of early closing (11pm), would-be rioters marched from one public house to another demanding to be served. Few innkeepers dared to oppose them. The next day, a Sunday, when closing time should have been 10pm, a large mob, including soldiers, gathered in the town centre prepared

continued on next page

General Charles 'Chinese' Gordon — and his 'ragged boys'.

General collects an army of 'slum boys from Gravesend'

January: To the dismay of more than 100 Gravesend 'ragamuffins', General Charles George Gordon, commanding officer with the Royal Engineers, has left his home at Fort House, Gravesend for a senior posting overseas.

For the last six years 'Chinese Gordon' has spent his spare time in the slums of this riverside town gathering poor boys so that he could teach them the rudiments of reading, writing and arithmetic. He found employment for many and gave them instructions in Christian belief.

General Gordon, who is 39, was commissioned in the British Army in 1852 and fought in the Crimean War. In 1860, during the Second Opium War, he took part in the capture of Beijing and a grateful Chinese Government made him commander of the peasant force known as the Ever Victorious Army, which helped to suppress the Taiping Rebellion.

He moved to Gravesend as a famous figure, popularly known as 'Chinese Gordon'.

The General immediately took the poor boys of Gravesend to his heart. When his day's work was done, he fed them, clothed them and showed great interest in their physical well-being. In fact he used one of the door frames at Fort House to measure the growth in height of the boys for entry in his logbook. His called them his 'kings' and even taught them to play cricket in what is known as 'the captain's field'.

Fort House and Fort Gardens are south of the moated Tavern Fort which was built about 100 years ago. It was remodelled this year to take 10 heavy guns, mostly nine-inch 12-ton rifled muzzle loaders.

General Gordon has made many keys for his garden gate at Fort House and gives them to selected old people. This extraordinary soldier says he is moved by a sense of the Unseen Presence.

Gravesend is looking forward to welcoming the General back when he completes his new posting as governor of Equatoria on the upper Nile.

See page 214

Better free than sober

(continued)

for another show of strength. On this occasion a military picket was ready for the men and 15 soldiers were marched back to their barracks while others were arrested.

The law is unpopular because it is seen as an attack on freedom. The Bishop of Peterborough said this week: "Better England free than England sober".

Peace in Europe was Napoleon III's greatest wish

January 15: Louis Napoleon Bonaparte III, Emperor of France and exile of Chislehurst, died at Camden Place on Thursday January 9. He was 65.

His lifelong friend, Dr Conneau was sitting with him at the time and the Emperor's last coherent words were: *"N'est-ce-pas, Conneau, que nous n'avons pas été des lâches, à Sedan?".*

The news was relayed to the Queen immediately who said he had borne his misfortunes with meekness, dignity and patience. "He has been a faithful ally to England and I remember the wonderful reception given to him in England in 1855 and his agreeable visit here in '57 and ours to Paris in '55".

Although the Emperor had been ill for some time he had long pondered over a scheme for establishing an International Council that would secure the peace of Europe.

"The day will come", he wrote, "when mankind will recognise that Napoleon III, the exile of Chislehurst, was the founder of this court of legislation and of judicial appeal for nations".He had even discussed it with Queen Victoria but did not live to see "the world rejoice".

For two days the Emperor's body lay on the iron bed on which he had died. He was watched day and night by two sisters of St Joseph and by members of the household.

On Saturday January 11 his body was embalmed and dressed in the uniform of a French General of Division. He was placed in a lead coffin.

The funeral took place today (Wednesday) in the chapel of St Mary's, Chislehurst and the service was conducted by the Catholic Bishop of Southwark. *See page 204*

Mort de L'Empereur Napoleon III. The funeral was held at St Mary's Chapel, Chislehurst when a procession walked from the wrought-iron gates of Camden Place. It was headed by a deputation of Parisian workmen whose leader carried the tricolour. The hearse followed, drawn by eight horses. Behind, alone, walked the Prince Imperial followed by his mother and other members of the Imperial family. Only 200 were allowed inside the tiny church but thousands, who had lined the route across the Common, surged to the front of the chapel while, in the distance, the funeral bell tolled from the Protestant church of St Nicholas. Lady Cowley, wife of the British Ambassador for Paris, described the service in a letter that was shown to the Queen. "There was not a dry eye in the church", she wrote.....All the pomps and obsequies at Notre Dame could never equal the scene in little St Mary's".

Snodland policeman murdered on duty

December 2: Thomas Atkins, a labourer with the Burham Cement Company, has been sentenced to 20 years penal servitude for killing a policeman — the first in Kent to die on duty.

The murder charge, reduced to manslaughter by the judge at the Winter Assizes, followed an incident on August 27 outside the Bull Inn at Snodland, where Pc Israel May, the burly 37-year village constable, found Atkins lying on the ground being sick.

Pc May grabbed Atkins by the coat, pushed him against the wall and told him to go home. Atkins replied that he would like to meet the policeman somewhere in the dark.

At six o'clock the next morning, Pc May's mutilated body was found in a turnip field beside the turnpike road leading from Snodland to Malling, in the neighbouring parish of Birling.

Atkins was suspected immediately and after a massive search by Kent County Constabulary he was arrested near Kingsdown. He had not eaten for at least three days and had been hiding in a wood at Birling.

In his defence, Atkins said that Pc May had followed him and hit him with his staff. "We struggled by the hedge", he said. "I took the staff away and hit him on the head five or six times. I threw it away. I didn't know he was dead".

The policeman's funeral was held at All Saints' Church, Snodland with crowds watching the cortege pass through the village. One local person not present was Pc May's wife. She was forbidden to attend by the police "lest the sight of our universal mourning should prove too much for her".

In appealing for funds in aid of Pc May's wife and three children, the Rector of Snodland, J.Gaspard Le M. Carey wrote: "The murder of a police constable is happily an event of rare occurrence; such a thing has never happened before in the county of Kent".

This is Pc Joseph Herbert Russell, a rural policeman stationed at Westerham, who would have mourned the loss of his colleague, Pc Israel May.

243 drowned as ships collide in the Channel

January 23: The *Northfleet*, a fully-rigged ship of 876 tons — named after the town where she was built in 1853 — sank in the English Channel yesterday with the loss of 243 lives. It is Kent's worst-ever shipping disaster.

On board the *Northfleet* were 343 passengers, most of them railway workers and their families who were sailing to Tasmania to work on the island's new railway line. The ship was also carrying 450 tons of iron for tracks and other materials for building a railway.

The *Northfleet*, commanded by Chief Officer Edward Knowles, had run into a storm that raged in the sea beyond the Thames Estuary. After a terrifying two days she dropped anchor in some 11 fathoms of water about 2° miles off Dungeness.

At 11pm last night she was rammed broadside by a Spanish steamer, later identified as the *Murillo*. The impact holed the wooden sailing ship below the waterline and it began to founder.

As panic broke out among the passengers, many of them in their nightclothes, distress flares were fired and a lifeboat lowered. Vessels which hurried to the scene from Kingsdown and Dover took 86 survivors to the National Sailors' Home at Dover. Those who drowned in the icy waters of the Channel included Captain Knowles and 23 of his crew of 34. His wife was rescued.

See page 199

May 20: Alexander II, the Tsar of Russia and Edward, Prince of Wales were accompanied by their wives on a visit to Crystal Palace. The picture shows the royal party passing up the Nave. Later they reviewed the Royal Artillery on Woolwich Common and toured the wonders of the Royal Arsenal. There are no longer any Sappers in Woolwich. To the great regret of the townspeople they moved to Chatham when the Board of Ordnance came to an end after the Crimean War.

Prize fights for £1000 a side

March 15: Time, energy and considerable resources are being expended by Kent police in attempting to prevent the business of prize fighting. But despite many arrests and harsh sentences there is no sign that the evil is being suppressed.

Two years ago a prize fight took place at Long Reach marshes and one of the combatants was killed. His killer and two accessories were charged.

The following day, unknown to the police, the same group organised another fight on Monkton Marshes, Thanet. It was arranged in great secrecy but still attracted a huge crowd.

The police suspect the directors of the railway companies are aiding and abetting this blatant breach of the peace. They know that a train of 34 carriages, containing 2,000 spectators left London and actually put their passengers down between stations. A ring was hastily erected in a field near Meopham for the purpose of a prize fight. The same thing occurred again between Headcorn and Pluckley but on this occasion two superintendents and seven constables arrived in time to stop the third fight.

Apparently the men fight for as much as £1000 a side and when the police arrive the crowd become as hostile as the combatants.

Permanent home in Kent for two army regiments

August: One of the major changes instigated by Mr Edward Cardwell since he became Minister of War has been to localise the regiments of the British Army and to reorganise them all into more professional and scientific units. He has also introduced a pairing system.

This means the 50th Foot has been given an official home at Maidstone as a single battalion regiment and paired with the 97th (Earl of Ulster's) Regiment. They will now have exclusive recruiting rights in West Kent and South London.

The Buffs have come to roost permanently in Canterbury and installed in barracks built during the Napoleonic War under the shadow of the Cathedral's famous Bell Harry.

Prime Minister Gladstone is delighted with his minister's pairing system which allows battalions to arrange alternate tours at home and overseas with regular exchanges of drafts. Cardwell is a quiet and tenacious man and has opened a new era for the army of advancement by merit.

In Maidstone, where relations between the regiments are most cordial, the depot is known as No 46 (West Kent) Infantry Sub-District Depot.

In Canterbury the Buffs have been issued with breach-loading rifles and the option of discharge after six years colour service in place of 21 years.

June 1: The London Chatham and Dover railway line has been extended from Otford to Maidstone East. **October 9**: South Eastern Railway has opened a line to Hythe and Sandgate.

Canterbury Cathedral has been saved from destruction by fire thanks to the sterling efforts of the local brigade under the captaincy of Bill Pidduck. The blaze occurred when plumbers were working on the roof and a spark set a quantity of twigs and sticks alight which had been carried into the roof space by jackdaws. The fire began to spread rapidly and the local volunteers were quickly mobilised.

Greenwich — the prime meridian?

AN International Geographical Congress in Antwerp today recommended that Greenwich should become the prime meridian — the universally recognised zero longitude and a date line for the world. The delegates at the conference will now report to their governments.

A lightship has been placed on the dangerous Goodwin Sands off the coast of Deal.

New churches in Kent this year are St Michaels, Blackheath (built with a 172 foot spire); Christchurch, Erith and St Mary's, Lewisham.

Mark Sever Bell, an Australian-born lieutenant with the Corps of the Royal Engineers has won the Victoria Cross in Ashanti where the local tribe under King Kofi Kari-Kari has been threatening British interests. Bell encouraged an unarmed working party of Fantee labourers to work under fire without a covering party during the Battle of Ordashu, contributing to the success of the day.

Anyone for tennis?

July: Benjamin Disraeli, at the age of 70, has become Prime Minister for the second time — succeeding his great adversary, William Gladstone, who went to the country in February promising to abolish income tax.

One of Disraeli's key Conservative ministers is William Hart-Dyke of Lullingstone Castle, Eynsford, a former English racquets champion and a member of the All England Croquet Club at Wimbledon.

Unable to show the same wizardry on the racquets court at the age of 36, Hart-Dyke has transferred his passion to the new game of tennis and has laid out on his lawn what is believed to be England's first tennis court.

In fact, tennis has been so popular at Lullingstone house parties this year that the All England Croquet Club has been encouraged to add Lawn Tennis to its title. They now plan to lay out several grass courts.

When he is not playing tennis William Hart-Dyke will be helping his prime minister to introduce an extensive programme of social reforms to improve the conditions of the labouring classes. Playing tennis will not be included! Lullingstone Castle is a magnificent Queen Anne house surrounded by a great park. *See page 238*

Four more dockyard fortresses

March: The fear of a French invasion of England has abated in recent years but that has not stopped engineers from going ahead with the construction of four land fortresses to defend Her Majesty's dockyard at Chatham. The forts will be built in a ring, each 1° miles from the River Medway at Borstal, Bridgewood, Horsted and Luton. The distance is in line with the increased range of enemy guns. It will take the navvies many years to build the forts but when completed they will occupy the best terrain for commanding the land approaches to the dockyard in an arc from the Medway Valley at Borstal to the riverbank at Twydall. The largest fort at Horsted will have a regular chevron plan and will be surrounded by a deep ditch. Concrete is being used for structures under mounted rubble and earth. Accommodation and stores will be protected in casements. The other forts will be smaller but similar in design with heavy fixed guns placed on the ramparts.

How Lord Harris was persuaded to play cricket for Kent

April: Kent Cricket Club, a founder member of the county championship which was inaugurated two years ago, has appointed Lord Harris of Belmont, Faversham as its regular captain and secretary.

Harris, who inherited his title from his father three years ago, has been involved with the administrative side of the club for many years and was responsible for Kent's amalgamation with the Beverley club of Canterbury in 1870.

The new captain first played for the county in 1873. "I was going up to London to see Eton v Harrow and, on the day before, to play for the Lords and Commons against I Zingari", he said, "when I bumped into my old friend, Herbert Knatchbull-Huggeson of Mersham Hatch at Faversham station.

"He was on his way to watch Kent v Lancashire at Gravesend and tried to persuade me to change my plans so I could play for the county.

"Impossible", I said. "I'm engaged to play for the Lords.

"Herbert reasoned with such effect that at Strood I got out of the train, wired to Lord's explaining my defection with profound apologies and turned up at the Bat and Ball ground, Gravesend. Someone most kindly stood out. I got 26 and 6 and we won the match".

This year Kent will play most of its matches at Catford Bridge which has been made available by the Private Banks Cricket Club.

Harris says his first task is to try and improve the financial situation and he intends to appeal for subscriptions.

Lord Harris of Eton and Oxford, a fine, free and stylish batsman.

In an attempt to improve conditions for cross-Channel travellers two experimental ships have been introduced on the Dover to Calais crossing — the *Castalia* and the *Bessemer*.

The *Castalia* consists of two half hulls with a pair of paddle wheels working in tandem between them. The *Bessemer* incorporates a suspended and pivoted saloon and anti-rolling mechanism to overcome the pitching and rolling of the ship.

The church of St Thomas of Canterbury, the only Roman Catholic church in the city since the reformation, has been dedicated by Cardinal Manning .

A new church, St Luke's, has been dedicated at Matfield.

Old John Timbs, a journalist and author of more than 100 books has died at Edenbridge, aged 75. He was the editor of Samuel Pepys diaries.

More than 40 people have died in a major outbreak of scarlatina in Sittingbourne, Sevenoaks, Chatham, West Malling and Maidstone

Mariner swims the Channel: an extraordinary feat of endurance

Captain Matthew Webb is helped ashore at Calais after completing his historic swim

August 25: Captain Matthew Webb, a 27-year-old merchant naval officer, today became the first man to swim the English Channel. According to many experts it is a feat unlikely ever to be repeated.

Webb put his feet down on French soil at 11 am this morning having spent 21 hours and 45 minutes in the water, covering a distance of nearly 40 miles. He was helped up the beach by a group of Frenchmen who sang *Rule Britannia* and was then taken by horse and trap to the Hotel de Paris at Calais.

Today he is sleeping. When he awakes he will find himself a national hero and an international celebrity. Webb is not the first swimmer to attempt this great test of endurance. During the Napoleonic Wars many French prisoners escaped from the hulks but all were drowned in their quest to swim the 21 miles to Cap Gris Nez.

Born in Shropshire, the son of a doctor, Matthew Webb learned to swim in the River Severn, developed a great passion for water and joined the merchant service.At almost six foot tall and weighing 14° stone he is in perfect health.

One month ago he swam the Thames from Blackwall to Gravesend on the ebb tide. It was a distance of 20 miles and he achieved it in under five hours. A few days later Webb swam round the coast from Dover to Ramsgate in eight hours 40 minutes. At times he was pitting his strength against the tide.

His first attempt to swim the Channel failed because of bad weather but his exploits fired public imagination and a group of businessmen working for the Stock Exchange each offered him 25 guineas if he could achieve his greatest ambition.

At one o'clock yesterday Webb jumped into the sea at Admiralty Pier, Dover, greased in porpoise oil. The sea was calm and the swimmer, sustained by hot coffee, beef tea and ale, made such good progress that the oarsmen in the accompanying lugger had difficulty in keeping up with him.

He didn't swim alone all the way. A school of porpoises escorted him for several miles and then jellyfish joined in the fun, stinging him so painfully that he took brandy for some relief. More welcome was the sight of cheering passengers on the cross Channel ferries which had altered course.

Some three miles from France the tide turned and Webb found himself swimming almost parallel with the coast and making little progress. This continued for five hours until eventually he was able to wade ashore.

August 15: The man who conquered the Straits of Dover returned to the town today a hero. The 24th Regiment gave him its '24 honours salute' and the Burmese Silver Cup and the Mayor of Dover told Webb before thousands of clamorous people: "The nation will be proud of you. Yours is a feat that may never be repeated". Later today at the Stock Exchange he will receive a cheque for £1,400.

See page 210

'I am a child of the beach at Ramsgate' — Vincent van Gogh in a letter to his brother

May 12: An accomplished and prolific Dutch artist, just 20 years old, has arrived in Ramsgate to take up an appointment as a teacher at Mr Stokes schoolhouse, 6 Royal Road, Ramsgate.

Vincent van Gogh is already spending much of his spare time making sketches and drawings of the locality which he sends home to his family in Holland.

There wasn't enough room to accommodate young Vincent at the school so he took lodgings nearby believed to be at 11 Spencer Square.

Recently he wrote to his brother Theo: "There are many bugs at Mr Stokes' but the view from the school windows makes one forget them".

In another letter, he writes: "I saw the sea last Sunday night, everything was dark and grey but at the horizon the day began to dawn. It was still very dark but a lark was singing already. So were nightingales in the gardens near the sea".

The descriptive letters home have continued. "After dinner", he wrote to his parents, "we took a walk on the shore; it was beautiful. The houses on the shore are mostly built of yellow stone in simple gothic style and have gardens full of cedars and other dark evergreens. There is a harbour full of ships, shut in between stone jetties on which one can walk. Then there is the unspoiled sea and that is beautiful".

This week he wrote to his brother again: "If there should be no human being that you can love enough, love the town in which you dwell...I love Paris and London though I am a child of the pine woods and of the beach at Ramsgate.."

Vincent van Gogh, aged 19, taken just before he arrived in Ramsgate.

June 17: Two months after his arrival at Ramsgate Vincent left for London, a distance of more than 100 miles. He walked and in a letter to his brother described what he had seen on the way. "That was quite a walk", he wrote. "It was very hot on the way so I rested frequently and went on eventually arriving in Canterbury in the evening. I found a few large beech trees and elms near a pond so there I rested for a while".

At 3.30 in the morning he started his journey again. "It was good to walk then", he wrote. He went from Canterbury, through Harbledown, Boughton-under-Blean, Ospringe, Sittingbourne and Chatham "where one can see the Thames in the distance, full of ships".

Eventually he got a lift in a cart for a few miles until the waggoner stopped at an inn and van Gogh completed his journey alone..

With attendance at schools now compulsory, more and more children are receiving a good Christian education. Almost 60 new schools have opened in Kent since the setting up of School Boards following the Act of 1870. Some towns have even found it necessary to build a second or even third school.

Prime Minister Benjamin Disraeli, former MP for Maidstone and a man who has entertained and infuriated the House of Commons for the past 39 years today made his last appearance in the lower house. Queen Victoria has created him Earl of Beaconsfield so he will lead the Government from the House of Lords.

Police say that more than 100,000 immigrants from South and East London are arriving in the Kentish hop gardens.

An open air bathing pool has been built by ther River Stour in Canterbury.It is proving very popular.

Edward Sharp has opened a grocery shop in Week Street, Maidstone selling special sweets made by his wife.

Churches restored this year are St John, Margate and St Mary's, Upchurch. New churches are Christchurch, Beckenham, St Michael and All Saints', Maidstone and St Saviour's, Tonbridge.

August: W.G. Grace, a large, bearded cricketer, scored 344 runs for the MCC against Kent at Canterbury. It took him six hours and 20 minutes and he didn't give a single chance. It takes his aggregate in eight days to 839 runs.

Home at last: This painting which hangs in Shoreham church shows Verney returning to the village. The African boy who is standing with him in the carriage was freed by Said Ibn Salim, the Arab Governor of Unyanyembé in November 1873. He says he intends to make his home in Shoreham.

Hero's welcome for African explorer

April 20: Lieutenant Verney Lovett Cameron, a 32-year-old explorer, was given a hero's welcome today as he returned to his home village of Shoreham with news of his great expedition to Africa in search of Dr David Livingstone. With him was a young African boy, Jacko who had accompanied Cameron on his adventures.

As they stepped off the train at Shoreham station they were decorated with bay and laurel. A band played *Hail the Conquering Hero* and a Mr George Wilmot presented Cameron with a congratulatory address.

The villagers then took the horses out of the traces of the waiting carriage and themselves pulled it up the hill preceded by a band. The explorer's mother and father, the Rev Lovett Cameron, vicar of Shoreham, were waiting at the church with the rest of the village.

It was three years ago in 1873 that Lt Cameron was chosen by the Royal Geographical Society to head an expedition to Africa to search for Dr Livingstone. The Scottish missionary and explorer had been seen a year earlier by the Welshman, Henry Stanley, on the edge of Lake Tanganyika, who famously lifted his hat and said: "Dr Livingstone, I presume".

Stanley's words were the first Livingstone had heard spoken by a European in five years.

The two men spent the next four months exploring together, trying to find the source of the Nile, but when Stanley tried to persuade the frail doctor to return home with him, he refused.

A few months later Lt Cameron set out with W.E.Dillon, a naval surgeon and Lt Cecil Murphy. Not long after they left Zanzibar they met Livingstone's servants bearing the dead body of their master. Dillon and Murphy turned back but Verney Cameron continued his march until he reached Ujiji on Lake Tanganyika in February 1874. There he found Livingstone's papers which he sent back to England.

The explorer, with his young friend Jacko, pressed on following the course of the Lualaba river. They crossed the entire continent reaching the Atlantic coast at Benguella in November. Cameron was the first white man

(continued on next page)

Kentish piers: bruised and battered by the waves

January 2: More than 40 terrified New Year's Day revellers spent the entire night marooned on the seaward end of the pier at Margate yesterday as heavy seas crashed against what was left of the 24-year-old structure.

The drama began in the afternoon when a storm-driven wreck crashed against the pier and sliced it in half. Several people escaped, including those who were thrown into the sea, but the others were not rescued until early today.

As town officials assess the extent of the damage to the jetty and droit office there are reports of more dramatic events right round the east Kent coast as far south as Hythe.

Here workmen were digging out shingle from the banked-up beach for the construction of a sea wall along the front at Stade Street when a south-westerly blew in.

The sea, enlarged by a spring high tide found the cut made by the builder's men, breached the landward side and rushed towards the town centre. Within minutes water had flowed over the raised banks and bridges of the Royal Military Canal and into the cellars of High Street shops. One man has died.

With the sea water rising rescue work was carried out immediately by firemen and policemen in boats. Today Marine Walk and the High Street are still inundated and a flood relief fund is being initiated. *See page 242*

It has taken almost five months for railway navigators to clear the line of chalk and rubble near the southern end of the Martello Tunnel between Folkestone and Dover following a gigantic landslide on January 12.

The landslide came a week after the New Year Day storm which washed away the foot of the cliff and undermined 60,000 cubic yards. It left a mound more than 110 feet deep. Sadly, three railway workers were killed. Desperate to open the line, the navvies began immediately to clear the rubble and the first line was opened on March 12 in the presence of Sir Edward Watkin (shown here wearing a Cossack cap) and other directors of South Eastern Railway.

He fought to suppress slavery

continued from page 193

to make such a journey.

In recognition of his achievement he has been promoted to the rank of Commander and has received the Gold Medal of the Royal Geographical Society.

His heroic exploits in Africa has stirred the people of Shoreham who have known the Cameron family since they moved into the village in 1860. Verney was then 16 and had spent three years in the Royal Navy. He was later appointed senior lieutenant on *HMS Star* of the East African Slave Squadron, formed to frustrate Arab purchasers of African slaves.

The experience of seeing at close hand the horrors of the slave trade convinced him that more missionaries were needed in the interior of Africa, fighting for the suppression of slavery. He studied Swahili and offered his services to the Royal Geographical Society.

November 24: In another terrible storm a schooner carrying coal from South Shields to Devon has crashed into Deal pier, smashing the cast iron pillars and ripping up the wooden deck. Three people have been killed.

Margate has not escaped and, according to Keble's Gazette, "the scene of devastation and ruin is so complete that the only parallel is in a nightmare".

More than 20 vessels have been driven ashore between Westgate and Westbrook and the Margate lifeboat *Friends of All Nations,* has helped to rescue 130 people.

See page 242

Kentish explorer dies in an African whirlpool

July: Kent's well-known African explorer, Frank Pocock has been drowned in a whirlpool somewhere near the mouth of the great Congo River.

The tragic news of his death has reached his home village of Upnor. There are few details but it is known that his distinguished explorer companion, Henry Stanley is so distraught that he plans to return from his 7,000 mile odyssey across some of the most hostile terrain in the world.

In 1874 — three years after finding Dr David Livingstone — Stanley returned to Africa on an expedition from Zanzibar to the mouth of the Congo.

With him travelled 347 natives and white assistants, Edward and Frank Pocock who were born and brought up in Upnor where their father is a fisherman. In volunteering to accompany Stanley through tropical Africa they promised they "would stick beside him to the death".

Sadly, that is exactly what has happened. Edward died of a tropical disease some months ago along with more than 150 natives. But Stanley and Frank Pocock pressed on. They circumnavigated Lakes Tanganyika and Victoria and traced the course of the unexplored Congo River losing more men on the way to disease, war with hostile tribes and sheer exhaustion.

On June 3 1877, some 150 miles from the mouth of the Congo, Frank Pocock was swallowed by a whirlpool. He disappeared within seconds.

It is believed that Frank's diary, which contains vivid descriptions of battles with warriors, the tragedy of losing so many willing companions and the excitement of finding the Congo river, has survived.

It will be returned to his family in Upnor.

Henry Morton was born in Wales in 1841 and grew up in a workhouse. He sailed for New Orleans at the age of 16 where he was adopted by a cotton broker named Stanley. Adopting this name he found work with a newspaper in St Louis and excelled as a journalist. In 1868 he persuaded the New York Herald to send him to find Livingstone who was 'lost'.

Rochester diocese exclusively in Kent

THE diocese of Rochester has been reorganised at last. It will now embrace more parishes from Kent, together with some from London south of the Thames and say goodbye to those in Essex and Hertfordshire, which it has looked after since 1845. These will be transferred to the new diocese of St Albans.

The clergy are delighted with the reforms. Measures have been taken to increase the annual incomes of bishoprics by reducing that of Canterbury and increasing the poorer Rochester.

Bishops in each diocese are now empowered to require every parish church to hold two full services each Sunday which will include a sermon or lecture. There will also be a major reform of the Cathedrals with the number of resident canons restricted to six each.

Home in Rusthall for the Queen's fourth daughter

June 30: Her Royal Highness, the Princess Louise — the fourth of Queen Victoria's five daughters — today laid a memorial stone to the west of Camden Road, Tunbridge Wells "where the Friendly Societies of the Wells will henceforth congregate".

Princess Louise and her husband, the Marquis of Lorne live at Dornden, Rusthall, an elegant but modest mansion of Gothic style built from the designs of the late Charles Barry. The couple moved to the 170-acre estate in 1874 and have received many members of the royal family who travel to Tunbridge Wells by the royal train.

Princess Louise is the Queen's only child to be married to a commoner — and that has not happened since 1659 when the Duke of York married Anne Hyde. Queen Victoria did consider the Prince of Orange, heir to the Dutch throne, but he was ruled out because of his reputation for loose living. She did not want Louise marrying into the Russian Imperial family and moving to St Petersburg and marriage to a Catholic, particularly a Bonaparte, was quite unacceptable.

So Queen Victoria encouraged her daughter to attend gatherings where bachelors of suitable background and income would be present. The Marquis of Lorne, eldest son of the 8th Duke of Argyll, was one of those young men. The couple were married in 1871.

Looking round for a suitable house not too far from London the Marquis chose Dornden which he bought for £30,000. Sadly the couple cannot stay. Next year Lorne will take up the appointment of Governor-General of Canada and will have to dispose of the property.

The medieval stone bridge over the River Medway at Maidstone is to be replaced with a new bridge of three arches which will give a clear waterway of 149 feet. The designer is Sir Joseph Bazalgette, the engineer of the Thames embankment and the cost of the bridge and its approaches is in excess of £55,000. The opening is set for August next year when a medal, struck specially for the occasion, will be presented to 5,000 local children. This painting of the old bridge by Albert Goodwin has been bought by public subscription.

Arthur Sullivan's *Lost Chord* heard at Hothfield

WHEN Arthur Sullivan returned from Leipzig as thc first holder of the Mendelssohn scholarship he asked the secretary of the Crystal Palace, George Grove if his *Tempest* could be performed in the great glass dome on Sydenham Hill.

Grove, so taken with the engaging young man of 19, agreed and on Saturday April 5, 1862 Sullivan became the first unknown composer to perform in the Crystal Palace. His music created a sensation and charmed all those who heard it including Charles Dickens who immediately went round to meet Sullivan, grasped his hand and said: "I don't pretend to know much about music but I do know I have been listening to a very great work".

In this way, at the Crystal Palace, was laid the foundation of Arthur Sullivan's musical career. He rented a room over a shop at Sydenham, composed *Sapphire Necklace* and was appointed Professor of Pianoforte and Ballad Singing at the Crystal Palace school of art. He began to compose hymns, cantatas, piano pieces, songs and orchestral works.

Today, Sullivan is best known for his highly successful collaboration with William Schwenk Gilbert. As a librettist-composer team their operettas are enjoyed for their satirical wit, comic plots and characters and tuneful music.

Their first collaboration, *Thespis* was not successful. *Trial by Jury* (1875) was unusual in being a one-act operetta without spoken dialogue. *The Sorcerer* (1877) began their public acclaim as well as their association with Richard D'Oyly Carte's company.

Last year they introduced *HMS Pinafore* and this year the brilliant *Pirates of Penzance*. Their fame has even extended to the United States.

Sullivan's work is not confined to his collaboration with Gilbert on comic operas satirizing Victorian manners. In 1871 he composed the music to the hymn *Onward Christian Soldiers* and followed that, in 1877, with *The Lost Chord.*

Soon after he finished this great composition he was invited to dine with Lord and Lady Hothfield at their mansion, Hothfield Place. So eager was he to try out his new music that he walked across to the village church, sat down at the organ and played. The delightful strains of *The Lost Chord* echoed across the fields of Hothfield.

1,576 NCOs and men were slaughtered at the British base of Isandhlwana

Sevenoaks boy dies in the blood of Isandhlwana

January 29: Several soldiers from Kent are among the 1,576 NCOs and men slaughtered in South Africa this week by Zulu warriors. Apparently only 40 Europeans escaped the massacre which occurred at the advance British base at Isandhlwana.

The disaster, was brought about by a clever Zulu manoeuvre, which drew Lord Chelmsford and his main force away from the camp and by the inept positioning of the garrison which was scattered over a large area.

One man who died was Francis (Frank) Holcroft who lived at the southern end of Sevenoaks High Street where his father is a solicitor. Holcroft had sailed to South Africa and joined the locally-raised 1st Natal native contingent as a lieutenant. He was in the British force sent to deal with the aggressive King Cetewayo of the Zulus who, after the slaughter, triumphantly claimed that his warriors had "washed their spears" in the blood of the garrison.

News reaching Kent this week tells that Holcroft and his fellow defenders fought gallantly until their ammunition ran out. Many of those who got away rode to alert the 130-strong garrison left behind at Rorke's Drift.

The Buffs, who left their base at Canterbury for South Africa some weeks ago, are luckier. As the British forces marched into Zulu territory they were split into five columns. The Buffs were in the first column, commanded by Colonel Pearson, which crossed the border and fortified a missionary station at Ekowe. It was the second and third columns which were wiped out at Isandhlwana.

Like those at Rorke's Drift it is believed the lst column is preparing to withstand a long siege. The Zulus have not yet attacked but the Buffs are waiting and praying in the hope that a relief column may soon be able to reach them.

February: George Langridge, whose family live at Buckhurst Avenue, Sevenoaks, has miraculously survived the Zulu assault at Rorke's Drift. On January 23, he was one of 130 men of the 2nd battalion of the South Wales Borderers' who held out for 12 hours while 4,000 spear-carrying warriors mounted attack after attack. It is being hailed as the greatest rearguard action in military hisory.

George enlisted with the Borderers at 18 and was 21 when he accompanied his regiment to the British base at Isandhlwana where the Zulus first attacked. George was among those who gallantly rode to alert the smaller garrison at Rorke's Drift.

continued on page 198

Crimean hero weds captain's daughter

REAR Admiral Charles Lucas, hero of the Crimean War and the first man to win the Victoria Cross, has married Frances, only daughter of Sir William Hall of Mereworth, who was captain of *HMS Hecla* when Lucas performed his great act of courage.

Lucas has always been a man of action. Apart from his heroics in the Crimea, he saw a great deal of the Burma Campaign of 1852-3 and was present at the capture of Rangoon.

He rose to captain in 1867 and by successive stages to that of Rear Admiral. His home today is Great Culverden, Tunbridge Wells.

TWO officers with the Corps of the Royal Engineers, **Captain Edward Leach**, 31 and **Lieutenant Reginald Clare Hart**, 30 have been awarded the Victoria Cross for their extraordinary acts of bravery in the Second Afghan War.

On January 31, Lt Hart rescued a wounded sowar of the Bengal Lancers who was lying in a river bed exposed to the fire of the enemy on all sides.

On March 17, Captain Leach with some men of the 45th Sikhs charged the enemy and killed three men himself while receiving a severe wound. He saved his whole party from annihilation.

Prince Imperial slain by Zulus in Africa

July 11: Thousands of people, including Queen Victoria and members of European royal families, watched as the coffin carrying the body of the last pretender to the title of Emperor Napoleon of France crossed Chislehurst Common today on its way from Camden Place to the Roman Catholic Church of St Mary.

The Prince Imperial, who was slain by spear-carrying warriors in South Africa during the Zulu War, was the last of the Napoleonic dynasty. Like his father and great uncle he died on alien soil. He was a popular young man who had grown up in England and the crowds, lining the route of the funeral procession, were the greatest Chislehurst has ever seen.

Five years ago, in 1874, when the Prince Imperial celebrated his coming of age, hundreds of French Bonapartists set up tents on the Common and marquees in the grounds of Camden Place in a show of loyalty designed to persuade Prince Louis that he could, one day, inaugurate the Third Empire.

The Prince may have harboured such ambitions but he needed military experience and a commission from the British Army in order to fight in the Zulu War. There he hoped to join his friends from the Royal Military Academy at Woolwich. Concerned about his princely status the army agreed he could travel as an observer only.

In South Africa, Lieutenant Carey, an officer in the Army's Quartermaster-General's Department, was given command of a platoon that included the Prince Imperial and told to make sure the headstrong 26-year-old was well protected by his bodyguards.

On one expedition the party decided to find a new camp site, settled at a suitable

Prince Louis, the Prince Imperial — last of the Napoleon dynasty

spot by the Inyolozi river and unsaddled their horses. Within minutes they were surrounded by chanting, spear-carrying Zulu warriors who made their intentions quite clear.

Carey ordered his men to mount and make a dash for freedom which they did. But the inexperienced Prince Imperial, unable to resaddle his horse, was left behind with only a service revolver for defence.He faced the now-charging Zulus head on and fought bravely but was speared to death".

Lt Carey was immediately charged with 'indiscretion' and court-martialled. He was then sentenced to death. Back in Chislehurst, Princess Eugenie was told about her son's death and collapsed in grief. She received a telegraph of sympathy from Queen Victoria and then learned about the fate facing Lt Carey.

"This will achieve nothing more than another widow", she said. "Let the sentence be quashed". It was. Carey returned to duty and Prince Louis Napoleon's body was returned to Chislehurst.

continued from page 197

There has been no news yet of George Langridge's role in the siege but it is believed his battalion was attacked by 4,000 of Cetewayo's warriors. They held out until the Zulus retreated after 12 hours. The Buffs are still marooned at Ekowe.

An artist's reconstruction of the collision in the Thames. The steamer* Princess Alice *broke into three parts.

More than 600 drowned in Galleons Reach

AN INQUIRY has been ordered into the tragedy of the pleasure steamer, *Princess Alice,* which was run down by a screw collier in Galleons Reach, Erith in September last year, drowning more than 600 people. It is the worst disaster the river has ever known.

The London Steamboat Company paddle-steamer was returning from an excursion to Sheerness when she was rammed by the *Bywell Castle*. She broke into three parts and sank immediately. It is believed there were more than 800 people on board, most of them women and children.

The accident is being blamed on the exceptionally heavy traffic on the river Thames. *Princess Alice* was one of a number of large saloon steamers which daily ran return excursions from London to Sheerness via Gravesend.

On this occasion she left London Bridge with 700 day trippers and dropped many of them at Rosherville Pier, Northfleet so they could enjoy a day in the 20-acres of pleasure gardens west of Gravesend. *Princess Alice* took the remainder to Sheerness.

She returned at 4.15 pm, picked up the trippers at Northfleet and steamed up the Thames with John Eyres at the helm and skipper William Grinstead giving orders.

The sky was clear and there was a light breeze but the river was typically busy and it was no surprise for those on deck to see a massive screw collier *Bywell Castle* moving down river. Tragically, it soon became apparent the collier was on a collision course.

The collier's bows sliced through the paddle steamer which immediately began to sink. There was pandemonium. Some people jumped into the water and others tried to climb the funnels but they were badly burned and fell back into the water.

Small craft from both banks of the river went to the aid of those in the water and rescued many. By that time the *Princess Alice* had sunk in just 18 feet of water and all around was the sight of drowning people.

Fewer than 200 people were saved.

Edward Coley Burne-Jones (left), a 46-year-old artist is pictured here with his friend and colleague, William Morris with whom he shares the Pre-Raphaelite's concern with medieval settings. Burne-Jones, who was trained by Dante Gabriel Rossetti, designs stained-glass windows, mosaics and tapestries for Morris and Company. Among his more recent commissions is ten windows for the Gothic revival church of St Mary's, Speldhurst. Other Kent churches with Burne-Jones stained-glass windows are those at Shoreham and Edenbridge.

1880-1889

1880: Every child between the ages of five and 13 is now legally bound to attend school.

April: William Gladstone wins the general election and the Queen is forced to invite the man she dislikes to form a government again.

September 10: 160 miners are killed in an explosion at Seaham colliery, Durham.

George Newnes introduces a new popular magazine called *Titbits.*

1881: January: A great freeze grips Britain. All roads in Kent are impassable.

Tenants are granted fair rents and greater protection from eviction in a new Bill.

The results of the national census shows that Kent is slowly becoming a 'middle class' county as the ranks of the commercial, managerial and professional salary earners expand.Chatham is still the largest town.

1882: The Church Army, a body of lay evangelists, is founded to spread the gospel.

Australia has beaten England at cricket prompting the *Sporting Times* to announce the death of English cricket and sending the Ashes to Australia.

1883: Railway companies offer a cheap workman's fare so that all classes may be able to travel and work in London.

A few railway companies have begun to introduce an electrically-powered lighting system in their stations.

1884: The Prince of Wales makes a speech in the House of Lords on the condition of the poor.

An earthquake in Essex lasting a minute is felt in Kent. Several buildings are damaged.

Queen Victoria has bestowed a peerage on Alfred Tennyson, the poet laureate.

A society, the NSPCC, is formed to protect children. It will work closely with the Barnardo homes.

South Eastern Railway Company opens a branch line to New Romney.

Ramsgate is incorporated by Royal Charter.

A Kent College boarding school for boys is established in Canterbury by Weslyan Methodists. There is a companion school for girls at Folkestone.

1885: Terms for the partition of central and eastern Africa have been agreed by delegates from 15 nations.

William Gladstone, Prime Minister, resigns after the defeat of his budget. Lord Salisbury is appointed caretaker Prime Minister.

A new safety bicycle is manufactured in Coventry. It will be cheaper and safer than the existing 'penny farthings'

Lydd is incorporated by Royal Charter.

J and E Hall of Dartford celebrates its centenary year.

1886: Lord Salisbury's government is defeated by 329 votes to 250 on the Queen's speech. Gladstone begins his third term as Prime Minister.

The Irish Home Rule issue dominates a turbulent political year as Liberal rebels throw out Gladstone's bill.

Women suspected of being prostitutes who refuse a medical examination may now be imprisoned following a tireless campaign by Josephine Butler.

1887: The Kent harvest is badly damaged as a severe drought hits the county.

A great fire at Knole, home of the Sackville family, threatens to engulf the house and its priceless trreasures. Sevenoaks, Tonbridge and Tunbridge Wells fire brigades attend while the Chief Constable of Kent and a large force of police officers keep spectators out of Knole Park.

There are celebrations all over the world to mark the golden jubilee of Queen Victoria's reign. The empire now comprises three quarters of the earth's land surface.

Sherlock Holmes, a fictional detective and Dr Watson his colleague are introduced by their creator, Arthur Conan Doyle.

1888: John Dunlop, an Irishman, invents a pneumatic tyre with rubber treads for his 10-year-old son. It is hailed as the invention of the year.

A man who is being dubbed 'Jack the Ripper' is terrorising London having already murdered five women. More than 600 policemen are hunting for him.

Queen Victoria's grandson succeeds to the throne of Germany as Emperor William II.

1889: An inquiry shows that one in three are living below the poverty line in London, the world's largest city.

A former schoolmaster Jerome K. Jerome writes a book about the occasion that he and his two friends took a leisurely trip up the river Thames. *Three Men in A Boat* is a massive bestseller.

A month-long strike by London's dockers ends with employers agreeing to a new pay deal of 6d an hour. It is a breakthrough for the socialist movement.

Robert Louis Stevenson, author of *Treasure Island* and *Kidnapped* builds himself a house on the island of Samoa.

Tonbridge ruffians paid to riot by defeated Liberals

April 24: Rioters rampaged through Tonbridge today following the surprise defeat of the town's once-popular Liberal candiates, Edward Cazalet and W.A.Elphinstone in the general election.

Police reinforcements from Maidstone eventually quelled the rebellion but not until an all-day battle had ended. During that time 500 ruffians pelted 94 officers with flour and rotten eggs.The windows of many buildings in the town have been smashed and debris lies everywhere.

Chief Constable William Ruxton says the victorious Conservative candidates, Sir William Hart-Dyke and Sir Edward Filmer foolishly drove into town in an open carriage and it was this ill-judged action which caused the eruption. It is believed the ruffians were paid to cause trouble by the Liberal Party.

Despite the Liberal reversal at Tonbridge and other Kent towns, William Gladstone has won a spectacular victory and will be forming a new government.

Sandwich disenfranchised in election scandal

October 25: Parliament is to abolish the Sandwich Constituency following allegations of widespread bribery and corruption during the general election contest earlier this year.

The decision to disenfranchise will be ratified by an Act of Parliament next year — and the good name of Sandwich will be blackened before the whole country.

At the last election the borough returned two Liberal members to Parliament, Henry Brassey and Mr Knatchbull-Huguesson. This year the latter member was raised to the peerage and his seat became vacant so the Liberals nominated Sir Julian Goldsmid, a wealthy baronet. Standing against him was Mr Crompton Roberts, a London businessman .

Mr Roberts won and Sir Julian immediately presented a petition alleging bribery and corruption had been rife — producing evidence to support his claim.

A Commission of Inquiry appointed to hear the case were given details of the corrupt practices which included large sums of money being handed over by the Conservative Party for canvassers to visit public houses and pay for votes. The Liberals, having heard about the payments, appointed 16 "watchers" at a pound each to walk the streets at night to prevent the voters "being tampered with".

There were other irregularities concerning the use of payments in gold by Sir Julian and extravagant expenditure on both sides.

This week the *Deal Chronicle* in a leading article wrote: "Sir Julian Goldsmid made the loudest professions of his horror of bribery and then furnished funds to be spent on the wholesale debauchery of the electors of Sandwich. He was righteously indignant that someone else should do the same and set to work to avenge his rejection by procuring the disenfranchisement of the Borough. Some will be scandalised at the cynical hypocrisy of the representative Radical."

The Commission says laws have been broken and legal proceedings must be taken against both parties at the Kent Summer Assizes next year. They also recommend the Sandwich Constituency be abolished.

Museum gift from the grocer-scientist

BENJAMIN Harrison, the 'grocer scientist' of Ightham village has presented to the Maidstone Museum his amazing collection of flint instruments which he has discovered around Oldbury, the prehistoric camp less than a mile from his home.

The collection, believed to be the finest in the world, has attracted antiquarians of note from the far corners of the earth to the small village between Sevenoaks and Maidstone.

A few years ago, Harrison — who began collecting fossils at the age of 12 — found Roman relics at Oldbury and this led to his search for flint instruments. He was able to prove that man lived on the back of the Wealden dome in bygone days.

As the country's foremost geologist his advice has been sought by railway engineers and surveyors throughout the country.

Roman Catholics have finally opened a church in Maidstone after years of conflict with the town's protestants. St Francis Church has been designed by C.G.Wray.

Campaigning newspaper, The *Gravesend Reporter,* is leading the way in Kent in urging the town to introduce an early closing day for shops. "Assistants become tired after working 86 hours a week and should be allowed to close at 1pm on Wednesday (the quietest day)". There is every chance this drastic reform may be adopted.

Greenwich Mean Time has been legally adopted as the official time zone for the world following an Act of Parliament this year. The time is now calculated by the movement of the sun in relation to the Greenwich meridian.

New churches this year are St John the Evangelist, Bromley, St Paul's, Four Elms and St Mary's, Sevenoaks,

Combe Bank, Sundridge, the home of William Spottiswoode

Kentish village witnesses the wonder of electricity

THE small community of Sundridge near Sevenoaks marvelled tonight at the sight of a glass bulb glowing "with great splendour" from the top of Combe Bank, an 18th century mansion owned by the remarkable William Spottiswoode.

The bulb is powered by a form of electricity invented by Joseph Swan, one of Mr Spottiswoode's colleagues in the Royal Society — the nation's most prestigious scientific institution.

Inside the house are further electric light fittings. They have been installed by Mr Michael Faraday, the experimental physicist, who was responsible for the discovery of electromagnetism earlier in the century.

Combe Bank's electric light burns carbon in a bulb exhausted of air and gives off a light "as bright as sunshine". It appears that Messrs Swan and Spottiswoode are winning the race to produce light by means of electricity. Certainly Combe Bank is one of the first houses in the country to have an electric light.

Spottiswoode is an inventive character. He is a member of the famous printing family by the same name and he has written a major scientific work entitled *The Polarization of Light*. He believes, one day, all homes should be able to switch to electric power.

He has lived in Combe Bank since 1865 when he was President of the Royal Society and the host to a glittering succession of famous personalities who were invited for the weekend. Mr Spottiswoode would send coaches and four to the newly-opened Sevenoaks railway station and pick up such well-known people as Professors Huxley and Pollock, Herbert Spencer, the evolutionist philosopher, Professor and Mrs Tyndall, Matthew Arnold, Moncure D.Conway, Oscar Wilde, Charles Darwin and, of course Michael Faraday who undertook the lighting work.

A few weeks ago the Chinese Ambassador came to stay and was nearly killed when the apparatus, generating the electricity current, accidentally blew up.

There is one concern for the British electricity pioneers and that comes from the New World where Mr Thomas Edison has devised an alternative system using metal filaments. Other inventors are striding in the same direction.

The race is on.

100 barges lost in 'mightiest blizzard since 1836'

January 19: One hundred barges on the Thames were sunk and several lives lost yesterday as a violent blizzard, accompanied by hurricane-force easterly winds, struck Kent. Newspapers are describing the gale as the "mightiest ever known". Old timers say it is certainly the worst since Christmas Day 1836.

The sea has rarely behaved so angrily and widespread damage has been reported all round the Kent coast.

At Folkestone most of the promenade was washed away and, in the harbour, dramatic scenes were witnessed. The sea dashed over the pier and breakwater, burying it in debris.

As the snow fell it was drifted by whirlwinds into every sheltered spot. At Ramsgate a train was buried under 16 feet of snow and at Dover the wind blew with such force that it was impossible to stand.

Post Office telegraphs were suspended, mail vessels were unable to leave port and trains were abandoned between stations.

The most dramatic occurrences were on the Thames. At North Woolwich 26 barges were missing and three men were drowned. Two dock constables are also missing and two are lost in the Albert Docks.

Mob of 600 on rampage through 'dirty' Chatham

November: Five years ago the official handbook to the county of Kent had this to say about the town of Chatham. "It is a very different style of place to Rochester; a dirty, unpleasant town devoted to the interests of soldiers, sailors and marines".

Chatham's reputation for lawlessness reached new depths this week when rioters attacked the police station in New Road in a failed attempt to 'rescue' Robert Merritt, a coal whipper accused of assaulting a respectable looking woman.

It took several members of the local constabulary and a detachment of military police from the barracks to take Merritt into custody.

Two weeks earlier, on Guy Fawkes Day, a mob of more than 600 gathered between Globe Lane and Military Road and rampaged through the town throwing fireworks indiscriminately.

Law abiding citizens say violence, prostitution, drunken brawls and the use of filthy, vile language on every corner of Chatham's streets is a direct result of the town's lack of organised authority.

Large scale riots are associated with seamen returning to or leaving port. They are known to march along the High Street, stopping to demand drinks at various pubs. Whenever they meet the soldiers, violence breaks out and, according to the *Chatham Observer* "respectable people are being roughly used and knocked about".

Chatham has one police inspector and 12 constables for a population in excess of 26,000 whereas Rochester has a Chief Constable and 28 constables for a population of 12,806. The unruly town is hindered by a lack of police manpower and the authorities are demanding an increase in the number of officers.

Minster Abbey 'sympathetically restored'

Minster Abbey on the Isle of Sheppey, founded in 640AD by Queen Sexburga and believed to be the oldest church in the country, has been in a bad state of repair for years. With the decision to make Minster a separate parish from Sheerness, village life has returned and the Abbey is being sympathetically restored. It commands fine views of what many people consider a 'desperately isolated and inhospitable island'.

Empress Eugenie has left Camden Place, Chislehurst to take up residence in Farnborough Hill, Hampshire where she has instructed Gabriel Destailler to build a French church of 16th century style over a Romanesque crypt, where she will lay the bodies of Louis and her son.

South Eastern Railway has opened a new line from Dunton Green to Westerham.

The 50th and 97th Regiments of Foot have been amalgamated to form the Queen's Own Royal West Kent Regiment.

A new church at Shipbourne was consecrated this year. The benefactor is Edward Cazalet, a merchant from Russia, who came to Kent 10 years ago keen to set up as an English gentleman and win a seat in Parliament. Cazalet bought and improved a rambling mansion, Fairlawne and, to the alarm of many villagers, set about modernising the village of Shipbourne.

Jezreelites of Gillingham

December 17: James Jershom Jezreel, a self-declared Messenger of the Lord and leader of a religious sect known as the Jezreelites, today married the daughter of one of his many followers, Clarissa Rogers.

Jezreel, real name James Rowland White, his new wife and their supporters live communally in Gillingham. Each member of the sect gives money to a community chest managed by Jezreel. He pays all the living expenses including the rent of the homes they occupy.

The sect's official name is the New and Latter House of Israel and is enrolling new members rapidly. Even the descendant followers of Joanna Southcott have joined the Jezreelites and embraced the teachings of this well built man with a big beard, long flowing hair and piercing eyes.

Sadly, there are no pictures of Jezreel or his wife. The Flying Roll, the doctrinal tract of the sect, bans the making of graven images and the taking of photographs.Those who know him well say he is a charming man, an articulate and persuasive speaker with a sound business sense. *See page 215*

July 31: ***A Ramsgate lifeboat,*** **Bradford III,** ***has saved 11 of a crew of 29 from a fully-rigged ship,*** **The Indian Chief** ***which ran onto the Long Sands during the height of a fierce gale. It has been described as one of the greatest rescues in the history of the RNLI. Having battled through heavy seas to reach the ship the coxwain, Charlie Fish, found the crew had taken to the rigging. Tragically, the mizzen mast collapsed and 16 were drowned. The lifeboat, together with a harbour tug, stayed close to the ship all night and at first light picked up the survivors.***

Baroness Emma Orczy, who writes historical novels, has moved from her native Hungary to Bearsted.

The fifth ***HMS Kent*** has been broken up and her figurehead preserved at the main entrance to Portsmouth Dockyard.

The Channel Tunnel luncheon guests are lowered by bucket to the bottom of the shaft below Shakespeare Cliff.

A tunnel under the Channel to France

March 4: Forty gentlemen from London today inspected Sir Edward Watkins' giant "mole hole" which has appeared below the Shakespeare Cliff between Dover and Folkestone. Arriving by special train, they descended the shaft, walked a thousand yards under the sea and admired the working of Colonel Beaumont's compressed boring machine. Illuminated by electric lights the gentlemen sat down to a sumptuous luncheon in a side chamber.

In a stirring speech, Sir Edward, chairman of the South Eastern Railway Company, said a pilot tunnel would be driven under the Channel from coast to coast within five years. His great dream of linking England and France would soon be a reality.

The shaft for the tunnel is sunk in the chalk cliff, about 160 feet in depth. The opening is circular with boarded sides and the descending apparatus is worked by a steam engine. At the bottom of the shaft is a square chamber protected by heavy beams. The heading is more than 1,100 yards long, 500 under the sea, and is advancing at 100 yards a week in the direction of Admiralty Pier, Dover.

The boring of the tunnel follows more than eight years of protracted negotiations with the Chemin de Fer du Nord, the London Chatham and Dover Railway Company, Her Majesty's Government and the French Government — for it was nine years ago that the English Channel Tunnel Company drew up a bill to purchase land and commence exploratory work. Progress since then can be summed up as follows:

April 1875: Peter William Barlow, railway engineer and builder of London's first Tube railway, the Tower Subway claims that a floating steel tube could be laid across the Channel in a year. There is no suggestion as to how ships might avoid it. His idea is rejected.

August 2, 1875: Both the French and English Bills are passed. In England the English Channel Tunnel Company is empowered to raise £80,000. The LCDR and Messrs Rothschild and Sons promise £20,000 each on condition the balance of £40,000 can be obtained.

August 1876: No more than £15,000 is forthcoming and the concession runs out.

December 1876: Mining engineers, geologists and hydrographers complete an extensive survey of the Straits of Dover in order to prepare a geological map.

October 1877: While the French sink two shafts to the west of Sangatte and drive a number of short headings, the penniless English Channel Company remains dormant.

March 1880: Sir Edward Watkin and the South Eastern Railway Company step in. Sir Edward asks Francis Brady and Colonel Frederick Beaumont, an engineer well known for his work on compressed air tunnelling machinery, to arrange trial borings.

June 1881: The Beaumont boring machine — a rotating horizontal shaft at the end of which is attached a cutting head driven forward by hydraulic pressure — drives a tunnel 897 yards parallel to the cliffs. The machine excavates a seven foot diameter heading through the chalk at the rate of two or three revolutions of the cutter every minute.

July 1881: The South Eastern Railway Act enables Watkin to invoke the previous Act. Engineers take possession of land in the parish of Hougham. Work begins on the Channel Tunnel.

September 1881: Watkins admits he will be unable to raise sufficient capital to build the tunnel. He asks the Government to help. They decline.

December 1881: The Submarine Continental Railway Company is registered with a capital of £250,000 in £1 shares. Watkin offers the LCDR access to the tunnel via the Elham

continued on next page

A self portrait of Dante Gabriel Rossetti as a young man. He said to William Morris: "If a man has any poetry in him he should paint, for it has all been said and written and they have scarcely begun to paint it". Rossetti, who was 54 when he died, was a leading spirit of the Pre-Raphaelite Brotherhood.

Reclusive Rossetti dies in Birchington

April 9: Dante Gabriel Rossetti, son of an Italian refugee, brother of the famous poetess Christina, a founder member of the Pre-Raphaelite Brotherhood, poet, artist and author — a total recluse and obsessed by persecution mania — died at Birchington-on-Sea today.

As a younger man Rossetti studied art under Ford Maddox Brown and shared a studio with William Holman Hunt, an association which led to the birth of the Pre-Raphaelites. Formed in 1848 when Victorian art was in a reactionary period, the work of the Brotherhood flew in the face of convention. Protests were only stilled when John Ruskin came to the rescue with a spirited defence of their work.

Rossetti was married to Elizabeth Siddal, a red-haired beauty who was first his model, then his mistress. When he confessed that the intense love he felt for her would be even stronger if she were to die, she took him at his word and committed suicide.

The artist, in grief, placed all his unpublished poems in her coffin — only to have them retrieved some years later. He then turned to Jane, wife of William Morris, for affection and embarked on another long-standing affair.

In 1871 Morris and Rossetti became joint tenants of Kelmscott Manor, Oxfordshire which Morris declared to be "heaven on earth". He lived there when Rossetti was not in residence. The next year Rossetti attempted suicide with an overdose of laudanum. Jane remained by his side.

His health never recovered. He moved alone to Birchington a few years ago and became paralysed by a lethal cocktail of morphia, laudanum and chloral — plus whisky, brandy and claret. He became a virtual recluse but still communicated by letter to Ford Maddox Brown and Jane Morris.

Tunnel to France *(continued)*

Valley line by means of a connection.

January 1882: The Channel Tunnel Company, dormant since 1877 prepares its own Bill. To Watkins this is an open declaration of war and he refuses to work in co-operation with the rival company.

February 1882: A Government committee is told by the Admiralty that an enemy army could, by taking possession of the tunnel, march on London.

March 1882: Scathing attacks on the tunnel by Lord Dunsany and others appear in the magazine *Nineteenth Century*. An anti-tunnel petition gains the support of Robert Browning, Alfred Tennyson, T.H.Huxley, Herbert Spencer and Sir George Sitwell.

March 1882: As work progresses on the headings, Watkins organises the first of what he promises will be many lavish luncheon parties.

April: As expected, Sandwich has been disenfranchised by an Act of Parliament and terms of imprisonment have been given to perpetrators on both sides. Sandwich is now a minor part of Thanet Constituency and Deal and Walmer have merged with Dover. Sandwich Council has been told to put £2,139 towards the cost of inquiry expenses. They are in total shock.

March 8: The Chancel of Sundridge church has been severely damaged by fire.

Penenden Heath has been granted to the the people of Maidstone in perpetuity by Charles Earl of Romney of Mote Park as a public pleasure ground.

A racecourse has opened at Wye.

South Eastern Railway has opened a branch line from West Wickham to Hayes.

New churches consecrated this year are St Cyprians, Brockley and St John the Evangelist, Bexleyheath

Charles Darwin, the scientist who changed human history, dies

April 19: Charles Darwin died peacefully last week at Down House, aged 73, after an illness of 10 years in which his pace of work never slackened. His fine book *The Expressions of the Emotions of Man and Animals*, published in 1872, was his 'hobby-horse', as he described it in a letter to a friend, because it discreetly laid the foundations of comparative animal psychology and ethology in the field of modern evolutionary theory.

In 1876 Darwin wrote his *Autobiography* for his family and friends. The following year he took a strong line on vivisection which he defended as vital to the progress of medical science, although he called for the greatest humanity towards animals.

His last book was *The Formation of Vegetable Mould, through the Actions of Worms, with Observations on their Habits.* This highlighted the important role these creatures have played throughout geological history. Since then he has continued with his experiments at Down House on the action of chemicals on plant tissues and animal behaviour When his day was finished he would sit in the drawing room and listen to his wife play the piano.

Darwin was buried today at Westminster Abbey. His family, close friends and a large gathering of people from the worlds of science, politics and even religion were present to see the man who attempted to separate science from God receive the homage of the Church of England.

He is renowned across the world for his controversial theory of evolution by natural selection which was inspired by observations made on the voyage of *HMS Beagle* more than 50 years ago. Since then he has struggled against religious ideology and creation mythologies but avoided direct confrontation, which he always considered would do more harm than good.

Darwin died on April 9, the same day as Dante Gabriel Rossetti.

Charles Darwin was given a state funeral and buried in Westminster Abbey after an emotional memorial service on April 26. He will be remembered for his theory of evolution by natural selection and the controversy that surrounded it.

Repair work on the 21-year-old South-Eastern Railway line at Chelsfield.

Rail companies at war again

A BITTER battle is raging again between Sir Edward Watkin, chairman of the South Eastern Railway Company and James Staats Forbes, of the London, Chatham and Dover — this time over a continental service from Sheppey to Flushing in Holland.

About six years ago the Dutch Zeeland Company inaugurated a steam service to Holland operating from a substantial wooden quay at Queenborough, owned by the LCDR. Because of the through facilities it offered to passengers to and from Germany, the service enjoyed great success and was awarded a contract by the Dutch government.

Sir Edward was incensed. He immediately established a company called the Hundred of Hoo and from the opposite shore of the Medway constructed a short line to Port Victoria. From the pier there, a ferry connects with the Dutch steamers at Queenborough.

As Forbes considers his next move, fate has taken a hand. The Queenborough quay has been destroyed by fire and the service transferred to Dover.

Some years ago the Government tried to eliminate competition between the two companies by introducing a Continental Traffic Agreement under which receipts for all traffic between London, Folkestone and Dover were to be pooled and shared.

That worked well for a number of years but Sir Edward now claims that the South Eastern railway stations at Radnor Park and Shorncliffe Camp 'are not serving Folkestone'. He has withheld receipts from the pool. Another legal battle ensues.

Aveling steam roller in New York

THOMAS Aveling, pioneer of the the steam plough but perhaps better known as the 'father of the traction engine' has died, aged 57.

Soon after taking out his traction engine patent in 1859 he teamed up with Richard Porter to establish a company in the field of steam haulage and was the originator of the "horn-plate" traction engine.

In 1867, Aveling produced a road roller, sending the first example to his agent in Paris. Subsequently, rollers of this type were sent all over the world; one of them became the first steam roller in America and helped to build, among others, the network of roads in Central Park, New York.

Although Aveling travelled extensively he never forgot his Kentish roots. He was mayor of the Corporation of Rochester in 1869 and long-time President of the Medway Yacht Club.

Stockbroker builds a home in Polecat alley

THE opening of the Hayes and West Wickham railway line has prompted many bankers, stockbrokers and those who are 'somebody' in the city of London to build their own houses in this highly desirable area where Lord Chatham once lived and William Pitt the second was born.

Many stately mansions, surrounded by large gardens are under construction and here the businessmen and their families will live with their indoor staff of parlourmaids, ladies' maids, cooks and kitchen maids. Outdoors there will be coachmen and gardeners. It will be the duty of the footman to take the master of the house to the station to catch his morning train to London. The carriage will be waiting for his return in the evening.

Among the wealthy men to move into the area is a Dutch stockbroker, Walkter Maximilian de Zoete who has leased six acres of land to build Warren House, Hayes. It stands in a wooded valley known locally as The Warren because of the number of rabbits. Here the locals come every day with their polecats and ferrets.

1883

Webb dies in the rapids of Niagara

July 25: Captain Matthew Webb, who became the first man to swim the English Channel just eight years ago, drowned yesterday attempting to swim the whirlpool rapids at Niagara from America to Canada — which he had earlier described as "the angriest bit of water in the world".

Many people told Webb that his mission was impossible and he would be committing suicide but the world-famous swimmer had great confidence in his own ability. "When the water gets very bad I will go under the surface and remain there until compelled to come up for breath", he said. "When I reach the whirlpool I will strike out with all my strength to keep away from the suckhole in the centre. My life will depend on my muscles and my breath with a touch of science behind them".

Webb, who hoped to earn $10,000 for swimming the rapids, was taken by Ferryman McCloy down river towards the two suspension bridges. The river was 95 feet deep and the current, running at 39 mph, was already so bad that McCloy tried to dissuade Webb going any further.

At 4.45 pm he dived into the water and was immediately at the mercy of the battling waves which gave sledgehammer blows to his ribs and pounded the air from his body. Like a ship without a rudder he was tossed and hurled around. He kept lifting himself above the torrent but, battered into total submission, he slipped into unconsciousness. Somehow he swam on until the impact of a huge wave almost threw him out of the water.

Webb's arms shot up in the air and his body seemed to hang for a brief second on top of the waves. The whirlpool then dragged him out of sight.

The whirlpool rapids between America and Canada — the 'angriest bit of water in the world'

Country parson acquitted of murdering girl, 16

THE Rev Timmins of West Malling, a country parson for more than 40 years, has been acquitted of the manslaughter of 16-year-old Sarah Wright after a sensational trial.

On December 14 last year Timmins visited the home of the Wright family where Sarah was ill. Having examined her he decided to administer a dose of medicinal arsenic with a glass of water. The girl took the arsenic but refused the water. A short while later she foamed at the mouth, vomited profusely and collapsed. She was dead.

The vicar was charged with manslaughter but several local chemists appeared on his behalf to say he knew how to administer 'oil of bitter almonds' as this treatment was known. The girl's refusal to take it with water led to her death.

The Hon Ivo Bligh (centre) with the team he took to Australia in 1882-3 to reclaim 'The Ashes'. The captain returned with an additional prize.

Edward White Benson, former headmaster of Wellington School, Chancellor of Lincoln and the first Bishop of Truro, is the new Archbishop of Canterbury. A high churchman whose delight is to be on his knees at a cathedral service rather than in the House of Lords, Benson is one of the most distinguished scholars to come to Lambeth and Canterbury.

The £3 million extension of Chatham Dockyard has been completed and the workforce there has grown to 4,199. The dockyard boundary now crosses into Gillingham. Some skilled observers have doubts about the prospects for the new yard in view of the growth of the battleship, the tortuous navigation of the Medway and the insufficient depth of water.

New churches built this year are: Ascension, Blackheath and St Mark's, New Cross. Christ Church, Luton has been repaired.

Ivo claims the greatest prizes

April 10: The Hon Ivo Walter Francis Bligh, the hard hitting Kent batsman entrusted with the captaincy of England, has returned from his successful tour of Australia with a lady whom he intends to marry and a small urn, suitably inscribed, containing the ashes of a cricket bail. This urn reposes on his drawing room mantlepiece at Cobham Hall.

Ivo Bligh learned to play cricket from George Bennett who was engaged on his father's estate. He said this week that his team were extremely lucky not to have ended the voyage in Davy Jones's locker; for in the Indian Ocean, a little south of the Equator, the team's boat *Peshawar* was involved in a serious collision and some members of the touring party were injured.

"By a curious fatality", he said, "the *Austral*, which was the alternative boat recommended to us, was sunk on arrival in Sydney Harbour, so we were unconsciously given the unusual choice between a ship that was run into and a ship that sunk".

The tour lasted seven months and England won two of the three Tests, so avenging the defeat at Kennington Oval last year when an Australian XI beat the finest side England had ever fielded. After that match the *Sporting Times* carried an obituary notice mourning the 'death' of English cricket and adding: "The body will be cremated and the ashes sent to Australia".

Soon after the final match in Australia Ivo Bligh was presented with a small urn by a group of Australian ladies. Inside were the ashes of a cricket bail which they had ceremonially cremated.

But Ivo did more than bring back the ashes. He carried the war into the enemy's camp by appropriating the pick of the ladies, the lovely Florence Murphy, the reigning beauty of the New Continent. Somehow the English captain found time to woo and win this supreme prize. The couple are now planning a summer wedding.

1884

Fear of invasion halts the tunnel

IN the face of opposition from militarists a parliamentary select committtee has recommended that Sir Edward Watkin's plans for a Channel Tunnel be abandoned. The digging must stop immediately.

The War Office believes the French could use the finished tunnel as a road to invading Britain, so avenging their defeat at Waterloo.

"It is the equivalent to draining the moat surrounding a fortress", said General Sir Garnett Wolseley. "I can envisage a battalion of picked troops crossing by boat and seizing the Channel Tunnel as a bridgehead."

Admiral Sir Astley Cooper Key, First Lord of the Admiralty agreed: "The enemy would need to control the tunnel for only four hours to assemble an army of 10,000 men on English soil".

Among the hundreds of witnesses called before the committee was Sir Edward who said he had already drawn up schemes for the destruction of the tunnel should an invasion occur. It included flooding the entire length, pumping it full of steam or poison gas, laying mines or choking the Dover entrance with shingle.

THE RIOTERS: Sevenoaks residents tear down the posts at the entrance to Knole.

Angry crowd storms Knole Park

June 19: An angry mob of residents from Sevenoaks broke down the posts across the entrance to Knole and, singing *Rule Britannia*, marched on the great house last night where they deposited the posts at the main door. They are planning to besiege the house again tonight with a party "in excess of 1,500 people".

Their dispute is with Mortimer Sackville-West, the owner of Knole, who has decided to close the deer park to the public because of "the promiscuous way they gallop around the place".

Mortimer had not envisaged the extent of the public outcry. Knole Park is treasured by the inhabitants of Sevenoaks and far beyond. Hundreds of people like to take a summer evening stroll, mothers and nursery maids wheel their children in perambulators along the paths, people from nearby villages ride on horseback or in carts across the park to the Sevenoaks shops. Everyone in the town, particularly shop and hotel owners, benefits from the passing trade that the park attracts.

The owner, who has a reputation as a disagreeable man for falling out with his relatives, rightly claims that the paths across the park are not a public amenity. He dislikes the changing social ways brought about by the improvements in the railway network and the introduction of bank holidays and half day closing.

There are 30 trains to Sevenoaks every weekday and 15 on Sundays. Knole is a popular destination for the day trippers who like to visit the largest family home in England and look at its magnificent collection of furniture, textiles, Old Masters and portraits. In the last few years there has been in excess of 10,000 visitors a year.

It was the opening of Hampton Court in 1839 that initiated this new age of country house visiting. That has fixed hours and admission charges. Mortimer Sackville-West prefers to simply shut the doors.

September: Mortimer Sackville-West has left Knole to live at the Grand Hotel, Scarborough or St Leonard's in Sussex. He says he will return when the Chief Constable of Kent increases the number of policeman stationed at Sevenoaks.

One in five relies on railway employment

WITH the building of the railways more, rather than fewer, horses are required to pull road vehicles to towns and villages throughout the county. In fact horse-drawn traffic has increased threefold in the second half of the nineteenth century.

A major passenger and goods traffic service has been created to and from railway stations, primitive 'country buses' convey villagers to the nearest stations and carriers drive in from faraway places with cheaper food and coal. Perishable goods, such as fish, move efficiently across the county and, of course, travel by road to local markets continues. Roads in backward areas like the Weald have been improved showing that door-to-door transport has its advantages.

Some local producers are not happy by this progress in movement. Forty years ago there were 4,448 boot and shoemakers in Kent but they are being slowly ousted by the mass producer. It is the same with building materials. Many homes today are likely to have roofs made of cheaper Welsh slate, as against the traditional Kentish peg tiles.

On the positive side more than one person in five of the occupied population of Kent now relies on railway employment while some 350 wheelwrights shops and 600 smithies are totally dependent on road transport.

Cold air machine for cargo ships

THE Dartford engineering firm of J and E Hall is once again proving itself to be a leader in the field. This time it is refrigeration.

When John Hall's son Edward died in 1875 the firm was in the doldrums and much of the machinery obsolete. It was rescued by Everard Hesketh, the chief draughtsman, who looked for a new branch of engineering in which he could specialise. He found it at the Paris Exhibition of 1878 — a cold air machine.

A steam engine compressed the air in a separate cylinder, a water jacket removed the resultant heat from the compressed air which then expanded through pipes to the refrigeration chamber, becoming very cold as it did so. Hesketh ironed out the snags in Hall's design and produced a compact unit for cargo ships.

There has been considerable rivalry but the Dartford company has supplied the refrigeration plant for shops to bring meat from South America and Australia. This will mean the end of 'salt horse', scurvy and live animals penned on the deck.

Everard Hesketh — cold air pioneer.

Next year J and E Hall will celebrate its centenary. It employs 275 people and is set to dominate the ever increasing market for cold storage.

Sidcup musician praised by Tchaikovsky

ETHEL Smythe may not be the most celebrated composer of her age but this talented young woman from Sidcup,who has studied at the Leipzig Conservatorium, is making a big impression among her contemporaries — including the great Pyotr Ilyich Tchaikovsky.

The Russian composer has complimented Ethel on her *Violin Sonata*. Her first important composition has been so successful that she is planning to write an opera to "perform all over Europe". Her many influential friends, who admire her talent, enthusiasm and strength of personality, believe she will succeed.

Ethel was born in 1858 the only daughter of an Indian army general. In later ycars shc travelled from her home in Sidcup to all the major concerts and was soon determined to become the first great female composer. At Leipzig she met influential friends such as George Henschel who wrote: "Our circle was brightened by the meteor-like appearance of a young, most attractive girl. None of us knew what to admire the most — her wonderful musical talent or her astonishing athletic prowess jumping over fences and chairs".

It has been said that Ethel is more attracted to women than men but this year she met Harry Brewster, a married American writer, and fell in love. He is campaigning to have her work performed. Other great friends include Edward Sackville-West who calls her "a brilliant woman" who feels violently about almost everything" and Empress Eugenie, who has introduced her to Queen Victoria.

General Gordon is killed in Khartoum

January 27: General Charles Gordon, the man reputed to lead his troops into battle with a bible in one hand and a cane in the other, was killed today on the steps of the palace of Khartoum after a five-month siege.

Soon after 'Chinese Gordon' left his home at Fort House, Gravesend in 1872 he became governor of the vast and unruly Egyptian province of the Sudan where he succeeded in pacifying the area and returned to England.

In his absence the Mahdi (the Muslim equivalent of a Messia) and his followers threatened the Egyptian garrisons and Gordon accepted a call to relieve them.

Instead this Christian soldier found himself besieged in Khartoum for five months while Prime Minister, Gladstone in London dithered over whether to send a relief force. That force has not yet arrived.

Yesterday the city wall was breached and the entire garrison slaughtered. Some say Gordon was hacked down by the swords of the Dervishes, others that he was hit by a rifle shot. It is known that his head was put on display by the Mahdi who had wanted to take him alive.

For 60 years the Sudan has been pillaged by slavers. Gordon, the hero of the anti-slave lobby, the scourge of the Taiping rebels in China has been a hero in England for many years.

He will be particularly missed in Woolwich, where he was born and trained, and in Gravesend where he fought tough battles for the poor and needy.

The news of Gordon's death has reached his former home at Fort House, Gravesend, where he spent so much time with the local boys. Most of them are older now and have work in the town. They are stunned, almost beyond belief.

All in vain for brave West Kents

January 29: A battalion of the Queen's Own Royal West Kent Regiment was part of the Relief Force sent by Gladstone to "rescue the beleaguered General Gordon".

Equipped with lightweight grey uniform and ready to go they suffered several delays through government indecision but eventually joined the Mounted Infantry Camel Regiment under the command of General Wolseley.

The battalion was conveyed up the Nile as far as Wadi Halfa in steamers provided by Thomas Cook and Son. Thereafter they rowed against the current and unloaded the cargo and hauled the boats through every rapid. By the time they reached Khartoum their hands were raw, their uniform ragged and many had died on the way from the effects of diarrhoea.

Worse still their effort was in vain. Khartoum had fallen, Gordon was dead and Wolseley's Desert Column had suffered an undeserved blow. Today they have been given the order to withdraw and told to make their way north.

Among the senior officers on this abortive mission is General Horatio Herbert Kitchener, a 34-year-old soldier with a reputation as 'a brilliant strategist'. He is determined to return to the Sudan to exact revenge on the Mahdi, the man who murdered his friend and fellow officer.

Born in Ireland, Kitchener came to Kent in 1871 to study at the Royal Military Academy at Woolwich and the Royal Engineers HQ at Brompton. Since then he has served as Intelligence Officer in Palestine, Anatolia and Cyprus.

Gentlemens' cycling clubs are springing up across the county. Here are members of Folkestone club with their Stanley 'Royal Salvco' tricycles which were developed a few years ago. In fact this cheap-to-produce safety tricycle could make cycling available to everyone. Only one rider in this photograph is perched on a penny farthing and he can be seen at the back of the group. These are now considered difficult and dangerous to ride.

The hero who stammered

NEWS has been received in Kent that Francis Jeffrey Dickens — third son of Charles and Katherine and now a member of the Canadian North West Mounted Police — helped to quell a rebellion in a remote area of Saskatchewan known as Maidstone.

Apparently a troublesome Red Indian, Louis Reil and his followers disliked the presence of white settlers who used a trade route across their land between Fort Battleford and Big Gulley Creek. The rising was suppressed but Inspector Dickens and his detachment of Mounties were forced to retreat on a raft down a dangerous fast flowing river.

Francis Dickens, always called Chickenstalker by his father, stammered badly as a child and was packed off to Germany to learn the language. The long 'portmanteau' German words cured his impediment and when he left school he joined the Bengal Mounted Police and then the Canadian North West division.

It seems likely that Maidstone, Saskatchewan was given its name by an emigrant from the county town — but no-one is certain.

Death of 'an immortal'

March 2: James Jeezreel has been translated directly into the hereafter. At least that is what his followers are saying following his death at Woodlands, Gillingham this week from a broken blood vessel.

The funeral service of the self-confessed Messenger of the Lord ,who had preached his own mortality, will be held at Gillingham cemetery. There will be sadness but no show of grief among his thousands of supporters in the Medway towns.

Before he died Jeezreel drew up plans for a great tower on the top of Chatham Hill, 144 feet in length, breadth and height. It will be the biggest church in England, capable of holding more people than St Paul's Cathedral and will house his printing presses and sectarian literature. The estimated cost is £25,000.

Money for the building has been pouring in and work is due to begin in September .

Thousands of acres of Romney Marsh, a vast tract of rich pasture land claimed from the sea, has been divided into fields and enclosures for the rearing of sheep. The land-owners employ a man called a Looker to look after their valuable stock.

The Bromley National School, one of the oldest in Kent, came into being in 1814 when it absorbed the Old Charity School. In 1855 the Combined New National School was opened east of Bromley College for 700 children. Here are the children of the infant class, pictured this year, with their two charming teachers.

Lads from Dial Square FC say 'call us The Gunners'

More and more young men are playing football, the game that was introduced some 25 years ago by boys at English public schools.

Now factories and workshops are forming teams and among them are a group of lads from the Woolwich foundry who play to a high standard on Plumstead Common.

In fact, they are enjoying so much success that they have changed their name from Dial Square — the name of the workshop— to the Royal Arsenal FC. To their loyal supporters they are simply known as 'The Gunners'.

The immediate aim of the Royal Arsenal is to win one of the three cups which senior sides are competing for — The Kent Senior Cup, the London Charity Cup and the London Cup.

Salvation Army — disturbing the peace in Tunbridge Wells

July: The Salvation Army, a Christian Mission founded by William and Catherine Booth eight years ago, is having a troubled time in its attempts to "rescue the poorest people and bring them to Jesus".

At Tunbridge Wells this month a group of louts calling themselves the Skeleton Army paraded their death's head and skull across the path of the band as it emerged from its citadel in Golding Street. This was followed by a riot. The big drum was smashed, a Salvationist was stabbed in the leg and elderly women supporters were roughly handled.

The police had anticipated trouble between the two 'armies' and five young labourers were arrested.

Tradesmen in Tunbridge Wells blame both parties for the trouble and agree with the comments from one influential resident, Mr D'Aubigny Hatch, who says the Salvation Army is responsible for the uproar and disturbance to public peace. "They appear to think they have to parade with a frightful noise and uproar to assail the Devil", he said.

There has been trouble in other towns but General Booth says he will continue to take his message to the poor people, providing them with food and shelter. His members will wear Army uniform and, to lure people to their services, they will march to the evocative tune of *Onward Christian Soldiers*, recently composed by Arthur Sullivan.

Since the formation of Kent County Constabulary in 1857 policemen on patrol in hospitable areas have carried a wooden rattle in order to communicate with colleagues. This is no longer the case. A police whistle has been issued to every constable on the beat. Pictured here are the policemen of the Tonbridge division.

Second railway station for Gravesend

LED by its ambitious chairman James Staats Forbes, the London Chatham and Dover Railway continues to march across Kent. In the last two years it has opened a line from Maidstone to Ashford, extended the Greenwich branch and opened a branch from the Swanley to Strood line to a new station called Gravesend West.

The station has yet to be built but a handsome viaduct is in place and the LCDR is ready to compete for passengers with the South Eastern railway line to Gravesend Central.

The foundation stone to the new Skinners "middle grade" School has been laid in Tunbridge Wells following a 20-year battle for the privilege with its 'mother town' some four miles away. Tonbridge, however, is soon to get its own second school — thanks to the generosity of the Skinners Company and local benefactors.

It will not compete with the larger and impressive Tonbridge Grammar School which now reaches out to the sons of wealthy families from afar.

Fordwich, three miles from Canterbury, which nestles on the River Stour and was once famous as the port for Canterbury, has ceased to be a borough. The 15th century town hall remains but there will no longer be a mayor to conduct corporation business.

Following the disastrous fire which destroyed Chatham's famous music hall The Palace of Varieties in 1879, Lou Barnard — son of the late proprietor — has opened another theatre in the town.

This one is bigger and better than the original and incorporates two bars into the design. It is known as Barnard's New Palace of Varieties.

The original theatre in the High Street was believed to be the oldest variety theatre in the country.

A special breed of hen, called a Buff Orpington, has been introduced this year by William Cook, a well-known poultry farmer. This small north Kent town, once a village which straggled along a High Street, is notorious for its winter floods.

New churches built this year are St Lawrence, Catford and St Luke's, Bromley Common

Charles Parnell, the Irish nationist leader who has put Home Rule on the political agenda and has formed an alliance with Gladstone, is said by the *Pall Mall Gazette* to be residing at the home of Mrs Katherine O'Shea in Kent. She is the wife of William O'Shea, one of Parnell's supporters.

See page 227

In honour of "the greatest ever monarch", commemorative 'golden jubilee' clock towers have been erected at Gravesend (left) and Margate. In Maidstone, the Archbishop's Palace, Maidstone has been purchased by public subscription.

Kent celebrates Victoria's golden jubilee

June 21: Kent celebrated Queen Victoria's golden jubilee in great style today with a display of rejoicing that has given the county a new sense of cohesion. Everybody had a day off and took part enthusiastically in parades, street parties, presentations and firework shows. The sun shone all day and in the evening hundreds of bonfires were lit.

Many people took the train to London to see the Queen pass in procession through the capital to Westminster Abbey for a jubilee thanksgiving service. The procession included 47 carriages bearing royalty from India and Europe and, at the abbey, a choir of some 300 voices sang music by the late Prince Albert. The diminutive Queen, dressed in a white bonnet and simple black dress perched on the coronation chair and heard the Archbishop of Canterbury thank God for her long reign.

Kent has marked the occasion in more tangible ways than parades and parties. New roads, springing up in almost every town, have been given the name Victoria Street and almost every new-born baby girl has been christened Victoria

Commemorative clock towers at Gravesend and Margate have been erected in honour of the "best-loved" monarch ever, a Victoria Pier has been opened at Folkestone and the Archbishop's Palace at Maidstone has been purchased by public subscription in honour of the great lady.

This morning the bells were ringing in every church with a bell tower and this afternoon children throughout the county were presented with commemorative medals and cups. Flags and streamers hang from almost every building throughout the county of Kent.

A new railway, known as the Elham Valley line, has opened from Shorncliffe to Barham.

New churches built this year are Christchurch Bromley, St Augustine, Grove Park and Christchurch, Sidcup

Dinah Craik — the author who adopted an abandoned child

October 12: The well-known author, Mrs Dinah Craik, who died at her home in Shortlands, Bromley today, will always be remembered for one book which became a best-seller in Britain and America.

John Halifax - Gentleman has already sold more than a quarter of a million copies and many Americans sailing to Britain make certain they visit the town of Tewkesbury where the novel is set.

Mrs Craik, born Dinah Mulock in 1826, has written numerous novels and children's stories, the best known being *Cola Monti* and *The Ogilvies*, published in three volumes.

Seven years ago she wrote *Little Sunshine*, the story of a little girl who had been abandoned.

It is based on a real-life event. On a winter's morning a workman, walking past the junction between St George's and Bromley roads, came across a baby lying near some bricks and carried the child to Beckenham police station. Mrs Craik heard about it and managed to legally adopt the child.

Dockyard crisis as 1,000 are dismissed

THOSE concerned about the future of the Royal Dockyard at Chatham, following its massive £3million extension into Gillingham, are right to be worried.

Business is bad and this week more than 1,000 dockyard workers were dismissed. Some blame the sudden change in government policy, others say that the Medway has an insufficient depth of water for the massive battleships currently being built.The fact is that Chatham needs to economise.

Many workers who were on a hired-only status have returned from whence they came but a crisis faces the local unemployed and hundreds of families have thrown themselves on the Guardians of the workhouse.

The *Chatham Observer* tells of a woman who needs assistance while her husband seeks work elsewhere. The Guardians have agreed to give her and others out-relief rather than order them to report to the already overcrowded workhouse.

Meanwhile, protest movements are growing in Chatham among the unskilled workers who still have employment. Many have joined the Society of the Dockyard Labourers, led by James Kingsland and William Lewington. Their first campaign is for a pay increase.

Victoria Pier, Folkestone, opened this year by Viscountess Folkestone, at a cost of £24,000. Thousands of holidaymakers heard the Viscountess say the pier will put Folkestone in the front rank of British watering places.

'Bloody Sunday' in Trafalgar Square

December 9: William Morris's radical views have been strengthened following the shocking events of November 13 when police broke up a protest meeting in Trafalgar Square with such violence that two protesters were killed and hundreds injured.

Morris led a contingent to that meeting, called by radicals and Irish sympathisers. It has been described by newspapers as "Bloody Sunday"

Appalled by what he saw he joined his friend Alfred Linnell, the artist, and hundreds of other radicals a week later to protest again — this time against the unnecessary use of police force. On this occasion Linnell was run down by the police and died of his injuries.

More than 10,000 supporters gathered for Linnell's funeral today in the biggest gathering since the funeral of the Duke of Wellington and Morris gave the graveside oration.

William Morris no longer lives in Bexleyheath. He moved from the Red House to Kelmscott Manor near Oxford in 1871 and then to a house at Hammersmith on the River Thames.

1888

Fabians support the Match Girls' Strike

June 30: To the disgust of *The Times* newspaper and many Tory ministers, the well known husband and wife writing team, Hubert Bland and Edith Nesbit have persuaded their colleagues in the Fabian Society to support a strike by 1,400 women who work for the Bryant and May match factory in London.

The couple live at Halstead Hall near Sevenoaks and have been with the Fabian Society from its inception. They are friendly with Annie Besant, editor of *The Link* newspaper, who has written an article entitled *White Slavery in London*. It describes how the health of the women making the matches has been severely affected by phosphorous which causes yellowing of the skin, hair loss and a phossy jaw, a form of bone cancer.

Miss Besant has also discovered that the women work 14 hours a day for a wage of less than five shillings a week and suffer considerably from a system of fines set up by the management for talking, going to the toilet without permission or dropping matches.

Soon after the article was published Bryant and May asked the women to sign a statement saying they were happy with their working conditions. A few refused to sign and were sacked. The response was immediate; the rest went on strike.

Bland and Nesbit immediately joined Miss Besant in her campaign for better working conditions at the factory. So did William Stead, editor of the *Pall Mall Gazette*, Catherine Booth of the Salvation Army and George Bernard Shaw. Conservative newspapers said they were socialist agitators and blamed them for the dispute.

A few of the Match Girls who went on strike.

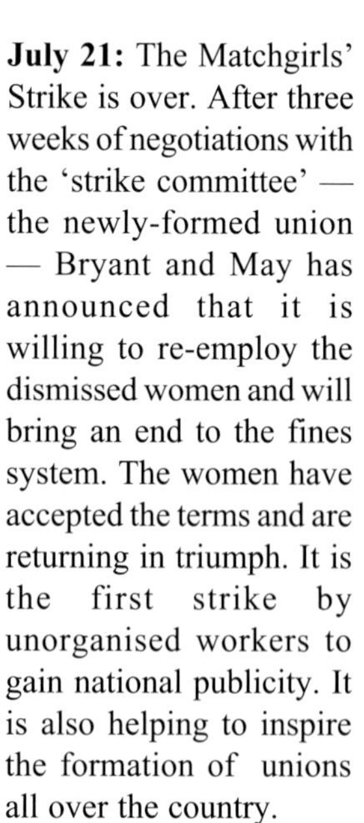

July 21: The Matchgirls' Strike is over. After three weeks of negotiations with the 'strike committee' — the newly-formed union — Bryant and May has announced that it is willing to re-employ the dismissed women and will bring an end to the fines system. The women have accepted the terms and are returning in triumph. It is the first strike by unorganised workers to gain national publicity. It is also helping to inspire the formation of unions all over the country.

See page 221

Bland and Nesbit like an 'open marriage'

EDITH Nesbit and Hubert Bland were married in 1877 and have three children. The youngest is a boy called Fabian. At the time of their marriage Hubert was a failed businessman so Edith peddled her writing on Fleet Street and inspired him to show an interest in journalism.

The couple approve of what they call an 'open marriage'. He has a mistress, Alice Hoatson and Edith likes to be surrounded by male admirers, who sometimes become her lovers. One of her friends recently described her as a "raffish Rossetti" because she smokes incessantly and her long cigarette holder is "an indissoluble part of the picture".

Edith is very tall and, on festive occasions, likes to wear a trailing gown of peacock blue satin with strings of beads and Indian bangles from wrist to elbow.

January 9: The bodies of Napoleon III and the Prince Imperial have been removed from St Mary's, Chislehurst and conveyed by rail to Farnborough where they will placed in a specially built crypt.

January 22: Countess Darnley of Cobham opened Rochester Grammar School for Girls today so helping to redress the balance between the sexes. Almost twice as many boys receive grammar school education as girls.

September: After 12 months of controversy and disruption a new bridge spans the River Medway at Tonbridge.

It was opened this month amid great pomp when members of the Local Board drove up the High Street in a three-horse landau,

The old Castle Inn, which provided cheap beds for bargemen working for the Medway Navigation Company, has also been rebuilt.

Tunnel engineers discover coal beneath the Shakespeare Cliff

January: The discovery of several seams of coal some 1,157 feet below the base of the Shakespeare Cliff is causing a flurry of excitement among geologists and those who are looking for new mines to develop.

The possibility of a coalfield in Kent was suggested many years ago by Henry de la Beche. However, test borings in 1870 were disappointing.

In 1873 Joseph Prestwich was engaged on the Report for the Coal Commission and suggested the driving of a Channel Tunnel would assist in locating coal beds.

He was right. Sir Edward Watkin put his engineers to work on more conclusive trials using the machinery of the Submarine Continental and coal seams were struck.

Coal is the commodity which, more than any other has made possible Britain's lead in the Industrial Revolution and today the country is the world's leading producer.

Many are saying that a tunnel under the sea is nothing more than a pipe dream, but Kentish coalfields, a real possibility.

See page 242.

Kent says goodbye to four 'northern' boroughs

August 9: A new managerial body for Kent came into being today with the passing of the Local Government Act. Kent County Council will now be responsible for all the county's administrative and financial affairs and will be controlled by a chairman, aldermen and councillors. It is one of 62 new elected councils for England and Wales and represents a significant landmark in the development of local government.

The mandatory qualification for someone to stand for election is that he must own his own property — either as a peer of the realm or as a parliamentary voter. Each councillor will stand for a term of three years after which he must seek re-election.

County councils will replace the old system of rule through the justices of the peace, who retain judicial power as magistrates. A local government board will decide the number of county councillors.

One new county has been created by the act and that affects Kent considerably. The county boundaries have been re-drawn allowing Deptford, Greenwich, Lewisham and Woolwich to be transferred to the newly-created London County Council.

The responsibilies of the new councils are wide ranging. Kent, for example, will charge rates, fix the salaries and fees of all paid officials, finance the police and provide gaols, court houses and new county buildings.

It will be responsible for licensing public houses, providing lunatic asylums, maintaining all roads and bridges in the county and much more.

The first meeting of Kent County Council has been fixed for April 1st next year at Sessions House, Maidstone. Elections will precede that inaugural meeting.

See page 222

Kent welcomes its county council

April 1: Following several provisional meetings the first full meeting of Kent County Council took place today at Sessions House, Maidstone. It means that the administration of the county by justices of the peace has come to an end after more than 100 years.

The new organisation inherits a balance of £10,756 but loses 35 per cent of the rateable value through the loss of the four northern boroughs. Kent will also have to compensate LCC for one third of the value of county buildings. Canterbury remains a county borough.

KCC is made up of 72 elected county councillors (39 urban and 33 rural) who have elected 24 aldermen to make up a council of 96 members. About a quarter of the members are former county justices who had attended general sessions.

Sir John Farnaby-Leonard who presided over today's meeting said that people with whom he had worked at general sessions were brother justices and personal friends who had known each other for many years. "The new system brings together more people from all over the county but it should work well".

Other key appointments are George Marsham of Loose as chairman of the county's first finance committee and Lord Harris of Belmont, who becomes vice-chairman.

Those with strong links with the former general sessions are the eighth Earl of Darnley, who brought the original cricket 'ashes' back to England, the Hon John Stewart Gathorne-Hardy, the sixth Lord Stanhope of Chevening, Sir David Salomons of Broomhill, Southborough, Charles Whitehead of Barming, an authority on agriculture and George Arnold, a Gravesend solicitor and several times Mayor of Gravesend.

Elected councillors who are likely to put forward an opposing view to the ruling elite include Charles Smith, a draper from Chatham and Adam Stigant.

Of the many lengthy debates the most controversial was how best to organise the maintenance of more than 600 miles of rural main roads which is likely to be the county's largest expenditure. It was decided that local highway authorities must continue to repair these roads but the county will now meet the whole cost.

Kent County Council is also responsible for the financing of the Kent Police Force.

Silas M. Burroughs and Henry S Welcome — a factory in Dartford

Tabloid medicine made in Dartford

THE famous pharmaceutical firm of Burroughs Wellcome has moved to a spacious site in Dartford which was previously a paper mill employing more than 400 boys.

First established in Wandsworth in 1880 when a deed of partnership was completed between Silas M Burroughs and Henry S. Wellcome, the company is famous for the production of compressed medicines or tabloids as they are known among doctors and chemists. Tabloid, registered in 1884, is now the most renowned of all trade marks.

The company will employ hundreds of people from Dartford who will be trained to produce such major products as tabloid medicines, Cod Liver Oil and Malt, Toilet Lanoline, Hazeline Snow, saccharin, artificial ear drums, tea in tabloid form, tonics and laxatives.

H.M.Stanley, the famous explorer carried a medicine chest prepared by Burroughs Wellcome when he went in search of Livingstone in 1874.

Lord Rosebery, Chairman of the three-day old London Council Council, today opened the Woolwich Ferry — the first free ferry in the kingdom. More than 500 passengers, two carriages and two pairs of horses made the trip across the river on the steamer **Gordon.** ***The 2nd and 3rd Kent Volunteer Artillery and the 3rd Kent Rifles provided the guard of honour and kept the ground. A Friendly Societies' band provided the music. Later, a second ferry boat,*** **Duncan** ***steamed across the river.***

Man who has saved thousands of lives

SIR Joseph Bazalgette's mammoth task in building intersecting sewers, pumping stations and treatment works and so improving London's primitive system of sanitation, has been completed after 30 years. He has transformed life in the city, cleansed the river Thames and helped to banish cholera and other water-borne diseases.

But these are not the only elements in Bazalgette's contribution to the development of London. He has reclaimed land from the Thames to construct the Victoria, Albert and Chelsea embankments, he has constructed bridges across the river at Battersea, Putney and Hammersmith and built new thoroughfares including Charing Cross Road, Southwark Street, Northumberland Avenue, Queen Victoria Street and Shaftesbury Avenue.

In Kent, he has inspired the establishment of the Woolwich free ferry and proposed the building of two tunnels under the Thames — one at Blackwall and the other at Rotherhithe. He has also supervised the reconstruction of a huge network of smaller sewers in and around the capital.

This week — his life's work completed — Joseph Bazalgette retires and hands over the Metropolitan Board of Works to a newly-constituted authority known as London County Council or LCC.

During the time he held office as Chief Engineer Sir Joseph spent in excess of £20 million on behalf of the board — £4m on main drainage, £2°m on the embankments, £12m on new streets and £7m on strengthening and re-building bridges. He moved almost 40,000 people from in-sanitary properties to newly-built ones.

He is hailed as a genius whose contributions are of far greater importance than that of his good friend Isambard Kingdom Brunel. He has certainly saved more lives than any single Victorian public figure.

Joseph Bazalgette has this to say about the scourges of cholera, typhus, smallpox and other water-borne diseases which had carried off tens of thousands of citizens during the epidemics of the mid-nineteenth century.

"The river (Thames) was in such an abominable condition that they were obliged to close the windows of the Houses of Parliament and there was talk of Parliament having to shift to other quarters altogether. The drains of London were pouring down their filth into the river at low water. There was no outflow from them at high water...When the tide ebbed it all came down and so kept oscillating up and down the river, while more filth was continuously adding to it until the Thames became absolutely pestilential."

Joseph Bazalgette

Before embarking on his gigantic programme Bazalgette visited Northfleet and later specified the use of Portland cement in the construction of the sewers, the first large-scale public work in which it was used. He said it was stronger than other kinds of cement owing to the vitrification process that occurred during manufacture. On every delivery of Portland cement his engineers and pupils carried out tests to ensure that it was sufficiently strong.

Sir Samuel Morton Peto who build the great viaduct at Folkestone, the final extension to Woolwich dockyard, many of London's clubs, parts of the Great Western, Great Eastern and South Western railways, part of the new Houses of Parliament and, most notably, Nelson's column, has died at the age of 80. He is buried at Pembury.

James Stirling, chief engineer of Ashford works and chairman of the Association of Locomotive Engineers has won the gold medal at the Paris exhibition for one of his Ashford-built locomotives.

A new church completed this year is St Matthew's, Southborough.

Wilkie Collins, the writer who achieved such popular success with *Woman in White* and *The Moonstone* has died aged 65. He lived at Broadstairs.

Tunbridge Wells, a bustling, beautifully-sited inland town, with a sizeable common, a famous cricket ground and charming buildings dating from its period of high fashion, has been incorporated. The best known street is Ye Pantyles — a terraced walk with shops behind a colonnade and a row of lime trees. It has existed since the first row of shops and houses were destroyed by fire in 1687 and Queen Anne provided funds for the 'Walks' which were paved from end to end with square earthenware tiles, known as pantiles. They were later replaced by Purbeck flagstones and these remain today.

1890-1899

1890: Joseph Merrick, a 27-year-old man with an acute disfiguring disease, dies today in London. Joseph, known all over Britain as the 'elephant man', escaped from a workhouse in 1883 to join a freak show — his extraordinary deformity attracting huge crowds. For the last three years he has been a patient in the London Hospital.

All-electric trains are introduced on London's underground railway line.

1891: A submarine cable is laid under the English Channel and those people in London who have a telephone can now speak to their friends in Paris — the first overseas city to be linked up. There are 20 telephone exchanges in London.

W.H.Smith refuses to stock a new book by Oscar Wilde called *The Picture of Dorian Gray* because it is "too filthy". Wilde says there is no such thing as a moral or immoral book.

Education is now available to all families in England and Wales, however poor, thanks to the new Elementary Education Act.

1892: Thomas Cook, who organised tours from the Midlands to see the Great Exhibition in 1851, dies after building up the world's biggest travel agency.

1893: A 15-week coal strike called by the Miners' Federation, ends. Unionism has grown strongly since the 1889 London dock strike.

William Gladstone's Home Rule Bill is resoundingly defeated on its second reading in the House of Commons.

1894: Gladstone's successor as Liberal Prime Minister is Philip Archibald Primrose, the Earl of Rosebery.

Engineering achievements completed this year include the Tower Bridge in London, the Blackpool Tower and the Manchester Ship Canal.

A son is born to the Duke and Duchess of York.The Queen's first great grandchild becomes third in line to the throne.

Diptheria, typhoid and influenza strikes in the village of Cuxton, reducing the school attendance from 100 to 40. Polluted drinking water is blamed.

Edward Watkins retires as Member of Parliament for Folkestone leaving his dreams of an Eiffel tower at Wembley Park and a tunnel to France under the English Channel unfulfilled.

1895: Oscar Wilde is imprisoned after being convicted of homosexual practices — four months after his play *The Importance of Being Earnest* opened at the Haymarket.

With the introduction of the pneumatic tyre, the current craze of bicycle riding is become popular with women.

1895: Lord Rosebery resigns as Prime Minister over a dispute concerning the lack of production of the explosive material cordite. Lord Salisbury will lead the Conservative party back to power.

Northern clubs who want to pay their players have broken away from the Rugby Union and formed their own Rugby League.

1896: Queen Victoria overtakes the record set by her grandfather, George III, for the longest reign — 59 years and 96 days.

Tension rises in South Africa following an attempt to seize the Boer republic of the Transvaal. It was launched with the backing of Cecil Rhodes, Prime Minister of Cape Colony.

1897: A gallery founded by sugar manufacturer, Sir Henry Tate is built on the site of the old Millbank prison.

Electric tramways are opening in many of Britain's major cities.

Taximeter cabs are now operating in the City and West End of London.

The formation of the Association of Men of Kent and Kentish Men — also Maids of Kent and Kentish Maids — takes place at Holborn Viaduct Hotel.

A typhoid epidemic breaks out in Maidstone.

1898: Charles Lutwidge Dodgson, a mathematics lecturer at Oxford, dies. He is better known by his pseudonym of Lewis Carol, author of *Alice's Adventures in Wonderland.*

July: The Prince and Princess of Wales are guests of Lionel Lord Sackville at Knole, Sevenoaks.

William Gladstone dies, aged 87. He was first elected to the House of Commons in 1832 and was Prime Minister on four occasions.

Liberal MPs are campaigning for an eight-hour working day. It is now the practice for workers to enjoy a half day holiday on a Saturday.

1899: Marylebone Station opens as the terminus for the Manchester, Sheffield and Lincoln railway. It could be the last of Britain's mainline railways.

War breaks out in South Africa between the British and the Boer republics. Boer commandoes have laid seige to Kimberley, Ladysmith and Mafeking.

The British empire now covers more than one-fifth of the landmass of the globe and is continuing to expand. One in every four human beings lives within its boundaries.

Canterbury artist famous for his cattle and sheep

IN his early life Thomas Sidney Cooper was a coach painter. Today, as a member of the Royal Academy, he has devoted his life to capturing on canvas the essential image of the English landscape and is mostly associated with pictures of cattle and sheep.

Cooper was born in Canterbury in 1803 and quickly showed his artistic talent. His family were unable to afford to give him any systematic training but his drawings and sketches came to the attention of the British Museum who invited him to paint for them. He was then admitted as a student of the Royal Academy.

Returning to Canterbury, Cooper earned a living as a drawing master and by the sale of his sketches.

He painted *Summer's Noon* in 1836, *Drover's Halt on the Fells* and, famously, the *Half-past One O'Clock Charge at Waterloo.* Other well-known paintings include *Pushing Off for Tilbury* (1884) and *On a Farm in East Kent* (1889). He has enjoyed a prolonged career as an exhibitor.

A few years ago he presented the Thomas Sidney Cooper Art Gallery to Canterbury, built on the site of the house in which he was born.

Hiram Maxim is working on another invention — a rifle with a silencer.

Machine gun has firepower of 100 rifles

HIRAM Stevens Maxim, famous in England and America for his contribution to military technology, has relocated his workshop in Crayford where, with the help of local workers, he will continue to manufacture the world's first automatic single-barrel portable machine gun.

Born in Maine just 50 years ago Maxim was apprenticed at the age of 14 to a carriage maker and became interested in the wonders of the electric light. He was appointed chief engineer of the first electric light company before coming to England to organise electricity services in this country.

In 1881, his interest switched to automatic weapons and at his factory in Hatton Gardens he worked on an effective machine gun. Five years ago he gave a demonstration to the British Army.

To his delight it was adopted by the Army in 1889 and the following year he was given contracts by the Austrian, German, Italian, Swiss and Russian armies.

Maxim's machine gun uses the energy of each bullet's recoil force to eject the spent cartridge and insert the next bullet. It can therefore fire until the entire belt of bullets is used up. Trials have proved that the machine gun can fire 500 rounds per minute and has the firepower of about 100 rifles.

The Prince of Wales is among many distinguished people intrigued by Hiram Maxim's new weapon. The inventor now lives in a house near Crayford called Stoneyhurst.

A new lighthouse, at Dungeness commissioned by Trinity House, will soon be beaming its warning messages across the Channel. Since one tragic year early in the 17th century when more than a thousand lifeless bodies of shipwreck victims were collected at or near the Ness there have been a succession of lighthouses on the point. Shingle is currently growing at the rate of 18 inches a year so the day will come when the new lighthouse has to be replaced.

It is believed that more than 250,000 hoppers are now working in the Kentish hop gardens — about 70,000 of them come from London.

New churches consecrated this year are St John's, Dunton Green, St Barnabas, Gillingham and St Luke's, Gravesend.

The 240-feet long Margate jetty, with a pavilion at one end, has been jam-packed with visitors this summer. Steamers, such as the **Royal Sovereign** *(pictured here) are coming and going all the time. Margate is the largest resort in Kent with a reputation for cheerfulness and vulgarity with its fun-fair image of picture postcards and mass amusements.*

Parnell admits affair with Katherine O'Shea

November: Katherine O'Shea, the young and beautiful wife of Irish MP Captain William O'Shea, who lives in a grand home in North Park, Eltham has admitted to a long and passionate love affair with Charles Parnell, the great Irish patriot and leader of the Home Rule Party.

Cited as co-respondent in a divorce case, Parnell has also confessed to the affair. *The Pall Mall Gazette* has called for his resignation on the grounds that his inolvement with Katherine could seriously injure the future of the Home Rule Bill in the House of Commons.

Eltham, a small town on the southern borders of London is the centre of a scandal which has dominated the gossip columns and aroused the interest of the whole world.

Katherine is the niece of Mrs Benjamin Wood, of Eltham. Some years ago she married Captain William O'Shea, an Irish Member of Parliament who passionately espoused the cause of nationalism.

O'Shea and his bride bought Wornesh Lodge, North Park, Eltham so Katherine could attend to her "Aunt Ben". The couple immediately began to live the privileged life which is enjoyed by the upper classes.

The O'Shea's admiration for 44-year-old Charles Parnell, the protestant Irish leader, is well known. They admire his efforts to turn self-government for Ireland from an impractical dream into an attainable goal. They dislike the way the government has treated him as an advocate for violence through his agitation for land reform.

In the 1885 general election Parnell's party won 85 seats, exactly the number of votes separating the Liberals from the Conservatives and because of this William Gladstone announced his support for a Home Rule bill and — with Irish support — became Prime Minister for the third time.

It is now known that Katherine O'Shea's admiration for Parnell goes beyond his skills at manipulating Gladstone. Some 10 years ago she tried, on several occasions, to persuade Parnell to dine with her at Eltham but he always declined. Piqued by these frequent refusals she drove to the House of Commons and sent a message for him to join her in her carriage, which he did.

Charles Parnell is a massive political figure, whose determination that Ireland should be governed by a parliament at Dublin, dominates his every waking hour. But he found room for romance, became Katherine's lover and during the Land League prosecutions remained concealed in an unused room at Wornesh Lodge, Eltham.

It appears that Captain William O'Shea was unaware of his presence in the house and the loyal servants turned a blind eye to the many visits that Katherine made to the room. The subterfuge did not last.

Captain O'Shea discovered Parnell's portmanteau at Eltham — an incident which so unsettled his mind that he challenged his leader to a duel. This was averted but divorce proceedings were not. Gladstone may now force the Irish party to choose between Parnell's leadership and his own support for a Home Rule Bill. *See page 228*

Parnell dies three months after his marriage to Katherine

October 2: Charles Parnell, exhausted by the scandal of his affair with Katherine O'Shea, which led to political ruin,and riddled with rheumatism died at Brighton today at the age of 45.

He married Katherine on June 25 and said he was determined to fight the next election and revive his political career.

A grief stricken Katherine Parnell has now spoken about the affair and the ability of statesmen to turn a blind eye to "social irregularities". She said: "For ten years Mr Gladstone had known of the intimacy between Parnell and myself and had taken full advantage of the facility this intimacy afforded him in keeping in touch with the Irish leader.

"In view of the fact that Mr Gladstone and his friends were so pained, surprised and properly shocked when Parnell was publicly arraigned as my lover, the frantic way they applied to me when they were unable to find him was afterwards a source of considerable amusement to us both."

The ruins of Rochester Castle which was purchased from the Earl of Jersey . Sadly much of the castle has been dismantled and the timbers sold to a brewery. The first castle was built on this site by the Romans to protect the bridge across the River Medway. Bishop Gundolf started work on the current castle on behalf of William the Conqueror in 1087.

Great welcome at Crystal Palace for Kaiser Willy

KAISER William II of Germany, who is in England to visit his grandmother, Queen Victoria, has visited Crystal Palace to see some of the great attractions it offers.

William succeeded to the German throne in July 1888 following the death of his father, Frederick II at Potsdam.

The Queen was broken-hearted by the news and urged her grandson to look after his mother, Victoria. His behaviour, though, worried her. She wrote at the time: "How sickening it is to see Willy, not two months after his father's death...at banquets and reviews..."

Hundreds of people travelled to the top of Sydenham Hill to catch a glimpse of the German king. Many travelled on the London Chatham and Dover railway which delivers its passengers at a high level station connected directly to the Palace grounds by a brick-vaulted tunnel running underneath the building.

William II is not the only member of a royal family to tour the palace. The Sultan of Turkey (1867), the Khedive of Egypt (1869), the Shah of Persia (1873), Tsar Alexander II of Russia (1874), the Sultan of Zanzibar (1875), the King and Queen of Greece (1876) and, of course, Queen Victoria, have been regular visitors.

The most popular event is the Grand Firework Display when flights of more than 5,000 rockets are set off to discharge great plumes of fire, cascading down in gold and silver stars. The speciality is the Niagara of Fire, a magnificent cascade which covers an area of some 25,000 square feet and burns a ton of iron filings.

September 16: A monument to Christopher Marlowe, the first great English dramatist, whose early plays were produced before those of William Shakespeare, has been unveiled at Buttermarket, Canterbury by Britain's most celebrated actor, Henry Irving.

While Kent's professional photographers enjoy a great trade in portrait photography, the amateurs are no less busy. Here are members of Tunbridge Wells Photographic Society at Scotney. They carry their dark room with them — a black cloth on bamboo framing and a box with a lens at one end and a watertight compartment at the other.

W.H.Smith, Lord Warden, dies at 66

October 6: William Henry Smith, Lord Warden of Walmer Castle but better known as the proprietor of the largest chain of newspaper/bookshops in the country, has died after less than six months in office. He was 66.

He was a sick man when appointed in March but that did not prevent him from setting up a trust to safeguard much of the furniture and mementoes at Walmer, which had been given by previous Lord Wardens such as Pitt and Wellington.

As soon as he took office, Smith showed great interest in Walmer's history and was concerned with preventing the removal of items with historical associations; this had already happened to many of Wellington's possessions.

Smith formulated an Act of Parliament detailing the conditions and listing all the valuable items or 'Heirlooms' which could not be removed from Walmer. He stipulated that the framed list was to hang in the corridor at Walmer and made provision for additions to be added by future Lord Wardens.

W.H. Smith took over the London newspaper shop which had been opened by his grandparents in 1792 and used the railways to develop the business into a national retail chain. In 1848 he secured a contract to place stalls on the platforms of many stations and saw them flourish in an age when novels were produced in instalments.

As a Conservative politician, W.H.Smith enjoyed a distinguished political career. He has held office as financial secretary to the Treasury, First Lord of the Admiralty, Secretary for War and, at his death, Leader of the Commons.

The new Lord Warden of Walmer is the Marquess of Dufferin and Ava, who has given W.H.Smith's son, W.F.D Smith permission to complete the Heirloom formalities.

Gladstone's tour

April: There was drama and near tragedy at Charing Cross when several officials, waiting for the arrival of the train carrying William Gladstone, fell off the station platform and had to save themselves by clinging to the engine coupling.

The incident was caused by several hundred people surging forward to catch a glimpse of the great Liberal statesmen. The shocked officials escaped without injury and the train left for Tunbridge Wells on the first stage of a Twenty Towns Tour of Kent and Sussex.

Ramsgate Sands has been a fashionable sea-bathing resort for more than 100 years and the donkey and pony rides for children have added to its popularity. Nearby is the Royal Harbour, so named since George IV's visit in 1821. It is 46 acres in size with a non-tidal inner basin and once subsisted largely on fishing and smuggling.

New Kentish forts to protect London

ENCOURAGED by the war office, who have grave doubts about the Royal Navy's ability to give absolute protection, a defensive ring of fortresses is to be built around London and three of them will be in Kent.

The plan is for an entrenched line along the North Downs and in Essex. They will be manned by London Volunteers who will dig the positions themselves in the week a warning is given. Negotiations are well under way for the purchase of land in Farningham, Halstead and Westerham on which to build the forts.

The case for building a defensive ring round London was presented to Parliament a few years ago by General Hamley who was supported by Viscount Wolseley, the Adjutant General and Edward Stanhope, the war minister.

The plan is for 10 defence positions, each covering an approach to London. A pontoon bridge at Tilbury will connect the positions north and south of the Thames. Two extensions could be ocupied to close gaps in the line, and an outlying position at Wrotham could join the line to the Chatham ring of defences.

At a recent debate MPs avoided using the word 'fort' and the Opposition was asked "in the national interest"not to press for details.

Bessie tells of life in rural Kent

BESSIE Marchant, a 30-year-old, six-foot tall, former schoolteacher, who earns her living writing articles and stories for magazines, has published a book about life in rural Kent during her childhood.

Largely biographical it is entitled *Pease Granock's Father* and tells, in Kentish dialogue, about the countryside around Petham where she joyously 'skivved from school to pick stones off t'Maisters fileds and shave 'is 'op poles'.

Bessie's father was a farmer at Debden Court who leased a second farm at Bodsam Green and built a mission chapel. To those who lived near Elmstead it was known as 'The Chapel in the Woods'.

Bessie moved from Petham National to a private school in Canterbury and quickly qualified as a teacher. She found a house in London and married fellow teacher and priest Jabez Ambrose Comfort. Today, her articles are anxiously sought by publishers.

The Napoleon family have been reunited in the crypt of St Michael's Abbey, Farnborough following the death this year of Empress Eugenie.

Wye Grammar School has been converted into an Agricultural College.

New swing bridge will carry the heaviest loco

December 6: A substantial new iron swing bridge has been built over the Stour at Sandwich — strong enough to withstand the weight of steam locomotives which now cross the river so frequently. No longer do the drivers have to give 24-hours notice before they cross but they must not exceed a speed of two miles an hour.

With the opening of the bridge, older residents have been recalling the days (as told by their grandfathers) when communication between Sandwich and Thanet could be made only by ferry.

It was in the mid-18th century that a wooden drawbridge was built to allow ships "to pass and repass as often as they have occasion". The ferry was closed and it was illegal for any unauthorised persons to ferry passengers, animals or goods. The fine for doing so was 1s.

In those days a bridge man was on duty day and night to collect the tolls — two shillings for a coach, chariot, landau, berlin, chaise, chair, cabash drawn by six or more horses and 9d if drawn by only one.

Some 40 years ago a new wooden bridge was substituted and the tolls were revised but the councils began to get worried by the appearance of locomotives on the roads and it was decided to build a third bridge. The opening took place today in front of a large gathering of townspeople.

***Right:** Alfred Tennyson when young. After a sketch by Dante Gabriel Rossetti in 1855, entitled 'Maud'*

Boxley prays for Tennyson

October 7: Special prayers were said in the church of St Mary and All Saints, Boxley this week for Alfred Lord Tennyson, poet laureate since 1850, who has died at the age of 83. He will be buried in Westminster Abbey.

Tennyson, greatly admired by the Queen, was once a frequent visitor to the village, just two miles from Maidstone at the foot of the North Downs.

It is believed that one of the Boxley streams, a tributary of the river Medway, was the inspiration for his poem, _The Brook_. Some time later, stimulated by his visits to Boxley Abbey and Park House, he wrote his prologue to the _The Princess._

The poet laureate's sister, Celia, lived at Park House and Tennyson was a regular guest.

He was a witness to the marriage of Celia into the Lushington family in 1852 and that occasion almost certainly inspired his passage from _In Memoriam_ of "maidens of the place that pelt us in the porch with flowers".

It is possible that he wrote much of his finest work in Boxley, in a little thatched lodge in the grounds of Park House, surrounded by glorious Kentish countryside.

The pictures tell the story. More than 200 buildings were damaged, many beyond repair, at Sandgate yesterday when the hillside, undermined by weeks of heavy rain, gave way.

Fabians say new Labour Party 'too revolutionary'

January 13: More and more "thinkers" and "young intellectuals" are joining the Fabian Party which propounds the socialist cause and aims to work towards a democratic socialist state.

Among the more active members are Hubert Bland who was born at Wood Street, Woolwich and his wife Edith Nesbit, who played a crucial role in the Match Girls' strike of 1888.

Bland, together with George Bernard Shaw, Sidney Webb and Annie Besant, were present today in Bradford at the formation of the Independent Labour Party but left early because the programme seemed too revolutionary.

Keir Hardy, a former Lanarkshire coalminer is chairman of the Labour Party. He says he is "determined to create a political party that represents the interests of the working class"

Hubert Bland writes for the Fabian Society and contributes a column under the pen name "Hubert" for the *Sunday Chronicle.*

The couple live at Halstead Hall, a red-bricked house between Bromley and Sevenoaks, situated near a railway cutting.

Malling Abbey, which has been in private hands since the dissolution in 1538, has been purchased by Mrs Charlotte Boys for an Anglican community of nuns founded by "Father Ignatius" of Llantony and is thus restored to nomadic use. Built by Bishop Gundulf in 1077, little of the original building is still standing apart from the Norman tower and a section of the nave.

The Daily Graphic, Britain's first illustrated daily newspaper, has been launched by W.L.Thomas. It is the first British newspaper to carry half tone pictures and marks a major step forward in press photography.

An outbreak of diphtheria and typoid in Cuxton has been blamed on bad drainage and polluted drinking water. Last year a influenza epidemic reduced the school attendance in Cuxton from 100 to 40.

Edward Watkins is to retire as MP for Folkestone, leaving unfulfilled his dreams for an "Eiffel Tower" at Wembley Park.

Admiralty Pier, Dover, completed a few years ago, is known as the Gateway of England. Here the paddle steamers carry continental visitors across the Channel on a journey that takes just two hours. Work began this year on a new Pier — the Prince of Wales — which will take many years to complete.

The railway map: a journey to prosperity

WITH the opening of the branch line from Paddock Wood to Hawkhurst, the railway network of Kent is virtually complete.The only new line sanctioned is that to link Sheerness with Leysdown on the Isle of Sheppey.

The railway has brought prosperity and a greater population to every Kent town it serves — and that means all of them except Tenterden.

The story began in 1842 with the building of the South Eastern Railway from London, then through the Weald of Kent via Tonbridge, Maidstone Road (Paddock Wood) and Ashford, reaching the coast at Folkestone in 1843.

This dead-straight rural line, with few gradients, was chosen because of the opposition of landowners in the developing towns in the north of the county.

To the disgust of the directors of the South Eastern who enjoyed a monopoly of railway transport, the East Kent Railway obtained Parliamentary sanction to construct a line from Strood to Canterbury with stations at Chatham, Sittingbourne and Faversham.

War was declared.

The rivalry grew. The East Kent changed its name to London, Chatham and Dover and extended its lines both eastward and westward, reaching Whitstable in 1860, Herne Bay and Dover in 1861 and Margate and Ramsgate in 1863.

As competition for the lucrative Channel traffic at Dover intensified, the towns in the west of the county began to share London's rapid expansion. Branch lines opened everywhere, enabling thousands of men and women to continue to live in the country and travel daily to the capital. With it came a change in character for Bromley, Beckenham, Sidcup, Chislehurst, Erith, Bexley and Orpington and all the smaller communities they serve.

People in Sevenoaks, Dartford, Gravesend could also get to London in less than an hour. The commuter age was born

Machine in flight — for 600 feet

Hiram Maxim's biplane has a wing span of 105 feet and weighs 7,000 lbs. It took to the air at 42 mph.

'Success is near', says Hiram Maxim — 'I will be flying soon'

July 31: History was made today when Hiram Maxim, the brilliant and eccentric British inventor, attempted the first powered flight in an airplane by man. It took place at Baldwyns Park, Bexley and was witnessed by a number of delighted, if anxious spectators.

It was actually Maxim's third test run and he was on board with a crew of three. As his 'biplane' raced down a specially-designed track the engines and boilers were coaxed to deliver greater and greater pressure. At a little more than 42 mph, the whole structure took to the air, lifting with such force that it broke the restraining track. It flew for about 600 feet —then crashed. It is believed that a lifting force of some 10,000 pounds had been generated.

It was in the mid-1880s that Maxim began his experiments at Baldwyns Park. Famous for his invention of the Maxim machine gun, from which he made a fortune, he began to explore heavier-than-air flight having relocated his engineering works at Crayford.

His first biplane weighed 7,000 pounds and had a wingspan of 105 feet. The machine had two Naptha-fired steam engines, each producing 180 hp and turned two propellers, each 17° in diameter.

Maxim, who lives nearby at Stoneyhurst, was wise enough to understand that getting a machine airborne and controlling it while in flight were two different things, so his was guided by rails, 1,800 feet long which, while allowing a degree of 'free' flight, restrained any serious deviation from the straight and narrow. This prevented a 'crash and rebuild' from start as had faced so many other experimenters.

This week Mr Maxim described the famous flight. "After running for about a 1,000 feet", he said, "one of the restraining axletrees doubled up and this put the whole lift of the machine onto the other three. The upper track

continued on next page

The flying brothers from Ohio

HIRAM Maxim is not the only person attempting to launch a flying machine.Two brothers from Dayton, Ohio, Orville and Wilbur Wright are conducting tests with kites and gliders and the results have been encouraging.

They are keen to solve the essential problem of controlling an airplane's motion in rising, descending and turning. Then they have to find a light and powerful engine or, in the words of Mr Maxim — "one horsepower with the weight of a barnyard fowl".

The brothers' interest in self-propelled transport began in the 1880s where they formed the Wright Cycle Company to build and sell bicycles in Dayton, Ohio. They are interested in coming to Kent. *See pages 247 and 251.*

Maxim's flying trials have cost £20,000

continued from previous page

was broken, the machine was liberated and floated into the air, giving those on board the sensation of being in a boat.

"However, a piece of the broken track caught in one of the screws and at the same instant I shut off the steam and the machine stopped and settled into the ground, the wheels sinking into the soft turf without making any other mark.

"It was the first time in the world that a powered flying machine had actually lifted itself and the crew into the air" said Maxim, "and the first machine to have flown from substantially level ground."

The engineer is now convinced that success is near. He has already towed the broken machine back to its enormous shed and will soon start on redesigning and constructing a stronger outrigger undercarriage. His team has been joined by a young English naval engineer, Percy Sinclair Pilcher who has thrown up his job as a lecturer in naval architecture in order to learn about the art of flying.

There are two setbacks to Maxim's plans. Having already spent £20,000 on the trials he now has to raise more money and is hoping that his backers will not havc cold feet. Baldwyns Park, Bexley is to be sold to Kent County Council for a mental home. *See page 247.*

The Open comes to Sandwich

THE Open, the world's oldest international golf championship, which has been played annually since 1860, will be held this year at Sandwich — the first time the competition has been held outside Scotland.

It was a Scot, Laidlow Purves, who laid out the links on the long stretch of flat sands. He called it St George's, bought the freehold of the ground and built a clubhouse.

The first Open Championship was played over three rounds of Prestwick's 12-hole course on October 17, 1860. Just eight men played in that first challenge and Willie Park of Musselburgh beat Tom Morris by two strokes.

A bronze tablet has been placed in St Edmund's church, Dartford by the parish council to commemorate the work of Richard Trevithick. At Westminster Abbey a stained glass window has been commissioned in his memory.

The pleasant Sussex village of Lamberhurst which sits on the River Teise close to the Kentish border has voted itself to be wholly in Kent because hops fetch a higher price in Kent.

Oliver Jocelyn Ellis, chief designer at J and E Hall of Dartford is one of the victims on the *SS Aberdeen* this year.

September: Major Henry Herbert Edwards, a deputy governor of Pentonville Prison and formerly of the Royal Welch Fusiliers, has been appointed chief constable of Kent following the retirement of Captain Ruxton after 37 years.

Ruxton, the only surviving member of the original Kent County Constabulary, resigned in August following the death of his wife and the fact that he is now 77. There were 70 applications for the post, mainly from military personnel.

Major Edwards has many critics who say that he lacks police experience and he was appointed only because he is the son-in-law of the chairman of Kent County Council.

Now Gladstone sacks the village squire

January 1: No longer are the squire of the manor, the parson and the schoolmaster the accepted leaders in their own village.

Thanks to William Gladstone and his cabinet, parish, rural and district councils have been set up in Kent along with some 6,000 other communities in the country. The Local Government Act or "the village revolution" as some are calling it has been passed.

This means that more people can have a say in how local affairs are managed and the squire may not be among them. Life will never be the same again.

In piloting the Act through the Commons last year, Gladstone met much opposition; for example there were more than 8,000 amendments during its passage through the House.

The Act will not only make great changes in the way Britain is administered. It increases the rights of women voters in local affairs. Qualified single women have been able to vote on local affairs since 1882. Now married women may do so and they can also be elected to councils.

Kent's villages were ruled by the Lord of the Manor during Norman times and this continued through the ages with parish priests and schoolmasters later joining in a kind of ruling clique.

In 1601 church vestry meetings were established and given the responsibility of levying the poor rate or local taxes. Everyone in the parish was entitled to attend but few bothered. By 1834 the responsibility for poor relief had passed to the Poor Law Unions.

The new authorities will have substantial powers although their spending has been limited to the equivalent of a 3d rate.

Thames frozen in this winter of discontent

February 10: **Soup kitchens and bread queues have been established in hundreds of communities as the Great Frost tightens its grip on Kent and temperatures fall to the lowest ever known.**

The Medway has been frozen from shore to shore for almost a fortnight and river traffic is at a standstill. The Thames is also frozen at Dartford and Gravesend and many ships have been damaged by ice.

Outdoor work is impossible. In the Medway towns thousands have been put out of work and great crowds have been seen fighting their way to the doors of those distributing bread. The *Chatham News* described it as "an extremely touching scene".

The intense cold has brought tragedy. At Sheerness a barge mate was frozen to death, at Chatham a prison warder froze to death at his post and at Maidstone a father of six has been drowned in icy waters.

There have also been some lighter moments. Children have been seen on the Thames, jumping from iceberg to iceberg while scores are enjoying night skating on the Gravesend and Higham Canal.

National Trust formed to save our heritage

MISS Octavia Hill, a lady committed to the ideal that green open spaces and historic buildings should be saved for the nation is one of the principal figures behind a new organisation called the National Trust. Miss Hill lives at Crockham Hill, near Edenbridge and has already formed a Kent and Surrey Commons Preservation Society. Her co-founders are Sir Robert Hunter and Canon H.D. Rawnsley, who now hope to acquire land and buildings for the nation.

Sir David Salomons (with beard) is seen here at the horseless carriage exhibition with his friend the Hon Evelyn Ellis.

Motor pioneer says: 'repeal red flag law'

October 15: An exhibition of horseless carriages was held at the agricultural showground in Tunbridge Wells today. It was organised and funded by Sir David Salomons, a wealthy inventor and electrical pioneer who lives at Broomhill, Southborough.

Sir David sees enormous potential in the motor vehicle and has already made many journeys to France where the craze is sweeping through the country. In fact his single cylinder Peugeot — purchased in Paris and capable of a sustained and quite illegal 15 miles per hour — was one of the exhibits at today's show.

Also on view was a Panhard Levassor, driven by his friend, the Hon Evelyn Ellis, a motorised Victoria carriage, a De Dion barouche and three tricycles, all made in France.

The exhibition was attended by more than 5,000 people, the majority of whom had never seen an automobile. They saw a hill-climbing demonstration by the Peugeot and the Panhard, watched with fascination as Sir David's Victoria glided round the show ring and were amused by the antics of Tunbridge Well's fire brigade as the men pitted their horse-drawn steam pump against a Daimler petrol tender.

Sir David and many other motorists are campaigning to end the tyranny of the man with the red flag who has to precede every motor-powered vehicle in order to warn horse drivers. "The law must be repealed" said Sir David this week. "We are not steam-traction engines and should not be restricted to four miles an hour in the country and two miles an hour in towns. I have personally no interest whatsoever in the manufacture of these vehicles, except so far as to possess a few of the best carriages which can be produced."

Another pioneer keen for reform is William Arnold of East Peckham who has already been prosecuted for "proceeding at a speed greater than four miles an hour".

See page 239

Sir William and Lady Hart-Dyke at Lullingstone Castle. Sir William, statesman, politician and sportsman, was the world racquets champion in 1862 and raised the money to build the first covered racquets court at his old school, Harrow in 1864. It was here at Lullingstone that he and friends, including the Prince of Wales, devised the rules for the game of lawn tennis. In the background leading to the 15th century manor house is one of the earliest brick-built gatehouses in England.

Dover mountaineer lost in 'eternal snows'

September: Mr A.F.Mummery, the Dover mountaineer who has conquered the Matterhorn and many other Alpine peaks, wrote in his recently-published book: "It is true that the odds are on the side of the mountaineer but the off chance excites to honesty of thought and tests how far decay has penetrated the inner fibre...No-one can look down its gloomy death-roll without feeling that our sport demands a fearful price".

These are strikingly prophetic words. On Sunday the news was wired to Dover - "Mummery and two Ghoorkas lost". It is now known that Mr Mummery died in his attempt to climb the Nunga Parbut, which rises above the western Himalayas to a height of 26,629 feet. On one side it is so steep that snow cannot lie on it, hence its name Nunga, meaning naked.

Apparently Mr Mummery left the military station of Astor accompanied by his companions, Mr Hastings and Dr Norman Colly and established a camp some 10,000 feet up.

The next day, with two 'Ghoorka' guides, he went exploring but failed to return. His colleagues believe they fell into a crevasse and "there they will continue to lie, far up among the eternal snows".

Alfred Mummery was the son of a former mayor of Dover, who lived at Maison Dieu house and ran a tannery business in the town. He took over the business when his father died in 1869 but so enjoyed his mountain escapades in the Alps and the Caucasus that climbing became his lifelong passion. The passion increased when he first gazed upon, then conquered, the mighty Matterhorn.

"As soon as I have ascended a peak it becomes a friend", he wrote, "but it is a delight to seek fresh woods and pastures new.... I am always open-eyed to their perils".

Alfred the little, a 'pompous' poet laureate

ALFRED Austin, a disenchanted barrister, author of a two-volume novel and a number of satirical poems, has surprised the literary world with his appointment as Poet Laureate.

The man who follows in the exalted footsteps of William Wordsworth and Alfred Lord Tennyson lives at Swinford Old Manor, Hothfield, a house of "charm, solitude and some antiquity, down three miles of Kentish lanes from the station, which I found with the help of a rubicund railway porter".

For many years Austin was the editor of the *National Review* and a staunch supporter of the Conservative party. When Tennyson died in 1892 he made it clear he was prepared to fill the great man's shoes but it has taken three years, three months and three prime ministers for the post to be finally offered by Lord Salisbury.

During that time there have been many more appropriate contenders such as William Morris (who refused), Rudyard Kipling (too young) and Algernon Swinburne (too impossible). Austin, however, was popular with the people and his *Garden That I Love* — about life at Swinford Manor — is into its fourth edition.

Many academics do not approve of the five-foot tall Alfred Austin whom, they say, writes bad poetry and has a pompous personality with no sense of humour. Among them is William Archer who recently wrote: "He is praised by none, derided by all and pipes on imperturbably".

Alfred the great — a tycoon, aged 34

October: A sporting, motor-car crazy, innovative young journalist from Broadstairs has launched a new style of newspaper which he hopes will appeal to the newly-educated masses. It is called the *Daily Mail*, it sells for just a halfpenny and is on course to become an enormous success — the average daily sales for the first two weeks were in excess of 200,000.

Alfred Harmsworth is just 34 and has modelled his "bright and breezy" newspaper on those currently selling well in the United States with snappy headlines and a greater variety of reports and reviews.

The oldest of 13 children of an English barrister and an Irish wife, Alfred edited his school magazine with much encouragement from the headmaster, Mr J.V. Milne. Smitten by journalism he joined George Newnes' *Titbits* magazine and then started his own magazine called *Answers to Correspondents.* For just a penny he gave the public just what they wanted and then hit on a brainwave by offering a "pound a week for life" to the reader who could most exactly estimate the value of gold and silver on that day in the Bank of England vaults.

There had to be a winner and there was. A reader guessed to within £2, won the prize and gained 3,000,000 new readers for Alfred Harmsworth who rapidly introduced new features including 'comic cuts' and 'chips'. His former headmaster was not impressed: "You've killed off the penny dreadful", he wrote to Harmsworth, "by producing a halfpenny dreadfuller".

Since then the young, now-notorious tycoon, with the shrewd business brain, has gone from strength to strength. Two years ago Harmsworth bought the *Evening News* and then his own horseless carriage. Campaigning for the repeal of the Red Flag Act which he hoped would spur Britain into joining the great motor vehicle craze which is currently sweeping through America, he helped to organise a London to Brighton motor run earlier this year. It was so successful that the restriction requiring vehicles to be preceded by a man carrying a flag has been lifted and the speed limit raised from four miles and hour to 20 mph.

Satisfied by the part he played in this famous victory, Harmsworth has acquired a fleet of cars and built modern garages to house them. A few weeks ago his chauffeur, driving rather too swiftly, swerved to avoid a horse near his new home in Broadstairs and overturned.

The tycoon was thrown out of the vehicle and temporarily paralysed. It was the first recorded motor car accident in Kent.

The Pleasure Gardens Theatre is the centre of Folkestone's entertainment and shows plays and concerts of a high standard. It is appropriate that the theatre, originally the home of the National Art Treasures Exhibition of 1886, should première the moving films.

Moving pictures are seen in Folkestone

July 6: Last night Folkestone became the first town in Kent to introduce a 'moving picture show'. Hundreds of people who crammed into the Pleasure Gardens Theatre to welcome a wonderful invention called a *Vivaceographe*, watched with growing bewilderment as whole crowds actually walked into a station. They saw the arrival of a train in a station, porters loading up the luggage and passengers getting in and out of a train.

Described by the promoters, Messrs Banks and Graves as 'the sensation of the age' and 'the electric marvel of the day' this animated picture show has already become the talk of the town. It has to be seen to be believed.

This morning the *Folkestone Herald* urged that "all should make a point of seeing the *Vivaceographe*, which presents with unerring accuracy animated pictures of everyday life...the movements of which are strikingly lifelike". The *Folkestone Up To Date* is not so enthusiastic saying "the animated pictures are blurred and indistinct".

The 'flickers' - as many people call them - are the consequence of almost simultaneous inventions on both sides of the Atlantic; by Thomas Edison in America and the brothers Louis and Auguste Lumière in France. They are more appealing and realistic than the old magic lantern shows where pictures were made to move in a revolving drum.

Moving pictures were introduced in Paris in December. By March this year the Lumière brothers were wowing audiences at the Empire, Leicester Square with their *Cinématographe* but were not the only ones with moving shows. Rival operators were soon showing films in London.

'Topsy' Morris dies at Kelmscott

October 3: William Morris, artist, painter and poet, who lived at the Red House, Bexleyheath from 1860 to 1871 died today at his home at Kelmscott aged 62. He employed his friends Rossetti and Burne-Jones to help him design furniture, stained glass, tapestry and wallpaper and he took English design away from the massed produced manufacturer. Topsy, as he was known to his friends, campaigned vigorously in the streets on behalf of socialism and, in 1884, formed his own Socialist League.

Help at last for the 'Little Hoppers'

September: When Father Richard Wilson of St Augustine's Church, Stepney and three volunteer nurses decided to establish a "Little Hoppers Hospital" in the Kentish village of Five Oak Green they had no idea of the real value of their enterprise.

But their arrival co-incided with an outbreak of smallpox and scores of sick children of the hop pickers have been nursed back to good health by these Good Samaritans.

Father Wilson first came to Kent with the hop pickers last year and was horrified by what he saw. The only drinking water from the entire camp was drawn from a pond and the only lavatories were the nearest ditch which drained into the same pond.

This year he has rented a cottage for his work but he hopes to establish a permanent hospital for Little Hoppers.

Cherry trees are in abundance in the villages that link Sittingbourne with Faversham and so are the cherry pickers who have been working in the fields ever since Richard Harris, fruiterer to Henry VIII planted hundreds of acres with cherry trees imported from Flanders. Today, fruit, paper production and brick making are Sittingbourne's staple industries.

The famous Invicta locomotive — a replica of Stephenson's Rocket — has been gifted to Canterbury thanks to the generosity of Sir David Salomons of Broomhill, Southborough.

The loco, which pulled Kent's first passenger train between Canterbury and Whitstable in 1830, was consigned to the scrap heap by railway officials. Mr Salomons, however, considers it of great historical value. It will be restored and sited in the city.

Benenden bells peal on a diamond day

June 22: Once again the people of Kent have reason to celebrate the long, distinguished reign of Queen Victoria, who presides over the largest and richest empire in the world. Diamond jubilee events have been held all over the county in brilliant sunshine and many lasting memorials are in place as a mark of respect for the lady who has seen the advent of steam, the coming of electricity, the telephone and motor cars. Among the memorials is the Lewisham clock tower while, in the village of Benenden, six church bells have been rehung. Today they are peeling merrily.

Shakespeare Colliery miners — eight of their colleagues were killed.

Miners drowned at Shakespeare Cliff

March 7: Tragedy struck at the Shakespeare Colliery, Dover today when eight miners, working at a depth of 3,000 feet, were drowned. Several other men managed to clamber to safety.

It was early last year that the Kent Coalfields Syndicate was formed to exploit the workings of the Shakespeare Cliff. Sadly the results were so poor that when a party of shareholders took up a long-standing invitation to inspect the progress they were shown wagon loads of superb coal brought down from Newcastle the previous day.

Undaunted, the work continued on the sinking of two further shafts and by July one had reached a depth of 360 feet when a sandy water-bearing strata was struck. Here, operations ceased immediately, but boring continued on the second shaft which was called Simpson Pit after the name of the Syndicate's managing director.

The disaster will not deter the directors from continuing their search for coal but effective pumping equipment will have to be found. Meanwhile borings and sinkings are taking place in other areas of East Kent.

Nine die as Margate surfboat turns turtle

December 2: The gale that raged across Thanet and the East Kent coast this week has claimed the lives of nine members of the crew of the Margate surfboat, the *Friend to All Nations.*

The surfboat, along with the lifeboat *Quiver* had set off to the aid of a stricken vessel on Nayland Rocks. It was blowing heavily from NNW when the *Friend* was struck by a massive wave. Before she had time to recover a second wave ran up the sail and she overturned. Of the 13 crew members, nine died

The upside down boat drifted in before the wind and eventually four were rescued — one under the boat and three somehow clinging to the outside.

This morning *Keble's Margate* described the tragedy: "Out of a full complement of 13 men, including Mr C.E. Troughton, superintendent of the Margate ambulance corps, who invariably accompanies one or other of the boats on their errands of mercy, only four were saved. No such shocking and appalling catastrophe has happened to Margate since the eventful 5th January 1857 when the

continued on next page

Medical student braves the streets of Lambeth

October: William Somerset Maugham — Willie to his friends — a recently qualified medical student, has published a fictional account of the working class London life which he has seen in the streets around St Thomas's Hospital. The book is entitled *Lisa of Lambeth* and Willie hopes it will lead him to a literary, rather than medical, career.

Born at the British Embassy in Paris in 1874, where his father worked as a solicitor, Willie Maugham lost both his parents before he was 10 years old and went to live with an uncle, the Rev Henry MacDonald Maugham, vicar of All Saints Church, Whitstable.

Robbed of his parents and his nanny, who was dismissed, Maugham spent the next five years with a man he detested. He was not allowed to play with the local boys and the sea, beach and harbour were out of bounds. He was forced to wear a velvet knicker-bocker suit, which invoked taunts of Little Lord Fauntleroy, and suffered emotional starvation under a severe regime in a cheerless vicarage.

His only enjoyment was books and he had the run of a large library which included some of the best adventure stories ever written — by authors such as Scott , Captain Marryat and Harrison Ainsworth

As a pupil at King's School, Canterbury, the oldest in the land, Willie Maugham was bullied relentlessly and developed an humiliating stutter. After what he described as "four years hard service" and much hard work he became a King's Scholar, enjoyed the advantage of being a senior boy and the dignity of wearing a gown. The bullies were still evident but this well-read, more assertive boy now counter-attacked with a wounding wit.

Maugham left King's, declined a Cambridge scholarship and travelled to the South of France, then Heidelberg University to study philosophy and literature. Returning to England he spent five years as a student at St Thomas's Hospital.

At nights he walked the local streets around Lambeth, always carrying a black bag which saved him from would-be assailants in this most perilous and seamy area of London. From this sprang *Lisa of Lambeth* and some encouraging reviews.

continued from page 242

lugger *Victory* was lost with her crew of nine hands".

It has been a terrible week for Margate. On Monday a tidal surge, accompanied by hurricane-force winds, unleashed its full fury on the town, destroying the jetty, stone pier and Droit office.

Sea walls, coastal defences, buildings and roadways were washed away. The great tide also destroyed the promenade at Westgate, the colonnade at Ramsgate and breached the pier at Broadstairs.

Keble's Margate said: "It is hardly an exaggeration to say the face of Margate has been changed for ever. Through the mist of the spray, huge masses of water could be seen rising mountain like, their created summits roaring in a majestic splendour high above their prey."

Hundreds of onlookers watch the funeral procession as the coffins of the nine crew members of the* Friend to All Nations *is carried to the parish church of St John.

W.G. moves to Kent: his wife teaches women to throw stones

October: W.G. Grace, the most successful and the best-known cricketer in England, has left his native Gloucestershire to live at Mottingham. At the age of 50 he has accepted a £600 a year post as cricket manager at the Crystal Palace and will captain a cricket eleven called London County.

The Old Man, as the bearded W.G. is known, has scored more than 50,000 runs and taken almost 3,000 wickets in a first-class career spanning 28 years. Three years ago he became the first batsman to score 1,000 runs in May and, at the Bat and Ball ground at Gravesend, he was on the field throughout the match.

His highest score — and the record individual score — was 344 against Kent at Canterbury in 1875.

Grace will make his debut for London County in April and will spend the winter recruiting players.

His wife is no less active. A fine athlete herself, she has been teaching women in Bromley and Beckenham how to throw stones — hard, fast and accurately. As a member of the National Union of Womens Suffrage Societies she is keen to use every tactic possible to persuade the government to give woman equal opportunities in education and employment.

The Suffrage movement has many champions in north Kent. Among them is Miss Mary Louisa Heppel, head teacher of Bromley High School, Kate Harvey, wife of a local councillor, the Rev William Welsh curate of St George's, Beckenham and Lloyd Phillips of the same town. All share in a dislike for the way women are treated as second class citizens.

Kitchener avenges death of Gordon

September 3: General Sir Herbert Kitchener's long held desire to recover the Sudan and avenge the death of General Gordon has been achieved. Yesterday, at Omdurman a huge Sudanese army was destroyed by the Maxim guns of the Anglo-Egyptian force. It is estimated that the Sudanese lost 10,000 warriors while British losses were less than 30.

Kent has played a significant part in the Sudan campaign. General Kitchener, commander-in-chief of the British-run Egyptian army lives at Barham, near Canterbury. Hiram Maxim has relocated his factory at Crayford and lives at Stoneyhurst. One of the heroes of yesterday's battle is a 32-year-old private with the 21st Lancers, Thomas Byrne, who lives at Canterbury

Yesterday the Sudanese, led by Khalifa Abdallahi, courageously attacked the Anglo-British encampment by charging Kitchener's rear and the battle ended in a huge cloud of dust and a charge by the 21st Lancers. One of the men, Lieutenant the Hon Molyneux — galloper to Lord Kitchener — was unseated from his horse and found himself surrounded by Dervishes. Thomas Byrne immediately came to the aid of his officer but was shot in the right shoulder and lost his lance. Wielding his sword in his left hand he attacked and routed the enemy and brought Molyneux to safety.

A colleague, a young officer Winston Churchill, was a witness to Byrne's gallantry. He said: "It was the bravest thing I've ever seen".

The victory followed months of meticulous planning by Kitchener. He designed his own gunboats for the passage up the Nile and commissioned his own railway to carry his armies to Khartoum. He celebrated the victory with a requiem service at the shattered remains of Gordon's house when the Union flag was triumphantly raised and three cheers were called for Queen Victoria. Apparently Kitchener was so overcome with emotion that he was unable to dismiss the parade. *See page 247.*

Victoria Cross for Kent heroes

October: As Kitchener continues to impose order in the Sudan, the Corps of the Royal Engineers and the Buffs have been involved in heavy fighting in India.

Two officers, Lieutenants James Colvin and Thomas Watson of the Engineers and Corporal James Smith of the East Kent (the Buffs) have been cited as recipients of the Victoria Cross.

The three men were among a party of volunteers who went into the burning village of Bilot in the Mamund Valley in north-west India in an attempt to dislodge the enemy who were inflicting losses on our troops. Watson was incapacitated by wounds but Colvin and Smith continued to fight and to carry the wounded to safety under heavy fire.

Martians and Morlocks and roads without horses

September: Herbert George Wells, author of another highly popular science fiction book, *War of The Worlds*, is moving to a new home by the sea — by order of his doctor!

Wells has suffered from ill health since his boyhood in Bromley, where his father ran a failing china shop. Some months ago his doctor suggested he find a home in dry air on dry subsoil so he set off on a cycling tour in tandem with his second wife Catherine (Jane) Roberts and lighted on a sunny plot of land at Folkestone, high above the sea at Sandgate.

He has bought Spade House but will not complete the move until his architect has redesigned the property to his liking.

H.G. Wells is one of many literary and artistic figures who have been caricatured by the pen of Max Beerbohm in his highly individual style. Beerbohm, half brother of the actor, Beerbohm Tree, shows Wells conjuring up a masculine-looking woman of the future holding her very brainy offspring.

Herbert Wells was originally apprenticed to a draper but after attending lectures given by Thomas Huxley at the Royal Society he decided to be a teacher. His troublesome kidney frequently kept him at home so he wrote short stories and immediately found a new lease of life as a prophet of what science may one day bring to pass.

His first books were *The Island of Dr Moreau* and *The Invisible Man*. Last year, while lodging in a flat at Eardley Road, Sevenoaks, he published *The Time Machine* and transported his readers ahead to the year 802701 into a world of moonless nights, flower people and the man eaters, the Morlocks. In his latest book *War of the Worlds* he produces the classic scenario of Martians invading in a rocket. They destroy London and the survivors exist with difficulty until... this science fiction fantasy is causing as great a stir as Wells' prophecies.

In his articles for the *Fortnightly Review* he questions whether the railway will remain the predominant method of land locomotion of the future. He says that automobiles will one day be capable of travelling 300 miles in a single day and that the horse and pedestrian will be segregated from the high road.

JOSEPH Conrad, a man who enjoyed adventures all over the world, has moved to an isolated farmhouse near Aldington where he plans to write novels about his experiences abroad.

Conrad is the adopted name of Teodor Josef Konrad Korzeniowski who was born in a part of Poland under Russian rule 41 years ago and left home at 17 to go to sea.His adventures brought him eventually into the British Merchant Navy and he was naturalised in 1886. Although Conrad only learnt the language in his 20s he has become a master of the English prose.

His wife Jessie bemoans the remoteness of their home but Conrad is delighted to be among such literary figures as H.G.Wells (Sandgate) and Henry James (Rye).

A few weeks ago, a sickly Wells came to lunch on the farm to a carefully prepared meal only to dine off a glass of milk and two aspirins.

Conrad is currently working on a book called *Heart of Darkness*, a personal insight into Africa and colonial exploitation.

Thanks to the enterprise of two ladies, Miss C.F.Philpotts and Miss K. Holmes, the ancient craft of weaving has been revived in Canterbury in its original setting. The ladies have moved into an old house on the banks of the Stour opposite King's Bridge which was one of the buildings used by James Callaway in the last years of the industry.

Kent welcomes two famous women

FRANCES Hodgson Burnett, the British born, American educated author who made a fortune out of her novel *Little Lord Fauntleroy*, has leased a new home in Kent where she will continue with her writing.

Great Maytham Hall is a spacious 18th-century house near Rolvenden which was built by a Captain Moneypenny RN out of the prize money won for the capture of a French man o' war.

Frances Burnett is adored by thousands; her near neighbour in the Weald of Kent, actress Ellen Terry, is loved by millions.

Ellen has recently bought Smallhythe Place, a 16th century converted farmhouse near Tenterden. The village of Smallhythe was once a trading port but the sea has receded and this charming place has been left high and dry among the fields.

Renowned as England's leading lady of the stage, Ellen Terry has achieved many major Shakespearean triumphs — as Portia in *The Merchant of Venice*, as Ophelia in *Hamlet* and as Beatrice in *Much Ado About Nothing*. Her partnership with Henry Irving, actor and manager of the Lyceum, is the most celebrated in the history of the theatre.

Ellen's private life is more complex. In 1868 when she was 21 she eloped with the architect, Edward Goodwin, a friend of William Morris and James Whistler. They were never legally married but Ellen bore two children and enjoyed many escapes to country retreats such as Ightham Mote, near Sevenoaks. The couple broke up in 1875.

Today she is single with many admirers. Oscar Wilde was so smitten by one of her performances that he wrote a sonnet — "In that gorgeous dress of beaten gold....No woman looked upon was half as fair as thou whom I behold".

And George Bernard Shaw wrote that "the name of Ellen Terry is the most beautiful in the world; it rings like a chime through the last quarter of the 19th century".

Steam motor bus takes spectators to the cricket

July: Cricket supporters find many ways of getting to Canterbury Cricket Week. Hundreds walk from the city centre or take the horse bus which links the East and West railway stations. Many use the bicycle or penny farthing while the wealthy take advantage of the abolition of the red flag law by driving a motor car to the ground. This month saw the most novel of all — the introduction of a 20-seat steam motor bus.

It is not the first in the county. In early April , two demonstration buses were on show at Tunbridge Wells and on April 24, Mr E.A.Livet introduced a twice-a-day service from Canterbury to Herne Bay with a Daimler wagonette.

Since then there have been services between Dover and St Margaret's-at-Cliffe and Dover to Deal. These buses were built by the Liquid Fuel and Engineering Company of Cowes and were able to maintain a speed of seven mph on level road.

This month Folkestone Motors Ltd began a service to Hythe using a wagonette manufactured in Coventry.

November 27: There was great excitement in Woolwich today when a bottle-nosed whale was found stranded in the Thames mud.

Percy dies on his famous flying machine

Percy Pilcher taking off for his last fateful flight.

October 2: Percy Pilcher, one of Britain's most famous flying pioneers, died in hospital today two days after crashing his famous Hawk glider during a demonstration at Stanford Hall near Market Harborough.

His death is a tragedy because Pilcher was close to becoming the first man in history to achieve a powered flight. His gliding experiments took place in a peaceful area of the Darenth Valley at Eynsford where the steep sides of a hill provided ideal launching sites. He would run down the hill in strong winds, jump into the air and his glider would fly above the slope for a distance of more than 300 feet.

Percy Pilcher came to Eynsford in 1896 and, at the invitation of Hiram Maxim, he worked on the construction of a flying machine at Crayford. Maxim's machines were too heavy so Pilcher branched out on his own and, in a great shed between Lower Austin and Upper Austin Lodge farms, he built his feather-weight Hawk from bamboo and fabric. It weighed 50 lbs and had a wing span of 23 feet 4 inches.

Percy continued with his experiments. He attached his glider to a pulley system and flew for 250 yards at almost 25 mph and then took out a patent for the design of a powered aeroplane. Working alongside a fellow engineer, Walter Wilson, he designed a four horsepower petrol motor for his Hawk which weighed just 40 lbs.

Percy completed the building of the engine just a few weeks ago and announced that he was to attempt a powered flight. Sadly, it was not to be. The great engineer had agreed to take his gliders to Lord Braye's country seat at Stanford Hall and there, during a demonstration in front of distinguished guests, he crashed to his death.

Boer War fund opens in Kent as casualties grow

December 30: The agitation and the tension between the British and the Boer republics in southern Africa, which flared into conflict a few weeks ago, has caused a great surge of patriotism here in Kent. Most people expected the war to be over by Christmas but the Boers are showing greater superiority in numbers, arms and tactics. As Rudyard Kipling, the author, said: "We are being taught no end of a lesson".

Boer commandos have cut through the British lines and laid siege to Ladysmith, Mafeking and Kimberley and severe defeats have been inflicted on the British at Colenso and Magersfontein. The British Regular Army, supplemented by numerous volunteer contingents is stretched to its limits to contain the activities of 60,000 Boers under arms.

Nowhere is the emotion greater than in West Kent where people of every town and village have responded to calls for aid for the wounded and the families of the men at the front. In Maidstone the mayor has opened a South African War Fund and, in support, many prominent people are organising

General Kitchener from Barham, near Canterbury — on his way to South Africa.

continued on page 249

Sir Edward Watkins of the South Eastern Railway Company — known in Kent as The Railway King.

Railways rivals unite — the battle is over at last

THE fierce antagonism which has existed between the South Eastern and the London, Chatham and Dover Railway Companies has ended peacefully — in amalgamation.

The two companies will now work together under a single management without any of the hostility and rivalry which has blighted railway progress in Kent.

It is known the destination of the two companies were governed by two strong and obstinate men in Edward Watkins and Forbes who each wanted the mastery of rail traffic — across the Channel in the case of the LCDR and under in the case of SER. Each successive Channel Tunnel Bill promoted by Watkins was vigorously opposed by the LCDR directors who thought it should not be constructed at all.

Unlike the militarists they were not frightened about the security of England. Their objections simply reflected the poor financial state of the Chatham line.

Gladstone once admitted that he was not so much for the tunnel as he was against those who objected to it. He said: "The army and the military host and the literary host were backed by the opinion of what is called Society and Society is always for the enjoyment of a good panic".

Old Waterloo recalls the greatest battle of the nineteenth century

There are few men alive today who took part in the Napoleonic Wars at the beginning of the century — but one who remembers an uncomfortable journey on a rambling baggage waggon from Quatre Bras to Waterloo and is in great demand to tell the story is not a man but a woman.

In the village of Rolvenden, where she has lived for many years, she is simply known as *Old Waterloo* and she can relate, with great clarity, the days when wives and children often followed in the wake of their soldier husbands and fathers.

Her father was in the British army and she followed him in a wagon through France and Belgium. She married Philip Moon in 1838 and moved to Rolvenden, where she raised 11 children.

More and more 'chain' stores are opening in Kent. Among the more popular are W.H. Smith (newsagents and booksellers), Home and Colonial (grocers), Liptons (grocers) and International Stores. In Maidstone a branch of Boots (chemists) will soon open.

Mrs C. Prescott-Westcar of Strode Park today formally opened Herne Bay pier which has been completed at a cost at £60,000. This is the third pier for Kent's newest seaside resort. The first wooden pier was demolished in 1871 and replaced two years later by a 320-foot long iron structure. An application for parliamentary powers to build a deep-sea pier enabling Herne Bay to resume steamer services was granted in 1891.

An electric tramway known as the Chatham and district light railway has opened — a first for the Medway towns.

A new entertainment centre — the Theatre Royal — has opened in Chatham. Further along the High Street, Barnard's Palace of Varieties, believed to be the oldest theatre in the world, continues to attract some of the top entertainers.

Defending Mafeking. Colonel Robert Baden-Powell has become a national hero.

'No surrender', says London

(continued from page 247)

numerous concerts and entertainments.

The chief attraction at many of these functions are the bands of the 3rd Battalion (Militia) and the 1st Battalion (Volunteer) of the 50th (Royal West Kent) Regiment.

A large number of applications are being received at Regimental headquarters from ex-soldiers keen to return to the Colours. One comes from a man of 52 who was discharged with a pension 15 years ago. He claims he can speak the Boer and Kaffir language fairly well. He has been enrolled.

This week no fewer than 371 Reservists of the Regiment assembled at the barracks. After they had been medically inspected, fitted with clothing, equipped and paid they were granted short leave and will sail for South Africa in the New Year. Already a number of ladies connected with the Regiment have begun to collect money for "comforts" for the troops. They plan to buy some 30,000 Woodbine cigarettes, 300 lbs of tobacco, 400 pipes and 300 sweaters.

Meanwhile Sir Revers Buller the British Commander-in-Chief — having lost 2,000 troops killed and 12 heavy guns captured — has asked London for permission to surrender but has been refused. Instead, Lord Roberts, the commander-in-chief of the British Army in India and General Kitchener are on their way to Southern Africa to try and restore the British position.

The Kent newspapers, many with correspondents in South Africa, are reporting the war in great detail but news of individual regiments and companies is coming through slowly. It is believed the 23rd Company of the Royal Engineers are holed up at the besieged garrison of Ladysmith. And many other Kent men are at Mafeking, now under siege for more than two months.

Here Colonel Robert Baden-Powell is defending the garrison with great courage.

Baden-Powell holds out at Mafeking

DURING the siege of Mafeking, which began in October, Colonel Robert Baden Powell has become the hero of every small boy, especially those who remember him as a schoolboy at Rose Hill School, Tunbridge Wells. Having lost his father at the age of three he was living with an aunt at Speldhurst and every day he set off on a four-mile trek to his school.

Later he won a scholarship to Charterhouse and in the woods around Godalming he would stalk his masters and learn to catch and cook rabbits, being careful not to let the tell-tale smoke give his position away.

Baden Powell joined the army and was commissioned into the 13th Huzzars, serving with great distinction in India, Afghanistan, South Africa and Malta.

Shortly before the outbreak of the Boer War, Baden Powell wrote his book *Aids to Scouting*. He sailed for South Africa and during the siege has put his own principles to good effect by using boys for responsible jobs and is delighted by the great response to some serious challenges.

His book has now been published and is winning a far wider readership than the military one for which it was intended.

There are nearly 1,000 bottle kilns clustered along the estuaries of the Thames and Medway, billowing evidence of the amazing growth of the cement industry. The rivers are alive with sailing barges carrying vital raw material and, in the chalk quarries, thousands of shovels continue to dig relentlessly.

NOTES

Page 12: Holwood House, Keston was sold for £15,000 and 20 years after Pitt's death it was pulled down and a new building erected in classical style. All memory of Pitt at Keston died with the demolition of the house.

Page 53: Birth of Alexandrina Victoria on May 24, 1837. This day in later years was adopted as Empire Day and subsequently Commonwealth Day.

Page 64: Sir Thomas More was canonized in 1935.

Page 67: In 1924, a farthing dated 1799 and two scraps of paper were found between the joints of the pulpit presented to Trottiscliffe church. The paper contained the names of the choiristers present at the instalation of the Knights of the Bath in Henry VII's chapel on May 19, 1803 and the other records the repair of the pulpit. We may imagine the choir boys at this fine pageantry climbing up the pulpit to hide the names.

Page 68: Hall's Engineering works was supplied with Dartford Gas in 1943. By 1946 the DGC had made a profit in excess of £2,000.

Page 68: Robert Colgate and his son William laid the foundation of the international commercial enterprise of the Colgates. The descendants of Robert never fail to visit Filston, Shoreham when they are in England.

Page 70: After five years of back-breaking toil in Tasmania, George Ransley earned a pardon and was joined by his family. For several years he ran a farm of some 200 acres, worked by his own gang of former convict smugglers. He died at River Plenty, North Norfolk.

Page 91: The Royal Fountain Hotel in Margaret Street, Canterbury was destroyed by Nazi bombs during the Baedeker raid on the city in 1942.

Page 97: Courteney and his disciples died near Dunkirk, where a church was built to combat the lack of moral leadership and remains a memorial to this day. The uprising is said to be the last occasion in which a soldier was killed in combat on British soil.

Page 111: Richard Dadd was arrested in France, extradited to England and eventually incarcerated in the recently-built Broadmoor. He continued to paint until his death in 1886.

Page 112: The prize-fighter who killed the constable, Thomas Clark was never found. His father and brothers appeared at the Assizes but were acquitted. One of them later stole a cheese and was transported to Australia.

Page 117: Thomas Waghorn died on January 7, 1850. He was buried at All Saints, Snodland. A memorial to him is on the south wall of the nave.

Page 122: Thomas Streatfeild's manuscripts of his great unpublished history of Kent still lie in the British Museum.

Page 133: The elaborate interior of the Houses of Parliament, designed by Augustus Pugin, is still fashionable today and survives, except in the chamber of the Commons and the adjoining lobby, which were destroyed by bombs in 1941.

Page 138: Catherine Marsh later wrote and published the story of her work under the title *English Hearts and English Hands* and out of that book the Navy Mission was formed.

Page 140: In 1936 the Crystal Palace was destroyed by fire along with its contents. The park survived and in 1956 became one of the sports centres run by the Sports Council.

Page 142: Albert Mitchell joined Cranbrook police in 1862 and published a book in 1884 about the *Relief of the Light Brigade*. Fiennes Wykeham Martin, later to become Lord Cornwallis, died in 1867. Henry Boxall moved to Tunbridge Wells in 1892.

Page 162: Victoria, the illegitimate daughter of Lionel and Pepita Sackville-West married her cousin Lionel and became the mistress of the great house of Knole. Her daughter Vita grew up at Knole, married the biographer, Harold Nicolson and inspired the creation of Sissinghurst Garden.

Page 172: Hop picking by hand — and the end of the London invasion of Hoppers — ceased in the 1960s when machines were introduced. Kent continues to be the premier county for growing hops although the total acreage is far less.

Page 175: The temperature reading on that July day in 1868 found its way into the *Guinness Book of Records* and for a long time was regarded as Britain's hottest day but the reading (100.5F) was taken in a stand open at the front. In order to achieve standardisation all measurements were later made in a Stevenson screen designed by Thomas, father of the famous writer and poet Robert Louis. The official record is 101F observed at Gravesend on August 10, 2003.

Page 175: Flood Lane in Sevenoaks was later renamed Oak Lane.

Page 181: Charles Dickens was buried neither at Gads Hill nor Rochester Cathedral. Westminster Abbey demanded the honour and he was buried without the razamataz that is usually reserved for such great men. For two days thousands filed past his open grave.

Page 190: Lord Harris, the fourth Baron, continued to captain Kent until 1889. He died in 1918 aged 73.

Page 191: It was another 51 years before the first woman swam the Channel and that was Gertrude Ederle from the US in 1926. Since then many hundreds of men and women have achieved the feat. In 1987, Philip Rush of New Zealand completed a triple crossing.

Page 192: Vincent van Gogh died on July 29, 1890, having shot himself in the chest following years of mental illness.

Page 204: Chatham Dockyard closed in 1984 and is now a museum.

Page 206: The Channel Tunnel scheme of 1875 foundered some 20 years after preparatory work by engineers and was not revived again until 1957. No serious progress was made until 1968 when a firm commitment was made to a privately funded twin-track tunnel with drive-on facilities for cars. The official opening ceremony took place in 1994.

Page 213: Ethel Smythe became one of the most celebrated composers of her age. She wrote *March of the Women* and *The Mass* which was performed in the Royal Albert Hall. Her first opera was *Fantasia* and was a brlliant success, then followed *Der Wald* and *The Wreckers*, a Wagnerian style grand opera based on the legendary wreckers of Cornwall. *The Wreckers,* performed at the Queen's Hall, directed by Sir Thomas Beecham became the anthem for the Suffragette movement. She had many lesbian love affairs, the final one being with Virginia Woolf which lasted until Virginia's death in 1941. Ethel Smythe died in 1944 aged 86.

Page 216: Arsenal joined Division Two of the Football League and were promoted in 1904. Apart from two years (1913-14) they have played continuously in the top division and have won the championship more times than any other club.

Page 220: Members of the Fabian Society retained its close links with the Labour Party and were responsible for establishing the London School of Economics.

Page 221: Many of Edith Nesbit's books acquired the status of classics. She wrote *Five Children and It* in 1902 and *The Railway Children* in 1906. She died in 1924 aged 68.

Page 228: Katherine Parnell died in Brighton in 1911.

Page 230: Bessie Marchant had 152 books published by the time she died in 1941, including *Held at Random* (1900), *Three Girls on a Ranch* (1901), *A Girl Munitions Worker* and *The Girls Realm*. She believed that girls should have as exciting adventures as boys and enjoyed research in Oxford's Bodleian Library.

Page 234: Hiram Maxim was naturalised in 1900, knighted in 1901 and his company amalgamated with the Erith-based firm called Vickers. He died in 1916, aged 76.

Page 235: The Wright brothers did come to Kent and worked closely with Horace, Eustace and Oswald Short at Leysdown on the Isle of Sheppey.

Page 236: By the turn of the 20th century the National Trust owned 210 houses, including some of the greatest stately homes, 100 gardens, 50 villages and some 230,000/ha of countryside. Octavia Hill died in 1912.

Page 239: Alfred Harmsworth died in 1922 as Viscount Northcliffe. After starting the *Daily Mail* in 1896 he followed this up by founding the *Daily Mirror*. His younger brother, Harold Viscount Rothermere, was a partner in his ventures.

Page 241: Father Wilson established a permanent Little Hoppers' Hospital at a disused public house, the Rose and Crown, Five Oak Green where he turned the skittles alley into a children's ward. In 1927 that was replaced by a purpose brick building in the village.

Page 242: Coal was disovered in East Kent and pits were opened at Snowdown, Betteshanger, Tilmanstone and in many small villages. The mines were finally closed by the Thatcher government in 1989 after many years of uncertainty.

Page 243: Somerset Maugham became one of the country's most prolific novelists and playwrights. Many of his stories became classics and he was described at one time as "the greatest living Englishman". He died in 1965 aged 91.

Page 244: W.G. Grace was captain of London County until 1904 when the club disbanded. His final match was played on July 25, 1914 at Eltham when he made 69 not out. He died at Fairmount, Mottingham in October 1915 aged 67.

Page 245: H.G. Wells wrote many novels about lower-middle-class life such as *Love and Mr Lewisham, Kipps* and the *History of Mr Polly*. But he made his mame with science fiction and his later works include *The First Men on The Moon* and *The Shape of Things to Come*. He was a member of the Fabian Society until he quarrelled with George Bernard Shaw. He advocated sexual freedom and had a long relationship with Rebecca West.

Page 246: Dame Ellen Terry died at Smallhythe Place in 1928 aged 81. She carried on a brilliant and flirtatious correspondence with George Bernard Shaw which was published in 1931.Today her home is kept as a museum.

Page 246: Frances Hodgson Burnett wrote *The Secret Garden* in 1907. Much of the story was based on her walled garden at Great Matham Hall, Rolvenden. She died in 1924.

Page 247: Herbert Lord Kitchener died in 1916 when the cruiser *HMS Hampshire*, taking him to Russia, struck a mine. He was Secretary of State for War and his was the face on the best-known of all 1914-18 war recruiting posters.

Page 248: The final link in the railway network was completed in 1905 with the opening of a branch line from Headcorn to Tenterden. Lines serving the East Kent coalfields were opened after the 1914-18 war.

SUBSCRIBERS

The following kindly gave their support to this book.

Doreen Allibone
H H Judge Andrew
Sally G Anning
Charles Armitage
Roy Arnold
Vic Ashlee
Eric John Atkins
F E Austen
Carole A Bailey
Sally Balcon
Frank Ballard
Valerie & Heidi Bamber
Jennifer Barton
W J Beazley
Francis J Bellingham
H Belsey
Peter and Myra Benford
Leonard Bennett
Mr & Mrs L P Best
Bethany School
Richard Bird
J Bishop
Janet Bishop
M & S Blundell
M V Borner
Geoff Boxall
J Branson
Ruby & Mary Breeds
W J Brenton
Mr & Mrs M A Brett
D E Brittenden
Rachel Anne Brooker
Bob Brooks
Elizabeth Brown
José S Brown
Peter Brown
Elizabeth A Bruce
Jean Bunnett
Trevor Burrage
Maureen & Arthur Burr
David Bushell
Mary Button
Ron & Joyce Cambridge
R G Cannon
F A Causton
Drummond and Robin Champion
Anthony Chapman
Shirley Chapman
Betty J Church
Dennis Clare
Julian Clark
Margaret & Sydney Cliffe
Mr & Mrs H B Clifford
Marjorie E Cocker
Richard A Collins
Dr J W Comper
Mr G A & Mrs P Coombs
J M Cook
Cyril & Iris Crane
Mrs Jean Crisfield
Richard P Cross
Peter W Corrie
Ivan Curtis
Margaret Dance
Simon Daniel
Stan Darnell
A Davidson
Ken & Margaret Davies
John Hanks Day
Alan Deares
Val Dennett
Rosemary Denton
Les Dickson
M J K Dodsworth
John F Dorling
Eunice and Peter Doswell
Janet & Tom Dowd
Katharine Draper
J & R Drover
Mr & Mrs P G Dunk
Peter Dunscombe
Mark Dutton
Charles Dyer
David Easton
David William Easton
Stan & Barbara Edgell
E C Edghill
Lesley Edmeads
Douglas H Elks
Rachel & George Elvery
Percy Entecott
Richard R D Ewing
Mary Feltham
E Fitzgerald
Nicholas Folkard
Rae Fowler
Colin Henry Fox
Emerald M Frampton
Pauline Freeland
Valerie Fry
Bernard Fuller
George Fuller
Marion Furner
Dean Garrett
Michael Gater
Stuart & Lydia Gay
Jan Golding
Martin Goord
Iris P Gosling
Tony Graves
José Gray
Janet Green
Eileen Gunnell
M Gutteridge
Mary Hackney
Brian D Hall
Marion Hall
M I Hamill
Barbara Hammerton
Joan Hammon
Wendy Hance
Mr & Mrs B Hanson
Angela & Barrie Harber
Kendrick J Harding
Berni Harrad
Derek Harris
R C Harris
Ken Hayes
Alan & Marion Healey
Gerald A Heath
Fred & Betty Hebert
Brian Heselden
Marjorie Hewes
Guy Hitchings
David Thomas Hobbs
V Holdaway
Joseph Holness
Brian A Holyland
Jim Homewood
Roy & Audrey Hooker
Edith Hopkins
John Hori
A E Horner
Mary Hover & Family
Sheena Hughes-Nurse
Sue & Chris Huke
Molly Horn
David R Hull
Maureen Humphrey
Elizabeth Jaecker
P S Jarvis
Betty Jeffery
Kevin Jeffrey
A W Jeffreys
Tony Johns
C L Jones
Paul & Julie Jones
Ray & Brenda Jones
Steve & Jane Jones
Lynn Jung
Jean Kay
Derek Kemp
Kemsing Heritage Centre Association
John & Sheila Kettel
Peter & Joyce Kiff
M Kitchingham
A J Ladd
Andy & Kay Laimbeer
Lamberhurst Local History Society
O C Lambert
T A Lampard
A J Lathey
David Lewis
Iris N Lilley
C T Lindsay
Maggie Lipscombe
John London
B J Longley
Martyn Longstaff
D E Lovelace
Lyminge Historical Society
D McCall Smith
Timothy F P McGrane
Ron Machey
Colin Mackinlay
J Macro
Ian Martin
Jean Martin
Ron Martin
Brian & Jill Matthews
Clifford Matthews
Colin Philip Matthews
Pete Matthews
Pam Meridew
F L Merrall
Francis & Sue Meynell
Chris Miles
Chris Miller
Geoffrey Milne
John Milton
Rodney Mintern
John Miskin
Clive Mitchell

Shirley Morris
Doreen Morrison
Queenie Mortimer
Tony & Maralyn
Mulcuck
Bill Morton
Gary D Mullins
Brian & Muriel Neal
Ann & Roy
Nicholson
Brian Nobbs
Richard Nobbs
Sue O'Connor
Richard (Dick) Olive
Len Olive
Peter O'Sullivan
Alison Painter
H A & R Parkes
John Pateman
Mr & Mrs B B
Payne
James E Peall
Mollie & Tony
Pearce
Gerard Pearson
Leslie Pearson
Lucy Peatfield
John S Penn
Dave Piggott
Cyril & Vera Pile
John Pluckrose
Janet E Pollitt
George Pott
Brian Price
Hugh R Pryke
Janet & Alec
Ramage
Roy Randall
Paul & Denise Rason
Margaret Rawlings
Colin Reffell
Ian & Eileen Reid
Pam Ridout
Bob & Ann Roffe
Peter Rogers
Martin Rolls
Bertha Rose
Malcolm Round

Edward Rubie
R D H Ruston
E L Sands
Rita & Fred Scales
Ian Scott
Michael Scott
Paul Scott
Enid Self
Trevor Simons
Jenny Simpson
Joan Slinn
Sevenoaks Society
Mary & Annette
Shaw
Tessa & Mike
Sheeres
Maurice G Short
K E & B M Silver
Elizabeth Sinstadt
Joan Slinn
Alan Smith
Michael J Smith
P A Smith
Louise Spreyer
Mick Springate
Fred Standen
Ronald H H Stokes
W Stotesbury
D G & C Stevens
P M Streets
Magda & Tony
Sweetland
Alison Taylor
George & June
Taylor
Maureen Thatcher
Valerie Thatcher
Frank M Thirkell
Troye R Thomas
Geoff & Adrienne
Thompson
Paul Thompson
Angela Thorn
E A B Thorneycroft
Jennifer Thornton
Conrad M B
Thrower
John R Toms

Vivienne & Brian
Tremaine
J Tresize
Eve Tucker
David H W Turner
& Family
David W Twining
J G Thorne
L W Thorne
Barbara Twinn
Stella D Underwood
Ced Verdon
Marshall Vine
B Wadhams
Barbara Wakeman
Bruce Walker
Patricia Walsh
Philip Wanstall
John H Warner
Mike Warren
David Watts
Christine Webb
Gordon Webb
Alan Weeks
M Wellings
Alan R Wells
Keith Wells
Carole West
E M White
Ian & Eileen
Whitehead
Richard Whitenstall
Gillian & Chris
Whittingham
John Willmott
Sidney G Willson
R A Wilson
Brian Wingate
Jack Wingate
George & Mary
Winton
P F & S M Winton
David Witherspoon
Christopher Wood
Ronald & Patricia
Woodgate
Mick Worrall
Patricia Wright

INDEX

Bob Ogley has travelled thousands of miles — to every town and most of the villages of Kent — in compiling this book, which has taken more than two years to research and write. It is his 22nd book and, at 256 pages, by far the largest and the most difficult to complete.

Bob is a journalist by profession and an author by courtesy of the greatest storm of the century. *In The Wake of The Hurricane* sold almost 250,000 copies in its varous editions, remained in the top ten bestseller list for eight months and changed his life.

He was then the editor of the *Sevenoaks Chronicle* and on course to remain so for a few more years. Today he is a full-time writer, a local historian, a regular contributor to BBC Radio Kent and continues to travel extensively in pursuit of information and photographs.

Many of his books about Kent have been county bestsellers. They includes *Biggin on The Bump, Doodlebugs and Rockets, Kent at War, The Kent Weather Book* and his four-part *Chronicle of Kent in the 20th century.*

Bob was born at Sevenoaks and has lived in the county all his life. He is in great demand to tell his unique story. On the charitable side his books have raised many thousands of pounds for such worthy causes as the RAF Benevolent Fund, the RNLI, the National Trust and Demelza House, the childrens' hospice.